CREEPY CRAWLING

*For my mother, who always encouraged me to read all the books
I could reach—even the scary ones.*

Other books by the author:

9/11 Culture: America Under Construction (Wiley-Blackwell, 2009; Arabic translation by Azza Alkhamissy, 2010)

Immigration and American Popular Culture: An Introduction, with Rachel Rubin (New York University Press, 2006)

Race and the Modern Artist, eds. Josef Jarab, Jeffrey Melnick and Heather Hathaway (Oxford University Press, 2003)

American Popular Music: New Approaches to the Twentieth Century, eds. Jeffrey Melnick and Rachel Rubin (University of Massachusetts Press, 2001)

Black-Jewish Relations on Trial: Leo Frank and Jim Conley in the New South (University Press of Mississippi, 2000)

A Right to Sing the Blues: African Americans, Jews, and American Popular Song (Harvard University Press, 1999)

CREEPY CRAWLING

CHARLES MANSON AND THE MANY LIVES OF AMERICA'S MOST INFAMOUS FAMILY

JEFFREY MELNICK

Arcade Publishing • New York

Arcade Publishing books may be purchased in bulk at special discounts for sales promotion, corporate gifts, fund-raising, or educational purposes. Special editions can also be created to specifications. For details, contact the Special Sales Department, Arcade Publishing, 307 West 36th Street, 11th Floor, New York, NY 10018 or arcade@skyhorsepublishing.com.

Arcade Publishing® is a registered trademark of Skyhorse Publishing, Inc.®, a Delaware corporation.

Visit our website at www.arcadepub.com.

10 9 8 7 6 5 4 3 2 1

Library of Congress Cataloging-in-Publication Data is available on file.

Print ISBN: 978-1-62872-893-4
Ebook ISBN: 978-1-62872- 894-1

Printed in the United States of America

Table of Contents

Introduction

Creepy Crawling through the Sixties: Charles Manson and History

The year 2019 will mark the fiftieth anniversary of the Tate-LaBianca murders that made Charles Manson a household name, and the man and his Family are still everywhere. In 2016 they were on network television with the return of Season Two of David Duchovny's *Aquarius* to NBC's schedule. They are at the center of Emma Cline's debut novel, *The Girls*, which has been prominently reviewed all over the mainstream press, hitting the *New York Times* Best Seller list within two weeks of publication. They are in the news in the developing story of the most recent parole hearing of Family member Leslie Van Houten, a dear friend of filmmaker John Waters.

During 2016 and early 2017, Manson's presence—at once frightful and comic—took on added resonance in the context of Donald Trump's campaign for, and ascension to, the presidency of the United States. Given that Manson has served for decades as a kind of shorthand for charismatic pathology, it would have been hard to resist Manson/Trump juxtapositions. So, during the campaign multiple Internet rumors about Manson's putative endorsement of the candidate circulated; more than a few compared Trump to the cult leader with respect to the power he held over his followers. In the early days of 2017, when Manson was rushed to the hospital for an undisclosed health emergency, Andy

Borowitz (at the *New Yorker*) and other comic writers suggested that now the president-elect would have to take the cult leader's name off his shortlist to fill the Supreme Court seat of Antonin Scalia that had been denied Merrick Garland by Republican obstructionism. Others noted similarly that when they saw Manson's name trending on social media after his health scare they at first assumed it was because Trump must have named him to a cabinet position. Most efficient of all was a widely circulated GIF that simply put video footage of Trump and Manson side by side so that viewers could observe and draw conclusions from the similarities in their exaggerated facial expressions, which often take the form of non-verbal insults.

We also find that Scott Michaels is continuing to do brisk business with his Helter Skelter van tour (part of his larger Dearly Departed "tragical history" business). The tour, as Michaels has explained, brings "victim people" and "Manson People" together to drive around Los Angeles and see everything from the restaurant where Sharon Tate and her friends ate their last meal to the apartment where the daughter of Leno and Rosemary LaBianca lived with her boyfriend—who, according to the tour guide, was definitely a biker, and *may* have been tied up with the Manson-affiliated Straight Satans club. When I took the tour it became clear to me that part of Michaels's business involves using the Manson case to entertain folks who are celebrating birthdays and other major life events.

As 2017 began, Manson's staying power was undimmed: there was a major survey of the art of Raymond Pettibon in New York featuring numerous Manson-inspired works, a heavily promoted Family documentary on ABC, early word of a new film project based on the meeting of Manson and television host Tom Snyder in 1981, and online whispers suggesting that the year might also finally bring us the long-rumored indie film project, *Manson Girls*. Manson was present in trailers for a narrative film—*Bigger Than the Beatles*—released in 2017 that traced out the relationship of Manson and Beach Boy Dennis Wilson, and in well-promoted teasers about Manson-related movies from prestige film directors Quentin Tarantino and Mary Harron.

Manson's death in November 2017 is not likely to change much about how he has operated in, and on, the American consciousness. The coverage of his demise at eighty-three did not show any indication that the volume was being turned down: the sober paper of record, the *New York Times*, headed its obituary with a phrase that described Manson as the "Wild-Eyed Leader of a Murderous Crew." Twitter was briefly aflame with the news—and was largely taken up with baby boomers instructing millenials why they should not be commemorating the event with "RIP Charles Manson." As the year ended, Manson appeared near the top of almost every list of major celebrity deaths, and rarely was he treated with anything other than the ritual horror that has so often attended mention of his name. The *Times*'s predictably detailed coverage repeated at some length the narrative first proposed by prosecutor Vincent Bugliosi at the 1970s trial, and then later codified in his 1974 book *Helter Skelter*, that suggested Manson directed his "murderous crew" to kill seven people over two nights in August 1969 as part of his evil plan to incite a race war. While Bugliosi worked hard at the trial of Manson and his followers to develop this story and never stopped working on it up until his own death in 2015, this Helter Skelter story has become much more important as a cultural script, meant to explain a good deal about the chaos of the American 1960s even if it could not necessarily hold water as a full or coherent explanation for Manson's actions. "Wild-eyed" also appeared in *Vox*'s coverage of Manson's death, in a piece that also uncritically quoted Bugliosi on Manson's race-war plans and his centrality to the culture. "Manson," according to the prosecutor, "has become a metaphor for evil, and there's a side of human nature that's fascinated by pure unalloyed evil." Our continued investment in Manson suggests that we are taking on the role played by the talent manager Col. Tom Parker who, upon the death of Elvis Presley, was asked what he planned to do: "Why, go right on managing him." There is every indication that we plan to go right on managing Manson, who shows no signs of becoming any less useful to us in death than he has been as a living presence for the past fifty years or so.[1]

The past few years have been relatively strong for Manson-related cultural chatter but this is really a question of marginal degree. Since August 1969, when a few members of the Family spent two nights killing seven residents of Los Angeles in what generally travels under the banner of the "Tate-LaBianca murders," the Family has never slipped from the American radar for long. We have rarely been able to talk about "the sixties" (or "the seventies") without Manson and his "girls" somehow entering the discussion; many of our most important cultural conversations about teenagers, about sexuality, drugs, music, California in the sixties, and yes, about family, mention the Manson Family in one way or another, whether we're always fully aware of it or not.

What is it about Manson, about the Family, that fascinates us and feeds our imaginations, and that hosts a range of artistic and cultural conversations? How and why they do they seem to matter, still, to so many of us? *Creepy Crawling: Charles Manson and the Many Lives of America's Most Infamous Family* will explore these questions. While Vincent Bugliosi, Ed Sanders, Jeff Guinn, and others have told and retold the story of the actual movements of Manson and his followers in the second half of the 1960s, what they have not done is offer a sustained exploration of the Manson Family in the deep context of the late 1960s and early 1970s, and as a cultural force to this day. How has this small-time con man and his ragtag minions creepy crawled through our social, political, and cultural life for close to fifty years now? While Manson and his followers gained their notoriety in connections with the killings of August 9 and 10, 1969, it was creepy crawling, more than murder, that was their emblematic crime, and it is creepy crawling that gives this book its frame.

I want to be clear here that I understand that Manson and the Family are most well-known for the murders of 1969, and that these murders provide an abundance of salacious, terrifying, and bizarre details: the writing in blood on the wall (RISE and the misspelled HEALTER SKELTER at the LaBianca house), the stunning dialogue reported from Cielo Drive, the post-murder snacks and showers at Waverly Drive—there is a generation's worth of film, fiction, and song built from the basic elements of the crimes. But I am not interested in the crime itself, and this is not a true crime book in any conventional sense. I will not take you back to those two nights when everything came down fast. As will become clear over these pages, I am much more interested in what went down in and around Los Angeles before the murders to bring Manson and the Family into the center of this Southern California culture, and how their crimes and their overall presence have been impossible to shake after their dark fame was established. It is in this light that I focus on creepy crawling rather than murder. The murders were bounded events. They happened, investigations and trials ensued, the convicted were incarcerated. But the creepy crawl never ended: Manson and his followers continue to make challenges to our sense of family, to our legal and judicial systems, to our minds. The Family, in short, has been central to the construction of American identity from the last days of the 1960s through our own time.

What the Family meant by creepy crawling was at once simple and profoundly upsetting. Leaving their communal home at Spahn Ranch in the San Fernando Valley, the Family would light out for private homes. Once inside, the Family members would not harm the sleeping family members. Instead, they would rearrange some of the furniture. That's all. Stealing was sometimes part of the agenda, especially toward the end, but it was not the raison d'être. (At the Manson trial, Family member Linda Kasabian sort of tried to explain this stealing with a spiritual/political framework: "[Y]ou take things which actually belong to you in the beginning, because it actually belongs to everyone.")[2] No dead bodies, no blood on the wall. Just the bare minimum of evidence that the sanctity of the private home had been breached—that *the* Family had paid a visit to *this* family. When trial prosecutor Vincent Bugliosi wrote about the creepy crawl in *Helter Skelter* (1974), he recounted that he trusted the jury would understand that the creepy crawl was a dress rehearsal for murder. It was not, but that was prosecutor talk, an argument launched by a lawyer who never really stopped trying the case.

The significant cultural legacy of the Manson Family is embodied in the creepy crawl. The central claim of this book is that we have yet to reckon with how much "furniture" the Family has moved around (or had moved around in its name). Our understanding of Manson and the Family's place in our national history has been too often hampered by cliché, above all that they represented the "end of the sixties," which is tempting, and convenient: after all, the murders took place in August 1969 and Manson and his confederates were indicted that December. It *was* the end of the 1960s. But that only gets us so far. There is little question that the Manson Family has held *sway* (to borrow the title of Zachary Lazar's Manson-inspired novel, which Lazar borrowed from the Rolling Stones' own end-of-the-sixties song of the same name) over our minds for almost half a century now. The power of the Manson Family goes well beyond matters of body count and even beyond the manifestly gruesome details of those two August nights—or the night in July when Gary Hinman was killed by Family associate Bobby Beausoleil and a few Family members. When we talk about Manson and his Family we only sometimes talk about Sharon Tate, Jay Sebring, Abigail Folger, Voytek Frykowski, Steven Parent, Rosemary LaBianca, and Leno LaBianca. While those seven tragic deaths certainly form one starting point for all the conversations we have about the Spahn Ranch commune, their details tell little about how we *use* Manson, Squeaky Fromme, Sadie Mae Glutz, Cupid, Ouisch, Snake, Tex, and all the rest in these wide-ranging and weighty discussions.

The Family appears so many places, communicating so many different claims about who we are, what we fear, and how we got here, that is has long been necessary to develop a key to crack the Manson Code. My hope is that *Creepy Crawling* provides that key. The central job the book takes on is a kind of detective work that Vincent Bugliosi was not inclined or trained to do. *Creepy Crawling* starts with the same question that *Helter Skelter,* and really all mystery stories, are organized around: whodunit? The major difference between these works and mine is that *they* are interested in the question of "who" and I accept that we already know that (sort of). The question we really need to attack has to do with the "it": what is the "it" exactly that we are accusing Manson and the Family of having done? Murder, of course, but what else? Misreading song lyrics? Eating garbage? Having too much sex? Doing too many drugs? Loving one another?

It is important to keep in mind that the sheer fact of our obsessive repetition of Manson lore is a big part of the story I am after here. Sarah Churchwell has written convincingly about such repetition in her book on Marilyn Monroe. "Repetition can itself be a pleasure," she writes. "It creates and fulfills expectation at the same time, and provides an illusion of control. We get what we were expecting, and what we wanted."[3] When it comes to Manson, it is not just that we ritually retell the facts of the case, or name-check Manson and his minions in song, story, film, and so on; we use "Manson" as a historical shortcut, a quick and efficient way to tell much larger stories. Here's an example. Joan Didion was one of the many journalists to find gold in the Manson case. Relatively early on she cozied up to Linda Kasabian who had turned state's evidence and according to some reports was planning to write a book about the former "Manson girl." Didion did not write that book, but she did write about the murders at length in *The White Album* (and I imagine some of you reading this could probably chant this along with me): "Many people I know in Los Angeles believe that the Sixties ended abruptly on August 9, 1969, ended at the exact moment when word of the murders on Cielo Drive traveled like brush fire through the community, and in a sense this is true. The tension broke that day. The paranoia was fulfilled."[4] There is plenty to argue with in Didion's actual "insight" as well as with her writing persona. (Barbara Grizzuti Harrison took care of the latter: "I am disinclined to find endearing a chronicler of the 1960s who is beset by migraines that can be triggered by her decorators having pleated instead of gathered her new dining room curtain."[5]) I have been researching *Creepy Crawling* for some years, and I only wish I had kept count of how many times I came upon these words of Didion, repeated as gospel; without an accurate count, the best I can offer at this point is an indefinite hyperbolic numeral along the lines of "umpteen" or a "gazillion." (Plenty of observers drew much more modest conclusions than did Didion: for instance, Dean Martin's daughter Deana, who was very much tied up with rising class of entertainers at the center of the Hollywood scene, remembers assuming that the Tate murders were likely the outcome of a "drug-crazed" burglary gone wrong.)[6]

Charles Manson and members of his Family were convicted in 1971 for crimes connected to seven murders committed in August 1969. From the time Manson and his followers were arrested up until today, the Family has also regularly been prosecuted for killing the counterculture, the "free" love movement, hitchhiking, the freak scene, and the 1960s as a whole. Along with the doomed concert sponsored by the Rolling Stones at the Altamont Freeway in California just a few days after the decisive break in solving the case, Manson quickly became a punchline and an epitaph. The spectacular murders of August 9 and 10, 1969, five at the Cielo Drive home shared by actor Sharon Tate and director Roman Polanski, and then two at the Waverly Drive home of Rosemary and Leno LaBianca the next night, contributed an enormous amount of energy to a story that got told over and over again, in many different forms, about how this was a tragic but necessary reboot: the counterculture had gone "too far" and these murders were somehow the natural result of too much *something*— with drugs and sex the most commonly cited villains. Critic Rob Sheffield has captured this cultural love affair with putative endings quite elegantly: "Manson-and-Altamont became the new Beatles-and-Stones, providing Nixon's America with the perfect twin metaphor for why kids were in need of some restraints. You still see Manson and Altamont cited as examples of why freedom doesn't work."[7] It may or may not be true that Family member Tex Watson announced at Cielo Drive that he was the Devil, doing the Devil's business; no amount of incorrect repetition can make it be true that "Sympathy for the Devil" was the song the Rolling Stones were playing when the Hells Angels killed audience member Meredith Hunter at the Altamont concert. But insisting that

"Sympathy for the Devil" was in the air sure makes for a good story.[8]

Decades are weird and unstable fictions. Michael Denning has reminded us that "decades are by no means the most adequate way of periodizing cultural history" and encourages us to think (in his example about what we usually refer to as "the thirties") about "generations" instead.[9] But it long ago became common-place to refer to the period from around 1965 to 1974 or so as "the sixties"; the cultural investment in the sixties is focused on organized liberation movements and countercultural challenges to mainstream traditions, morality, and rituals. And it is in this framework that Manson is alleged to have done his dirty deeds. Insofar as we have developed a collective belief in a meaningful and recognizable stretch of time that we agree to call "the sixties," there is a surprising consensus that Manson somehow helped to end the era. The stunning amount of investment that has been made in this construction should remind us above all that plenty of people were *really* eager to shut the door not just on Manson but on all the hippies, Yippies, and freaks he came to stand for. For sheer destruction of human life, the Tate-LaBianca murders do not rise to the level of the daily horrors inflicted at the same time by American forces in Vietnam, but we do not have the same tendency to imagine that this war "killed the sixties." The uncomfortable truth is that Manson was quickly converted into a weapon used to discipline the unruly generation in which he had immersed himself.

Joan Didion's words have contributed a great deal of energy to this cultural effort. This apocalyptic tale-telling had a clear case to make about the promiscuous cultural mixing that had been rife in the previous half decade. As the story goes, this was all bound to lead to a crack-up. Didion has not carried the torch by herself, of course. The end-of-the-sixties rhetoric has become a standard feature in voice-over documentary narration (what Twitter regulars have come to refer to more generally as *Ron Howard voice*), in journalistic feature stories, and in the work of plenty of professional scholars such as Todd Gitlin, who frames his reading of the Manson affair as belonging in the "realm of the demonic": "There was a sense of doom in the air," Gitlin informs us. "The culture," Gitlin explains, was "full of intimations of ending." A "hunger for an end."[10]

Newspaper coverage in the moment of Manson's arrest was much less likely to indulge in this kind of mythmaking. Take, for instance, an article that appeared in the *Sandusky Register* (Ohio) in mid-December, 1969, under the headline HOLLYWOOD: WHERE ALL WALKS OF LIFE MINGLE. This wire-service story made a clear case that one way to understand the Tate murders was as an unfortunate side effect of the relative cultural openness of Hollywood. This center of film and music production, according to the article, is a community where a person's "pedigree or background is of no consequence." One result is that the area is particularly vulnerable to "bums, losers, drifters and hustlers."[11] A similar story appeared a day earlier in the *Raleigh Register* (West Virginia) written by UPI's Hollywood columnist, Vernon Scott. Scott's basic take was that in Hollywood it was too easy for untrustworthy people to insinuate themselves into elite culture because (unlike in, say, Denver) there are no "background checks" or "questionnaires" to fill out.[12] To put it simply, the crimes of Manson and the Family very quickly made a very big impact in national and local media across the United States.

I don't want to take up too much space in this introduction prosecuting a case against Didion, Gitlin, and their latter-day followers who want to use the Manson moment as an occasion to shut the door on a number of the most ambitious movements and social experiments of the 1960s. There are plenty of Latin phrases you could throw at these forces of simplification and generalization (*post hoc ergo propter hoc*, for example), but what I care most about is how they participate in building a cult(ure) of Manson. The creepy crawls were short-term and episodic, but the whole point of this book is that even locking up a number of the key members of the Family has not done much to expel Manson from our midst. From Didion to Sanders to Bugliosi to the dozens, if not hundreds, of artists who have kept him present in our midst, the creepy crawl abides. Manson's Family have proven to be the (uninvited) guests who never leave.

There is a video found in the AP archive dated 1971 (and now on YouTube) that shows five women associated with Manson literally crawling through the streets of Los Angeles. This is, as the AP record puts it, a "stunt"—the young women are making sure that the people of Los Angeles know that even with their sisters and brothers behind bars, the creepy crawl lives on. It is pretty fascinating to track the reactions of the people they encounter. First a young man walks by, content with the apple he is eating and not paying much attention to the crawling women: this is Los Angeles and who knows what else he has seen on his walk. Then, after the camera shows us that they are crossing the intersection against the "Don't Walk" sign, we see the Family women pass a *very* square-looking white woman in matching sweater and skirt, white handbag slung over her forearm. This woman makes a slightly alarmed move to give these crawlers a wide berth, but then cannot help but turn back in order to get another look at the fascinating sight. At the same time, two youngish looking African Americans pass the women but appear not to even notice them. On the next block a fairly hip group of young white people comes out of an office building to watch the show. For the most part they are having a good time, except for one woman who is nervously chewing on her fingers. Two construction workers continue to do their work. A woman with a brown paper sack catches up to the crawlers and bends down to feed one of them; it is not clear if she is part of the stunt or not. The final significant figure, who I hope received an Oscar for Best Supporting Actor in some alternate universe, appears in the final seconds of the clip. He is white and middle-aged. He is mostly bald and his pants are hiked up a little bit higher than the national average. When we first see him he is pointing with alarm at the group—it seems possible he is trying to enlist somebody else to help him rectify the situation. But then we see him again as he crosses the street to get closer to the action: with one of the

most eloquent shrugs in film history, this Angeleno has under-
gone a change of attitude. Our furniture is being rearranged, his
shrug seems to say, and I guess there is not a damn thing we can
do about it. Over the course of the 1970s it got more and more
difficult to shrug the Family off. We wrestle again and again with
what the new arrangement of furniture means.

How wonderfully apt that Manson's most lasting cultural innovation was named after a Mattel product that now regularly shows
up on lists of the most dangerous toys ever produced. The Creepy
Crawlers were toy bugs, made of cooked molded plastic. Things
got hot and hands got burned. There was something big going on
("We get to use a really hot oven") and something really little too
("Mine is grosser looking than yours"). The Family's creepy crawlers similarly combined elements of serious adult activity—the
challenging of the boundaries of middle-class safety and private
property—and carnivalesque kid stuff ("Let's watch them sleep!").
In a strange and captivating way, the Manson Family has combined elements of adolescent precocity and adult infantilization.
This cultural stew has proven to be relentlessly compelling.

Over the years, Charles Manson himself has regularly alter-
nated between describing himself as a mythologically endowed
Bad Man and as a simple, almost childlike ward of the state. At a
1981 parole hearing, Manson insisted to the board, "I don't read or
write too good and I've stayed like a little kid. I stopped thinking
in 1954." On the other hand, some ten years later he told a similar
group, "I'm an outlaw . . . and I'm a gangster and I'm bad."[13] But the
wild variations in Manson's self-presentation (you can track the
evolution in the hair, the beard, the giggle and the cackle with very
little effort via YouTube) has not had all that much of an influence
on the larger culture's habitual invocations of California's most
famous convict or of his followers. The Manson Family lets us
talk about the banal unholy trinity (sex, drugs, rock and roll) in
all its many forms, but also about historical time itself: they are
the main characters in an origin story about the end of the 1960s.

Novelist Tony O'Neill has gotten at this quite efficiently in
Sick City (2010), in which he has a character ruminate that "over

the years the whole fucking incident got so mythologized that it's almost like it never happened in concrete reality. Like it was always some fucking awful movie about the death of the sixties." O'Neill's own failure of imagination (well, maybe it is actually Ed Sanders's limited imagination he is borrowing) won't let him get much beyond this insight; all he can really come up with is that maybe there were *other actual movies* that got lost in the chaos of the moment—movies that showed a party at which "everybody takes off their clothes"—even Mama Cass—to "take a pop" at Sharon Tate.[14] But for the most part it has been nearly impossible to avoid superficial summaries—such as the one offered up by television journalist Diane Sawyer in 1994—that these murders embodied a "savagery that brought an end to the decade of love."[15] The "decade of love," apparently, had been able to live through the firehoses turned on civil-rights marchers, a handful of heartbreaking assassinations, and a desperately brutal war in Southeast Asia. But it could not make it past some writing in blood on a couple of walls in Southern California.

Ultimately, while O'Neill briefly resists what he rightly points to as the mythologizing of Manson, he also participates in promoting the rumor culture and literary and journalistic hand-wringing that was ignited in Los Angeles in the second half of 1969 and really took off once prosecutor Vincent Bugliosi started dropping hints about the race-war/Helter Skelter angle. Bugliosi's linkage of the murders to Manson's obsessive, delusional Beatles fandom helped turn the end-of-the-1960s hot take into something like conventional wisdom. This is not to say Joan Didion and her disciples have gone unchallenged. Among others, Bobby Beausoleil, who, in his many decades in prison, has provided some of the most incisive commentary on the Family, the crimes, and the cultural fallout, has challenged the approach taken by her and so many others. ("I guess, because I know the truth, to me that explanation seems ridiculously simplified. How can anybody not see through that? Murder by Beatles records—this is what happens if you listen to Beatles' records and take LSD!? What could be a more blatant attempt to discredit the youth movement of the sixties than that?")[16] But sensible testimony offered by Beausoleil and others cannot even begin to stem the Manson tide. As Curt Rowlett has correctly noted, the arrest, public discussion surrounding, and trial of Charles Manson and members of his Family, helped energize the creation of a consequential new cultural figure, the "crazed hippie"—joining the parallel development of the "crazed returning veteran." (The most significant appearance of the "crazed hippie" in the immediate wake of Manson's imprisonment came with the case of Dr. Jeffrey MacDonald, accused of having murdered his wife and two children in early 1970. MacDonald claimed that his family was killed by hippies chanting, "Acid is groovy, kill the pigs.")[17]

In an earlier book of mine, on American cultural life after 9/11, I recounted a great line Joe Biden used when he was running for president in 2007. Mocking former New York Mayor Rudolph Giuliani's own campaign for the White House, Biden claimed that every sentence Giuliani uttered consisted of "a noun, a verb, and '9/11.'" It's a sick burn and I will shamelessly repurpose it here because in many ways this book seeks to understand the meaning of the many sentences that have been articulated over the past forty-five years or so that consist of a noun, a verb, and "Charles Manson." Invocations of Manson and his followers are so routine that it becomes interesting to think about how much weight is actually being carried by such references. By exploring this dynamic, the book is in a way an unruly history of our time—a history of the counterculture, but also of the mainstream culture it was in dialogue with, of children and their parents, of rock stars and groupies, of Los Angeles as a vibrant center of American life and also as the site of death and destruction.

The uncanny thing about repetition—with its alternating currents of pleasure and fear—is that it does not necessarily lead to anything like greater insight. This is why, for all of the gallons of ink and miles of film and so on that we have devoted to the Manson Family, it still made sense, not that long ago, for Bill James to write that the "cultural impact of the Manson murders is enormously *under*-appreciated." But even James cannot get out from under the rhetoric of end-of-the-sixties inevitability: "A culture based on categorical trust and unconditional acceptance was a balloon waiting to burst and Charles Manson was the needle."[18] So wait, the hippies were a balloon? An overfilled balloon? Because? They were too nice? Writer, director, and actor Buck Henry says that the Tate-LaBianca murders were "the defining event of our time"— not Nixon's 1968 election; the assassinations of Martin Luther King Jr. and Robert Kennedy; the escalating war in Vietnam; or the multiple race riots of the second half of the 1960s, but these seven killings. Van Dyke Parks, an associate of the Beach Boys and *sui generis* musician in his own right, argued that Manson "took a crap in the mess kit" of the 1960s and in doing so "scattered what had been a unified social field."[19] Shitting in our food, popping our balloons, changing our whole damn world—what can't Charlie Manson do?! With only a smidgen of perturbed hyperbole, Peter Vronsky has summed up this whole tendency by suggesting that Manson and the Family are "the shadow in every baby boomer's sweet memory of another time long past. Manson represents in our collective consciousness how the sixties came to die."[20] Much more nuanced is Phil Proctor of the Firesign Theater, who resists talk of inevitability and doom and argues more cogently that the Tate-LaBianca murders represented an "aberration and a warning."[21]

Of course "the sixties" did not "die." The decade ended, as decades do—that is, if you believe in time as linear and coherent. What Manson did was offer an opportunity for plenty of people, situated all over the social spectrum, to wipe their brows, exhale a sigh of relief, and retreat into their privileged positions of (relative) individual power. Few have written more trenchantly about the abandonment and suppression of this era's modes of cultural resistance than Jonathan Crary, who fiercely defends the anti-consumerism and collectivization that marked the sixties. Crary mourns the loss (or renunciation) of the insight that "happiness could be unrelated to ownership, to acquiring products or to individual status." In an analysis that is not about the Manson Family in any direct way,

Crary offers a remarkably useful framework for understanding the threat they posed (and the decades-long effort to characterize the Family as *only* the dark culmination of evil forces that had shot through the entire culture). As Crary puts it, "new forms of association" such as communes "introduced at least a limited permeability of social class and a range of affronts to the sanctity of private property." The Manson murders did not "end" the 1960s but rather helped build an arena for what Crary calls the "counter-revolution"—a terrible backlash that has been constituted, at least in part, by the "elimination or the financialization of social arrangements that had previously supported many kinds of cooperative activity."[22] What Crary says about communal life in general has been devastatingly true about the Manson Family: it has become impossible to think of anything having to do with them outside of the notion that the group represented a terrifying caricature of the dominant culture. Where Richard Schechner and his Performance Group took the challenge of the Manson Family seriously and wrestled with questions it raised about collective living and power, few others in the aftermath of the murders were willing to do anything but run screaming.[23]

Emma Cline's 2016 novel *The Girls* is one good corrective to this: among other things, Cline is able to suggest, tentatively at least, that the women of the Manson Family were able to construct autonomous pockets of activity marked by sisterly support and thrilling unconventionality. The work of *Creepy Crawling* is to build on the challenges made by Phil Proctor, Emma Cline, and a handful of others who have refused to place their bets on the conventional wisdom about this moment, and have chosen instead to explore how we have continued to live with all the messy complexities presented by the case.

Creepy Crawling moves all over the geographical map and all over the cultural map. Charles Manson and the many women (and a few men) who joined him are central characters in my account, but here they share space with many others on the complex landscape of a broader cultural history. A roll call of some key figures in the book might help give some sense of the scope: there is the late Vincent Bugliosi, of course, along with his freaky shadow, the poet and provocateur Ed Sanders, whose book *The Family* (1971) was the first major work published on the case. While Sanders has no doubt played an important role in our understanding of the power of the Family, it is Bugliosi who requires the larger portion of my attention. Manson's conviction for his role as mastermind of the Tate-LaBianca murders was delivered in early 1971; over the next five years Vincent Bugliosi continued to prosecute him—in public appearances, documentary films, and most significantly by far, in the book (1974) and televised (1976) versions of *Helter Skelter*. If these two immensely appealing texts frightened a generation of young people, including me (quick experiment: do a Google search of "helter," "skelter," and "bejesus"), Bugliosi's work also promoted a "true" crime narrative that brought the horrifying threat of Manson and his Family to light only to show how utterly that threat had been contained—mostly by the good work of an energetic prosecutor. And yet the Manson Family creepy crawl has continued unabated.

Another prominent figure in the book is Terry Melcher, son of Doris Day and a prominent music producer. Manson was a talented amateur songwriter and musician (Neil Young thought he could have been great with the right band and the proper production) who invested in the fantasy that Melcher would provide him with access to music-industry glory. Melcher, who worked with the Byrds and Paul Revere and the Raiders, among others, was first introduced to Manson by Dennis Wilson of the Beach Boys, who had become close to the Family, even letting a few of them live at his house for a while. Melcher got creepy crawled by the Manson Family in more than one way. In fact, aside from the seven people actually killed in August 1969 and members of the Family itself, there are few people who appear to have been as devastated by their contact with Manson as Melcher was. This privileged young man previously had counted himself—with the hunky Beach Boy Dennis Wilson and their mutual friend Gregg Jakobson—a charter member of a group whose reason for being was captured in its name: the Golden Penetrators.

But Melcher seems to have lost his cockiness fairly quickly after encountering Manson. Melcher visited Spahn Ranch officially to see what he thought about Manson's potential as a recording artist. That was not going to happen, of course: Melcher left the ranch lighter by fifty dollars ("they looked hungry," he told Vincent Bugliosi at Tex Watson's trial) and with something of a crush on Ruth Anne "Ouisch" Moorehouse, who was probably seventeen when Melcher met her. For quite some time after the murders, before deputy district attorney Bugliosi would unveil his Helter Skelter scenario, the dominant explanation of Manson's motivation in sending his followers out to kill was that he was exacting revenge on Melcher for dashing his music business dreams.

Melcher lived, but the Family was not done with him. According to numerous reports, they creepy crawled the Malibu home of Doris Day, where Melcher and his girlfriend Candice Bergen had gone to live after leaving their Benedict Canyon house on Cielo Drive, a house soon to be occupied by Sharon Tate and Roman Polanski. What is clear from all available evidence is that Melcher, a perfect representative of the rising class of cultural movers and shakers in Los Angeles in the late 1960s, was undone by the Manson Family. In *Creepy Crawling* I present an underappreciated story of how the Manson Family interacted with the new elite of Los Angeles (and beyond), separated by deep fissures of class, but trying to work out new methods of interaction. The scope and number of such meetings in and around the Manson case—before and after the murders—are staggering. Not just Melcher, but also Dennis Wilson and Dennis Hopper, Neil Young, and many others met with Manson and various members of his Family; Joan Didion met with Linda Kasabian; Kenneth Anger (and later Truman Capote) met with Bobby Beausoleil; filmmaker John Waters met with Leslie Van Houten.

Terry Melcher spent years after the Tate-LaBianca killings trying to sort out his relationship to the Manson Family. I move Melcher from the margins of this story to the center, because he stands as the best example of how the Manson Family reorganized the cultural landscape of Los Angeles in their moment of fullest social integration and also continued to shape individual consciousness and artistic productions for years to come. Melcher treated Manson and the Family as if they were part of his entourage—as "groupies," really. But Charles Manson creepy crawled from the fringes of the culture industry and insinuated himself into the center of Southern California's cultural life for a brief but significant moment. Whatever delusions might have accompanied his travels through the rock-and-roll clubs, homes, and studios of Los Angeles, it is clear that Charles Manson had taken the notion that the music world was characterized by class fluidity, that it was an arena where talent and charisma and commitment would be rewarded. But these Wilson brothers, these children of Doris Day and ventriloquist Edgar Bergen, were not so eager to see the gates opened to all freaky comers. While some report that Manson and perhaps Tex Watson socialized at 10050 Cielo Drive, ultimately Watson would have to scale those gates by brute force when the Family wanted to make its most dramatic impression.

Creepy Crawling is not a straightforward narrative history of the Manson case. We have shelves groaning under the weight of Manson true-crime books, memoirs, and biographies. I'm more interested in sifting through the contexts and the implications of the murders, life at the Ranch, the Family in Los Angeles, the way the case shaped modern true-crime literature, and the place Manson has come to play in American popular and "high" art. While I follow a roughly chronological scheme in *Creepy Crawling*, a central point is that Manson (as Mojo Nixon sang about Elvis in 1987) is everywhere.

I have been living with the Family since I first discovered *Helter Skelter* on my parents' bookshelf in the mid-1970s and watched the 1976 miniseries. (*Helter Skelter* was a main selection of the Book-of-the-Month Club, and I know I am not the only child to read Bugliosi and Piers Paul Read's *Alive* at far too young an age.) I have made my way through piles of pulp and literary novels, watched a scary number of 1970s splatter films, tracked down every hip-hop Manson shout-out I can find (and listened to one hip-hop collective called the Manson Family *and* one group known as Heltah Skeltah), immersed myself in the vast literature that developed in the early 1970s about runaway youth and communes, figured out the relationship of the Pixies' 1989 song "Wave of Mutilation" to Manson and the Beach Boys, read true-crime accounts of the Family that *predated* even Ed Sanders's work, collected all Manson-related rumors I could find, and spent hours puzzling over a sculpture made by John Waters featuring baby-Manson and baby-Michael Jackson playing together.

I came to the project knowing that significant courtroom dramas often come to hold a remarkable amount of cultural energy. Since I developed a deep interest in the Sacco and Vanzetti case as an undergraduate, and the Leo Frank case some years later, I have rarely moved far from my commitment to teach and write about major trials and their cultural fallout. Manson, though sentenced to death at his original trial, had his sentence commuted in 1972 when California changed its death-penalty law. But increasingly the actual Manson has become an unimportant shadow of our "cultural" Manson. This is how cultural history often works: the presence of the real cannot help but enter into a dialogue—often a very thrilling, productive, and colorful dialogue—with the claims of the fictional.

That dialogue is very much at the heart of *Creepy Crawling*. Cultural meaning develops in fits and starts, not so much with clear, defining moments or conclusive statements, but rather out of tensions, eruptions, projections, and contradictions. The obsessive interest American artists and audiences have demonstrated for Manson and his girls is not a simple matter of "attraction," nor can it easily be dismissed as rubbernecking repulsion. What makes it fascinating, to me as a cultural historian, is its *capacity*. If I might flirt with a cliché for a moment, it might be said that the Manson Family is not a historical destination, but a vehicle. In *Creepy Crawling*, we will find ourselves riding in dune buggies to all sorts of interesting places, from meaningful countercultural margins to the absolute dead center of Americans' efforts to define themselves in a time of great chaos.

The book is divided into four main parts. In the first section, "Creepy Crawling Family," I get right down to business and try to start figuring out how Charles Manson and *his* Family have shaped all of *our* families in the half century or so that they came to public consciousness. While Manson himself has consistently denied that he ever referred to his Spahn Ranch collective as a "family," this group of young people not only came to be called "the Family," but were generally understood as having launched a major challenge to the conventional family of modern America. In this opening section of *Creepy Crawling* I explore how Manson and his "girls" emerged as a nightmare vision of what had gone wrong with American households in the late 1960s. The fact that these young women still generally get called "girls"—in historical narratives, in film, and in fiction—begins to hint at our confusion regarding who they were and how they lived. There was a wide range of women who came to be known as the Manson girls: some were exploited and abused minors, while others (Catherine "Gypsy" Share comes to mind) seem to have exercised a fair amount of power in the Family context. The girls were vulnerable runaways, pragmatic sister-wives, and terrifying tricksters. In an era when the basic terms of what counted as a family were being rearticulated, the women of the Family were offering complex evidence about how these social negotiations might play out in real time.

This was a patriarchal clan, and Manson was, by far, its most powerful man. One of the most uncomfortable truths presented to us by the members of the Family is that their families of origin were also characterized by numerous broken taboos and trespasses of various significant boundaries. After the Tate-LaBianca murders came to light, numerous attempts were made to marginalize and pathologize the everyday life of the Family. But a preponderance of evidence suggests that the Family operated in many recognizable "family" ways—doing important socializing over meals, following the dictates of a central male figure, and so on. A caricature of the nuclear and patriarchal family to be sure, the Spahn Ranch community also shined a bright light on some major contradictions of the sexual- and gender-liberation movements of the late 1960s.

Among other things, the group that settled at Spahn Ranch was what was generally called a commune in the late 1960s. The Manson Family created a problem that never really went away for other countercultural groups settling in communes on ranches, farms, and in urban settings. As Neil Young would later say, "It was the ugly side of the Maharishi. There's this one side, with flowers and white robes, then there's something that looks a lot like it, but isn't at all."[24] Additionally, although rarely discussed in a focused way, a good number of Manson's young compatriots were runaways. The problem of the runaway formed a major crisis in the late 1960s and early 1970s and a great deal of political and media attention was expended on attempts to diagnose and solve this problem. Manson's girls hardly ever received the sympathetic attention bestowed on other runaways, but it is important to stitch them into this history in order to explore the possibility that they deserved something more humane and nuanced than the severe neglect and punishment that came their way. Over the course of this section I try to reckon with how this one infamous Family contributed crucial data to an ongoing conversation about how families should be organized and how their members should act.

In the second section of the book, "Creepy Crawling Los Angeles," I put the Family in its proper place—the chaotic, fascinating, and ultimately punishing world of Southern California in the second half of the 1960s. Here I examine in detail how the Tate-LaBianca killings forced observers to envision California as both a place of horror and darkness and as a landscape of creation. What did Manson and the Family do *to*—and get *from*—the rising class of creative artists (mostly in the film and music industries) as they creepy crawled through the Valley and the canyons, the Strip, and the beach? While Ed Sanders, Vincent Bugliosi, and so many others have pushed us to think of the Manson collective as a sort of marginal eruption—a social disease—here I put them back where they belong, near the center of the cultural life of Los Angeles in the last few years of the 1960s. Manson used the power he held over his young female acolytes to carve out a temporarily comfortable place for himself in and around Los Angeles. I offer up a much more detailed picture than previously available of the social hierarchy of a transforming Los Angeles and how Manson slotted himself into this fluid social order.

Manson and his followers operated in an interesting space in this new Los Angeles. They were not rock stars or film actors (though Bobby Beausoleil had already enjoyed some success as a musician, and he and Catherine Share had both appeared in a softcore porn film—shot, coincidentally, at Spahn Ranch). Nor were they simply—or only—the kind of devoted fans often referred to as groupies (although Family member Cathy "Cappy" Gillies may have been, with Buffalo Springfield). While I have mentioned that Neil Young is the rare celebrity willing to describe Manson as occupying a central role in the social and cultural world of hip Los Angeles, there is plenty of evidence that the "scruffy little guru," in the words of one Beach Boy, assimilated quite well. Manson donned the mantle of the "freak," an identity related to but distinct from "hippie," as he made his way into the hearts, minds, and homes of some of the most powerful players in Los Angeles. I also discuss how fully and quickly this loose collective of "freaks" was ejected from the center. It did not take long for an informal conspiracy of denial to take hold, as many of the young power brokers guiding the direction of the entertainment industries worked to expel the traces of Manson from their midst. These people—from major actors to a wide range of LA musicians—have been upfront about their backlash against young freaks: no more picking up hitchhikers, no more open doors in the canyon, no more crash pads.

In Part Three, "Creepy Crawling Truth," I take a look at the complex ways the Manson Family has become a central figure in true-crime writing of the past forty-five years. Here I explain how Manson has captivated audiences, mostly through the strategic work carried out by Vincent Bugliosi inside and, more significantly, outside the courtroom. For too long Bugliosi has appeared as an objective reporter, a sort of "just the facts, ma'am" figure.

But the prosecutor was a complex character, and in this section I reintroduce him as such. There are really two main characters in this section: Vincent Bugliosi and Ed Sanders. Bugliosi, of course, was the prosecutor in the original trial and later the coauthor of *Helter Skelter.* Sanders was a poet, provocateur, rock musician, and reporter for the *Los Angeles Free Press*, one of the most important alternative newspapers in the country. Sanders, like many other members of the counterculture, initially found Manson and the Family to be sympathetic characters. But Sanders undertook a fascinating journey during his time covering the trial, and ultimately came to denounce Manson. He provides us with a crucial case study for understanding how Manson first creepy crawled his way onto the landscape of the counterculture and then was exorcised by some of its key figures. Sanders has revised his book numerous times and more recently published a (re)hash of it in the form of a biography of Sharon Tate. Like Terry Melcher, Ed Sanders seems never to have really gotten over Manson.

In the book's final section, "Creepy Crawling Art," I wrestle with the remarkably robust afterlife of the Manson Family. It is difficult to convey an accurate sense of how amazingly *present* Charles Manson and the Family have been in the cultural life of the United States from 1969 forward. Manson has been a regular reference point in our discussions of mass murder, the dark arts, California, rock and roll, evil, and sex, just to name a few obvious areas. In this section I first draw a cultural map of all the places the cult leader and his followers have made their presence felt in American culture. Mike Rubin, writing in a fascinating article in *Spin* in 1994, wondered about the process by which Manson imagery had "creepy-crawled out of the fringes" right into the center of American culture. The only problem with Rubin's piece is that his basic premise is faulty: from the moment he came to public consciousness in late 1969, Manson has never been far from the heart of things.[25]

What I am calling "Manson Art" ranges from serious book-length investigations and extended musical works to (seemingly) thoughtless shout-outs, which on their own might serve to undercut Manson's scariness but also, collectively, act to underscore the cult leader's centrality to American conceptions of terror, class, sexuality, race, family, and so on. (There are, for instance, countless contemporary mystery novels that feature a police officer or private investigator saying some version of "I hope we don't have another Charlie Manson on our hands.") Signs of Manson and his followers are far-flung and include writing on the wall in blood, unconventional family arrangements, sexy/weird female hippies, and charismatic men with beards and "Southern" accents. Manson never got his musical voice recorded in a culturally significant way and worried about not getting his voice heard during his trial. But his major post-conviction interviews (with Tom Snyder, Geraldo Rivera, Diane Sawyer) have formed an important archive—as stand-alone cultural artifacts and as a deep reservoir of hip-hop samples. For every Killer Mike, using Manson soundbites as basis of serious and sustained political commentary, there are literally hundreds of rappers who dip into this material as easily available intensifiers in crime narratives.

While I try to box the cultural compass in this section, I also suggest that some works of Manson art require more attention than others—either because of their impact or their complexity. Neil Young's *On the Beach* (released in 1974, the year of *Helter Skelter*), for instance, from the dark and hilarious album cover to the music in the grooves, is a prime example of a work of popular art just drenched in Manson. *On the Beach* represents an effort by a major Los Angeles–identified artist to reckon with the wreckage left behind by the Family. As with so much of the work inspired by Manson, this is the art of "aftermath," part of a loose, collective effort to sort out what comes after the apocalypse. It is simply impossible to imagine post-1960s American culture without Manson and the Family somewhere near the center.

*

Part I

Creepy Crawling Family: Charles Manson in Our Homes

*

Mother Father Sister Brother

"Picture in your mind that I am your father." According to Susan Atkins, a.k.a. Sadie Mae Glutz, a key early member of Charles Manson's tribe of followers, this invitation was a crucial part of her initial seduction by Charles Manson in the Haight-Ashbury district of San Francisco in 1967. Whatever Manson's warmed-over Scientology-jargon-as-sexual-come-on lacked in subtlety, it worked exceedingly well on Atkins. "[I]t was," as Atkins put it during her Grand Jury testimony in December 1969, "a beautiful experience."[1] Atkins's own father, more or less a blank space, has never commented on the particulars of his daughter's involvement with Manson except to admit that he had (obviously) miscalculated the danger he posed. In a bit of testimony that seems like it could have been scripted by Damon Runyon, all Edward Atkins was ever able to offer up with respect to why he had not tried to intervene more forcefully in the life of his delinquent daughter is that he thought the young hippies who constituted the Family were just a "slap-happy bunch of kooks."[2] Edward Atkins was not the only "straight" to underestimate the challenge that Manson and his followers were posing to conventional norms of family as they existed in the 1960s.

While Manson and his girls did not invent sexual liberation, the generation gap, or group marriage (just for instance), after the arrests of 1969 they very quickly came to represent a dark burlesque of the alleged decline of the "traditional" American family. Sociologists, politicians, journalists, and other sympathetic observers were working assiduously in the late 1960s to make it clear that young runaways were, frequently, responding to a staggering number of challenges at home. But a popular discourse developed around the Manson Family that suggested the degradation and downfall of the young women was mostly a result of bad choices made by immature, impulsive, and possibly pathological rebels.[3]

There is no unanimity on whether this "slap-happy bunch of kooks" even consistently referred to themselves as a family. In her grand jury testimony, Atkins insisted that "among ourselves we called ourselves the Family, a Family like no other Family."[4] Terry Melcher's aide-de-camp Gregg Jakobson insists that he was the one who first described the ragtag group at Spahn Ranch as a family. For his part, Charles Manson denies that the group used the word to describe its social arrangement; according to the leader there "was no Manson Family" until the moment of arrest: "There was a music group known as The Family Jams, but . . . that Manson Family thing—the DA put that together."

Manson put an even sharper political point on the whole question. What the straight world called "the Family," its leader insisted, was made up of young people that same world had rejected, "so I took them to my garbage dump."[5]

For their part, *Rolling Stone*'s reporters wanted its readers in 1970 to know that this was indeed a Family. "The press likes to put the Manson family in quotation marks," David Dalton and David Felton wrote, but "it's a real family, with real feelings of devotion, loyalty and disappointment. For Manson and all the others it's the only family they've ever had."[6] Susan Atkins herself would insist on this in her first autobiography, arguing that "family" feelings were developing even before the young renegades moved south from San Francisco to Los Angeles.[7]

There were a number of obvious reasons for the American media to flip its collective wig in the wake of the Tate-LaBianca murders and subsequent arrest of Manson and his compatriots.

Not least among these is that the freaky residents of Spahn and Barker Ranch most certainly were operating as some kind of family. But from the second half of 1969 until, really, our own time, Charles Manson, Susan Atkins, Leslie Van Houten, Patricia Krenwinkel, Lynette Fromme, and all the rest have posed a remarkably robust challenge to conventional ideas about what a family should look like and how it should operate. On a very meaningful level Manson and the Family were social entrepreneurs. They recognized that the post–World War II experiment in family reorganization (essentially the move to a male-directed nuclear family that lived under one roof with no other relatives present) had run its relatively short course and needed to be replaced with other forms of collective life. In the late 1960s the Family was surrounded by many others who were also actively innovating new forms to replace the increasingly irrelevant nuclear, patriarchal family. The new institutions created were called "communes" and "crash pads," "shelters" and "families." The breakdown in what had been conventionally (and misleadingly) called the "traditional family" contributed a considerable amount of energy to wider conversations taking place all across society that were concerned with child-rearing, gender and power, the best way to live in groups, and sex. These conversations were held at special White House conferences, on television shows, in encounter groups, at universities, and in works of popular psychology. There was a remarkable amount of cultural agreement that the American family was undergoing some kind of paradigm shift. Manson and his followers became grist for this mill even *before* they gained criminal notoriety in December of 1969.

David E. Smith, cofounder and director of the Haight Ashbury Free Medical Clinic, engaged in a study of Manson and his followers before they left for Los Angeles in 1968. While he didn't publish his findings until 1970, it is clear that Smith understood these young people to be launching a major protest against the rigid structures and undernourishing realities of conventional family life. Smith ultimately found much that was troubling about the communal arrangements hammered out by Manson and his followers, and in the article he ultimately published with his cow-riter Al Rose in the *Journal of Psychedelic Drugs* in 1971, Smith refused to use the term "family" to describe the group he insists was known as "Charlie's Girls": "Approximately 20 members of this commune referred to themselves as a 'family,' but we have chosen the term 'group marriage commune' because of the polyg-amous sexual relations."[8] Smith, of course, was engaged in some damage control here. As a dedicated countercultural provider, he was interested in creating distance between the Manson Family and the other alternative communities he came into daily contact with through his work at the Haight clinic. But these people were living under one roof (well, on a bus), having sex together in a male-dominated milieu, and procuring and eating food together. They might not have looked much like their own—or Smith's—families of origin, but they were certainly acting like a family of choice in this late 1960s moment.

The sociologist Donald Nielsen has helped us to understand why it was so hard to accept that the Manson group was a family. While plenty of cultural commentators were willing to acknowl-edge, and often mourn, the disappearance of the "traditional" family, most found Manson and his girls simply too unsettling in their modes of interacting. In the aftermath of their arrests, the Manson Family became "objects of terror and titillation," as Nielsen explains. The upset they caused was largely a result of how their behavior served to confuse "such usually distinct social relations as brother and sister, daughter, husband and wife."[9] The social webs constructed by Manson and his compatriots included elements of standard parent–child relations but also encompassed what Nielsen has called "a whirl of kinship terms." As a result of this, the members of the Family made it nearly impossible for representatives of straight society to understand them or develop anything like empathy for them.[10] If other counterculture upstarts were expanding the rhetoric of brotherhood and sisterhood in the 1960s—often in a recognizably progressive social and politi-cal way—Manson and his girls were doing so in an uncomfortably "creepy" way. Elected, appointed, and volunteer representatives of straight culture responded with incomprehension, anger, and discipline. "Incest" was the barely repressed term in all of this: Susan Atkins, of course, was frantically pointing at the missing word in her description of her first sexual encounter with Manson. Agonized attempts to explain what exactly was wrong with the Manson Family in the 1970s and beyond, without using the word incest, act as a poignant reminder that "incest is not the taboo." As literary scholar Christine Grogan has explained, "it happens too often" for that to be true. What *is* forbidden is "talking about it."[11]

It has always been much more comfortable to deny that the Family was a family than it has been to acknowledge how its configuration could cast a harsh light on more conventional American families. One obvious result of the refusal to acknowledge this group as a family fed directly into Vincent Bugliosi's surprising decision to prosecute the Helter Skelter motive. This was a value-added proposition to begin with. The deputy district attorney did not even have to provide motive to get a conviction against Manson. But when it came time to construct his account, Bugliosi landed on what was actually quite an implausible theory: the prosecutor wove together various strands of Manson's philosophy to suggest the cult leader organized the murders as part of a chaotic effort to inspire a race war that would leave him, essentially, as ruler of the world. Numerous commentators— from active participants in life in the Family to later critics—have attempted to draw attention to the rather left-field nature of Bugliosi's story.[12] Defense attorney Irving Kanarek made cutting reference to the notion promoted by Bugliosi that Manson had instructed Linda Kasabian to drop Rosemary LaBianca's wallet in a gas station bathroom in Sylmar, mistakenly believing this was a Black neighborhood: "Are we to believe that by means of a wallet found in a toilet tank Mr. Manson intended to start a race war?"[13] For his part, and insofar as he has ever given anything like coherent testimony, Manson has been fairly consistent in his claim that the Helter Skelter motive was Bugliosi's fiction; to the Family, its leader insists, Helter Skelter was simply a song and the name of an "after-hours nightclub" opened at Spahn Ranch "to make money and play some music and do some dancing and singing and play some stuff to make some money for dune buggies to go out in the desert."[14]

What does Bugliosi's fantastical Helter Skelter theory have to do with the integrity of the Manson clan as a family? Most directly it acted as a sly refusal to acknowledge what so many people saw as the much more obvious explanation for the murders: "love of brother." Once the Melcher hypothesis was discredited (that is, the idea that the murders were some kind of revenge Manson organized against the record producer for refusing to sign him)—most informed observers were certain that Manson and/or Tex Watson very clearly understood that Melcher had moved out of the Cielo Drive home that Sharon Tate and Roman Polanski now inhabited—it became easier for many to understand that the murders in August may have been intended to call attention away from the Family's role in the late-July murder of Gary Hinman. The short version of this story is that Hinman was killed by Bobby Beausoleil with the help of Susan Atkins and Mary Brunner (and possible assists from Bruce Davis and Manson himself) as a payback for a drug deal gone bad. The writing the Family members left on Hinman's wall— POLITICAL PIGGY with a paw print—was itself meant to hint at Black Panther involvement. Once Beausoleil was arrested for the crime, while driving Hinman's car, the other two nights of murder were carried out as a sort of false flag operation: if people were still being killed, with similar writing in blood left on the walls, then perhaps investigators would conclude that Beausoleil could not possibly be the right suspect in the Hinman murder.

But Manson and his band of nicknamed followers (Sadie, Squeaky, Ouisch, and the rest) were not a family in any way that Bugliosi was willing to recognize. It is worth noting that Bugliosi introduces himself as an "intruder" in *Helter Skelter* when he wants to move from being an "unseen narrator" to a character in the drama. After running down the basic facts of his professional resume and his intellectual bona fides, the prosecutor adds, "Married. Two children."[15] Bugliosi trusted that his readers would understand (as he knew the jury he had faced would understand) that Manson had a family too, but that this family was a travesty of "normal" families, an insult to the many people in the dominant culture who could capture their own reality by simply writing, "Married. Two children." Bugliosi did want to present the Spahn Ranch gang as the Family when it suited his goal of calling attention to what he saw as the delusional heart of the enterprise. But the gate swung shut when it came to allowing for the possibility that this group *acted* like a regular family, that it displayed loyalty, took risks for each others' benefit, and so on.

Why was it so hard for Bugliosi and so many others to accept that, as Donald Nielsen has finally insisted, the Manson Family murdered "out of love"? Nielsen, one of the wisest commentators we have on the case, acknowledges that Bugliosi's Helter Skelter scenario may well "have circulated in some form among the group members, but it certainly was not the actual motive for the Tate-LaBianca crimes. Instead, the motive was more mundane and integrally connected with the issues concerning social experience" in the present, rather than with fantasies about the future. Nielsen reminds us that numerous members of the Family *said* that the crimes of August were inspired by their loving effort to cover up the murder of Gary Hinman, "but no one could take such an account seriously."[16] None of this is to suggest that we develop any kind of late-game sympathy for the people who killed Gary Hinman and the victims at Cielo and Waverly Drives. But rather than continue to accept the seemingly natural logic of Vincent Bugliosi's Beatles/race-war theory it is important to imagine that the killers acted, in the summer of 1969, out of impulses that may well have been rooted in real family feeling.

The bulk of Manson's female followers were born in the first few years of what historians, journalists, and sociologists have come to refer to as the "baby boom." They were children of the 1950s and their mothers were the women Betty Friedan described as suffering under the "feminine mystique," that constellation of limiting social expectations she summarized in 1963 as the "problem that has no name."[17] The white, middle-class nuclear family of the 1950s was already being memorialized, mourned, and idealized by the late 1960s. This "elusive traditional family" (as Stephanie Coontz has described it) was the object of all sorts of intense projection during the moment of the Tate-LaBianca murders.[18] As the Manson Family came into focus in the late 1960s they served an important social function as a red flag: the Family got waved around as a warning and a call to action. The time was ripe for some retrenchment, some battening of the hatches, some scapegoating. The Spahn Ranch gang simply could not be legitimized as a social unit by the forces shaping mainstream opinion in the United States because of how this would undercut the status-claim of more conventional nuclear families. Vincent Bugliosi and his co-conspirators in the mainstream media worked assiduously to invalidate the notion that Manson and his followers could be understood as part of a wave of emerging alternatives to the much-bruited nuclear family.

From soon after the murders down to our own time, Bobby Beausoleil has been one of the most energetic supporters of the notion that Manson and his followers did form a family. Beausoleil is a fascinating figure in the story of the Manson Family. He was not a member of the immediate Family but something like a close cousin. Unlike Manson, he seems to have been generally understood to be a talented and professionally competent musician. Among other things Beausoleil played guitar in a band called the Grass Roots (*not* the "Let's Live for Today" Grass Roots, but a different ensemble) that featured Arthur Lee, later to front the important psychedelic act Love. He seems to have exerted something like Manson's power—without the spiritual mumbo-jumbo—over the women who joined him. As with virtually every single issue related to the Manson Family, its crimes, and its motivations, it is absolutely necessary to take insider testimony (from Family members, from Vincent Bugliosi, from Terry Melcher, and so on) as motivated and partial. In Beausoleil's case it is especially important to understand that once he went to prison he seems to have enjoyed, at least at times, the opportunity to play the trickster. This is especially true for the interview Beausoleil gave to Truman Capote in the early 1970s, ultimately published in

Music for Chameleons, which is full of rhetorical acrobatics (not to mention Capote's sly and provocative fictionalizing). Beausoleil has, in the years since the Capote interview, seriously challenged its veracity. But here (and elsewhere) Beausoleil is quite straightforward about his role at the center of the Manson family's crisis:

> The girls got on the stand and tried to really tell how it all came down, but nobody would listen. People couldn't believe anything except what the media said. The media had them programmed to believe it all happened because we were out to start a race war. That it was mean niggers going around hurting all these good white folk. Only—it was like you say. The media, they called us a "family." And it was the only true thing they said. We were a family. We were mother, father, brother, sister, daughter, son. If a member of our family was in jeopardy, we didn't abandon that person. And so for the love of a brother, a brother who was in jail on a murder rap, all those killings came down.

If our acceptance of the Beausoleil hypothesis (and our understanding of Manson and his followers *as* a family) must rely on the words of insiders with complex motivations, it is important to remember that the "love of brother" motive is not exculpatory: it is explanatory. In the wake of the arrests and the challenge to the workings of the Family as it had been most recently constituted at Spahn and Barker ranches, it seems to have been a matter of real moment for many of the key players to explain *who* they were and *why* they had acted as they did.[19]

What these people wanted to make clear—Charles Manson and Bobby Beausoleil, along with Patricia Krenwinkel, Tex Watson, Leslie Van Houten, Susan Atkins, Mary Brunner, Catherine Share, Sandra Good, Paul Watkins, Lynette Fromme, and many others—is that, whether or not they used the word "family," they had been living for an extended period of time connected by an ethic of nurture and commitment. In her late 1970s, post-conversion autobiography, Susan Atkins insisted that their Family had much in common with conventional ones, explaining approvingly that Barbara Hoyt introduced her to Manson's group in the Haight by telling her "this is another kind of family—a real one. We all live together and take care of one another."[20] The Manson Family, according to Atkins, followed many recognizable protocols; dinner, she writes, "was an important time for us—the time when we overtly drew together as a community or family."[21] Members of the Family procured, prepared, and ate food together; they made plans for the future; they gave birth to and began raising children according to their own sense of what was best; they fought among themselves and deferred to the authority of their powerful male leader.

It has become commonplace in accounts of the Manson Family to call attention to the difficult situations many of its members had experienced in their families of origin. Again, Donald Nielsen offers an apt summary: "in general their families of origin were experienced as damaged and troubled, either because of the death, divorce, or other absence of one parent, or the extreme domination of father over mother, or some other variant of asymmetry between parental roles."[22] Manson himself faced horrifying tribulations as a boy and teenager; speculation about just *how* bad has become something of a cottage industry for biographers and fiction writers. Many of the young women who joined Manson either lost parents to death, or suffered extreme abuse or neglect. Perhaps none suffered more family loss than Catherine "Gypsy" Share. According to Vincent Bugliosi, Share's birth parents were both members of the French Resistance and committed suicide during World War II. Her adoptive mother, a French woman who married an American man, was diagnosed with cancer during Share's teenage years and committed suicide when the young woman was sixteen.[23]

These individual stories of affliction rarely led to sympathy for Manson or the women. Observers were much more likely to indulge in blaming expressions of dime-store psychology. Here is a real piece of analysis offered up by an accredited psychiatrist in 1970: "They formed the 'bad' family, in caricature of their parents. It was a schizophrenic family, the outgrowth of early emotional deprivation. They were, in a sense, reenacting the primal scene. To a child's irrational mind, the sex act resembles a man trying to murder a woman (or a woman killing a man depending on the sexual position)." This "expert" witness, writing in a book called *I Hate My Parents: The Real and Unreal Reasons Why Youth Is Angry*, also suggested that Susan Atkins's killing of Sharon Tate's fetus might have been a displaced reenactment of how she felt when "her mother got pregnant with her little brother."[24] Maybe.

David E. Smith also wrote psychodynamically about Manson in his 1971 book on the Haight-Ashbury Free Medical Clinic, drawing on his own observation of the Family and on input from other professionals. Smith concluded that Manson was a delusional schizophrenic. He was, according to this account, trying to "find his parents" through a complex process whereby he would become "a parent himself to younger and weaker people . . . thereby nurturing himself by proxy."[25] Psychology, in short, was no help. Charles Manson had been the object of psychiatric reporting since at least 1951 (as biographer Jeff Guinn makes clear), and there has rarely been anything that could pass for helpful insight about his behavior in any of this writing. Manson himself told John Gilmore that when he was released from prison and found his way to the Haight-Ashbury he was gratified to meet some hippies who looked up to him: "I had someone to protect."[26] But Manson's own dime-store psychologizing seems no more trustworthy than that published by actual trained professionals.

Professional and amateur sociologists and historians of the family have much more to offer us than the psychoanalysts do. Radical activist Abbie Hoffman, for instance, understood by the late 1960s that much of what was taking place on the larger political landscape was energized by more localized battles taking place between parents and children. Hoffman was one of the major proponents of the idea that runaway teenagers were at the vanguard of social revolution—modern actors in what he came to call a "slave revolt."[27] Hoffman was also among the many who worried early and often about what kind of "surrogate" families the young people were finding when they reached the Haight, the Village, and other countercultural zones.[28] Ed Sanders shared this concern, describing the vulnerable flower children as being akin to "plump white rabbits surrounded by wounded coyotes."[29]

If we are going to understand anything about how the breaking news of the Manson Family's alleged crimes in the second half of 1969 circulated, we will have to understand just how widely held was the belief that the American family was in decline, if not utter chaos in this era. As historian Natasha Zaretsky explains, the alarm about the family "emerged out of the cultural ferment of the 1960s." The so-called traditional family was under perceived attack from the women's liberation movement, which expanded on Engels's vision of the subordination of women as endemic to life in the family under capitalism, and from the gay liberation movement, which made demands vis-à-vis "love, sexuality, and kinship" that could not be satisfied within the bounds of the conventional heterosexual family. According to Zaretsky, "Policymakers and social scientists claimed the institution of the family was under unprecedented strain."[30] One of the major elements of "crisis" obsessively repeated in these cultural conversations had to do with the absence or relative disengagement of fathers from American family life: by the early 1970s one in six American children was growing up in a family without a father; even fathers who were literally present were described by many observers as being alienated from and inaccessible to their children.[31] For his part, Manson always recognized that his own fatherlessness made him immediately suspect and tried, in his statement, to transform his experience into a critique of the cruel realities of American jurisprudence: "My father is the jailhouse," Manson said. "My father is your system."[32] Attempts to reckon with changes in American family life—changes wrought by the expanding presence of women in the paid workforce and changes wrought by a devastating shift to what would only some years later be recognized as a decades-in-the-making conversion to a post-industrial labor system—erupted into a panicky, multifront attempt to sort out just what had gone wrong.[33] The Tate-LaBianca murders were not infrequently brought into the hysterical discussion, as when one tabloid in the early 1970s insisted that not only were there "Twenty Million Charlie Mansons Running Loose" in the United States but that the cause was clear: "Doctors Say Parents to Blame."[34]

The young women followers of Charles Manson broke all sorts of mainstream norms regarding sexual activity, appearance, drug use, and consumerism. But it is likely the alleged violence of some of them that most disturbed the wider public. Some of the Family women, after all, were convicted of killing a pregnant woman, who begged for the life of her baby. It seems fairly clear that the fear created by the Manson girls was complexly tied up with social anxieties about women's liberation. Ann Jones has written persuasively about a destructive rhetoric that developed in the 1970s (mostly rooted in the work of criminologist Freda Adler) that essentially blamed the rise in crimes committed by women on the women's liberation movement. Seeing causation instead of a highly motivated anti-feminist correlation, Adler described the rise in crime as the "shady aspect of liberation."[35] Whatever sympathy the Manson women might have accessed *as* young women was forfeited because they had too much non-monogamous sex and then murdered a pregnant woman.[36]

The alleged crisis in the family was addressed in multiple contexts—from children's television shows to government-sponsored conferences. *Sesame Street* debuted in 1969, and viewers of later seasons might be surprised to find out how strongly the show threw in on the side of "traditional" families. In the "Father, Mother, Children" song, which debuted in the first months of its initial season, the puppets gave very clear definitions of each role. The first character to sing is the father, who explains that there are "a few things you need to be a father": "First of all you need to have a wife." In addition to being kind and being able to "fix anything," a father also "buys you food and clothes" and "works all day to get you those." A mother on the other hand, needs to have a husband, and does not seem to leave the house. The mother puppet explains that "a mother cooks, a mother sews, a mother washes all the clothes." The main job of the child-puppets is to make clear that this is a conventional nuclear family. Daughter puppet, in addition to making clear that she likes dolls (unlike her rascally brother who is busy making mudpies), announces that she is "a daughter, which means I have a mother and a father"; the son then identifies himself as her brother, which, he explains, means that "we have the same mother and father." Got that? "Family" means there are no single-parents, no blending, no anything other than mother, father, sister, brother. *Sesame Street*'s definition of "family" in 1969 had no room for Charles Manson, Catherine Share, Terry Melcher (who grew up with a stepfather), or the Waverly Drive family of Rosemary and Leno LaBianca, both of whom came to their second marriage with children born during previous marriages.[37]

In the topsy-turvy world of the United States in the late 1960s and early 1970s, *Sesame Street*'s family song was the site of norm-setting conservative politics, and the White House was the sponsor of heartfelt, radical efforts to come to grips with the new realities shaping the landscape of family life. The report of the 1970 White House Conference on Children and Youth still has the power to startle for how unblinkingly it confronts the challenges facing American families. The conference was made up of multiple panels of health professionals, politicians, administrators, artists, activists, media figures (Mr. Rogers!), and others. While we know now that virtually nothing recommended by the Conference participants was taken seriously by the government or by private industry, the discussions of family life and the welfare of children remains refreshingly unconventional. Among its many conclusions about why it was so hard to pass legislation and create programs that would support *all* families is the simple reality that "family" was still being defined in far too narrow and traditional a way as "the nuclear household of husband, wife, and their children—the male the breadwinner and the female the homemaker." This report noted that representatives of official culture too readily and too regularly assumed "that this type of home environment is the best for the child." With a daring directness, this subcommittee asserted that "children can and do flourish in many family forms other than the traditional nuclear structure."[38]

What is perhaps most striking about the committee reports is how fully they signed on to a progressive vision of how a family could be constituted. It is worth remembering that this report was issued just five years after the release of the so-called "Moynihan Report," which argued, among other things, that African American youths were being raised in a "tangle of pathology" caused mostly by the matrifocality of Black family life. The White House Conference on Children and Youth, accepted as a given that a family could be "single parent, traditional, dual work" or even "commune." While the report made clear that the participants in the conference believed that "the majority of children can find the conditions for character and personality development in the nuclear family," it was also important to establish that their recommendations for changes in policy, social infrastructure, and consciousness did not "favor any particular family form." (The report never makes clear whether this openness can apply to *all* families or is, rather, a privilege of whiteness.) As such, the report advocated unequivocally for the government to help "make visible the increased variability in family forms and to recognize the right of individuals to live in any family form they feel will increase their options for self-fulfillment."

This White House Conference did not only encourage the government to recognize changes in family structure and behaviors that had developed on an ad hoc basis during the years immediately preceding its meeting. The report also made clear that the executive and legislative branches had to get in the business, actively, of helping to sustain nontraditional families. In essence, the argument contained in the pages of the report argued for what, in the 1980s, would come to be called "wraparound programs"— community-based centers that would help tend to the educational, social, cultural, and health concerns of all children and their families. The conference suggested explicitly that the US Government needed to begin creating a model of what it called the "human service center," which would "provide a new approach to the socially isolated and the alienated and hopefully could partially replace the extended family and neighborhood supports of the past."

Instead of wringing hands over the decline or destruction of the "traditional" family, the White House Conference on Children and Youth implicitly acknowledged that "family" is always evolving, both in theory and in practice. The "quasi-familial institution" of the community center (which strangely, the subcommittee suggested might be housed in a variety of sites, including a department store!) was not meant as a band-aid for wounded families or as a consolation prize for have-not children. To the contrary, the recommendation was built on the premise that the diversity of American experience represented an opportunity for progressive social change that could potentially benefit *all* children—not only those of the "needy." The surprising conclusions and progressive suggestions for change made in this report largely went unheeded. They could not begin to calm the pervasive fears that had taken hold that the "crisis" in the family had to be met with swift and decisive rearguard actions.

Paying attention to this relatively underappreciated moment in American cultural and political life helps us better understand more about how the Manson collective was able to creepy crawl into our homes. The example they provided was consonant with the larger argument being developed in the culture that "real" and "traditional" families were under attack. The Manson Family did not have a coherent spiritual code or theoretical underpinning. Manson never got much beyond regurgitating bits from Scientology, Robert Heinlein, the Process Church, Dale Carnegie, and hippie bromides he encountered in San Francisco. At his trial, Manson insisted that he put no pressure on any young woman to join or stay with his family. According to his account all he did was "let the children loose and follow them. That is what I did . . . . That is what I was doing, following your children, the ones you didn't want, each and every one of them."[39] Bobby Beausoleil was similarly mystifying, telling John Gilmore (author of an early book on Manson) that what he had done was take young women from the "sterile and plastic world without truth that their mothers and fathers had made for them" and created for them "a whole new world of laughter and song and magic . . . a crazy, tilted, springtime world where love is king."[40] It seems likely Beausoleil was at least partly pulling Gilmore's leg here, and Manson's utterances have to be taken in the context of performance; he has never *not* performed wildly in court appearances and interviews. But the point remains that insofar as Manson and Susan Atkins and all the rest launched a fairly significant protest against traditional belief systems, it was mostly on a very sophomoric level. It is not so hard to shock the bourgeoisie, as the Doors did, with a round of "Father . . . I want to kill you/Mother I want to fuck you." (Or the other way around for Susan Atkins who, in her first book, wrote of her father that "I know he wanted to have an affair with me, especially after my mother died . . . . I was very well built, very attractive . . . . I actually did want to have an affair with him.")[41] The incoherent nature of the Family's rebellion should not interfere with our ability to see how its broad cultural creepy crawl helped energize the growing panic about the dissolution of "real" families in the United States. The Family was not an organized or methodical attack on the family. But to many observers it sure felt like it was.

In her young adult novel *Family* (2011), Micol Ostow imagines that the Manson Family was a "network of sisters and brothers, each of them shattered in some unique way."[42] There is no doubt that many of the individual members of the Family carried deep wounds from their past into their present lives. There are plenty of reasons to agree with *Life* magazine's reading of Manson's female followers as having been "lured . . . into a sisterhood of exploitation" through "flattery, fear and sex."[43] But all of the hand-wringing discussions in which the larger culture indulged about the particular pathologies of the Manson Family often served as a barely masked form of truth-telling about so many families—that the home is so often the site of the most intense and sustained abuse that children experience anywhere in their lives. If the Manson Family was sick, how much of its dysfunction was a next-generation effect that could be blamed on its members' families of origin? Manson may have acted, as so many observers have pointed out, as a kind of caricature of the dominant and hurtful father. But the grotesque cartoon of patriarchy that Manson animated could not have succeeded if his followers were not vulnerable to his ability to dominate them.

Not every Manson girl was in a situation quite as starkly heartbreaking as Ruth Ann Moorehouse, known as Ouisch to the Family. Ruth Ann Moorehouse joined the collective after her father, Dean Moorehouse, picked up Manson hitchhiking. Dean Moorehouse attempted something like a rescue of his daughter, but according to the best accounts, was soon taking LSD himself and beseeching Manson to let *him* join the family. His explicit agreement to let Ruth Ann stay with Manson, although she was still legally a minor, sent a clear message about how literally this one father was willing to participate in the exploitation of his daughter. Gregg Jakobson has more than once suggested that Manson was not the only man with designs on Ruth Ann Moorehouse. According to Jakobson, his good friend Terry Melcher was also smitten with Ouisch and considered moving her into the Cielo Drive home he shared with Candice Bergen to serve, in Jakobson's heartrending euphemism, as "a housekeeper." As Jakobson tells the tale, "Candy Bergen knew what kind of chores Terry had in mind and vetoed the plan."[44]

Dianne Lake, called "Snake" by the Family (as a commentary, Ed Sanders suggests, on the "transverse ophidian wiggles she made during intercourse") was also allowed by her own commune-dwelling parents to travel on her own.[45] Some accounts suggest that Lake's parents even gave her a note to carry around with her (though Lake has recently disputed this)—a permission slip for field trip with Manson—to make clear that she was free to follow her bliss.[46]

But in this place and at this time permission was just a kiss away from submission. Allowing your daughter to travel freely in countercultural circles, as Ruth Ann Moorehouse's father did, as Dianne Lake's Hog Farm mother and father did, and as, perhaps, Deirdre Lansbury's mother, actor Angela Lansbury, did as well, must have struck these parents as either a positive act of progressive parenting or as a reasonable compromise growing from their own hopelessness about managing their children.[47] But we must recognize that the sexual liberation and family reorganizations of the 1960s and 1970s often meant, in a practical way, that young women were ending up in positions of great vulnerability. Submission is stipulated as a social good in Charles Manson's song "Cease to Exist," which appeared in 1969 as the B-side of a Beach Boys single (and then on their LP release *20/20*). When the Beach Boys recorded Manson's song "Cease to Exist" as "Never Learn Not to Love" they also changed a crucial line in which Manson suggested that women must submit. Instead, the Beach Boys transformed the imperative sentence into a descriptive one simply by changing "give it" to "given." (Bobby Beausoleil has recently suggested that Manson's anger at the Beach Boys vis-à-vis this song had more to do with messaging than money: he was, apparently, upset that the group turned his statement of spiritual purpose into a song of seduction.)[48] When Manson used "brother" in his original version of the song (called "Never Learn Not to Love") he was most likely using it in its expanded countercultural sense of "comrade" or "lover"; Donald Nielsen reminds us that Manson was particularly invested in expanding the "'brotherly' rhetoric widespread in the 1960s counterculture."[49] But the Wilson brothers, who grew up in a "traditional" nuclear family headed by a father who wielded fear and humiliation as everyday weapons of control, were not able to wrap their vocal cords around the line as written and changed "brother" to "another." Perhaps Dennis Wilson and the others just thought that "another" scanned better than "your brother." (It does.) But one of the uncomfortable tales the Family had to tell in the late 1960s is that expressions of control were not incidental by-products of the "traditional" family; domination (and sometimes resistance) were foundational.

Brian Wilson, the Beach Boys' wounded genius, seems to know this. Wilson briefly summarizes the relationship of Manson to celebrity musicians like Terry Melcher and his own brother Dennis ("Terry was . . . the guy in the middle of the situation with my brother . . . and Charles Manson") and then notes that "Terry and Manson didn't get the right ideas about each other and they stopped being friends." Wilson then wonders for a second whether

Manson sent his followers to Cielo Drive to look for Melcher or "if it didn't make any difference to them who was in the house." The very next sentence is something of a surprise: "Families can be the strangest, most horrible things."[50]

Paul Watkins, one of Manson's most trusted co-conspirators, and author of what is perhaps the most interesting family memoir that we have, writes that essentially "Charlie's trip was to program us all to submit."[51] Manson did not invent the idea that the family operated along recognizable vectors (i.e., gender, age) of power. What Manson figured out is that helping to liberate children from *their own* parents did not necessarily imply a critique of all authority. If Manson's Family represented, as Todd Gitlin has suggested, a "parody of patriarchy," it remained unclear who or what was being parodied.[52] While plenty of commentators in the late 1960s and early 1970s recognized that young people were testing new social organizations that removed the scaffolding of generational power in favor of peer equity, it remained difficult for many observers to notice that Manson had substantial holdings in both the old ways and the new. As Paul O'Neil put it in *Life* magazine in December 1969, Charles Manson was "no hippie. . . . He was an entrepreneur."[53]

The Family That Slays Together

It was not easy to set right all the applecarts that were upset by Charles Manson and his family in the second half of 1969 and the years following. In the first half of the 1970s the makers of pulp and horror films devoted a considerable amount of energy to figuring out how we were going to live with these countercultural challenges to the "traditional" family. A major thematic concern of American films in the 1970s was how far mainstream (even "liberal") Americans would go to defend themselves and their families against intruders and aggressors. Sam Peckinpah's *Straw Dogs* (1971) is probably the most critically celebrated of these, and Charles Bronson's *Death Wish* likely the most successful in terms of box-office earnings. But Steven Spielberg's television movie *Duel* (1971), starring Dennis Weaver, and John Boorman's *Deliverance* (1972) also raised the question of whether mainstream Americans would fight back against marginal crazy people.

Perhaps most influential of all are the horror movies *Last House on the Left* (1972) and *Texas Chainsaw Massacre* (1974). The latter must have gained much of its resonance for audiences as a vehicle to process the fears raised by Manson and his followers. The family in *Texas Chainsaw Massacre* is literally made up of cannibals. They live by consuming (i.e., destroying) the members of other families. *I Drink Your Blood* (1970) also trucks with a Manson-like family and some measure of cannibalism (kicked off by a truly bizarre plot point involving rabies-infused meat pies). Wes Craven, who directed *Last House on the Left*, would pick up on the cannibal theme in his 1977 film *The Hills Have Eyes*, in which the crazy "hillbilly" family kidnaps a baby from the "normal" family because they want to eat it. For its part, *Last House on the Left* fits more snugly in the cluster that includes *Straw Dogs* and *Death Wish*. Here, two parents are driven to engage in extreme violence after their daughter has been sexually assaulted and shot by a gang of criminals that has a blood family at its core.[1]

This movie essentially organizes a battle between two kinds of family: Mari and her parents (a relatively stable nuclear family) fight for their lives against a criminal family, which includes some blood connections but also a non-relative named Sadie. (Sadie was played by Jeramie Rain, who according to numerous sources had already played Susan Atkins in an Off-Broadway stage production, and later moved into Sharon Tate's house on Cielo Drive reportedly *without knowing what had happened there!* Marilyn Burns, who played Sally in *Texas Chainsaw Massacre*, went on to play Linda Kasabian in *Helter Skelter*.) After Mari is forced to have oral sex with her friend Paige, then is shot and left for dead, her parents—as is so often the case in movies of this kind—become compelled to match the criminal family's level of violence. Mari's father turns murderous and her mother bites the penis off one of the gang members after she has seduced him into believing she wants to perform fellatio on him. The messages are confused, to be sure, in *Last House on the Left*. But one thing that is completely clear in Wes Craven's movie is that if American parents are going to keep their children safe at home, they will have to ratchet up their game and fight off the awesome power of these countercultural forces of destruction.

The Exorcist, from 1973, represents a slight variation in this two-kinds-of-family horror film. The top-grossing movie of its year, and second best-selling novel of 1971 when William Peter Blatty published it, *The Exorcist* makes the battle remarkably intimate. The demonic forces threatening the sanctity of the family are literally *inside* of young Regan McNeil, played by Linda Blair.

In the Blatty novel, the writer made it clear that he was interested in "manifestations of evil in the modern world," with references to the Holocaust and American war crimes in Vietnam. But the film, as Nick Cull has explained forcefully, "avoided the novel's epigrams and allusions to the spectacular evils of the age." Instead, as Cull notes, the film revolves around a concern with "inter-generational conflict." This agenda is prosecuted most directly "in early scenes of *The Exorcist* in which we learn that Regan's mother is an actress in a film portraying campus dissent. She is seen begging an angry crowd of students to 'work within the system.'" Overall, Cull argues convincingly, "the theme of a young girl's transformation into a demon-possessed beast played with America's growing fear of its youth." The devil is here to do the devil's business, and will do so from inside your daughter's body.[2]

Terror on the Beach (1973), starring Dennis Weaver as the conventional father, choreographs a similar, if slightly less gory battle between a traditional family and a scary hippie family than the horror movies did. In this decidedly TV-movie, Weaver is taking his wife, daughter, and son on a family vacation to the beach—driving them, interestingly enough, in a rented VW microbus, *the* automotive symbol of the counterculture. The movie quickly establishes its Manson investment by having the VW run off the road by a dune buggy driven by members of the hippie family; it turns out they have another vehicle that is broken down and needs a tow. The Glynn family helps the hippie family. Rather than express simple gratitude, the leader of the rogue family taunts Neil Glynn by saying "Thank you, Mr. Whitebread." Neil Glynn's son recognizes that the hippies are criminal—their truck is full of goods that he can somehow tell are stolen. But his father insists that the hippies' business is not their business.

The film wants us to understand that the Glynn children are alienated from their parents. In stagey scenes, first we observe Neil and DeeDee Glynn discussing how out of touch their parents are from the realities of their lives. Neil Glynn complains that they "don't seem to understand we learn, we grow." For her part, mother Estelle Glynn recognizes that her daughter has learned and grown, but dismisses her evolution as silly: "[T]wo years of college and you're ready to change the world." Things ultimately come to a head in *Terror on the Beach* after it becomes clear that the family of hippies means to torment the blood family. Among other tactics used by the hippies is to record the conversations of the straight family and then blast it back at them incessantly through a PA system they have rigged up. It is not clear exactly why these hippies want to torture these squares. The logic of inevitability structuring the film seems to be rooted in the notion that these different kinds of families cannot share the same social landscape. One type of family (guess which!) ultimately will have to run the inferior type off the American road.

Nothing is sublimated in *Terror on the Beach*. The climax of the movie comes with a literal fistfight on the beach between the two "fathers." The Glynn parents ascertain that this wild bunch conceives of itself as a family—or at least this is what the leader, Jerry, has been telling them. But the Glynns capture one of Jerry's followers and he seems pretty happy to switch sides. In the final fight he literally steps in to help Neil Glynn win the fight—while Estelle Glynn looks on approvingly, wearing her red-and-white gingham dress.

That "family" could come to signify, among other things, an engine of dramatic violence, could not have been too surprising to American audiences of the late 1960s or early 1970s. Mario Puzo's novel *The Godfather* was the second highest selling novel of 1969, and Francis Ford Coppola's film version was the highest grossing movie of 1972. *The Godfather* presents an interesting vision of how "family" could signal at once blood relations (along with adoptive kin) and a criminal and commercial enterprise, and that the most powerful men—Vito, Sonny, and Michael Corleone, and Tom Hagen—must constantly police the boundaries to make sure that the central animating principles of family life are being protected and nurtured. The family, Puzo and Coppola tell us, is always under siege and must be constantly defended against the forces arrayed against it—other families, drugs (how important it is for Vito to refuse to let his family get into the trade in illicit drugs!), and so on. *Terror on the Beach* hardly had the ambition or scope of *The Godfather*, of course, but like that film (and novel), and like *Last House on the Left*, it was organized around the idea that the modern family had to protect itself by engaging in acts of horrifying violence.

The cinematic hysteria about the decline of the American family seeped into more than just the horror genre in the wake of the Tate-LaBianca murders and the arrests of Manson and his co-conspirators. *Billy Jack*, the fifth highest-grossing movie of 1971, substituted a truly mesmerizing earnestness in the place of terror. Here the good family is the countercultural one—a collective made up mostly of the kids living at the Freedom School, a sort of experimental commune/boarding school/halfway house. Nathan Rabin has pointed out that this is a square's vision of the counterculture: there is plenty of time spent on having the young people at the school discuss social problems—they "rap it out"—but there are no drugs, no sex, no organized political protest.[3] The only conventional family we learn much about in *Billy Jack* is that of Bernard Posner and his father Stuart, who represent all that is cruel, parochial, and punishing about the townspeople who resist the innovations of Jean's Freedom School. Billy Jack himself is a fascinating combination of mainstream and counterculture: he is part Native American, a Vietnam vet, a loner, a martial-arts expert, and a lover of Jean and her marginalized charges. As with the horror films and *The Godfather*, *Billy Jack* argues that the work of the family (here represented by the motherly Jean, her partner Billy, and their countless needy children) is inseparable from the commission of violence.

Throughout the movie Jean, a pacifist, beseeches Billy to remain nonviolent—even after she has been raped. But the film makes clear that Billy Jack has no choice: his beautiful violence—the ballet that brings his right foot into contact with Stuart Posner's face—is politically, socially, and aesthetically right. While *Billy Jack* made no direct comment on the Manson Family, it participated in a cultural process that was made necessary, at least in part, by the frightening way that the Spahn Ranch gang threw some basic realities of American family life into stark relief. While Manson and his followers were outliers in what historian Rick Perlstein has named "Nixonland" in recognition of the power of that other murderous Californian on the landscape of late 1960s America, they also sang a song of family that sounded like a funeral dirge. The threat to the family represented by the Family *had* to be contained.

Humor was one strategy of control. Most notable here, as reported by *Rolling Stone* in its issue of May 14, 1970, was a skit performed at the seventeenth annual Installation Banquet of the Los Angeles Criminal Bar Association called "One Manson's Family: The Family That Slays Together Stays Together." The phrase in the subtitle followed a familiar formulation of course. Since World War II, the Irish-American anti-communist priest Patrick Peyton had been promoting a movement that came to be known as the Family Rosary Crusade, whose slogan was "The Family That Prays Together Stays Together." The template has been revised countless times, including by the Los Angeles rock band Spirit, who called their 1968 album *The Family That Plays Together*, in recognition of the relationship of band leader, Randy California, and his stepfather, the band's drummer Ed Cassidy.

In any event, the "family . . . stays together" formulation proved irresistible to Marvin Part, the lawyer who wrote the skit—and who had, briefly, been the court-appointed attorney for Leslie Van Houten. (Part seems to have been something of an amateur musician; his obituary in the *Los Angeles Times* notes that he got great joy in his later years from the time he spent with his ukulele group.)[4] In its piece on the banquet and the skit, *Rolling Stone* shielded its eyes a bit, noting that while it was still not clear whether or not "the charges against Charles Manson and his commune/Family are true," one thing that is clear is that "the whole gruesome affair does not inspire much laughter. In most people."[5]

The lawyers and their guests, however, were not most people. They counted among their number not only skit-author Marvin Part, but also William Keene, who had been the original presiding judge in Manson's trial, and Raymond Choate, who would go on to oversee Manson's trial for the murder of Spahn Ranch worker Donald "Shorty" Shea. When asked about the propriety of the event, Choate appeared remarkably unconcerned. The skit was perfectly within the bounds of propriety, according to Choate, who explained it away simply by noting that it was only performed for "a group of lawyers, their wives and close friends."[6] *Rolling Stone* only gave limited data about the actual content of the comic skit, but according to an account later published in *The Manson File* there seems to have been plenty of talk about money: "I want to sell your records," one verse went, "So I can get my fee." This song was sung to the tune of *West Side Story*'s "Gee, Officer Krupke," a song sung by "depraved" young gang members and now a vehicle for serial jokes about grubby lawyers. Another line from the skit imagined a different musical path to financial success, as the singing lawyers imagined that they could "take your story," and "make . . . a sequel to *Hair*."[7] "Charlie, bube," the lawyer promised, throwing in a little Yinglish in case it was not already clear that this was a Jewish lawyer talking, "There's plenty of money / We'll both make a pile / And we can share it / Family style."[8] While the lawyers could comfortably joke about monetizing their own clients, the skit also makes it clear that they think the Family was made up of "slap-happy kooks." These talented members of the Criminal Bar Association were, to use the lingo of the time, "squares": hippies hit their radar not so much as a terrifying challenge but as a humorous sideshow. (Leslie Van Houten's trial lawyer, Ronald Hughes, came to be known as "the hippie lawyer," because he demonstrated some actual knowledge of youth subcultures during his questioning and also, no doubt, because he had a beard. During a November 1970 recess in the trial, Hughes went on a camping trip and disappeared. His body was not found until much later.)

The lawyers were not the only ones to use humor as a tool of containment against the Family. Reporter Theo Wilson, who later wrote about her experiences covering the Manson trial for the *New York Daily News* in her book *Headline Justice*, acknowledges that journalists also found time to mock the Manson Family. As Wilson explains, reporters in Los Angeles were worn down by the tedium of the long trial; at one point, she writes, "we thought one of the jurors would leap out of the jury box . . . screaming, 'Oh, God, make it stop!' the way prosecution witness Linda Kasabian burst out when she described the killings at the Tate house."[9] It is interesting to observe Wilson struggling to sort out her feelings about all the key players she encountered through her work at the Hall of Justice. While it is clear that she was not particularly sympathetic to Manson's hippie family, she also had little patience for Vincent Bugliosi and his self-mythologizing: "The prosecutor had already irritated some of the reporters by telling them how to write their stories, and berating them for not recognizing the importance of his work in the courtroom. He also said, in all interviews with him, that he was dedicated so totally to the prosecution of the Manson Family that he had little time for his own family. So we didn't feel concerned about not inviting him to share our after-hours get togethers."[10]

One of those get togethers, in October 1970, was a "Helter Skelter party." Wilson still seemed quite tickled by the event when she got around to writing about it in her 1998 memoir—at least in part because she was taking the opportunity to spill the beans about an event that seems to have stayed secret up until that point. Wilson explains that "like all these parties it was for fun. And like all trial parties, it was strictly off the record and not one word about it ever surfaced." The party offered its participants "release from the truly awful events unfolding every day in the courtroom, letting us laugh in spite of the tragedy that had brought us all together."[11] The "fun" of the Helter Skelter party included invitations that parodied Family speak and the Beatles' "I Am the Walrus" all at once (the start time was listed as "Night is day and day is night and I am you and you are me" and the venue as "The Bottomless Pit"). Reporters dressed as their favorite trial "character," with Wilson offering her take on Linda Kasabian, wearing "a blond wig with long pigtails and a demure peasant dress" and carrying a doll meant to represent the child Kasabian left at Spahn Ranch when "she fled after the murders."[12] Other journalists dressed as 6' 5" Panamanian Juan Flynn, as Barbara Hoyt (carrying a plastic hamburger to represent the LSD–laced meal other Family members dosed her with in an attempt to prevent her from testifying at the trial), and as Susan Atkins, wearing all black "creepy crawlie" clothing. Prizes were given out for best costumes and, as Wilson tells it, a good time was had by all—except for the "house dick" who was made nervous by all these "hippies" wearing wild clothing and sporting X marks on their heads.[13]

But it is hard to imagine that anyone, even a hotel's stuffed-shirt hired detective, could mistake the journalists for actual hippies. Part of the "fun" of dressing up in costume comes with calling attention to the distance that separates the costume's object from the costume's wearer. Did the hotel detective really mistake Theo Wilson's friend Sandi Mettetal for Juan Flynn? A picture of this party has surfaced on various Manson websites and it is likely doctored—Vincent Bugliosi appears in it looking happy to be there—but it has elements that otherwise check out as legitimate (including a sign on the wall that quotes Tex Watson's "here to do the devil's work" line from the night of the Tate murders). One thing clear in this picture is that no sighted person who had been conscious in California over the past few years would have been fooled by these "costumes." The reporters are making fun of the Family—their dress, their ideology—and having (as far as this evidence demonstrates) a wild time doing so. The Family certainly presented a threatening set of frightful challenges to more mainstream observers, but this party of journalists, along with their legal compatriots and the horror film directors hitting the scene in the 1970s, developed a number of strategies that proved at least temporarily useful in exorcising the social and cultural demons troubling the American family. Fictive "good" families were taking back the social spaces the Family had seemed to threaten so frightfully.

Ranch, Hill, Farm

Charles Manson represented a dark provocation and a compelling spectacle. His usurpation of parental authority at Spahn Ranch and elsewhere was terrifying, to be sure, but terrifying in an utterly compelling way. Americans could not stop looking at and talking about the Family—in fictional forms like horror movies and in "real" life conversations. Part of Manson's achievement was to tap so successfully into (as Terry Melcher once put it) "what's going on today."[1] Manson played all the roles he wanted to play: he referred to other members of the Family as his "children"; he mocked the trial judge by shouting, "Hey dad . . . look at the truth over here"; he poignantly told the court that he had "stayed a child while I have watched your world grow up, and then I look at the things that you do and I don't understand."[2] Abandoned son, loyal brother, nurturing father—Manson's public persona stitched together a variety of significant familial roles.

The father business was, of course the most troubling to Manson's many audiences inside and outside the courtroom. Manson was, to use some anachronistic language, a Father with Benefits. He had sex with his children, and arranged much about their sexual lives even when he was not directly involved in the acts. He took the privileges of being a family patriarch without shouldering the usual burdens of providing food, money, or conventional markers of status. And he did all of this in a culture that was in the midst of scaring itself with terrifying stories about the dissolution of the "traditional" patriarchal family. R. D. Laing had been encouraging readers in the late 1960s to think of the family as a site of "micropolitics." Historian Andreas Killen has recognized the importance of Laing to countercultural youth and has persuasively argued that their disappointment in the failure of their own families to act as agents of progressive change led many to construct "wild travesties of patriarchal authority."[3]

Manson was not the only daddy walking this line: he was joined by a number of other older men attempting to capitalize on the father-hunger certain younger people were feeling. Perhaps most successful at occupying this role for his followers was James Edward Baker, better known as Father Yod. Father Yod's group, the Source Family, was organized in Los Angeles and lived there quite comfortably until a mid-1970s move to Hawaii. With a thriving health-food restaurant (also known as The Source) and a Family band as well (Ya Ho Wha 13, which sometimes included Sky Saxon, formerly of The Seeds, and oh, didn't they ramble), this group sustained important myths about the benevolence and magical power of its Father. Evie Shapiro described how she and her sister (who became Source Family member Electra) had grown up with a rigid and authoritarian father. In searching for a way out of the strictures of her family origin—"surprise, surprise," as Shapiro tells it—Electra found a replacement father, who was gentle, loving, and kind. Electra more or less supports this reading of her journey, explaining that many Source Family members were desperate to find a "loving, paternal figure." When Magus the Aquarian first went upstairs from The Source to meet Father Yod, he bent over to kiss the older man's feet. Father Yod responded first by saying "Far fucking out" and then by announcing to the younger man that "You are my son and I am your father."[4]

Perhaps the most important story that has been ritually retold by Source sources has to do with the first baby born to Father Yod's family. When Sunflower delivered this child it appeared in the world with the umbilical cord wrapped three times around its neck, and appeared to be stillborn. Father Yod sprang into action, breathed into the baby, and "five seconds later" he was alive and ready to be named Solomon.[5] There is by now plenty of evidence that Baker, a full generation older than his young followers (he was born in

1922), leveraged his graybeard status to take sexual advantage of his acolytes. But unlike Manson, this cult father seems to have been able to keep himself out of trouble and avoid unwelcome attention from straight culture. Father Yod also managed to die in 1975—crash landing after his hang-gliding debut (and swan song, as it turned out)—well before the most upsetting details of his warped "parenting" came to light. Father Yod's family has done a relatively effective job of protecting his name and even in promoting the Source Family's music to a later generation of rock fans and musicians (including Billy Corgan of Smashing Pumpkins).

Father Yod did his work literally wrapped in gauzy white robes and rhetorically cloaked in gauzy romantic visions of benign loving freakiness (he played his role as a sort of American Yogi Bhajan with a little Walt Whitman earthiness thrown in). But in the early 1970s there was only one "father" who could really compete with Charles Manson for his ability to both command a loyal following on the local level and inspire a national frenzy of negative media attention. Boston's Mel Lyman, who first came to visibility as the harmonica player for Jim Kweskin's Jug Band, established a commune in the Fort Hill section of Boston's Roxbury neighborhood. While relatively underappreciated as a cultural force in our time, Lyman did some serious creepy crawling of his own in the late 1960s and the 1970s. The height of media attention to the Lyman family came with a fear-inspiring two-part article published in *Rolling Stone* in December 1971 and January 1972; Lyman was the cover model for the first half of the article.[6]

This David Felton article (collected in the book by Dalton and Felton, with Robin Green, published in 1972 as *Mindfuckers: A Sourcebook on the Rise of Acid Fascism in America*) was meant to shock and made its position clear with a few direct comparisons to Manson. The subtitle for the first half of the exposé was "Inside the Cult Led by Mel Lyman, the East Coast Charles Manson." Scarier yet was a reflection by Jim Kweskin himself, in response to a question about the relationship of the two tribes. In what became the most oft-quoted part of the entire, very lengthy, investigation of Lyman's family, the one-time leader of an important folk-revival band had this to say: "The Manson Family preached peace and love and went around killing people. We don't preach peace and love. And . . . we haven't killed anybody—yet."[7]

The Lyman Family was more tapped into mainstream circuits of power than any of the other patriarchal cults under construction in the late 1960s and early 1970s, and had far more access to cultural (and financial) capital than most. Unlike the Manson Family, squirreled away at a decrepit old movie ranch, the Lyman Family lived on top of a hill and integrated into mainstream business culture *and* countercultural music and media activity in a way that the California group never could. This family included among its members a number of well-placed cultural figures, including Jessie Benton, who married Mel Lyman and who was the daughter of painter Thomas Hart Benton. This family also included rock critic Paul Williams, and actors Mark Frechette and Daria Halprin (who both starred in Michelangelo Antonioni's *Zabriskie Point*). One reason the Lyman Family was able to sustain itself so successfully even in the face of such tremendous negative attention is that they had a serious business plan. As with Father Yod and his followers, the Lyman Family knew how to make money. Lyman was able to attract a couple of financial "angels": the key venture capitalists of the Fort Hill project seem to have been Jim Kweskin and actors Frechette and Halprin. It is likely that a good bit of startup money also came from Jessie Benton, though Family spokespeople have long insisted that its continued ability to thrive is due completely to the work of its flagship business, the Fort Hill Construction Co.[8] The Lyman Family also used the pages of the alternative newspaper *The Avatar* to promote itself.

While Felton's account of Mel Lyman's family has come under regular attack since its publication in the early 1970s, some of its basic insights seem unremarkable and true. Like so many other communes of this moment, the Fort Hill settlement was organized according to very old-fashioned gender hierarchies and was especially focused on serving the needs and following the dictates of its mystically powerful male leader. While Mel Lyman remains something of a cipher, it is clear that some combination of personal charisma and strategic use of hallucinogens (the "acid fascism" of *Mindfuckers*' subtitle) allowed him to attain a great deal of power over his followers. Fort Hill was a closed and, at times, heavily guarded community, and even in Boston much of what passed for knowledge about the group was actually rooted in speculation and fantasy projection.

Virtually all coverage of the Lyman Family—from a gentle and earnest overview in the city's African American newspaper, the *Bay State Banner*, to a very critical article in the *Boston Globe* in 1970, to Felton's alarming *Rolling Stone* piece—agreed that Mel Lyman himself was something more than just "leader," or "chair" of the commune. The *Globe*, for instance, called attention to the "severe authority structure" on Fort Hill, and reminded readers that Lyman was accepted by his followers "literally as a god figure."[9] What Andreas Killen called a "travesty" of conventional patriarchal family life was in abundant evidence in Lyman's Family.

By 1972, Boston's *After Dark*, a forerunner of the alternative weekly the *Boston Phoenix*, would publish a scathing indictment of the gender politics built into Lyman Family life on the Hill. Written by Ellen Herst, and published under the title "Mel & Charlie's Women: The Souring of Street Life," what was assigned as a book review (of Ed Sanders's Manson book and Mel Lyman's *Mirror at the End of the Road*) immediately announces itself as something very different: "This isn't a book review. It's my response as a woman to reading all the gossip about Charles Manson and Mel Lyman. And, more than that, a response to the whole of hippie / freak culture and the 'place' of women in it. I mean, it may be total drag to spend your life at the dishwasher, washing machine, supermarket, etc.—and of course we know that—on the other hand it's not exactly a groove to hustle on the street, bake bread for your hippie farmer, serve the God incarnate, commit murders: to name a few options." Herst uses Manson and Lyman as an occasion to mourn the dashed hope that sexual liberation and other counterculture challenges to conventional family life would spell anything like equality for women. The real innovation of these new families, according to Herst, was in figuring out how to boil down and dress up the most exploitative aspects of patriarchal family life.[10]

While plenty of critics have called attention to the distressing sexism of so many New Left and countercultural men (and organizations), Herst's prose is particularly clear and direct. What is most important for Herst to establish is that the horrifying gender politics organizing the families of Lyman and Manson are both noteworthy, in a sense, because they are so familiar—rancid wine poured into a straw-wrapped Chianti bottle. Herst is adamant that Manson and Lyman not be credited as "evil geniuses." After all, Herst writes, the "evil they practice is the evil of sexism that each has adapted to his own needs." Herst is particularly struck by the fact that Manson's early criminal activities included pimping: her condemnation of both Manson and Lyman is rooted in the fact that both "thrived off the resources of women." Herst calls attention to how Manson and Lyman built their familial empires on the financial resources of women: "How fortunate for Mel Lyman to have fallen in love with Jessie Benton, falling heir to a great deal of Thomas Hart Benton's property in the bargain."[11] But the argument is much more than an attack on cult leaders—it is ultimately a reckoning of the links connecting this vision of sexual liberation, women's labor, and male pleasure. After noting Manson's early career as a pimp, Herst goes on to explain that living "off women is of course, what pimps do. How progressive of hippie men to have liberated themselves from the confines of straight jobs so that they can go and do likewise." Herst is not calling every hippie a Manson or Lyman, but she does want to emphasize that "freak women everywhere" are turning over the welfare checks and the money they make in sex work to their male partners.

The multifront attack organized by Ellen Herst in "Mel & Charlie's Women" is, among other things, a reminder that this conversation about communes, cults, and new familial configurations had especially high stakes for young women who considered themselves a part of the counterculture and/or the women's movement. The ideological and strategic heart of second-wave feminism was, by the late 1960s and early 1970s, embodied in the phrase "the personal is political," and Ellen Herst uses the rise of Charles Manson, Mel Lyman, and their less entrepreneurial male hippie peers to engage in what is essentially a meditation on power relations in contemporary sexual politics. The rise of Lyman and Manson represents to Herst the terrible but logical outcome of what she sees as a loyalty to very conventional, hierarchical gender relations in far too many counterculture relationships and institutions. "Boston's own happy family," Herst writes, "the Fort Hill commune, under the supreme guidance of Mel Lyman, shows striking similarities to the Manson ménage: total submission to the will of one male and total subjugation of women." While Lyman is not as immediately terrifying as Manson (his "method is softer . . . the mode of control is romantic, rather than violent"), his theoretical framework—"a whole myth about woman as slave"—is every bit as terrifying as that of his California colleague. Jessie Benton herself, when she finally gave an extended interview to Brian Burnes in 1986, confirmed that Herst was hardly exaggerating when she explained that the "women on the hill serve the men. There is a traditional division of labor, with the men doing the heavy work and the women rearing the children and keeping the kitchen."[12] This was not the first exposé of gender and power in hippie relationships, of course: the commune scene in *Easy Rider* (1969), some of the photography of Lisa Law, the casual, cruel sexism of the Grateful Dead's "Jack Straw," (1972) which promotes the idea that women can be passed around by men as easily as they share the communal wine bottle, just to name a few examples, were some of the raw data being considered by feminists disappointed in how fully men in the counterculture were embracing the privileges of their gender. (Law, one of the crucial chroniclers of this time and place, would later reflect that she actually did not enjoy "that kind of living. It always seemed that women ended up doing a lot more chores than the men.")[13] When Peter Lawford asked Family member Paul Watkins in a KABC-TV documentary (*Charles Manson: A Portrait in Terror*) why Manson wanted so many young women around at Spahn Ranch, Watkins answered simply "to do all the work."[14] Herst was, perhaps, most disturbed by how Lyman, Manson, and their minor-league brothers used the languages of domestic fulfillment and spiritual achievement to take advantage of a woman's right to pleasure. Herst is interested in the economic realities at the base of gender exploitation. She explains, for instance, that young women are often put in vulnerable positions because they are forced to rely on men for places to stay—a direct result of men having more access to making money in the street economy of selling drugs. But Herst also insists that the economic asymmetry is intensified by emotional needs, and here she gets *very* personal: "Shocked as I am by the particular viciousness of Manson's treatment of freak women . . . I'm not really surprised. Nor am I at a loss to understand why women take it. When I was 21 I had a boyfriend who reminds me of Manson and Lyman in more ways than I care to remember, and I still carry with me the fear that I, like Susan Atkins, etc., would be dominated by some man."[15]

"Mel & Charlie's Women" explores how women get "trapped by the promise of love and sexual gratification." Writing about the family arrangements of Manson and Lyman is Herst's method for getting at the much larger question of how women's need for pleasure and companionship can be taken advantage of by unscrupulous men. Lyman, as Herst explains, was able to cloak a "total contempt for and exploitation of women with a whole poetic trip." Manson worked in a slightly different vein. "What I find most insidious," Herst writes, "is the extent to which Manson used sex—by all accounts he was some kind of super stud—to dominate women." Herst's conclusion about Manson, in this respect, applies to all the countercultural men who trouble her: "This form of control is frightening because it's so hard to see through—since pleasure itself, which is hard to come by, becomes used against you."[16]

That the pursuit of pleasure was defined by already existing power relations was a familiar insight by the time Ellen Herst published this article on Charles Manson and Mel Lyman in February 1972 (the publication date was a day after Valentine's Day). What is striking about Herst's addition to this literature is the tone of urgency and desperation. Writing as Ed Sanders was, from within the counterculture, Herst rejects Sanders's tone of ironic detachment in favor of passionate engagement. She cares about Manson and Lyman, of course, but her real targets are found all over the counterculture, from alternative journalists, to Yippies, to your "average hippie guy." Herst condemns rock critic Nick Tosches, for instance, for including in his review of Sanders's *Family* an aside about what a "good lay" Manson was reputed to be. Yippie leader Stew Albert is taken to task by Herst for commenting on the sexual deprivation ("compulsory masturbation") Manson will suffer as a result of his prison sentence. Herst explains to her readers that Albert's statement "confirms all my basic suspicions about your typical male heavy . . . that he thinks that being cut off from a supply of willing and helpless females is a terrible and unjust fate." "It's enough," Herst avows, "to make many of us choose a course of voluntary masturbation." Name-checking the Rolling Stones album of 1971, Herst notes it would be better to have "sticky fingers than bloody hands."[17]

What Herst is after, ultimately, is a reconsideration of how the promise of sexual liberation (that it would be liberating!) had turned out to be a cruel lie. The new family was new only insofar as powerful men were gaining access to more vulnerable women than ever in terms of number and intensity. By the end of this extraordinary article Herst makes it clear that her goal is to encourage a reconsideration of sex and romance under capitalism as crucial elements of the false consciousness that keeps women in a subservient position. Herst's conclusions draw from her sober realization that "your average hippie guy and street freak doesn't have the elaborate poetic and financial power of Mel Lyman (8 homes at Fort Hill, a brownstone and loft in NYC, a duplex in Buena Vista, two houses in LA, 280 acres in Kansas . . . pretty good for an ex-folkie who just wants to be God), nor that satanic majesty of Manson, but he can make the myth of love work for him."[18] Writing particularly about the rigors of street life, but drawing conclusions that seem applicable to the larger landscape of the counterculture, Ellen Herst concludes that women continue to be hurt by their desire "to find some new man, some new pleasure that will make it bearable."[19]

The most at-risk young people, those living on the streets, were of special concern to radical and progressive members of the counterculture. Jeffrey D. Blum and Judith Smith, also writing in 1972, worried about the reality that so many young women did not seem "to be in control of their sexual situations."[20] As Blum and Smith put it, some aspects of the developing scene appeared to "be even more oppressive to women" than the older "regimen of monogamy." They write, "repeatedly, these young women were led into sexual relations that they did not want because to have refused to sleep with a man would have been 'unfair' to him and would have meant they were as outdated as brassieres." Blum and Smith concluded, "for an adolescent to feel committed to sleeping with everyone is as oppressive as to feel that one must not sleep with anyone."[21]

The major solution to the individualistic anarchy of the streets was supposed to be found, of course, in the era's great collective experiment—the commune. But as Blum and Smith make clear, even "in rural communes, sex roles are preserved: the males chop the wood, and the females bake the bread."[22] Robert Houriet published a fascinating book in 1971, *Getting Back Together,* which recounted his tour around a large number of American communes to collect data on how the project was faring. His experience bears out Blum and Smith, even as it underscores the absolute necessity of developing these new modes of relating. After visiting one commune in Pennsylvania, Houriet recounted that few of the residents "would talk of their parents or past, and when they did, it was bitterly." These young seekers had grown up in "comfortable sterile homes . . . in interchangeable suburbs with almost mocking names like Heritage Hills Estates. They were reared in families that were not families at all."[23] As with many of their peers around the country, many of the commune dwellers signified their break with the past—their "membership and adoption of a new family"—by "dropping their patronyms and assuming new names like Odessa,

Dancing Bear, and Vesta."[24] But these social innovators did not break with the gender rules that had structured their families of origin. Houriet explains that at High Ridge Farm, in Oregon, "as elsewhere in American society, the women as a group still bear most of the responsibility for the children." "Out in the country," Houriet contends, "there is a natural impetus to revert to traditional roles: Women stay inside, cook, and look after the children, while men plow, chop, and build roads."[25]

A different sell was made by residents and promoters of a number of communes. Wavy Gravy, for instance, described his Hog Farm commune as "an expanded family, a mobile hallucination, a sociological experiment, an army of clowns."[26] It would be hard to argue with the claim that many communes were populated by "expanded" families, but all too often the central fact of the expansion had to do with a scaling-up of male privilege. It was part and parcel of the sensationalist mainstream coverage of the Spahn Ranch community to refer to Manson's women followers as a "harem" or as what Jerry LeBlanc and Ivor Davis called an "army of modern day slaves and zombies."[27] Jeffrey Sconce has rightly suggested that one reason representatives of straight culture were so upset by Manson is that he acted, on some level, as a master of seduction, an "art that many males had been aspiring to understand through the sexual revolution of the sixties."[28] While no one would confuse Manson with the suave studs of the mainstream (Sconce points to the "airline pilot seducing young stewardesses" as an exemplar), it became something of a ritual for representatives of the dominant culture to make clear that whatever sexual license the cult leader was enjoying at Spahn Ranch, none of it came to him because he was *a real man*.[29] Manson might be the sexual king of his commune, but, as Sconce explains, articles in the popular press consistently referred to him as "diminutive" and "pint-sized." Manson, in this reading, had to be understood as some kind of otherworldly magician—a "psycho-Svengali" in Sconce's formulation—rather than one more man abusing women in some of the most familiar and horrifying ways.[30]

The Spahn Ranch commune bedeviled straight culture for the most obvious reason—its residents were at the center of a shocking murder case—but also because Manson and his girls embodied confusing elements of the New Freedom. The Family was a screen onto which a wide array of fantasies was projected (including the all-too-familiar "these little girls are really sexually hot"). It is instructive to see how desire and disgust battled it out in the mainstream media as the complex realities of commune life came to light. It comes as no surprise, on the one hand, to find purple material in *Movie Mirror*, *Silver Screen*, and *National Insider*, and all the other outlets anthologist Tom Brinkman collects under the rubric of "Bad Mags" or in pulp novels and films. But intense interest in the Sexual Life of the Commune was also expressed in *Life* and *Time* and most of the rest of the "good mags" as well and reaches us today as a form of voyeuristic violence against young women over and above the abuse the Manson girls lived through at the ranch and elsewhere. *Time*, for instance, took a moment to mention the "nude or bare-breasted" young women, "catering to" Manson's every whim—including performing a "sex act" on him while he discussed business with a "chagrined ranch hand." The ranch hand, or one of his colleagues, got his own close up in Gay Talese's borderline softcore article on the Family that was published in *Esquire* in early 1970. First off, *Esquire* titled the piece "Charlie Manson's Home on the Range" to make sure its readers understood that the Family commune at Spahn Ranch was some kind of horrifying caricature—a perverse mashup of Old West romance and New West freakiness.[31]

Talese ramps up the sexual energy immediately: "The horse wrangler, tall and ruggedly handsome, placed his hands on the hips of a pretty girl wearing white bell-bottomed trousers and casually lifted her onto a hitching post near the stable; then, voluntarily, almost automatically, she spread her legs and he stood between her, moving slowly from side to side and up and down, stroking her long blonde hair while her arms and fingers caressed his back, not quickly or eagerly but quite passively, indolently, a mood harmonious with his own." (Talese was a "New Journalist."

Along with some of his most esteemed peers in this field—Joan Didion and Truman Capote most notably—this means that he was as interested in presenting his research findings with a novelist's touch as he was with getting the facts right. But there was no requirement that the touch be as sexualized as this.) "Home on the Range" continues with the Ranch couple engaging in "their slow erotic slumber for several moments under mid-morning sun, swaying silently and looking without expression" into each other's eyes. Talese goes on to imagine that the couple are "totally unaware of their own lack of privacy"—or maybe getting off on it?—and also totally unaware of "the smell of horse manure near their feet." This is classic bad New Journalism: it is hard to know how a reporter could possibly know what his subject is currently smelling. But that is not the point here: Talese wants to marginalize the commune-dwellers by making it clear up top that not only do they "get after it" (as Ed Sanders would put it) in public, they "get after it" while sinking into shit.

That is the disgust part. The desire element is also here, as when Talese recounts how "voluntarily, almost automatically," the young woman "spread her legs and he stood between her, moving slowly from side to side and up and down." The phrase "voluntarily, almost automatically" should give pause to modern readers. The "voluntarily" is meant to be reassuring: these young women actually *want* to have sex with these young men! But "automatically" conveys a different mood and argues for a different conclusion entirely—this female Family member has apparently been so successfully controlled by Manson that she will have sex more-or-less on autopilot. Many elements of Manson-culture proved to be compelling to a very broad American audience, but perhaps nothing contributed to the mainstream investment in all of this more than the idea that this was a Family that hosted a nonstop orgy.[32] The radical writer Paul Krassner, who spent some significant time with Squeaky Fromme and other family members, got at this dynamic efficiently by recounting a moment of alleged overheard conversation that he claims a prison psychiatrist told him about. As Krassner tells it, an African American inmate confronted

Manson and said, "Look, I don't wanna know about your theories on race. I don't wanna hear anything about religion. I just wanna know one thing—how'd you get them girls to obey you like that?"[33] This captures well the "desire" side of the equation, but it is crucial also to attend to the disgust that always shadowed expressions of attraction. And what seems most thrilling to men hovering around the case is that young women were having their sexual lives directed by this one man.

Here we might turn to a legal filing made by Manson Family member Sandra Good (listed as "Goode" in the court papers) "in order to show cause in re contempt against Vincent Bugliosi." In this fascinating document, Good claims that Bugliosi had confronted her outside the Hall of Justice and called her a "goddam two-bit whore"; according to Good, Bugliosi informed her that "he knew that I 's-----d Charlie Manson's d---k'; that he has proof and he is going to bring it out in the trial, that I was a 'goddam f-----g tramp' ['whore' is crossed out on the document]; then he said, 'I have one thing to say—I'm going to get you and I'm going to get you good. I'm going to have you behind bars if it's the last thing I do.'"[34] Good's affidavit is less significant for whether it can prove its claims or not, but gains heft because of how clearly it lays out the process by which all the complex dimensions of Family life on its commune would be flattened out and sexualized when placed under judicial and media scrutiny. It is also noteworthy that Bugliosi regularly blamed young women for the actions they carried out while under the control of Manson. In constructing his legal strategy, it must be emphasized, Bugliosi normalized rape and held young women accountable for the violence done to them.

Charles Manson's ranch and Mel Lyman's hill offered liberatory opportunities to a few men and a new form of patriarchal control for most women. In his memoir, Tex Watson remembers life at the ranch with fondness, and recalls being served sandwiches "full of sprouts and avocado and cheese" by willing young women: "It was as if we were kings, just because we were men, and nothing could make them happier than waiting on us, making us happy."[35] The extreme gender hierarchies of Spahn Ranch and Fort Hill were outliers in the counterculture world, no doubt, but they were outliers in degree, not in kind. The upsetting truths revealed via the dramatic spectacle of Manson and the less studied but still influential example of Lyman were really open secrets. The innovative social organization promised by the reinvention of communes in the 1960s had turned out to be a terrible disappointment for many participants.

Even the most successful communes—the most obvious example being The Farm, in Tennessee—tended to be rooted in very traditional gender behaviors and relations. The Farm had its own guru, Stephen Gaskin, who was ultimately partnered with Ina May Gaskin, author of *Spiritual Midwifery*, widely considered to be a bible of the home-birth movement. While the Farm's large intentional community did quite a bit of progressive work (not only in midwifery, but also in sustainable agriculture and anti-nuclear activism) its gender ideology was retrograde. Maggie Gaskin, who was married to Stephen from 1967 to 1975, suggests a natural, immutable basis for this commune's arrangements: "The women . . . are very, very female . . . . There are a lot of children around that are there because they're wanted, and the women are going back and doing very feminine things, like weaving and cooking with a lot pride, doing it as a woman-thing."[36] As historian Timothy Miller explains, Ina May Gaskin's incredibly successful work as a midwife was situated in a broader Farm culture of anti-abortion and anti-birth control politics. Miller writes that in "its opposition to abortion the Farm made a remarkable offer: 'Hey Ladies! Don't have an abortion, come to the Farm and we'll deliver your baby and take care of it, and if you ever decide you want it back, you can have it."[37] The documentary *Manson* (1973) makes it clear that Family ideology promoted a similar approach to baby-making and baby-raising.

It is interesting to see that on its current webpage FAQ the Farm directly confronts the question of gender hierarchies at the commune. Under the question "How has the culture shifted over time regarding gender roles?" there is an answer that might be boiled down to "Not so much." "Gender roles have shifted," readers arc told, "as the first generation of children have left home enabling more women to pursue more varied and lucrative careers." That is not nearly the whole story, though: "However in the new families with young children . . . we tend to remain somewhat traditional, encouraging moms to be with the children with the dads being breadwinners, at least while the kids are still little. However dads change diapers, feed, bathe, and play an active role in their family."[38]

There were, of course, many, many meaningful and sustained efforts to transcend the limits of the conventional nuclear family among communards, and it is possible, if you look hard enough, to find media narratives that admit that all kinds of groups, from lesbian separatists to spiritual seekers, have done so. But for the most part our ability to *see* different communal models as successful was stunted first by the negative examples of Manson, Lyman et al., and next, and perhaps more profoundly, by what Jonathan Crary has called a "counter-revolution" that erased the gains of the 1960s generation. "The main thrust," Crary writes, "has been either the elimination or the financialization of social arrangements that had previously supported many kinds of cooperative activity."[39] Crary is correct to suggest that "the idea of a commune derived from any form of socialism" became intolerable in the wake of the 1960s experiments. He points not only to broadly popular cultural narratives about Soviet and Chinese collective efforts here, but also to the "countless narratives of cult-like communes of obedient converts ruled by homicidal madmen and cynical manipulators."[40] If Crary is right to criticize the use that has been made of Manson, Lyman, and their commune-betraying brethren by the forces of capital, it is important to notice that the collectivist dream of the 1960s was not only attacked from without, but also poisoned from within.

For all of the radical promise built into the commune movement of the 1960s and 1970s, it turns out that the lasting challenge to the conventional family of the post–World War II era would not come from hippies, Yippies, or the creepy-crawling

Family of Manson's invention. As Judith Stacey and other sociologists and historians have made abundantly clear, the deepest and most lasting changes came not in conscious proactive rearrangements, but in on-the-fly responses to the challenges of the shift from an industrial to a post-industrial economy and the claims made by women carrying the challenges of the second-wave feminist movement. For her part, Judith Stacey writes that the traditional "family is not here to stay. Nor should we wish it were. On the contrary, I believe that all democratic people, whatever their kinship preferences, should work to hasten its demise."[41] In its haphazard way, the Family certainly tried.

Hush Little Dropout

In his *Getting Back Together*, participant-observer Robert Houriet acknowledges that a sizable number of commune dwellers were "transients," many of whom were "pregnant runaway girls."[1] We cannot fully understand the story of the Manson Family or the hold its members had on the popular imagination if we don't take the runaway question seriously. It serves us well to at least ask why we have not been able to find a deeper sympathy for the vulnerable young women who joined Manson in San Francisco's Haight and at various spots in Los Angeles, including Dennis Wilson's house, the Spiral Staircase, the Yellow Submarine, and Spahn and Barker Ranches. Since the late 1960s, a loose coalition of Americans including government officials, journalists, filmmakers, fiction writers, and social scientists devoted considerable energy to outlining (and attempting to solve) the problem of the runaway. But few tears were shed for the runaways who found their way to Manson. The sexualization of *these* young women made it almost impossible to see them as vulnerable or available for rescue.

Given how much cultural energy was expended on the "problem" of runaways and what this phenomenon had to say about the state of the American family, about youth culture, about the "generation gap," it becomes more and more difficult to understand how *little* effort was made to stitch the Manson women into this cultural script of fear and concern. Jeffrey Sconce and others have made clear that the Manson girls were used as "a site of sexual fantasy, or at least fixation, for the culture at large," but rarely were they offered up as objects of parental concern.[2] In fact, one of the few people in or around the Manson case to express any interest in the welfare of the young women of the Spahn Ranch commune was Terry Melcher, who testified that "the reason I went back the second time, I felt sorry for these people. There were a lot of girls that were obviously young and I assumed that most of them were runaways, or whatever."[3] As with so many older men who noticed the fraught realities of life as a young runaway, Melcher might not have harbored the purest motives; his alleged interest in Ruth Ann Moorehouse suggests some dark possibilities. But it is striking how rarely observers even mentioned that the Family had become sort of a clearinghouse for runaways.

It might be worth taking a moment here to think about how those dark possibilities found troubling public expression in Los Angeles in the mid-1970s in the form of a band comprised of young women who called themselves the Runaways. Kim Fowley, whom we will meet again in the next section (rubbing his hands in glee over the pleasure he found in the all the young women streaming into Laurel Canyon in the 1960s), was at the center of all this. With an assist from Rodney Bingenheimer, the so-called "Mayor of the Sunset Strip," Fowley helped put the band together and contributed to their output as a producer and lyricist. For years, histories of Fowley have used words like "impresario" and "Svengali" (which at least hints at the power dynamic built into the relationship of this powerful older man and these younger women). But given recent autobiographical testimony from the band's bassist, Jackie Fox, and good journalistic work by Jason Cherkis, it has become clear that more accurate words to describe Fowley include "rapist," "abuser," and "exploiter." The story of the Runaways makes clear that (at least in the 1970s) Fowley was purposefully casting a net to catch vulnerable young women. Cherkis describes Kari Krome, an early contributor to the Runaways, as Fowley's "type": thirteen years old when she met Fowley, Krome was "a young girl who spent too much time dodging her violent stepdad and bouncing from apartment to apartment in various working-class neighborhoods." Fowley, as Cherkis puts it, took a regular interest in

Krome and became "the most responsible adult in her world."[4] In 2015 Cherkis published his *Huffington Post* article that described in terrifying detail how Fowley used a combination of drugs, emotional manipulation, and physical power to control these young women. His rape of Fox, with numerous others observing, was the fullest expression of his violent abuse of young women.

The bystanders who witnessed the rape of Jackie Fox serve as a reminder that the social investment in the safety of young women (particularly runaways with or without a capital "r") was shot through with remarkably damaging misogyny, one effect of which was to reduce *all* women to the status of sexual objects. There seems to have been no backlash, for instance, to Fowley taking out an ad in the June 1975 issue of *Back Door Man* that essentially invited women who were either above eighteen or "under 18 and legally emancipated (with paper work)" to come join the much older man as a paid sexual partner. (It probably goes without saying that the zine *Back Door Man* took its name from the Howlin' Wolf song, which features a man making "his midnight creep" who reminds listeners that men don't know what he is up to, "but the little girls understand.") Jason Cherkis also notes, correctly, that the behavior of Kim Fowley and others like him was enabled by countless rock journalists, writing of the band as the "Sex Kittens of Rock," who "saw the Runaways as little more than the teenage sluts of Fowley's imagination." Charles M. Young's infamous *Crawdaddy* article about the group was full of bizarre eruptions including the claim that, playing live, the band made "a direct sexual challenge, almost too threatening." This piece ended with an unparalleled bit of rhetorical violence/masochism: hearing from the band's choreographer that young men were masturbating at a San Diego gig, Young writes "I am overcome with the urge to jack off against the stage, get my teeth kicked out by a vicious roadie, claw my way through a thousand demented teenagers puking cheap wine and luded out of their cerebral cortexes, just so I could touch the platform boots of these 16 year old girls."[5]

The unwillingness or inability to situate the Manson Family in the context of the runaway crisis appears as what literary critics have taught us to understand as a "structured absence": the thing *not* said or *not* represented tells us not only about what the culture has decided must be repressed, but also speaks loudly about what we do want to privilege or make manifest. That these young women were generally construed as spoiled dropouts—as opposed to vulnerable runaways—is one of the many tragedies of the Manson phenomenon. What should have served, as Sconce writes, as "a cogent lesson about the excesses of male power" became instead "a parable legitimating a generation's retreat back into" more familiar tendencies of patriarchal control.[6] A major part of that control was the enshrinement of a type of bystander culture in which the physical and emotional safety of young women was demoted in favor of privileging the physical and emotional needs of men.

There were many ways to think and talk about runaway youth in the late 1960s. In his 1968 book, *Revolution for the Hell of It*, Abbie Hoffman insisted that runaways were "the backbone of the youth revolution." According to Hoffman, a fifteen-year-old "who takes off from middle-class American life is an escaped slave crossing the Mason-Dixon line." Hoffman also noted that an "underground railroad exists" to help these young radicals navigate their way around the country.[7] (Hoffman's claims here also serve as a good reminder that in the 1960s and 1970s "runaway" virtually always implied "white" as well.) It was possible, then—at least for some avowed members of the counterculture— to understand the phenomenon of young people running away from home as part of a larger social movement. Peter Coyote, one of the founders of the Diggers, a San Francisco–based street activist group, makes it clear that older radicals considered runaways to be a responsibility they needed to take on. Coyote explains, "Digger shelters, crash pads, and hippie communes helped develop the sense of extended family and linked underground communities." Coyote's use of the word "family" seems purposeful, a counterculture reclamation project. "There were all these way stations where you were welcome and you were extended family," Coyote writes.

There was this loose linked sense of family and sharing of resources and alliances. You'd go someplace and you stay for awhile, and you'd pitch in and work there and live . . . . Information about these shelters was transmitted by word of mouth, through underground press advertisements, postings in local counterculture business, and at times was even noted in the mainstream press . . . . Children who set out on their own had places to go other than the street.[8]

According to Coyote, the Diggers even had a lullaby that summarized the group's whole approach to runaways: "Hush little drop-out, don't make a peep, / Diggers gonna find you a place to sleep / And if your stomach stands in need / Diggers have a big Panhandle feed / And if of clothing you need more / Everything's free at the Digger store."[9]

Coyote's subtle invocation of the street opens up the troubling reality that many teenage runaways were not only living on the street, but also working the streets. Scholar David McBride has summarized, perhaps with more power than subtlety, that the two major alternatives facing female runaways were "prostitution and commune living," both of which were "hardly empowering." McBride suggested that "the degradation of prostitution was self-evident" but that commune life was also more than a little bit problematic: "[W]omen's majority status in communes belied the fact that 'leadership' was almost exclusively male."[10] Even if McBride overstates the case, it is clear that from the mid-1960s at least through the mid-1970s, a passionate conversation developed around young female runaways, which, as Karen Staller explains in her book on runaways, essentially presented these girls and women as "vulnerable and exploitable . . . and driven to deviant acts to meet their basic survival needs."[11] Family associate Bobby Beausoleil has claimed that during the time he lived in Hollywood in the late 1960s he tried to make sure that his basement apartment could serve as a crash pad for vulnerable runaways.[12]

In response to the relative defenselessness of *The Young Runaways* (that is the title of a 1968 film) a fairly extensive network of hip youth-service providers developed around the country. In hot spots such as the Haight-Ashbury (where David E. Smith worked at the Free Medical Clinic) and Greenwich Village, agencies providing housing, job leads, health care, social opportunities, and other services developed rapidly. These countercultural organizations attempted, Karen Staller writes, to respect the autonomy of these teenagers; often the service providers understood themselves to be part of a "civil rights movement" working on behalf of an oppressed minority. Young people had the right, in this framing of the issue, to leave "unhappy and unstable family backgrounds," in order to search for more evolved "substitute" families being developed in communes and elsewhere.[13] Ann B. Moses, a social-service worker and scholar, has offered a nice shorthand to understanding the cultural divide in approaching runaways. The mainstream press offered advice to parents on how to cope when faced with a runaway child; the underground press regularly published tips on how to avoid being caught.[14]

The Diggers were at the center of the effort to frame running away as a progressive choice, but they also recognized that counterculture elders needed to take responsibility for actively making it possible for young people to be on their own in the city. The construction of "Digger Free," Karen Staller explains, included "free food, store, shelter, education, on street survival, clinics, and referrals to other service." The Diggers' good works and outreach efforts came in for more than a little mockery. The mainstream media called them "mod monks" and "psychedelic social workers."[15] But whatever attacks were made on the Diggers, it is clear that the model they created was copied and built upon for years to come. From Huckleberry House in San Francisco (whose name invoked an earlier era's righteous and young fictional hero who headed West) to Covenant House in New York, agents of "alternative" social services drew inspiration from the work done by the Diggers.

The triage practiced by the Diggers, churches, and other social service agencies was made more difficult by the fact that much of the work they were attempting to do was illegal given that "most states had criminal laws against harboring a minor or interfering with custodial rights."[16] Richard Fairfield recounts a relevant incident at the Sheep Ridge Ranch commune in California, which is also notable for the parallel it draws between runaway youth (presumably female) and members of the military who have gone AWOL (presumably male):

> Early in the morning on October 31, 1969, a 25-man army of policemen, narcotics agents, juvenile officers, FBI agents, et al., had descended on Sheep Ridge Ranch without benefit of either invitation or search warrant. They said they were looking for juvenile runaways and Army deserters. When they arrested one of the female residents, Bill [a commune dweller] objected. Without warning, an officer swung around with handcuffs in hand and gashed Bill's forehead with them. This led to a melee of hitting, shoving, and pushing, and the subsequent arrest of Bill and four others on felony charges of assaulting an officer.[17]

Charles Manson, it is worth remembering, was charged in Mendocino County in 1967 with "interfering with the questioning of a suspected runaway juvenile, Ruth Anne Moorehouse."[18] Powerful forces in the mainstream culture were initially indifferent, if not hostile, to the efforts made by the counterculture agents. But before too long outright opposition to these efforts was joined by co-optation with the passage of the Runaway Youth Act of 1974, which codified many of the counterculture practices into federal law. In addition to striving for "normalization" (essentially acknowledging that running away was not pathological and trying to keep the legal system out of the picture), the Act also validated "alternative" services with a government stamp of approval.[19]

But I am jumping ahead with this mention of 1974—the year of this important new law and of Vincent Bugliosi's *Helter Skelter*. The "runaway" years to which I want to be sure to do justice here stretch from 1967 to 1973.[20] I pick these years as bookends because both 1967 and 1973 were marked by the murders of young people, murders that energized the national conversation about the vulnerability of runaways. The 1967 murder involved a young woman named Linda Fitzpatrick and her boyfriend, James Hutchinson, known as Groovy. The two were found dead in a boiler room in the East Village. The murders received a great deal of press coverage, including a major series of articles in the *New York Times* by J. Anthony Lukas, who strove desperately to explain how this privileged daughter of Greenwich, Connecticut, could have come to the terrible end she did. Lukas's major animus in his article is to demonstrate that while Greenwich and the East Village are less than an hour's drive from each other, the residents of the two places occupy completely separate spheres of existence. When Lukas interviewed Linda Fitzpatrick's mother, she told the reporter that she didn't even know there *was* an East Village: "I've heard of the Lower East Side. But the East Village?" Fitzpatrick was not, strictly speaking, a runaway; her parents gave her "reluctant consent" to move to New York, presumably to go to art school.[21]

Whether or not Fitzpatrick was technically a runaway mattered less than how her story would be narrated in the press. The *Village Voice*'s writer recognized that the murders would be used as a cautionary tale, "a reminder to Americans that freaking-out in the land of the free and the home of the brave can be fatal."[22] Ada Calhoun has written recently that the "happy-go-lucky" Groovy was known around the East Village "as someone who helped runaways find shelter."[23] This brought Groovy to the attention of New York officials. He was arrested in May of 1967, along with his good friend Galahad, a Digger, for "impairing the morals of a minor"—in this case a "15-year old run-away girl whom they had let stay in their apartment, called a commune."[24] Groovy was clear that he was providing a "safe haven to newcomers who would otherwise be living on the street."[25] The question Lukas ultimately posed to the readers of his *New York Times* article had to do with how these parents could know so little about their child—where she lived, what she was doing in New York, whom she was living with. 1967 was the year that a public service announcement debuted that has become the object of consistent parody since then. But when deep-voiced men intoned, "It's 10 p.m. Do you know where your children are?" every night, the question underscored the reality that many parents really had no idea. Denizens of the East Village processed the murders as a cataclysmic tragedy, as Ada Calhoun demonstrates in her history of St. Marks Place: "After the murders, many suburban kids were no longer allowed to visit the Village. Shops . . . suffered and the streets grew emptier . . . . Crime rose . . . there was a sense of looming apocalypse."[26]

Although the Linda and Groovy murders shook up plenty of observers, that dark tale of the generation gap was enough of an anomaly that it did not actually cause much hand-wringing or concrete change. The Houston mass murders of 1973, on the other hand, were so shocking in their details, so clear in the message the killings delivered about official neglect of young people (in this case boys), that a dramatic response became absolutely necessary. The Runaway Youth Act of 1974 grew, in large part, from the horrors of the killings in Houston by Dean Corll. At least twenty-eight young boys and men were kidnapped, raped, and murdered by Dean Corll between 1970 and 1973. This mass murderer in Houston seems to have taken his victims with impunity, and even had two teenage accomplices who worked with him to commit the crimes. Corll's family owned a candy factory—he was literally a stranger with candy—and he spent years on the hunt for potential victims to torture and kill.

More than the details of Corll's crimes, what's important here is how little the police in Houston cared about these young men, one after another going missing, being reported by their parents, not turning back up. In Skip Hollandsworth's long article on the murders in *Texas Monthly*, he reports that when "parents protested" about the lack of police interest in finding the young men, "the officer said that all sorts of kids were hitting the road, hitchhiking across the country, joining communes and being part of the 'hippie' movement. The investigators said that unless there was clear evidence of foul play, no official search could be conducted."[27] After Corll was killed by Wayne Henley (who, along with another teenager, David Brooks, was coerced to support Corll in his criminal activity), it became clear that the parents of victims had been turned away by the police again and again. As Hollandsworth tells it, "police barely investigated the boys' disappearance . . . . The officer who received the report on [one boy] labeled him a runaway after learning he had previously left home and stayed with friends because he had been having arguments with his father about such issues as the length of his hair. The officer who got [another boy's] report also labeled him a runaway, after finding out that someone thought he'd seen him at a house where runaways often gathered."[28]

The response was swift and appropriately critical. As far away as the Soviet Union, *Izvyestia* was suggesting that "indifference" and "murderous bureaucracy" were to blame for the killings. The police chief in Houston remained unmoved, suggesting that the parents had been responsible for neglecting their sons. Houston's mayor added that "the police can't be expected to know where a child is if his parents don't."[29] The captain of the juvenile division of the police department also suggested that "some parents don't want their children returned."[30] A minority discourse also developed that hinted that the victims "came from broken homes."[31]

The Linda Fitzpatrick/Groovy murders and Dean Corll's crimes suggest something about the complex set of feelings evinced by the group of insurgent young people most often referred to as runaways. The runaways got processed in many cultural forms, from comic books to art films, but nothing like a single point of view emerged. To develop an understanding of the relative lack of empathy expressed across the culture for the young women of the Manson Family it will help to take a brief tour through some of the major ways cultural producers in the United States expressed their complicated points of view about the runaway challenge to the American family. The arrest of Manson and his followers late in 1969 acted as a climactic moment in this ongoing crisis of the family. The challenges these young people embodied made it clear to many observers that it was now an urgent matter to organize a cultural course correction.

The trouble with sorting out the runaway problem in the late 1960s and early 1970s is that it was rare to find any clarity about who or what was to blame for the phenomenon. When Lillian Ambrosino wrote a sympathetic book simply called *Runaways* for the progressive Beacon Press in 1971, there was very little she could say concretely about why young people were "taking off" in such large numbers—the basic "push" and "pull" factors were rarely discussed with any specificity. While it was obvious in the 1930s that young people who hit the road were largely motivated by economic concerns, in the 1960s, to Ambrosino, the major push seems to have come from what she called "hypocrisy": "The youngster who leaves the 'hypocrisy' of his household, or society, goes in search of the warmth, integrity, and meaning he has been led to believe thrive within communes or among groups of flower folks." Trying rhetorically to save the runaways from an understanding of their identity as "spoiled" (as sociologist Erving Goffman put it), Ambrosino assures her readers that "many runaways actually love or respect their parents."[32] An earnest sociological study published a few years before Ambrosino's book in 1967, "Suburban Runaways of the 1960s" also struggled to understand the social landscape of running away. The authors of this study also make clear that economic factors seem irrelevant, given that their research was done during a period of "unprecedented national affluence." Trying to head off simple or blaming conclusions, the authors admit that the runaway is "more likely to come from a broken or reconstituted family" but argue that it would be "misleading . . . to assert a simple cause-and-effect relation between broken homes and running away. To do so would ignore the fact that half the runaways came from intact families." The authors also took pains to note that it is "popularly believed that families in which the mother works outside the home are functionally equivalent to broken homes. The working mother is frequently blamed for any deviant behavior in her child." While not directly taking issue with this assumption, the study's authors do note that their findings make clear that "the presence of a working mother does not seem to be a crucial factor in whether a child runs away from home."[33]

"Suburban Runaways of the 1960s" cannot offer much to explain why so many young people had been running away in this period except to suggest that they come from families that are perceived to be characterized by "conflict." The authors of the study also suggest that suburban boredom might be a real cause of teenage disillusionment and a factor in the ultimate decision to leave home. Using a phrasing that is especially interesting for our purposes, these sociologists contend that in "the helter-skelter suburbias with their minimal or nonexistent symptoms of public transportation, recreational activities typically are lacking, and what few exists are inaccessible to large numbers of adolescents."[34] Senator Birch Bayh, writing an introduction to a study of "boy prostitution in America" in 1976, suggested (after repeating the misleading claim that the victims of Dean Corll were runaways) somewhat vaguely that many flee their homes because of disappointments at school and "look for companionship, friendship and approval from those they meet . . . . The generation gap is very real."[35] One Digger, quoted in novelist Bibi Wein's 1970 study of the "runaway generation" tried to emphasize "pull" over "push" factors, arguing that young people were "not really running away": "They are running to something they think is there which isn't there. They think it's just groovy . . . oh boy, all these fascinating, you know, hip types, they don't have to go to school, they live in these groovy communes—which of course isn't true . . . . They think it's really an exciting thing. It's complete freedom, but they don't realize that it's kind of hard to have freedom if you're out panhandling for food, or selling the *Free Press* to pay your rent."[36] Journalist Robert Sam Anson, writing in the late 1970s about the exploitative use of the "million runaways" by the pornography industry, argued that the "talent pool is bottomless": there were, according to Anson, "unnumbered children who . . . simply belong to parents who don't give a damn."[37] Anson sharpened the focus even more by quoting a producer of pornography who informed him that these are children of "lawyers, doctors, policemen, preachers—who are attracted to older men because their fathers have no time or them. They are searching for a father."[38] Without wading into the dime-store psychologizing of the Anson-approved porn producer, it is safe to say that many of Manson's followers—Lynette Fromme (who had a "dictatorial" father), Susan Atkins, and Ruth Ann Moorehouse come right to mind—suffered dramatically from having fathers who parented on the sad spectrum that stretched from neglectful to abusive.

Perhaps the most poignant statement of all on how parental failure fed into the problem of runaways was Paul Schrader's 1979 film *Hardcore*, which is meant as a sort of summary statement on the crisis; a few years before this, Schrader had scripted *Taxi Driver*, another film concerned with a vulnerable young runaway. In *Hardcore*, George C. Scott plays Jake Van Dorn, a single parent whose daughter Kristen disappears from an amusement park she visits with her Calvinist youth group. Van Dorn hires a private investigator, Andy Mast (Peter Boyle) to hunt her down. Boyle takes on the work of finding Kristen but makes sure that Van Dorn understands the problem he faces: informing Van Dorn that "stag films" are legal and hinting that this might be where his daughter has landed, he invokes the dark heart of American captivity narratives stretching from the earliest days of Anglo settlement in the Americas through John Ford's *The Searchers* (1956), and warns the grieving father that "when I find her you may not even want her back." Schrader's reference to *The Searchers* is made manifest every time Mast calls Van Dorn "pilgrim," a usage that was noted by Janet Maslin in her *New York Times* review of the movie in 1979. It is important to keep *The Searchers* in mind here—*Hardcore* was initially slated to be called *Pilgrim*—because the claim made about Kristen is that whatever led to her "captivity" may have permanently damaged her and made her unfit for reintegration into straight society. It is not hard, of course, to see that this judgment was in the air around the Manson "girls." For his part, it seems clear that Schrader wants Manson in his picture, at least when he has the porn director in the film coach Kristen to get in the mood for her scene by channeling Susan Atkins: "[Y]ou're setting your mind free, you're thinking about your dad."

Van Dorn ultimately takes the reins of the investigation himself, enlisting the help of Niki, a sex worker who has been on the streets herself since the time she was fifteen. Supporting the two-distinct-worlds rhetoric of J. Anthony Lukas's Linda/Groovy coverage in the *New York Times*, Van Dorn tells Niki that she could never possibly understand him—"a man who believes in God, who doesn't pursue women, who believes in social order, and believes that at the end of his life he will be redeemed." When Van Dorn finally finds Kristen, the daughter is unwilling to let her father off the hook. "You never gave a fuck about me before," she says, and then adds "I'm with people who love me now." In his awkward speech that follows, Van Dorn meditates on gender, parenting, and expressiveness: "Baby, I do love you. I just never knew how to show you. It's very difficult for me. Nobody ever taught me." Encouraging the audience to see the wounded, emotionally repressed father as the origin of the problem afflicting the younger generation, *Hardcore* made a clear case that parents had contributed in a major way to the runaway crisis.

Hardcore was certainly not the first piece of American art to present the possibility that the problems faced by runaways were, in large part, created by the parents. Early in the decade, Milos Forman's film *Taking Off*, Horace Jackson's *Johnny Tough* (a revision of François Truffaut's *The 400 Blows* set in Black Los Angeles), and the fake diary *Go Ask Alice* (both from 1971), all made the case that the utter incompetence of contemporary parents was helping to make fleeing seem like a relatively sane choice for many young people. The 1974 television movie *Born Innocent* (starring Linda Blair) was similarly blaming of the parents: Chris Parker is forced to run away again and again to escape an abusive father and neglectful mother. Ultimately she is sent to juvenile prison where she is brutally raped with a plunger by other teenagers. The violent imagery was blamed by one parent for a copycat attack on her own nine-year-old. This horrifying series of events led to the creation of the Family Viewing hour, which lasted for one television season.[39]

Taking Off, Forman's first American movie, is an underappreciated comic tour de force that suggests that hapless parents bear a large percentage of the responsibility for the alienation of their children from mainstream culture. The movie plays as a sort of serious parody of the Beatles' 1967 runaway epic "She's Leaving Home," although here the daughter is searching for much more than "fun." Larry and Lynne Tyne are Forest Hills parents whose daughter Jeannie has run to the East Village. The main action of the film consists of scenes of the Tynes figuring out what to do in response to this family tragedy, intercut with scenes of Jeannie and other young women—including Carly Simon and Kathy Bates—auditioning for an unnamed musical opportunity. Gently skewering the musical pretensions of the younger generation (from earnest folkie performances about the time when "even horses had wings" to the lute-playing madrigal singer who tells her lover "you can fuck the lillies / and the roses too / you can fuck the maidens / who swear they've never been screwed" as long as she gets to be first in line). Forman saves his sharpest critique for the parents who appear to not have any idea about what matters to their children.

Taking Off mostly wants to tamp down the hysterical rhetoric surrounding the runaway problem. The film does acknowledge that running away has become epidemic; when Larry Tyne asks a lunch-counter employee to hold onto a picture of Jeannie to look at in case the girl shows up there, the woman tosses it into a box full of similar pictures. At the same time, *Taking Off* tries to defuse the panic surrounding the phenomenon through the implication that this has become, more or less, a rite of passage. Jeannie's flight does not seem to have been spurred by any major crisis—her parents are just sort of awful in a general way. One way Forman indicates that Larry Tyne is going to be no help to his daughter is that he pronounces "where" as if the "h" comes first.

What is clear is that the parents are not going to let the disappearance of their pesky children get in the way of having an enjoyable and educational night out. At a party sponsored by the

Society for Parents of Fugitive Children, the parents get *very* high after smoking joints provided to them by the leadership of the organization, who also arrange for a brief lecture on weed protocol by a character named Schiavelli, played by Vincent Schiavelli: "After you inhale, you take the joint and you pass it to the person sitting next to you. Do not—repeat—do not hold onto the joint. This is called bogarting the joint and is very rude." The Tynes end up back at their house, playing strip poker with their new friends, the Lockstons. They seem to have forgotten about Jeannie until she reappears in their midst, at a truly inopportune moment. Larry Tyne manages, awkwardly, to ascertain that Jeannie has run off at least in part because of a "boy." He insists that Jeannie bring the young man, Jamie, home for dinner.

It is at this climactic dinner that the real gulf between the parental and the younger generations becomes clear. Forman reveals in this scene that he has been using the whole movie to set his audience up for a mordant joke about the complexities of youth. Larry Tyne spends a good bit of the meal in the typical parent-as-inquisitor role; for most of the conversation Jamie refuses, or is unable, to talk. Jamie, as one recent commentator puts it, "to be frank, looks like Charles Manson c. 1970."[40] Tyne runs through the predictable questions and finally asks Jamie if he makes any money playing music: "Last year I made 290,000." Tyne responds, quite literally, with a spit take: "What, uh . . . what did you say?" Jamie continues to speak a few lines of dialogue, which given his earlier, shifty silence, ends up feeling like a complex dramatic monologue: "290,000. Before taxes. It's a very funny thing. Like, uh. You see a lot of things that, uh, say the government is doing that, uh, just, uh, makes you kinda angry, so you, uh, write some songs about it and, uh, you try and reach as many people as you can. And, uh, in the end you end up paying for those very same things that made you angry in the first place." There is a brief pause in the speech, just long enough for Jeannie's father to light one of the angriest cigarettes in film history. And Jamie continues: "But I guess, uh . . . I guess I accept contradictions." Before the dinner ends Jamie informs Jeannie's parents that he lives "frugally" (perhaps a jab at *Easy Rider*'s "simple food for our simple taste" commune scene?): "I'm saving up so I can buy an intercontinental ballistic missile. I think we should change the balance of power a little." The film ends, fittingly, with some more music. After Jamie refuses to perform any of his music for the Tynes (he is concerned that given the setup he will not be able to "get his rocks off") the parents themselves take the stage—with Lynne accompanying on piano, Larry belts "Stranger in Paradise," from *Kismet*. But then Forman cuts one more time to the audition scene, where a young woman is playing "Feeling Sort of Nice," a folk song keyed around the phrase "we're on our own side." The scene dissolves and the soundtrack segues into a group performance of the folk-gospel song "Amen"—popularized by Sidney Poitier in the 1963 film *Lilies of the Field* and then by the Impressions in 1964. Finishing his film with this marching song, Forman seems to be cosigning Abbie Hoffman's contention that runaways formed a vanguard of the youth revolution.

Where Forman uses elements of documentary style in *Taking Off* to emphasize the cluelessness of contemporary middle-class parents, Mormon youth counselor and fiction-writer Beatrice Sparks went full-on in the writing of her numbing book *Go Ask Alice*, a faux-teen diary that was presented, and often received, as authentic (with Sparks as the editor of the manuscript written by the now-dead teenager who is the book's subject). *Kirkus Reviews*, for instance, noted balefully that readers of the book would never get to meet "Alice," because she had died of an overdose.[41] The book reaches us now as a caricature—a joke about well-meaning adults and their complete inability to understand the first thing about adolescent drug use or the pressures that pushed so many young people to leave their homes. Historian Mark Oppenheimer has written cogently of how quickly everything falls apart for young Alice: "On July 9, the normal child Alice goes on her first acid trip. By Sept. 6, she is complaining, 'I'm getting so that no matter what I do I can't please the Establishment.' By December matters are grimmer: 'I can't believe that soon it will have to be mother against daughter and father against son to make the new world.'"[42] Sparks, as Brian Herrera has explained, was able to get the diary into print largely because of her relationship with television personality Art Linkletter, who gave the manuscript to his own literary agent. Linkletter had recently suffered the tragic loss of his own daughter Diane, who committed suicide. While no drugs were found in Diane Linkletter's system, her father insisted that her prior drug use had contributed to her death. Before long a fairly energetic rumor culture developed that held that Diane Linkletter had gotten so high on LSD that she tried to fly out a window.[43]

It seems clear that we should read *Go Ask Alice* as commentary on the generation gap and the runaway crisis. In one diary entry, "Alice" tells of a moment when she was doing some cleaning and the Beatles' song "She's Leaving Home"—the ur-text of this runaway moment—came on the radio. As the diary's author explains things, "[B]efore I knew what was happening I had tears dripping down my face like two spigots had been turned on inside my head. Oh that song was written about me and all the others of thousands of girls like me trying to escape."[44] The figure of Alice is complex, to say the least. For every moment of sympathetic vulnerability, Alice just as often pushes readers away with self-indulgent rationalizations: "I better take some of Gramps' sleeping pills. I'm never going to be able to sleep without them. In fact I think I'd better take a supply of them. He's got plenty."[45] The book's narrator ranges from absurd references to "the old Negro spiritual," which actually seems to be "Ol' Man River" from *Show Boat*, to girlfriend guides to hair care ("I wash it in mayonnaise and it's shining and soft enough to make anyone turn on.") to what should have been the ultimate giveaway for any conscious reader that this was the work of an adult—the mention of bringing "gelatin salad" to a potluck.[46]

Sparks was working in a tradition of American literary expression that dates back to the first half of the nineteenth century, organized around "mediated" first-person accounts of alcohol and drug use. These thrilling stories promise complex satisfactions—as a reader you thrill to the particular dangers the lead character faces, occasionally feeling some sympathy, but also take more than a little pleasure out of judging the shameful fall from grace. Many of the stories produced in the late 1960s and early 1970s about young runaways offered up just such delectable reading experiences—and *Go Ask Alice* was likely the most far-reaching of all. While it must have been difficult for some readers to understand "Alice" as a completely sympathetic character, it does seem clear that she is presented as (and was certainly received as) worthy of care and concern.

These examples reveal that the culture surrounding the Manson Family was open to the possibility that young women runaways were misguided but not irredeemable. They needed support—professional help—and could not be left to the wolves of the streets. One of the best summaries of this nuanced approach to the drug-using runaway is found in Paul Revere and the Raiders' "Kicks" from 1966—a top-five hit produced by none other than Terry Melcher. The song, written by Barry Mann and Cynthia Weill, is remarkably gentle with its object of address, a young woman who takes a "magic carpet ride" and thinks, the narrator explains, that she has found the answer to all of her problems in drug use. The song imagines its female protagonist is some kind of runaway—though "Kicks" carefully avoids making it clear whether she is literally on the road or just taking escapist trips in her mind. This is a corny cautionary tale, to be sure, but one with a generous spirit. From Mann-Weill's peer-oriented lyrics to Mark Lindsay's warm and compassionate lead vocal, the song is non-judgmental and at least a little hopeful. The song's narrator commits to helping the "girl" find her way to recovery—in fact the emotional heart of the song comes with the singer reminding the troubled young woman that all she really needs is some help. The gender politics of "Kicks" may reach contemporary listeners as patronizing; the song never allows for the possibility that the imagined drug-user is on the kind of visionary and spiritual quest that was so highly valued by and for male seekers in the 1960s.[47]

"Kicks" articulated a politics of care that has run through much of the rhetoric surrounding runaways from the 1960s to our own time. Across the political spectrum (from Abbie Hoffman to Art Linkletter), expressions of concern about runaways, and particularly female runaways, became a cultural shorthand—an efficient way to talk about a whole host of social, cultural, and political problems. Linkletter, for his part, received a Grammy for a spoken-word record he released soon after his daughter's death, an ostensible letter from a father to a runaway daughter, called "We Love You, Call Collect." (The flip side was Diane's response, "Dear Mom and Dad.") Linkletter, the popular television personality, could not have been more square and voluntarily served the forces of reaction whenever he could. While the persona he adopted in "Call Collect" was gentle, understanding, and patient, in the real world Linkletter was aggressively anti–youth culture. Linkletter pioneered a feature called "Kids Say the Darndest Things" on his radio and television shows, but in his public life he worked assiduously to censor expressions of the rising generation in popular culture. In 1969, for instance, Linkletter testified in front of a Congressional committee on drug abuse that a full 50 percent of songs on rock-and-roll radio stations are "secret messages to the teen world to drop out, turn on and groove with chemicals and lights shows at discotheques." Leaving aside the obvious questions—if the messages were secret, who broke the code for Daddy Art?—it is clear that Linkletter was using the runaway and drug crises, along with his own family tragedy, to organize a resistance to the developing economic, social, and cultural power of his daughter's generation.[48]

That said, Linkletter's "Call Collect" could only do its work by draping itself in the appearance of parental solicitude. "I've read there are thousands just like you," Linkletter intones, his voice dripping with mock concern, "searching for something they fail to find at home." This spoken-word record offers up little in terms of understanding *or* solution: what Linkletter comes up with, essentially, is that young runaways should come home because they make their parents sad. Unlike the empathetic narrator of Paul Revere and the Raiders' "Kicks," Linkletter's Grammy-winner has little to offer outside of a vague promises of stability and (relative) quiet. Linkletter must have noticed that the Byrds had a huge hit in 1965 with their version of Pete Seeger's "Turn, Turn, Turn," and so slips a little bit of Ecclesiastes into "Call Collect." Lindsay and the Raiders, of course, abjure such lofty language of a more conversational approach. Even so, I want to be clear that both Linkletter's record and Paul Revere's were signing a social contract that held that youthful drug users and runaways were lost, and could not find themselves without outside help.

In between the positions staked out by Abbie Hoffman on one end (Every Runaway a Revolutionary!) to Art Linkletter on the other (Respect Tradition!), there was a canvas filled with all manner of popular art having to do with these young dropouts. Historian Gretchen Lemke-Santangelo has written of a "series of prime-time programs" that aired on television between 1968 and 1970 about young women seduced into joining the drug culture by "older, guru-type males, drug pushers, or seemingly innocent boy-next-door figures." "The lucky ones," as Lemke-Santangelo explains, are saved by parents or the police; the rest fall into prostitution or try to fly out windows. Lemke-Santangelo makes a case for many of these young runaways as "remarkably resilient, resourceful, and determined to secure and maintain their freedom and autonomy."[49] Radical sociologist Lewis Yablonski made a similar case in 1968, when he wrote of the hippie movement more generally, but purposefully used the language of the runaway crisis: "The participants were running away from a plastic society—at the same time they were running toward the difficult-to-define and even more difficult-to-live-by human ethic of love."[50] The culture industries in the United States, however, entered this conversation with a much different agenda and had a much different tale to tell: these young women had been plunged into a social maelstrom, and they were lost and vulnerable.[51]

The Young Runaways, a 1968 B-movie, is a perfect example of the damsel-in-distress approach described by Lemke-Santangelo. The real problem the film lays out (as the title song performed by Arthur Prysock makes clear) is that too many current major social questions cannot be answered satisfactorily. As a result, a generation gap develops. As with so much of this Runaway Art, the parents are not so much evil as they are clueless. In this case, Raymond Allen is an ad man who realizes (too late) that he has spent his life trying to sell "our way of life" to teenagers, but has not really bothered to listen to his own daughter. The movie shows a culture that lacks the infrastructure to address these new challenges. In one canned speech worthy of a 1930s gangster movie, a police officer reminds Mr. Allen that there are fifty thousand runaways in Chicago alone, with only eight cops assigned to work with/on them. In a bizarre bit of pop sociology, this police officer explains to Raymond Allen that it is only youngsters from "good" homes who run away, largely because "ghetto kids" have a safety valve in "crime and gangs." The movie's real summary moment comes when the police officer notes ruefully that there is "something weird going on in this country."

This type of speechifying is echoed in the better known *Dawn: Portrait of a Teenage Runaway*, a television movie that first aired in 1976. Here a young man who has taken a friendly interest in Dawn gets told by a court officer that the "streets are crawling with liberated teenie hookers" who are, these days, "running at 8 and 9." When this young man, Alex, asks whether there might be a spot in a halfway house for Dawn, the bureaucrat reminds him that there is not enough funding to create spaces for all who need them: "So the streets win by default," the young man answers, incredulous. In *Dawn* the pimp takes the place of the cult leader, exerting total, warping control over a bevy of young women.

Two films from 1971, *Maybe I'll Come Home in the Spring* (which debuted on television) and *Runaway, Runaway* joined *The Young Runaways* in communicating a sense of utter bafflement about the breadth and depth of the problem of runaways without turning too judgmental about the young people in question. In *Runaway, Runaway* young Ricki is picked up hitchhiking as she runs from home by a nice guy named Frank who smartly says to her, "So you're a runaway!" and tells her that he is in the business of finding and returning young runaways to their parents—but only, he hastens to add, the rich ones. Ricki faces a number of dangers—street people! lesbians!—but mostly is taken care of by Frank, who turns out to be her own personal catcher in the rye, the kind of 1970s-style catcher in the rye who ends up in bed with his teenage charge.

Maybe I'll Come Home in the Spring is even messier, featuring Sally Field as "Dennie," a young woman whose parents are clearly the ones who are out of control. (It is probably worth noting that both of these runaway heroes have androgynous names; Carol Clover has taught us to notice that the "final girl" in slasher movies often is given a gender-neutral name as a hint to readers that she will access male power in order to survive the horrors facing her. These runaways will also stand relatively firm in the face of the social dangers facing them.)[52] While it would be foolish to pretend that this television movie has a clear or coherent argument to make, it does make plenty of effort to let viewers know that as things fall apart around her, Dennie should not be held responsible. We see Dennie meaningfully looking at her parents' single beds, and we learn something about their loveless marriage; we see young Dennie playing with a doll as the filmmaker immediately cuts to a hippie man "playing" with her body; we see an ice cream truck that says "Caution Children" on the back, and an exterminator's truck from a company called "Wonder." By the movie's end the one thing that is clear is that Dennie has become more of a parent than her own and will now try to save her sister from the injuries she has suffered herself.

These pulp films, whether appearing on television or in the theaters, held out the hope that young people would be saved, cleansed, redeemed. Taken together they establish a cultural baseline with respect to the crisis of runaway white youth: the situation is bad, but not too bad. There are good cops and court officers, halfway house administrators and friends, all these helpers, who are doing their best to make sure that the young runaways will find their way home and get some support. These "problem" films rarely communicate a sense of despair or permanent damage. From Milos Forman's *Taking Off* through these lower-brow offerings, there are strong suggestions that a cultural reboot will not take much more than what Art Linkletter prescribes in "Call Collect": some good talk—and especially some good listening— will help bridge whatever gaps are separating the generations. This context helps us understand just how threatening Manson's girls appeared upon arrest and during the trials. The well-developed cultural vocabulary and packed social toolkit organized to confront the runaway crisis would not be up to that task of saving or curing or redeeming these outliers.

The one cultural artifact I know of that might help us understand the total banishing of the Manson girls from the realm of cultural concern is John Avildsen's heartbreaking and terrifying (and largely forgotten) 1970 movie *Joe*. Film critic and historian J. Hoberman has puzzled over the fact that in our own time *Joe* is a "movie without a reputation," especially given that it made something of a splash in its moment of first release.[53] It is hard to do justice to the emotional (and physical) grotesqueries this movie presents. Perhaps it would be best if I cut to the chase and reveal that the film ends with one of its lead characters "accidentally" shooting his own daughter to death and for many viewers this will not even come close to being the most painful thing they have seen in the past hour and forty-five minutes or so. The basic plot is simple: Melissa Compton (played by Susan Sarandon in her first role) has left her parents' home to take up with her boyfriend, a drug dealer and wannabe painter in the East Village: there are faint echoes of the Groovy/Linda Fitzpatrick story here. After Melissa experiences a serious, but not fatal, overdose, her parents go to her apartment to gather her belongings, and her father, Bill Compton, "accidentally" kills her boyfriend.

The real action of the movie from this point forward mostly has to do with the burgeoning relationship between the elder Compton and Joe Curran (Peter Boyle), an angry, reactionary factory worker. Joe is delighted to discover that for all of his own talk about the evils of hippies, Bill Compton has actually done something about them. The movie traces the painful contours of their cross-class friendship and follows the men as they go on adventures that include visiting each other's favorite bars, trying to live through a dinner party at Joe's house, and ultimately joining a party of hippies, smoking pot, and having sex with some of them. When Joe and Bill are ripped off by some of these hippies, they trace them to a commune upstate and there the mayhem ensures. Joe kills the first bunch and then Bill jumps in to finish off the rest—including his daughter, whose face is not visible to him.

Joe and Bill are separated in this movie by profound class differences. But while *Joe* is centrally interested in the not-so-hidden injuries of class, it ultimately has a more dramatic tale to tell about the generation gap. The movie was originally slated, in fact, to be called *The Gap*. It was released, as Hoberman reminds us, just months after a group of workers on Wall Street attacked a large group of young protesters (responding to the Kent State killings) in what came to be known as the Hard Hat Riots. But the way that class acts as a wedge between Bill and Joe—a scene where Joe makes Bill tell him how much money he earns is especially hard to watch—is dissolved in the unity of their hatred for the younger generation. These men, the movie tells, feel that something has been stolen from them, a vision of how the world should work, the chance to enjoy the sexual, emotional, and spiritual gifts the young generation have taken as their due, a more general feeling of being able to express their authority. When they go on their rampage at the movie's end, it is a declaration of war against the people who they think have changed the rules of the game.

Up until the mass murder that ends *Joe*, it is possible to read the film's point of view as ambivalent. The film's young hippies are awful, to say the least—self-indulgent, casually cruel, unable to recognize the subjectivity of the other. But when Joe and Bill begin their hunting expedition the movie shows its hand. In the masculine ritual of defining and neutralizing targets (and the movie has let us know a number of times that Joe *wishes* Bill would go hunting with him—not least because it would level off some of the differences in power that have been plaguing Joe throughout the film) the men find the water they can most comfortably swim in. Peter Boyle himself was clear about the generational animus of *Joe*: "The message of the movie is very plain," he told the *New York Times.* "It says that we'd just better stop that war in Vietnam now; that we'd just better stop killing our children there or we're going to be killing our children in the streets here."[54] But Boyle was either indulging in naivete or being purposefully obfuscatory. Of course he knew that during this "working-class war," as historian Christian Appy has called it, the sacrifice of the sons of Joe and his blue-collar kin was a given. What the film *Joe* also begins to suggest is that certain American daughters, particularly those who had taken up with socially marginal men, would also prove to be disposable.

Perhaps in *Joe* we begin to find some indication as to why the Manson "girls" could not be plotted on the broad map of cultural concern that included so many other young runaways and dropouts. Because some of Manson's followers *did* engage in criminal acts, and all participated in what many members of the surrounding culture understood to be immoral behavior, it was difficult for contemporary observers to stitch them into the developing narrative of abandoned children (or, at the very least, "misunderstood" children) that was coming to form something like a field of conventional wisdom about young runaways of the late 1960s. Manson was no Digger, but he served a similar countercultural caretaking function as that radical group did. Donald Nielsen reminds us that "most of Manson's followers had run away from or been driven out of original families of birth," but in accepting Manson's ministrations they seem to have forfeited any support they might have otherwise accessed as vulnerable women living away from home.[55] There seems to have been something about the contract forged between Manson and these women, something about how the Manson girls had transferred their allegiance from the father at home to the father at the ranch, that undid many observers. The "scruffy little guru" had come to operate as a "hyperbolic" representation of the Father in a manner that felt like rebuke and even mockery to older men.[56]

The young women who collectively became known as the "Manson girls" were not going to be stitched into available American tales of heroic runaways stretching from Huckleberry Finn to the X-Men; girls and women have always had less access to this tradition, and it would, of course, be much simpler to imagine them as the ruined daughters of the captivity narrative—the powerful story that so often included more than a hint that, even after their kidnap and rape, these young white woman come to "feel" Indian and want to stay with their new daddies. Or at least they might come to appear "Indian" enough to white eyes that they could never be assimilated back into the dominant culture.

Perhaps if the Manson girls had been able or willing to act out a public renunciation of Manson's power over them in the days leading up to the trial or at the trial itself the father-injury might have been minimized. But their ritual scarification in the early days of the trial, their courtroom interruptions and witchy behavior on the streets outside the Hall of Justice, and their steady stream of press releases and other publicity efforts made it clear that these young women were not going to be renouncing the commitment they had made to the head of their Family. Media critic Jeffrey Sconce has argued that the "X" mark that Manson's followers carved in their foreheads served to interrupt or deflect the sexual objectification that had afflicted them since they first appeared in Los Angeles—and likely even before that. Additionally, the scarring acted as an act of identification with, and support for, Manson—the women were following his lead in doing so.

The scar is central here. We recall the moment in John Ford's captivity-narrative Western *The Searchers* when John Wayne's Ethan Edwards finally meets the "Indian chief" responsible for his niece's kidnap and rape: "I see why they call you Scar," he mordantly observes. While no scar is visible on the captive daughter, viewers understand what Ford is up to here—there will be no washing away of the essential Indian stain that has been left on the young white woman.

Unlike Patty Hearst, whose family would be able, half a decade later, to afford to hire expert witnesses like Robert Jay Lifton to testify to the complex processes that led her to identify with her oppressors, the Manson girls could not stitch their perceived betrayal into a tale of "brainwashing." The young women who had settled with Manson at Spahn Ranch had made a bet against the parental establishment in forging a relationship to the cult leader, and the response to their treason would include few elements of mercy. After the facts of the Tate-LaBianca murders were sorted out, numerous sensible and perceptive observers would find it hard to avoid communicating a sense of doomy paranoia about how this had all shaken out. In her book on Leslie Van Houten, the brilliant radical criminologist Karlene Faith summarized the feelings of many when she wrote that the "fear and harassment of hippies that occurred after the crimes was as destructive to healthy communes as it was to those already dysfunctional. It was as if the dominant culture, in cahoots with the media, had been waiting for the Manson 'family' to happen so they would have 'proof' that the hippie movement was no good."[57] That is certainly the sentiment expressed in the work of syndicated columnist Vernon Scott, who managed to bring together the Cielo Drive murders and the suicide of Diane Linkletter by assigning a healthy dose of blame: "The sub-culture of trippers, pot-blowers, speed takers, LSD addicts and amphetamine junkies contributed to both tragedies." (To his credit, Scott distinguished between garden-variety hippies who just went to music festivals and took off their clothes in "paroxysms of flouting the establishment" and this more ominous kind who engaged in "eerie, weird and freaked out" behaviors.)[58]

Manson's girls were essentially treated—by Bugliosi and in the popular press—as particularly toxic groupies. A basic definition of "groupie" in the late 1960s would have to go beyond the simple description "devoted follower of rock group" to incorporate a clearer statement about the sexualization and more-than-occasional dehumanization of these (often underage) people. When she reviewed the 1970 documentary *Groupies*, film

critic Judith Crist described the movie as an "unforgettable portrait of the lost ones—hard-bitten whores, teeny-boppers, girl-
next-door lovelies, neurotics and near-psychopaths."[59]

It is hard to know what Judith Crist was seeing (though not
hard to imagine what she was hearing in the everyday world she
was living in). The documentary *Groupies* introduces a wide
range of young women, many of whom seem to be anything but
lost. The testimony offered suggests on more than one occasion
that having some element of control in deciding when to have
sex, with whom, and on what terms, was being incorporated in
a framing of the self as liberated and powerful. "It makes me in
a way feel . . . superior," offers one of the young women. Perhaps
even more revealing is the testimony from another subject of the
film who (purposefully, it seems) cannot tell the camera with clarity which rock star she first had sex with: "Who did I start with?
Oh! Fuck! Forget it! The Box Tops!" This young woman's refusal to
list a particular person, her tongue-in-cheek naming of her sexual
conquest with the band-name-collective rather than by individual
name (and possibly with a punning reference to sexual position as
well) represents an insistence on female agency. In an offhanded,
yet summary way, another contributor underscores the benefits
of the "groupie" lifestyle: "You get to fuck the prettiest boys, you
get to smoke the best dope." Journalist Amanda Petrusich has
written recently that it is worth considering that "sex was not the
only option for these women, but it was their preferred option."[60]
While I want to take this liberationist approach seriously, it is
also necessary to take into account scholar Lisa Rhodes's more
nuanced approach to the subject, especially her reminder that
to engage with all of the issues surrounding young female rock
fans and their sexuality is also to confront very difficult questions
about the "sexualizing of children" and the matter of who benefits most from the "moral system" that establishes taboos and the
attendant modes of discipline and punishment.[61]

Charles Manson may not have become the kind of star he
hoped to be in Los Angeles, but there surely was a common
understanding of his female Family members as having the same

sort of "spoiled identity" that afflicted the young women of Los Angeles and elsewhere who came to be called "groupies." (It is worth noting that when news broke in 2013 that Manson might be marrying a young woman who had been visiting him in prison, numerous news outlets snickered at the news and identified Afton "Star" Burton as a groupie of the "serial killer.") Recall that Family member Sandra Good reported that prosecutor Vincent Bugliosi once accosted her outside the Hall of Justice at Los Angeles to warn her that he was going to "get her" because she performed oral sex on Manson. The act named and the partner identified seem equally suspect in this telling: in Good's anecdote, Bugliosi is targeting her for choosing to practice her sexuality in a way and with a partner who fall outside of the norms he is trying to establish as part of his case against the Family inside the Hall of Justice. The story Bugliosi told about the Family combined two time-tested American artistic forms—the captivity narrative and the Gothic horror story. The Manson Family tale as constructed in the popular consciousness was, then, a terrifying Western and a terrifying Eastern. While Spahn Ranch was, on the face of things, an outdated movie ranch that offered a home to numerous young runaways, the prosecutor was able to frame it as a poisonous site of imperilment and a secret chamber of horrors.

While Abbie Hoffman (and presumably many of his allies on the left) saw the runaways as constituting a "slave revolt," the much more common and powerful mainstream response was to suggest that the young female runaways had become enslaved *in the process of* running away. Max Lerner referred to the women as slaves in the *New York Post* and the teaser for an article by Jean Stafford in *McCalls* promised that the well-known writer would "ponder the meaning of the Tate murders" and consider how "the girls who tried so hard for freedom . . . won only the most awful kind of slavery."[62] Jerry LeBlanc and Ivor Davis, in their early journalistic treatment of the case also used the phrase "modern day slaves"[63]; Susan Atkins herself would later describe the process of her affiliation with Manson as a "drive for freedom" that led her into "the worst bondage possible."[64] It would take years for the more forgiving language of "brainwashing" to find a place in treatments of the case. But if this Family was constituted by one Master and dozens of slaves, why did so few put their minds to the issue of emancipation? How could the Manson girls be freed from these chains of slavery—even, or especially, the ones who would spend most of their adult lives behind bars?

The History of Consciousness

There would be no fancy expert witnesses to help defend the women of the Manson Family at trial, but there was a remarkable effort to aid in their self-liberation, made by a coalition of feminists associated with the History of Consciousness program at University of California, Santa Cruz, and the Santa Cruz Women's Prison Project. They were there at the invitation of Virginia Carlson, the warden at the California Institution for Women (CIW), which housed the Special Security Unit (SSU), where Susan Atkins, Patricia Krenwinkel, and Leslie Van Houten were imprisoned.[1] This is a remarkable—and still underappreciated—chapter in the history of the Manson Family, a moment when a group of radical feminist activists and intellectuals inserted themselves into an unfolding drama that had for the most part been organized around powerful men and the vulnerable women they exploited. These feminists were enacting a truly profound form of theoretically informed practice. Soon after the end of the trial and California's abolition of the death penalty in 1972, the women (and some men) of the Santa Cruz project recognized that the three convicted women would need to see themselves as belonging to a different community, a new family of sorts, that was rooted in the individual dignity of each woman and the power to be found in collective support and education. Prison administrators approved a program devised to raise the consciousness of the imprisoned women according to radical feminist principles. More than forty years after the experiment was devised and implemented it is still more than a little shocking that it was approved.

Feminist sociologist Karlene Faith was a central figure in this effort and has written about it in detail in her book *The Long Prison Journey of Leslie Van Houten* as well as in a monograph on women's confinement and resistance.[2] Faith, along with her entire cohort, really, has embodied astounding restraint and has kept a low profile with respect to her work in prison with these women. Susan Atkins, for her part, was not shy about promoting the importance of the work done by Faith. In her autobiography Atkins writes with deep gratitude about Faith, whom she refers to as a "light in the darkness." Through the Women's Studies curriculum that Faith and her collaborators brought to the SSU, Atkins was able to develop a new sense of how she had "walked into" her own oppression. Through the intervention of Faith and the other feminists, Atkins experienced a revolution in her mind: "suddenly I found myself free."[3]

Virginia Carlson, the prison warden, must have been some kind of feminist herself. According to Karlene Faith, Carlson wanted to "raise the women's consciousness to a point where they would be able to think clearly for themselves, and recognize how deeply their subordination and rote obedience to Manson had degraded their humanity."[4] According to Faith, the warden wanted the women in the SSU to "be introduced to the idea of women's liberation as a way of gaining self-sufficiency."[5] Now, of course, this is Faith retrospectively explaining her sense of things, but the fact is that from 1972 to 1976 Carlson invited "carloads of graduate student instructors, professors, law students, artists, performers and community activists from throughout the state," to "corrections valley" where they came to teach a curriculum that included studies of women and the law, ethnic studies, creative writing, and radical psychology.[6] In Faith's account the volunteers were especially affected by the work they did in the SSU with the Family women. Here they met "three young, attractive, intelligent and unexpectedly endearing and vulnerable women" who appear to have thrown themselves into their studies with great energy.[7] The program seems to have been in place for four years, with an interruption during the first year after Faith closed a letter to a prisoner with the suspect word "*venceremos*" (essentially "we shall overcome"), the slogan of Che Guevara.[8]

It is clear that this engagement was not completely comfortable for all participants immediately. Candace Falk, who was a graduate student at UC Santa Cruz and went on to become a historian and founder of the Emma Goldman Archive at University of California, Berkeley, noted that she felt some discomfort in hearing the three women talk about the erotics of murder and also by the fact they used some vocabulary (i.e., "revolution") that was central to her own vision—but they were using it in a much different way. Falk stayed committed to the goals of the program without ever feeling comfortable with the visits to the members of the Family.[9]

The conversations that took place among the jailed women and their visitors seem to have been wide-ranging and profound in impact. In addition to the regular instructors, the prisoners had visits from a number of key figures from the emerging "women's music" scene, including Meg Christian, June Millington, Holly Near, and Linda Tillery.[10] They learned about poetry from Judy Grahn, and took seminars with writer Paul Krassner and with scholars speaking on politics, the blues, and women's history. The women were also encouraged to share their own talents; their embroidery impressed many guests and, as Faith recounts in heartrending detail, the three also sang a beautiful "close harmony" version of Buck Owens's country-and-western hit "Cryin' Time."[11]

This was not "deprogramming" as it came to be familiarly called in the 1970s, but rather an acknowledgment that a holistic political, social, and cultural education was the most powerful tool to help convert Van Houten, Atkins, and Krenwinkel back into the "independent, promising young people" they had been before being turned into "obedient disciples who lost their ability to think for themselves."[12] Faith was a radical feminist and a radical criminologist and worked assiduously with male and female comrades to create spaces of potential self-discovery for Van Houten, Krenwinkel, and Atkins. In doing so the Santa Cruz collective never lost sight of the fact that the prison system itself was a the root of the whole tragedy. Faith was aware that their leader's patriarchal "dogma was an inventory of the flaws of the society that rejected him and infantilized him as a prisoner without choice or responsibility."[13] Given her broader goals surrounding reform of the legal, judicial, and penal system, it is not surprising to find that Faith had little patience for Vincent Bugliosi, who not only prosecuted the women but then cashed in with a "mass-market novel-like book" full of "inaccuracies" and "sensationalized myths."[14] Welcoming Atkins, Krenwinkel, and Van Houten into an ad hoc collective of conscious feminists would mean rejecting the dominant rhetoric of the powerful men who had, thus far, controlled their lives.

Aside from the Santa Cruz feminists, very few in the world of politics, journalism, academia, or popular culture have worried much about the intellectual or emotional well-being of the Manson women. This is prison, after all. While Atkins (like Tex Watson) underwent a religious conversion and attracted the notice of some who were putatively interested in her "soul," for the most part these women have never been the object of much public concern—not when they were vulnerable young women and not when they were aging prisoners (Atkins has since died). Film director John Waters's decades-long friendship with Leslie Van Houten is atypical to say the least. A-List Hollywood film and music figures were never particularly interested in following up on their late 1960s contact with the Manson girls. With little outside of Faith's book and Waters's writing on Van Houten in *Role Models*, Atkins's own autobiography, and some scattered academic work on the Family, there is little available to those who might be interested in understanding *anything* about the inner lives of the Manson women or how their crimes have been processed in the larger culture. Here we have needed to rely on the creative artists. While Manson himself has, of course, dominated the field of cultural representations, there is much fictional work to guide us in beginning to construct an understanding of the women. From Stephen Sondheim to Madison Smartt Bell, Cady Noland, John Kaye, and some others, there has been a fairly consistent stream of cultural representations that at least dignify the Manson women as interesting subjects of consideration.

But none of this could really have prepared us for the two months in 2016 that saw the publication of Alison Umminger's *American Girls* or Emma Cline's *The Girls*. Both are serious works of cultural criticism and neither has a plot that matters much. The most significant accomplishment of the two books is telegraphed by the titles: on some level "Manson" does not need to be in either title (and the massive pre-publication press Cline received makes this especially true) for readers to understand quickly that we are in this territory. But more important is that both Cline and Umminger want readers to entertain a reframing of the story that does not demote Manson but that does imagine overlapping circles of activity, some of which have him centrally involved, some of which do not include him at all. After all, the "Family" *was* mostly—both in terms of sheer numbers and in terms of the daily kinwork and survival skills necessary to prop the project up—organized around the young women. This is where Gretchen Lemke-Santangelo's work on women in the counterculture proves helpful as we begin to consider the fictional inventions offered up by Umminger and Cline. Lemke-Santangelo explains that the surface reality of conventional gender roles should not obscure the reality that counterculture women were "launching a subtle rebellion against prevailing class and gender norms." She writes, "Rejecting the suburban domesticity of their mothers, hippie women revived an older, agrarian ideal that assigned greater value and visibility to female productive labor. They also cast off the privatized nuclear family structure in favor of a type of communal living that, like large extended families of the past, permitted women to share chores, conversation, advice, and practical knowledge."[15]

Cline's novel insists on the sustaining power of these female relationships—at least for the relatively brief time that her narrator is part of a Northern California commune obviously modeled on Family life: "The men in this book are sort of unimportant," Cline has said in an interview, "even though they set things in motion. I liked the idea of the Manson character and cult leader being peripheral. It's really about the shifting relationships of the girls."[16] Family associate Bobby Beausoleil has offered his own support for this position, suggesting that he understood that Leslie Van Houten's initial attraction to the group had more to do with her desire to be around other women rather than somehow falling under the hypnotic power of Manson himself.[17]

There is little that is surprising about *The Girls*, except perhaps for the intensity of focus—Cline resists the temptation so many other creative artists have indulged to trot Manson out for some crazy-sexy-preachy close-ups. While many of the key supporting players (Dennis Wilson, Terry Melcher) are here in minimal disguise, the focus is on what Lemke-Santangelo has called "the arena in which they labored, and the sense of mission and purpose that informed their work."[18] The dumpster figures here as an important site of Family activity: Cline knows what the Diggers knew and what Lemke-Santangelo knows—that this scavenging was "a mode of resistance, a political act."[19] Commune historian Timothy Miller has proposed that the garbage at the Safeway supermarket was an important link in the hippie food chain and Cline makes sure to focus on this activity a handful of times—although she does anachronistically use the 1980s coinage "dumpster diving" to do so. What matters most to Cline is to sketch out the social webs connecting these young women who had "passed into a familial contract" and whose female togetherness proves so compelling to young Evie.[20] Cline's protagonist insists upon the magnetic force that issues from this female-centric collective. The novel starts, simply, with Evie remembering how she "looked up because of the laughter, and kept looking because of the girls."[21]

Cline encourages readers to think about how the girls changed the landscape with their resourceful presence. Finding nourishment in dumpsters flies in the face of conventional ideas about what counts as food and what as garbage.[22] Even more important than the garbage dump/food run in her novel is the creepy crawl. The women of the ranch—that "orphanage for raunchy children"—come to recognize how powerful their very presence is. Evie reminisces about how momentous the creepy crawl could feel: "We were ripping a tiny seam" in family life—just so the family in question would "see themselves differently, even if for a moment"[23] She recalls, "Homes had been reshaped. Turned suddenly unsafe, familiarity flung back in their owners faces, as if taunting them—see, this is your living room, your kitchen, and see how little it helps, all that familiarity."[24]

Even so, the narrator of *The Girls* recognizes her own marginality, at least as she has been rendered in the official story. She has read and noticed that she is not mentioned "in most of the books." Evie does not appear in "the paperbacks with the title bloody and oozing, the glossed pages of crime-scene photographs. Not the less popular but more accurate tome written by the lead prosecutor, gross with specifics, down to the undigested spaghetti they found in the little boy's stomach." Wonderfully, according to Evie, she only appears in a "couple of lines" in "an out-of-print book by a former poet."[25] Cline is not willing to take only this one shot at Ed Sanders, and continues by having Evie note that he had "gotten my name wrong." She continues, "The same poet also claimed the CIA was producing porn films starring a drugged Marilyn Monroe, films sold to politicians and foreign heads of state."[26] The wicked parody and critique of Bugliosi and Sanders holds a serious argument, about how little these men understood about the workings of the Family. All of the books, as Evie understands them, make it sound like "the men force the girls into it. That wasn't true, not all the time."[27] With this careful and ambivalent declaration of agency, Cline reminds us that this Family had complex power dynamics.

The question of force and the hierarchies of power that structure all families are at the heart of Alison Umminger's *American Girls*. This dark young adult novel is a metacommentary—a story about stories—on the Manson Family. The book opens with an epigraph from Manson himself, and it is one of his best lines: "These children that come at you with knives, they are your children." The rest of the novel is essentially a reckoning, an inquisition into *why* exactly your children are coming at you with knives. (Or stealing your credit card. Or running away from home. Or getting obsessed with the Manson Family.) The simple and profoundly disturbing answer is that these abusive and neglectful parents have it coming.

The framing narrative of *American Girls* features a family that has ceased to exist in any meaningful, functioning way. Anna's mother, Cora, has discovered, midlife, that she loves women and one woman, Lynette (yes, Anna takes note of how odd this name coincidence is) in particular. When Anna comes to realize, as her sister Delia did years ago, that their mother is unable to care for them, she runs away to Los Angeles where her sister is trying to make it the film industry. Anna steals Lynette's credit card to finance her trip, and makes explicit that she has now joined the tribe of Lost Girls exemplified by the women of the Family—with one major difference: "I would never have gone after my mother with a knife, not while a credit card was cleaner and cut just as deep."[28] After some settling-in time in Los Angeles, Umminger presents readers with the novel's one sort-of-deus-ex-machina. The ex-boyfriend of Anna's sister is working on a film that is partly inspired by the Manson Family and he hires Anna as a research assistant. This set-up allows Umminger to endow young Anna with a kind of Manson-omniscience, which then informs her understanding of gender relations, family dysfunction, and the nature of celebrity. As with so many YA protagonists, Anna works hard to achieve deep knowledge about the landscape surrounding her and the players who populate it. When Anna's sister appears in makeup she has been wearing for a role in a zombie movie, the younger woman concludes that "in Hollywood you couldn't tell the killers from the actors." Anna leaves unspoken what she has learned about women becoming "zombies" under patriarchal control.[29] Charles Manson, she comes to understand, was like a "psychopathic film director," giving hippies orders about what to do and when. The cult of celebrity, she concludes, is "vomit-worthy." It ultimately seems fairly straightforward to Anna why a young woman might want to become a Manson girl and kill Hollywood stars.[30]

What is most devastating about Umminger's novel is the insistence that we focus on the family (and not the Family) as the prime vehicle of violence in modern life. After a summer in Los Angeles and an immersion in the details of the Tate-LaBianca murders, Anna comes to realize that for most people, "the real danger wasn't violence like you saw on the television news, random and exciting," but the everyday violence of what is done to young women in their family's homes, and then out in the world when they take their vulnerable selves away from the primal scene.[31] The Manson women, as Evie comes to realize, were primed to commit violence by their own families of origin, "ready and willing, scarred by the silent cruelty behind those carefully locked doors."[32] Anna's revelation comes as a result of all of her reading, but seems especially informed by her reading of Jess Bravin's biography of Squeaky Fromme. (*American Girls* is a *very* academic novel, demonstrably informed by deep reading in the relevant literature.) While Anna begins her whole narration with a declaration that Leslie Van Houten was her "first Manson girl," it becomes clear that Lynette Fromme reaches her as the most representative and tragic of the Family.

"Squeaky Fromme should never have been Squeaky Fromme, and not just the nickname, the whole deal."[33] This is Anna's conclusion, as she readies herself to return home, after her strange Los Angeles summer, which has included a friendship with one of two very famous television twins (modeled on *The Suite Life of Zack and Cody*) and a brush with a Miley Cyrus–type character who is one hurt away, if that, from taking a knife to her own father. Or somebody. What Anna has learned about Lynette Fromme, the "no duh" of the biography she has been reading, is that she was profoundly abused by her father. (In his book Jess Bravin quotes Fromme as saying that her father taught her "everything about sex."[34] Given that Bravin otherwise paints a portrait of a man who cruelly withheld contact from his daughter—rarely speaking to her and forcing her to sit apart from the rest of the family at dinner—it is clear that Bravin is suggesting outright sexual abuse.) Anna ultimately acknowledges the likelihood that more than one motive drove the Manson Family as they committed horrible acts of violence in August 1969. But she also comes to believe that if she could travel to the past and send a message to her country that would improve the future, it would be this: "Please give your daughters sturdy bedroom doors that lock from the inside. And when they are hungry, give them a place at the table."[35] Physical safety and emotional security, the active acknowledgment of appetite—these, Anna learns during her strange Los Angeles summer, are the project of the family. But for too many young women the family is the site of danger and denial. (Short-story writer Laura Elizabeth Woollett joined Umminger and Cline in 2016 with her story "Charlie's Girls," which also tried to move beyond the usual shame and panic that previously character-ized narratives of Family life. Woollett constructs a liberationist framework around the women of the Family and ends her story with an incantatory call-to-arms, narrated by a Family member explaining the continued dedication of the girls: "We sing for those girls outside, who we love. For our daddies hiding behind their newspapers, our mommies crying over burnt meatloaf. For all the square-eyed people watching us on television. Until the whole world knows we're not afraid, we'll keep singing.")[36]

In 2018 these works were joined by an amazing film, Lonnie Martin's *The Last of the Manson Girls*. Martin's film—originally the final project for his MFA at American University—is organ-ized around journalist Paul Krassner's visit to (and acid trip with) Lynette Fromme, Sandra Good, and Brenda McCann in the early 1970s. The Krassner framing is important to the film, to be sure. Presenting the writer as a sort of shaggy Lenny Bruce (as played by Dustin Hoffman in Bob Fosse's biopic), Martin reimagines Krassner as a sort of trippy Jewish, slightly paranoid everyman. Carrying unresolved questions inspired by investigative radio host Mae Brussell, Krassner turns himself into a sort of countercultural private investigator. While the narrative of *Last of the Manson Girls* is centrally concerned with whether Krassner will crack the case—who is N. Dight? And what does this naval intelligence officer have to do with Manson?—Martin's real animus is to explore the relationship of these three women to each other and to the Family more generally. Krassner is welcomed into the fold, invited to try on the much-storied embroidered vest the Family's women made for Manson, and reminded that he has more in common with these marginalized young people than he does with the forces of straight culture arrayed against them.

But the central plot of *Last of the Manson Girls* ultimately carries much less weight than its contributions to our basic understanding of Fromme, Good, and McCann as actual human beings. To begin, Fromme makes it clear that she will not be called "Squeaky" anymore. Whatever allegiance she maintains to Manson and the Family, she has made a break with the more cultish aspects of her earlier life. The three women have dimension, they are witchy but also funny. They are intimidating, but also frightened. In a few key scenes (especially one that finds Fromme whispering into Krassner's ear, telling him the secret about her birth family she has been carrying so long) Martin reminds his viewers that the appeal of the Family had much to do with injuries sustained by these young women earlier in their lives.

Although Alison Umminger, Emma Cline, and Lonnie Martin are not the first people to try to call attention to the necessity of replotting the family at the center of the story of the Family, their achievement comes with the intensity of their focus on how the Manson girls came to be the Manson girls. The warped dynamics of the Family deserve the kind of attention these artistic works insist upon, not least because they serve as a reminder that these young hippie goddesses did not spring from the head of Charles Manson or from the heads of their own fathers. They were creating relationships, forging bonds, enacting violence that made some kind of sense in situations not mostly of their own making. It is worth remembering that the end of the Family was also the end of two other families, the Tate-Polanski family and the LaBianca family. Umminger repurposes a key line uttered by Susan Atkins as the final dialogue of the movie Roger is making: "I don't feel sorry for you, bitch" is what Atkins reportedly said when Tate pled for the life of the fetus she planned to name Paul Richard Polanski. The murders were a terrible punctuation on what the Manson girls had been saying all along with their creepy crawls: the family is not safe. Things got truly messy when this family tried to integrate itself into the chaotic celebrity culture of Los Angeles in the late 1960s. Just as the Manson Family created the illusion that it was challenging some of the most pernicious aspects of "traditional" American family life, so too did key figures in Los Angeles's music industry create confusion by signaling cultural democracy while insisting, ultimately, on protecting entrenched hierarchies.

*

Part II

Creepy Crawling Los Angeles: Charles Manson on Our Maps

*

High Rollers

Let us find our way back to Los Angeles at the moment of the Manson murders with Terry Melcher as our guide. Melcher, a major figure in the Los Angeles music scene of the late 1960s and possible target of the murderous Family, released a particularly tricky song on his second solo album (1976), *Royal Flush*. The song is called "High Rollers" and it is a bitter commentary on "making it" in Los Angeles in the late 1960s. Sung in the voice of a self-pitying "high-rolling stud," the song describes a culture in flux, defined by movement—movement of people around the country and up the economic ladder. "High Rollers" is addressed, with dripping sarcasm, to a would-be star, someone who has come to Hollywood to make it: Melcher makes a dumb joke in the song about his character wanting to be big like (Bing) Crosby, Stills, Nash and Young. The narrator's persona is complex—he is aware of (and seems to enjoy) his own privileged social position, invoking Joan Didion in a line that echoes the title of her 1970 novel *Play It As It Lays*. At the same time, the narrator of the song acknowledges the awkward position he occupies in modern Los Angeles, acknowledging that people like him are treated as untrustworthy by hippies and as bust-worthy by the cops. (Gregg Jakobson, Melcher's musical collaborator and long-time running buddy has made it clear that in practice the police in Los Angeles were more likely to let this famous son of Doris Day and his posse off the hook, even when they were shooting out streetlights in the Hollywood Hills.)

Charles Manson, of course, was one member of the rebel culture Melcher's narrator is trying to place in the lyrics of his song. By most accounts Manson's primary motivation in moving from the hippie homeland of the Haight-Ashbury in San Francisco (where he went after being released from prison) to Los Angeles was to try to make it as a popular musician. Having been taught guitar by Alvin "Creepy" Karpis—formerly a leading member of Ma Barker's murderous Depression-era gang—while serving time in the 1960s in California's McNeil Island prison, Manson apparently thought he had a real shot at becoming a high-rolling stud in Los Angeles. Karpis, who was a self-taught musician, believed that Manson had "a pleasant voice and a pleasing personality," but found him "unusually meek and mild for a convict" and thought it likely that Manson would prove too lazy to make a dent in the entertainment industry."[1] Manson also met Phil Kaufman, later an important music producer and manager, while they served time together and Kaufman—who was impressed by the "lilt" in Manson's voice (which reminded him of Frankie Laine)— offered to connect Manson up with music industry people he knew. But Manson was not part of the younger generation of hip Angelenos. While he did manage to spend a fair amount of time with Neil Young, Manson claims to have felt disconnected from the younger cohort: "[T]hat's not my generation. My generation's Bing Crosby."[2]

Built into Melcher's pun about Bing Crosby, [Stills], Nash and Young is a tacit acknowledgment that Melcher himself was instrumental in connecting the generations indicated by the wordplay. Melcher was born in 1942, the son of Doris Day, who, by the time Melcher was three, had become a dominant presence on the popular music charts in the United States. He was a high roller by birth. By the time he was in his early twenties Melcher had already established himself as a presence in the California surf and hot-rod music scene, first as a member of Bruce and Terry (with Beach-Boy-to-be Bruce Johnston) and then with the Rip Chords, who had a top-ten hit in 1964 with "Hey Little Cobra." Melcher's reputation rests not with his early recordings, though, but with the production work he later did at Columbia Records. Melcher, in short, was a key figure in the musical culture of Los Angeles from the early 1960s through 1969.

We will get a better understanding of the broad cultural environment surrounding Manson if we start with what Barney Hoskyns has called the "manifold interconnectedness" of the cultural scene in Los Angeles in the late 1960s.[3] Even Ed Sanders, who is deeply committed in his book *The Family* to expunging Manson and his followers from the mainstream of the counterculture, makes it clear that the cult leader had very successfully "plugged into the restless world of successful rock musicians and continued his adventures inside the interlocking circles of young sons and daughters of figures in the motion picture and music industries."[4] To understand the profound meanings of the Manson Family's creepy crawl over the landscape of film and popular music production in the late 1960s, it is important to take a closer look at the scene Charlie Manson so energetically attempted to break into and what that has to tell us about the reorganization of American cultural life in the late 1960s and early 1970s. The Family may have been happily experimenting with all kinds of new social arrangements in their various home places, but they were also very much "of the world"—and that world was Los Angeles's culture industries during a time of major social upheaval.

In the hands of Vincent Bugliosi, Ed Sanders, and so many others, the story of Charles Manson and his Family is told again and again as a cautionary tale, a story we tell ourselves so that we will remember not to go down the particular roads they traveled. But we never do get done with them, do we? The "many lives" of my subtitle is meant as a small reminder that since 1969 there has been a truly astounding cultural investment made in the Family. The work of this section is, in some ways, to orient the Family in actual time and real physical space so that in the second half of the book we can begin to make sense of all the cultural work they have done for us since 1969. David McBride has underscored the important point that we know so much about the Los Angeles counterculture, have so many images of its denizens, because well, it was Los Angeles. The local counterculture, as he explains, "had to exist under the watchful gaze of the locally-based mass entertainment industries always on the lookout for captivating, sensationalist fodder which they could package and market."[5] At the same time, as Gerry Carlin and Mark Jones have argued so persuasively, "the tarnished aura of Hollywood informs the Family's story, from its early days driving a Volkswagen bus with 'Hollywood Productions' lettered on its side, to occupancy of the Spahn Ranch, used in numerous classic westerns, B-movies, television series, and advertisements." The Family rejected "mundane reality" in favor a more "performative gestalt" (the Hollywood star factory) "in which role-play and ritual" reigned supreme.[6] So what we find in Los Angeles at this moment is an emerging new class of film-world entrepreneurs who liked to present themselves as anti-authoritarian and countercultural now being confronted by *real* outsiders. The Manson Family represented an unwelcome reminder (to Peter Fonda and Dennis Hopper and all the rest) that they only *played* cultural rebels onscreen while sustaining the energies of (hip) capitalism. Their confrontation with the Manson Family forced them to acknowledge the contradictions built into their position.

The Manson Family did not kill Terry Melcher on the night of August 9, 1969. Even so, the idea that Charles "Tex" Watson, Susan Atkins, Patricia Krenwinkel, and Linda Kasabian left Spahn Ranch that night (at the direction of Charles Manson) with the intention of either killing Melcher or putting a scare into him, immediately became a sort of given for the many people trying to come to terms with the horror in the wake of the summer tragedy. In this version of things, Charles Manson, incensed that Melcher had bailed on a promise to sign Manson and record his music, sent his minions to 10050 Cielo Drive to kill Melcher, or at least to send him some kind of message. Susan Atkins herself has promoted this argument at various times. It became something like conventional wisdom in the second half of 1969 that the murders were the work of a "failed musician" who was targeting entertainment-industry figures.[7] This aspect of the lore surrounding the Tate-LaBianca murders has now passed mostly into the domain of richly detailed rumor culture and has been demoted in the historical record—first by Ed Sanders's gonzo work *The Family* in 1971, which focuses on bad drug-deal fallout and the grimy occult influence of the Process Church, and then, of course, by Vincent Bugliosi's 1974 *Helter Skelter*, the true-crime bible of the case, with its killer hook—the theory that Manson ordered the murders as part of a larger plan to kick off an American racial apocalypse.

But in 1969 the Melcher hypothesis was, briefly, gospel—at least in Los Angeles. From this first principle—that the son of Doris Day was being targeted by a crazed band of hippies ("Grudge Against Doris Day's Son Linked to Tate Slayings" is how the *Los Angeles Times* put it)[8]—it was only a gossipy hop, skip, and jump, to imagine Frank Sinatra leaving town to save himself from being skinned alive while being forced to listen to his own music; Steve McQueen instructing his wife to sleep with a gun under her pillow; and the frightful possibility that the Family would soon send Richard Burton's penis and Elizabeth Taylor's eyes in a bottle to Eddie Fisher.[9]

The existence of the Melcher hypothesis offers us an opportunity to explore a relatively underappreciated moment in California's counterculture history, a moment when the hip aristocracy of Los Angeles's culture industries dallied with emerging figures from the margins, mingling in the homes of Laurel Canyon, mingling on the Sunset Strip, and mingling at the Manson Family headquarters of Spahn Ranch (the Western movie set that became, in 1969, a gathering point for these various tribes of Los Angeles).

As is usually the case with rumors, this hysterical tale-telling had a relatively clear case to make and it was essentially that the murders at 10050 Cielo Drive represented a sort of horrifying but necessary cleansing of the cultural scene. The wild cultural mixing that had been rife in the previous half decade—from the dancing at the Whisky a Go Go to the "orgies" at Mama Cass's house in Laurel Canyon, to the (alleged) S and M parties (allegedly) filmed at the Tate-Polanski house itself!—were bound to lead to a crack-up. This rumor culture that developed in Los Angeles in the second half of 1969 had, predictably, a disciplinary thrust; it was time to stop dancing with these freaks. Joan Didion owns the brand on this strand of LA mythmaking, as I have discussed in the introduction. In her essay "The White Album," a title mischievously borrowed from the Beatles album that allegedly inspired Manson's crazed race-war talk, Didion argues, "This mystical flirtation with the idea of 'sin'—this sense that it was possible to go 'too far,' and that many people were doing it—was very much with us in Los Angeles in 1968 and 1969." Speaking directly of the rumor culture that developed in and around the murders, she continues, "I remember all of the day's misinformation very clearly, and I also remember this, and wish I did not: *I remember that no one was surprised.*" Didion writes, "The tension broke that day . . . . The paranoia was fulfilled."[10] Simon Reynolds and Joy Press, in *The Sex Revolts*, pick up on this line and put even more emphasis on *inevitability*: "the Manson murders were the logical culmination of the counterculture's project of throwing off the shackles of conscience and consciousness, the grim flowering of the id's voodoo energies"[11] Music historian Barney Hoskyns seconds the notion that the crimes were inevitable, suggesting that there was "a palpable sense of evil in the air . . . that had more than a little to do with the ever-increasing decadence of the music scene."[12] Gail Zappa, who had a catbird seat in Laurel Canyon with her husband Frank Zappa, also endorses the notion that *everybody* knew that *something* wicked was this way coming: "If you were surprised by the Manson murders, you weren't connected to what was going on in the canyon."[13]

Cultural critic Greil Marcus is likely Didion's most slavish and unhinged follower in the logical fallacy sweepstakes: in his recent book on the Doors he reminds us that while Jim Morrison's band was not at Woodstock, they *were* at Cielo Drive, "looking back from what they already said."[14] While it is admirable that Marcus wants to read the Tate-LaBianca murders and Woodstock as part of a complex larger narrative of countercultural life in the late 1960s, his breezy conclusion is malignant. He basically argues that *if* the murders of "Sharon Tate and her house guests" had been solved in the week between the crimes and the opening of the Woodstock festival, and *if* it had been clear that these crimes had been "the work of a hippie commune," *then* press reports about the rock festival would *certainly* not "have been so fulsome." In writing her self-involved take on the case, Joan Didion at least had the decency not to pretend her claims had any particular currency outside of Los Angeles. Marcus acts as if there is an organic tie between Manson and his followers on the one hand, and the (largely) peaceful "450,000-strong hippie commune that briefly established itself as Woodstock" on the other. But the connection is retrospective and fantastical, the product of decades of investment in a mythology created by people like Joan Didion and Greil Marcus who both seem to very much love California but who also both seem to have been knocked off their game a bit by hippies. (It is probably worth noting that Marcus came of age in Berkeley during the Free Speech Movement and seems to have fashioned his identity, at least in part, as distinct from the less political hippies across the bay in San Francisco.)[15] I want to be clear here—there was a *very important chronological link* between the Tate-LaBianca murders and Woodstock: they both took place in August of 1969. But that does not mean that the Spahn Ranch commune had much to do with the pop-up "commune" that convened at Woodstock. Some participant-observers at Woodstock (Paul Krassner, for instance) also became important commentators on the Manson phenomenon—but usually without insisting upon the false equivalences structuring Marcus's work. The Manson case gets used over and over again as a way to throw the baby (hippies) out the with all that bathwater they were (allegedly) not using. As we make our way through this complex cultural landscape it will be important to remember that very few actual hippies have written or spoken at length about Manson and the Family. For all of the cultural chatter about the Family that has developed over half a century, voices from hippie communities are relatively scarce. Much more useful than Marcus's formulation is Mike Rubin's reminder (supported more recently by Rob Sheffield) that the synergy of Manson-plus-Altamont has completely trumped whatever might be learned from the juxtaposition of Manson-plus-Woodstock.

The strange rhetoric of inevitability that developed in the wake of the August murders had more than a touch of victim-blaming in it. In a book titled *5 to Die*, which made it into print by January of 1970 (months before any of the trials got started), Ivor Davis and Jerry LeBlanc did not hold back when it came to repeating rumors supposedly circulating in and around the canyons of Los Angeles: "Wild drug trips, gang bangs, ritualistic witchcraft practices, sadism, blindfolds and diamond encrusted whips: And wasn't Miss Tate pregnant and what was she doing with her ex-boyfriend Sebring? . . . The rumors were mean. After all, who really knew whether the baby was his?"[16] Davis and LeBlanc also wonder about the wealthy Abigail Folger (of the coffee Folgers) who was raised in "the fashionable hills of San Francisco," but also "probed the other side of life and was no stranger to the hippie center of the world, the dozen-odd ramshackle blocks centered on Haight-Ashbury." Thinking of the brief time Manson lived in the Haight, and the focused work he did there corralling his first followers, the authors ask rhetorically of Folger, "who knows who she might have met there"?[17]

The authorial attack is similar—although quite a bit more clear in its right-wing politics—in another book published in 1970, J. D. Russell's *The Beautiful People: Pacesetters of the New Morality*, a pulpy collection of work drawn from *Confidential* magazine. Here, hairdresser Jay Sebring is depicted as "slight" and "aesthetic-appearing" (we should probably read "aesthetic" as "gay"—it at least suggests Sebring was mildly kinky), and as "never" playing the role of the "overt hero."[18] A bit later in the book Russell suggests that Sebring was obsessively attracted to sadomasochistic scenarios. Filmmaker Roman Polanski is simply described as Sharon Tate's "Svengali," and 10050 Cielo Drive comes to light as the site of "wildly freaked-out drug parties with weird sexual overtones." Russell reports that police in Los Angeles had become interested (given the "sado-masochistic drug freak-outs" taking place at Cielo Drive) in exploring that "narrow line" that separates "the killer and the killed!"[19] Russell concludes that "the pace-of-life swing set of which Sharon Tate was a part left her vulnerable to the insanities of the environment she inhabited."

This is put even more directly in the first book ever published on the case, Lawrence Schiller's *The Killing of Sharon Tate*, which was rushed into print in 1970 (and written with the cooperation of Susan Atkins). According to Schiller, many of the "silent majority" found the whole thing oddly satisfying, watching "relieved, happy" as these two "out-groups" engaged in a battle royale.[20] In *5 to Die* Jerry LeBlanc and Ivor Davis report that one Benedict Canyon neighbor noted simply, with poetic smugness, that the denizens of 10050 Cielo Drive had gotten their just desserts: "Live Freaky Die Freaky."[21] Prosecutor Vincent Bugliosi was only slightly less blaming of the victims in his true-crime account of the case: "Given Roman Polanski's affinity for the macabre; rumors of Sebring's sexual peculiarities; the presence of both Miss Tate and her former lover at the death scene while her husband was away; the 'anything goes' image of the Hollywood jet set; drugs . . . almost any kind of plot could be fashioned."[22]

It was not only "straights" who read the murders at Cielo and Waverly Drives as some kind of critical commentary on countercultural life. In his memoir of the 1960s, novelist Robert Stone recalls that "the most extraordinary speculations as to motive and perpetrator went around. The most unsettling involved the number of people who suspect one another of having a hand in the murders. This included *famous* people who used not to do such things."[23] The list of names dragged through the rumor culture would include Roman Polanski himself, one Mama (Cass Elliot) and one Papa (John Phillips), and a number of other marginal film- and music-industry figures. Dennis Hopper claimed that the denizens of 10050 Cielo Drive had "fallen into sadism and masochism and bestiality."[24] Terry Melcher seconded this, reporting to his mother's biographer that he assumed the murders were somehow related to "the weird people hanging around" Roman Polanski's house," who had been making homemade "sadomasochistic-porn movies with quite a few recognizable Hollywood faces in them."[25] (Manson himself lent credibility to this explanation—well, if he had any credibility to lend, that is—telling Ron Reagan in an interview, that the whole Tate-LaBianca mess had to do with missing videotapes that featured Yul Brynner and Peter Sellers "gobbling on each other's knobs.")[26]

Many of the stories about what went wrong at Cielo Drive have to with films that may or may not have existed. This is a story about—among other things—the New Hollywood, and the case is complexly haunted by film—actual and imagined, "lost" and never found. There is the much-discussed homemade sex tape made by Polanski and Sharon Tate, which detectives removed from Cielo Drive and then, with great care, placed right back where they found it. There is the story told by Paul Krassner and so many others about a film made by Voytek Frykowski and Jay Sebring of their sexual torture of Billy Doyle, a drug dealer they claimed ripped them off: these two friends of Sharon Tate, as the rumor has it, took their revenge by lashing Doyle to a chair so that they could "whip him and then fuck him in the ass while a video camera taped the proceedings before a live audience."[27] (The story about Doyle seems to have made the rounds in and around Los Angeles; Bobby Beausoleil himself suggested to John Gilmore that the denizens of Cielo Drive "were dealing bad dope, burning people on dope deals—holding whipping parties and things like that." Beausoleil's pointed summary of this set of claims is that the people surrounding Sharon Tate "wore long hair and imitated things the young people were doing, but they were perverting it—making everything that these young people were doing that was beautiful and good—taking it and turning it into ugliness.")[28] Kenneth Anger wanted Bobby Beausoleil to star in *Lucifer Rising*, but killing Gary Hinman and going on the lam before being arrested took Beausoleil out of the picture. And then there are, of course, the Manson Family "snuff" films, much bruited by Ed Sanders, but which have never been found.[29] What Sanders could not seem to acknowledge is, as many have pointed out, that the significant snuff film of the moment was *Gimme Shelter*, the documentary about the tragic concert at Altamont.

All of these stories about film and bad (and sometimes criminal) behavior provides a snapshot of the culture of self-critique that developed almost immediately after the Tate-LaBianca murders. Marianne Faithfull, a major artist in her own right and also a member of the Rolling Stones' bohemian circle, notes in her autobiography that it was "devastating" to "hear of Hendrix's death, of Janis's death, one right after the other. The awful feeling that we must really have fucked up. The Manson murders as a judgment on us all."[30] Such recrimination is also articulated in 1969's *Easy Rider*, directed by Dennis Hopper and starring Hopper and Peter Fonda, and perhaps the most influential movie produced by the "New Hollywood"—when Wyatt responds to Billy's gloating ("We did it, man, we did it. We're rich, man.") with the devastating "We blew it."

Dennis Hopper met Charles Manson at least once. I say "at least" because that is what we know for sure (and this once is by Hopper's own admission). Hopper would not be the first major figure in Hollywood or the Los Angeles music industry to underplay his connection to the man Dennis Wilson of the Beach Boys called "the Wizard." Neil Young is one of the few figures from this time and place willing to acknowledge how central Manson was to the scene: Young goes beyond simply arguing that as a musician Manson was "great, he was unreal" and admits that he promoted Manson to Mo Ostin, president of Warner Bros. Records.[31] Calling Manson "one of the main movers and shakers" of the Southern California scene of the late 1960s, Young makes it clear that Manson very quickly insinuated himself into a world that included some of most powerful members of the New Hollywood and the new rock-and-roll aristocracy. Young also insists that a very quick revisionist history developed as soon as Manson was indicted in December of 1969, noting that many "well-known musicians around LA knew him . . . though they'd probably deny it now."[32]

As tempting as it is to speculate about, we do not need to sort out how "good" Manson was as a musician. What he sounded like in his moment, what he *could* have sounded like with the right band is irrelevant to the central issue of how Manson used whatever talents he did have to carve out a place of real significance in late 1960s Los Angeles. In any event, reports on Manson's musical ability are hopelessly tangled: for every Neil Young remembering Manson's music with fond appreciation there are plenty of observers who testified that while Manson had a definite magnetism in his spontaneous performance, he could not sing a lick when it came time to try to make tracks in the studio. For his part, Bobby Beausoleil (who briefly played in a rock band called The Milky Way with Manson) has offered up wonderfully contradictory evaluations in various interviews. To one interlocutor, Beausoleil—who had used his connection to Frank Zappa to try to advance Manson's musical ambitions—said the following: "Just between us, Charlie doesn't have a whole lot of talent. (Strumming chords) 'This is my song, my dark song, my dark song.'"[33] But on another occasion Beausoleil changed his tune and argued that Manson "was a very talented songwriter, good musician, lyrically, just excellent. He was somebody with an incredibly intense, vivid, expanded imagination."[34]

In *Easy Riders, Raging Bulls* (subtitled *How the Sex-Drugs-and-Rock 'n' Roll Generation Saved Hollywood*), Peter Biskind suggests that Hopper visited Manson in prison, at Manson's invitation. As Biskind explains, "Manson wanted Hopper to star in the film version of his life."[35] At first Hopper balked—out of respect, he says, for the memory of his "good friend" Jay Sebring. Curiosity "finally triumphed over scruple," as Biskind tells it, and Hopper went to meet Manson. According to Hopper, Manson said that "like, y'know, he was a big star and like, his whole life he had been acting out a movie, but there hadn't been any movie cameras there."[36] What is important here is Manson's oft-described belief that there had to be a prominent place for him in the culture of the New Hollywood and the Los Angeles rock-and-roll scene of the late 1960s. We need to credit Neil Young's claims about Manson's promise (all Manson needed was a "band like Dylan had on 'Subterranean Homesick Blues'") and take seriously Gregg Jakobson's insistence that what he really wanted to do—rather than get Manson signed to a recording contract through Terry Melcher—was make a film documentary of the Manson Family: "I said to Terry, 'This guy should be captured on film. You're never gonna capture this guy on tape.' It'd be like having footage of Castro while he was still in the mountains or something. This guy was a real rebel. It had to be movie footage."[37]

Charles Manson did not simply fantasize that he and his Family had come to have a place of some prominence in the volatile world of Los Angeles in the late 1960s. His "All right, Mr. DeMille, I'm ready for my close-up" interaction with Dennis Hopper represents simply one rather last-ditch attempt to draw on the credit he (reasonably) thought he had accrued with the rising sons of Los Angeles. Charles Manson and his Family were not bizarre outliers in Los Angeles in the late 1960s. We need to come to a new understanding of them, in fact, as key figures in this scene. One of the most treasured bits of lore surrounding Manson and his music-business contacts has to do with the time Manson and some of the girls spent living with Dennis Wilson of the Beach Boys in Wilson's house on Sunset Boulevard. Wilson (a charter member—along with Terry Melcher and Gregg Jakobson—of the self-styled club known as the "Golden Penetrators") not only enjoyed the apparently unlimited sexual access he had to the young women in his home, but regularly tried to "share" this access: no less an expert on sleaze than John Phillips recounted years later that he would "shudder" every time the other men would invite him over to participate in the sexual escapades of this group. Wilson himself would punctuate his experiment in communal living by claiming that all it had left him with was the "largest gonorrhea bill in history."[38] But Manson and his "girls" *were not a disease.* They were players in what, in other contexts, we call the "New Hollywood," or the "freak scene," or, simply, "Los Angeles." The intersection of Manson's Family with major stars in the New Hollywood and the Los Angeles music scene turned out to be a dangerous crossroads, but not because evil was "in the air" or because the counterculture held within it the seeds of its own destruction or any of the other nonsense that has been peddled by Joan Didion and her acolytes.

If it is true that Charles Manson turned out to be a delusional reader of the Beatles' "White" album and the mastermind of the multiple murders on August 8 and 9, it is likewise true that it was plausible for Manson to believe that he might find a prominent place in these new cultures—as an embodiment of what Laurel Canyon historian Michael Walker has nicely summarized as an "unprecedented breed of incipient celebrity." ABC news correspondent Dick Shoemaker remembers talking to his contacts in Hollywood right after the Tate murders and having many of them tell him that they were convinced that the Cielo Drive attacks had something to do with "celebrityism."[39]

Shoemaker's coinage ("celebrityism") is both awkward and quite useful. There was something new and unfixed about the celebrityism of Los Angeles in the late 1960s. Well before the night of August 8, Charles Manson had become something of a fixture on the cultural scene. Manson and his followers (not only his girls but some of the boys who followed him too) were at home in Dennis Wilson's house, on the Sunset Strip, at Venice Beach, at Frank Zappa's log-cabin home/crash pad, at Mama Cass's house, and maybe even at 10050 Cielo Drive, where at least a few of the Family are reported to have socialized well before the summer of 1969. Crossing paths with Doris Day's son, with Angela Lansbury's daughter, with the Byrds, Love, and the Beach Boys, just to name a few acts, the Manson Family was in a complex and dynamic relationship with Los Angeles's film and music (and drug and biker) cultures. While the Family's central strategy was *stealth*, and their major tactic the creepy crawl, they also made a full-frontal attack on the citadels of film and music production in Southern California in the late 1960s. From the slightly surreal home-base of Spahn Ranch, the superannuated Western movie and television setting, now a weekend horseback-riding attraction and hippie commune, the Manson Family launched a sustained charm offensive in and around Los Angeles before finally changing gears and resorting to a murderous harm offensive.[40]

Kim Fowley, who wore a number of different music business hats in Los Angeles, gives a good thumbnail sketch of the years from 1965 to 1969 with a special focus on the ways the music and film businesses helped define each other. The Byrds, according to Fowley, were at the center of all this. In 1965, Fowley explains, "the movie business really got into 'the music business' for the first time with the Byrds at Ciro's nightclub." Actors "started coming down every night to see the Byrds, and pretty soon you had Dennis Hopper and Peter Fonda checking out rock 'n' roll." Fowley goes on to note that in short order "Fonda got in with the Byrds, Nicholson got in with the Monkees and even Steve McQueen could be found announcing to the world that 'Johnny Rivers playing the Whisky a Go Go was god.'"[41] The first two cases would turn out to be especially significant, since Fonda would soon star in *Easy Rider*—a film that relies heavily on non-diegetic use of two Byrds' songs ("Ballad of Easy Rider" and "Wasn't Born to Follow") and Jack Nicholson would soon collaborate with the Monkees on the screenplay for their psychedelic movie *Head*.[42]

This was not, of course, the first time that Hollywood and rock and roll had crossed paths. From the use of Bill Haley's "Rock around the Clock" in 1955's *Blackboard Jungle*, Little Richard's appearance in *The Girl Can't Help It* (1956), and through Elvis Presley's tenure in Hollywood, the film industry took note of and consistently tried to capitalize on the success of rock-and-roll music. This was following an old Hollywood tradition of working assiduously to incorporate the advances in American popular music into the mainstream of film production, from the early 1930s hiring of Tin Pan Alley composers to come work in Southern California and major roles offered to singing cowboys in Westerns, to the regular adaptation of Broadway musicals into screen versions. Various and regular attempts were made to domesticate rock and roll as a proper subject and soundtrack for film productions. Hollywood film (and later television) studios learned to use sites of popular music production (whether in New York, Nashville, Bakersfield, San Francisco, or, increasingly, Los Angeles itself) as a sort of minor league—offering up players, styles, and stories as raw material for modern films and television programs.

Fonda and Hopper and their New Hollywood compatriots were not the first to take "today's music" seriously. In its own oddball and confused way, AIP's *Riot on Sunset Strip* provided a relatively sympathetic picture of the new youth cultures in and around Los Angeles. Released in 1967, this Sam Katzman production tried to offer a balanced view of the conflict between the police and the young people who milled around outside the rock clubs on the Strip. The voice-over that opens the film tells the audience that these young people "are not dangerous revolutionaries in a beleaguered city. . . . These are teenagers" who are simply demanding "the right of self-expression." The movie has its own traditionalist points to score—these poor wayfaring teenagers often come from "broken" homes and have not gotten enough attention or love. For what it's worth, one of these young women, Andrea, is the daughter of police officer Walter Lorimer; Lorimer attempts to make peace between the longhairs, the local business people who complain about them, and the police rank-and-file who seem mostly to want to bust some heads. "Getting together in groups" is not unlawful, Lorimer reminds his colleagues (and the viewers) and the film's argument is that, for the most part, if you leave young people to their own devices they will simply dance. Albeit interracially. Danger intrudes in the form of Herbie, son of a big Hollywood celebrity, who introduces Andrea to LSD. Havoc—including a gang rape of Andrea—follows from this dosing; a similar crime is committed in *Easy Rider* during a trip as well. While earlier *Riot on Sunset Strip* had been relatively neutral on the question of marijuana usage, here it takes a staunch anti-acid position. This all leads film scholar Christopher Sharrett to accuse *Riot* of having it both ways, "able to cater to its target market while also justifying adult paranoia about out-of-control teenagers." Sharrett notes that any sympathy the film has shown for its teenagers is undercut at the end with its warning that "half the world will soon be under twenty-five, so we must stay vigilant (or some such)."[43] But this sort of final statement has been deployed in Hollywood film as a sort of inoculation against claims of prurience since at least the 1930s (especially with respect to gangster films).

Riot on the Sunset Strip is what has come to be called an "exploitation" film. But unlike the cruel indifference of Buffalo Springfield's "For What It's Worth"—the most famous piece of

Hippies with Power

One crucial moment in the evolution of the new class of music-business stars came with the Monterey International Pop Festival of 1967. This event, the first major rock music festival, has often been heralded as the great first meeting of San Francisco's "rawer" and more "natural" music scene with the more "polished" and "commercial" Los Angeles industry. This festival was organized by Los Angeles producer and impresario Lou Adler, along with John Phillips, who convened a Board of Governors for the three-day non-profit event, which included Adler and Phillips, Donovan, Smokey Robinson, Brian Wilson, Johnny Rivers, Alan Pariser, Terry Melcher, Andrew Loog Oldham, Mick Jagger, Paul McCartney, and Jim (later Roger) McGuinn. The convening of this board has a few tales to tell—but one very obvious one is about Angeleno resistance to the San Francisco crowd. While representatives of the San Francisco scene were noticeably absent from the Board of Governors (and of course there were no women, and only one African American), Adler and Phillips knew that they needed to attract a number of the key bands from the Bay Area if the festival was to be the "seismic event" they hoped to host. Adler properly saw that the "San Francisco groups had a very bad taste in their mouths about LA commercialism. . . . And it's true that we were a business-minded industry. It wasn't a hobby. They called it slick, and I'd have to agree with them."[1] Adler and Phillips relied on the mediating influence of legendary jazz critic Ralph Gleason as well as San Francisco promoter Bill Graham, "whose entire modus operandi had always been about keeping one foot in hippiedom and the other in bottom-line business," along with David Crosby, who was Los Angeles–based but had numerous friends in the Bay Area groups.[2] Singer Jackson Browne later explained that, for him, Crosby was the "main cultural luminary": "He had this legendary VW bus with a Porsche engine in it, and that summed him up—a hippie with power!"[3]

A hippie with power! That phrase should give us some pause—it will strike some of us as a contradiction—given that one dominant cultural reading of "hippie" is as being in opposition to "power." But that one could be a hippie and not only *want* power but actually *have* power is important to understand as we come to consider how the Family enacted its creepy crawl across the entertainment industries of Southern California in the late 1960s. Peter Biskind recounts a telling anecdote in his book on the New Hollywood, about Donna Greenberg—a woman who "wasn't in the business" but who was "clever, wealthy, attractive, and had a wonderful home, with rooms and more rooms for guests, a swimming pool on the beach, and an expansive patio." As Greenberg later recalled "One beautiful, sunny Sunday morning, I was having breakfast on the patio with my four-year-old, the nanny, my husband, and our oldest son, who was thirteen or fourteen. . . . We had just had a paint-in, painting our seawall with peace signs, graffiti, that sort of thing. Suddenly the most frightening group of hippies walked onto our patio, stood around and stared at us, wandered through our house. I was petrified, but I didn't know what to say, and it was also the '60s, being nice to people who wore lots of beads and jewels and bandannas. There was a piano covered with all the pictures one collects of children and family and loved ones and everyone I knew. . . . They gathered around the piano and looked at the pictures. Then they walked out, leaving us shaken. They got down to the end of the beach, but they couldn't get out, and a police car came, and I found myself walking down there and telling the police to let them go, they were my guests. Don't ask me what the impulse was. It was the Manson family." Greenberg was not a hippie, not by any of the standard definitions, it is clear, but she is influenced by hippie culture (with her family's "paint-in" and its evocation of the hippie world of "be-in" and "love-in") and is willing to identify with this scary band of hippies as opposed to the straight world represented by the police.[4]

Without being in the business, Donna Greenberg was still situated right at the heart of the New Hollywood, with her house in Malibu Colony and her friendship with Bob and Toby Rafaelson (Bob Rafaelson helped bring the Monkees to television, directed *Head* and *Five Easy Pieces*, and produced numerous other key films of the era). It was perhaps just old-fashioned *noblesse oblige* that motivated Greenberg to protect her "guests" from the police. But there is something more complicated at work in the behavior of those members of the Southern California film and music cultural elite who expressed, in a variety of ways, some level of attraction for hippie culture and hippie people. Thomas Frank has taught us to notice how quickly and efficiently the forces of American consumer capitalism coopted the language, style, and sounds of the hippies, incorporating what seemed like rebellion—like a radical challenge to the dominant culture—into the everyday language of advertising. In fact, Frank rightly cautions us to resist the temptation of imagining that there is, or has ever been, some pure and authentic counterculture safely set apart from the corrupting influence of the dominant culture, noting that "from its very beginnings down to the present, business dogged the counterculture with a fake counterculture, a commercial replica that seemed to ape its every move for the titillation of the TV-watching millions and the nation's corporate sponsors." Frank goes on to note that every "rock band with a substantial following was immediately honored with a host of imitators; the 1967 'summer of love' was as much a product of lascivious television specials and *Life* magazine stories as it was an expression of youthful disaffection; Hearst launched a psychedelic magazine in 1968; and even hostility to co-optation had a desperately 'authentic' shadow, documented by a famous 1968 print ad for Columbia Records titled 'But The Man Can't Bust Our Music.' So oppressive was the climate of national voyeurism that, as early as the fall of 1967, the San Francisco Diggers had held a funeral for 'Hippie, devoted son of mass media.'"[5]

"Hippie" was a name for all manner of cultural, social, political, and economic activity. While Charles Manson, with his followers, was able to engage with the social world of the New Hollywood, the gate swung decisively closed when it came to his attempt to convert personal closeness into cultural prestige or financial gain. If Manson himself occupied a fairly ambiguous position, his girls were placed rather definitively in the scene as sprung go-go dancers—out of the cage and made available to the Golden Penetrators and just about any and all other comers, from Beach Boys to old men like George Spahn, owner of the ranch. Manson and the Family were welcomed into this kingdom of Dennis (Wilson and Hopper) as something like dancing bears, neat tricks to be enjoyed for a moment or two, but certainly not to be taken seriously as friends, as peers, as talent, or as co-workers. Gregg Jakobson has, since the original trials of Manson, Krenwinkel, Atkins, and Van Houten, been fairly straightforward about the fairly straightforward pleasures offered up by the Manson girls at Dennis Wilson's house on Sunset Boulevard and at Spahn Ranch.[6]

The Manson Family might creepy crawl into the bedrooms of the rich and famous (according to various accounts these nighttime raids brought them to the homes of Doris Day in Malibu, John and Michelle Phillips in Bel Air, and Dennis Wilson on Sunset Boulevard). They might live more or less as squatters at Dennis Wilson's house for months, eventually forcing the musician to seek refuge in Gregg Jakobson's basement. They might persuade Jakobson into arranging for Terry Melcher to come "audition" Manson out at Spahn Ranch. But Manson could not insinuate himself into the business culture of the new Los Angeles. Of all Manson's associates, it is really only Bobby Beausoleil who seems to have made any headway (in San Francisco and Los Angeles) as a performing artist. Beausoleil was a founding member of the Orkustra, who played around the Bay Area and, according to some accounts, became the unofficial house band of the Diggers.

Beausoleil was not only making inroads in avant-garde film; he was also professionally tapped into the Los Angeles rock-and-roll scene, particularly through his connection to Arthur Lee. Beausoleil briefly played with Lee in a band called the Grass Roots, soon to rename itself as Love.

The Manson Family engaged with a thriving and well-established Los Angeles bohemia, which—as cultural historian Rachel Rubin demonstrates in her book *Well-Met: Renaissance Faires and the American Counterculture*—hosted productive moments of contact between all manner of groups and individuals who had not, in fact, "met" very regularly in the past.[7] It seems pretty well-established in the historical record that Manson wanted something from Terry Melcher—he thought the producer could get him a recording contract. Various members of the Family have testified (in court and out) that whatever Melcher actually intended, Manson *believed* the producer was his route to music-business success. It is also clear that gaining access to the recording industry was crucial to Manson's sense of how he would spread his influence beyond the relatively narrow confines of the Family. To this day Bobby Beausoleil is insistent that Manson was not particularly interested in a contract per se but understood it as an important way to expand his platform.[8]

Given Manson's current status in American cultural life as something of a terrifying joke, it becomes somewhat astounding to recreate the moment of his fullest assimilation into the celebrity culture of Los Angeles. Dennis Wilson seems to have been the entry point for Manson during the time that has come, in the historical literature, to be referred to as Manson's "Sunset Boulevard" period.[9] Manson and Wilson came to a tacit understanding that revolved around Wilson having unfettered access to Manson's female followers and in return letting Manson and other members of the Family live at his house and meet a number of other key figures from the music world. Wilson seems to have first met Patricia Krenwinkel and Ella Jo Bailey, two of Manson's followers, in the spring of 1968, when he picked them up hitchhiking (two different times, in Malibu).[10] After the second ride,

Manson appeared late at night to greet Wilson in his driveway after the musician returned home after a late recording session. Wilson became intimately involved with Family life; he had sex regularly with a number of the women, paid to have Susan Atkins's teeth fixed, loaned his car out, and introduced Manson to Gregg Jakobson and other members of his inner circle.[11] When the power dynamics got too challenging to negotiate, Wilson essentially abandoned ship, moved in with Jakobson and told his manager to get rid of the Family.[12]

Dennis Wilson became something of an evangelist for the Family. He liked Manson's worldview and he experienced life with the girls as a sexual utopia. At first the appeal seemed primarily physical. A few years after Wilson's dalliance with the Family, the Grateful Dead would record a song, "Jack Straw," which begins with an exuberant reminder of how women (like wine) can be passed around from man to man. This seems to have been the standard operating procedure at Wilson's home on Sunset Boulevard. John Phillips recounts that Wilson (and according to Phillips, Melcher too) frequently tried to sell him on Manson: "He has all these chicks hanging out like servants. You can come over and just fuck any of them you want. It's a great party."[13] While Phillips claims to have rejected Wilson's regular offers, he had already memorialized the broader cultural phenomenon in the 1967 song "Twelve Thirty (Young Girls Are Coming to the Canyon)" which went top twenty in the United States.

Of course Dennis Wilson's house on Sunset Boulevard (formerly owned by Will Rogers!) was not the only site at which such sexual meetings were taking place. Kim Fowley insists that daily life in Laurel Canyon, since the advent of the Byrds on the Strip was characterized by these regular and transitory meetings of "civilian" women and industry men. Fowley, narrating this moment with a hyperbole that borders on critique, suggests that "All these chicks would hitchhike up to the Canyon Store from the Strip, girls from Kansas who'd heard about Laurel Canyon. 'Hi! Folk-rock musicians! I'll clean your house and fuck you and I'm vegetarian and I can make you macrobiotic stuff as you're shooting heroin."[14] With something like amazement, Fowley adds that he "was a creep, an ugly guy, and suddenly even creeps could get laid." "Get laid" should be read with great care here, given what we know about Fowley's predatory 1970s life in Los Angeles.[15] Dennis Wilson went well beyond appreciating the fruits of Charles Manson's experience as a pimp. To put it most plainly, Wilson seems not only to have been getting off, but was also getting off on getting off; part of Wilson's pleasure, no doubt, came from *talking* about all this with his male friends in the music business.

That said, Wilson and Gregg Jakobson, to use the painful coinage inspired by another cult leader, also seem to have drunk fairly deeply of Manson's Kool-Aid. Long after Wilson fled his house to get away from the Family, the Beach Boy was still speaking positively of Manson in an interview to a British music magazine, *Rave*, in which he called Manson a friend, dubbed him "the Wizard," and explained that Manson "thinks he is God and the devil. He sings, plays and writes poetry and may be another artist for Brother records."[16] Dennis Wilson's involvement with Manson was extensive enough to become a bother to the rest of the Beach Boys—one of whom described Manson to Vincent Bugliosi as a "scruffy little guru."[17]

While Wilson actually lived with the Family, Jakobson appears to have been even more taken with Manson as a thinker. Separated from this intense time by a span of decades, Jakobson remembers his main attraction to Spahn Ranch as being organized around the appeal of these available young women. But Jakobson's role in helping Vincent Bugliosi to "crack" the code of the case (i.e., his explanation of the Helter Skelter philosophy) and his acknowledgment during the Manson trials—especially Tex Watson's—that he had been in Manson's presence somewhere around a hundred times bespeak a much deeper investment. Jakobson, in fact, became quite deeply engaged with Manson's worldview. We need not credit the analysis of John Phillips (for instance) that the whole story could be reduced to sex. Barry Miles has been more careful in situating the Manson phenomenon as part of a larger set of cultural processes through which "underground" belief systems began to have an influence on "regular Hollywood."[18]

However much Manson may have shaped the worldview of Dennis Wilson or Gregg Jakobson, he did not get signed by the Beach Boys' Brother, or any other record label. The Beach Boys did release a version of his song "Cease to Exist" (now renamed "Never Learn Not to Love") as the B-side of their 1968 single, a cover of Ersel Hickey's "Bluebirds Over the Mountain" and then as a track on their hodgepodge 1969 LP *20/20*. "Never Learn Not to Love" is credited only to Dennis Wilson; while the song never became an important part of the Beach Boys repertoire, Wilson did step up from behind the drums to sing it on national television on the Mike Douglas show in 1968.[19] The Manson Family's creepy crawl over the cultural landscape had put them right at the heart of American popular music production in the late 1960s.

The matter of credit and royalties for "Never Learn Not to Love" is not inconsequential.[20] For all of his success at insinuating himself into the musical life of Los Angeles, Manson was clearly ill-equipped when it came to dealing as an equal with music-business professionals such as Dennis Wilson, Terry Melcher, and Gregg Jakobson. During the trial of Manson Family member Charles "Tex" Watson during August of 1971, Melcher admitted that he went out to Spahn Ranch in April of 1969 at Gregg Jakobson's urging, in order to audition Manson. The April meeting served as a makeup session after Melcher failed to appear in March at a Family home in Canoga Park when the Family was first expecting him (and for which some of the girls had baked cookies).[21] After listening to Manson perform, accompanied by naked humming women from the Family, Melcher then spoke "briefly" with Manson and asked him a few questions: "I gave him a few basic suggestions and found out that he wasn't in any union . . . and therefore he couldn't really professionally record."[22]

The most interesting thing that happened at this meeting is that Melcher ended the interaction by handing Manson some money. At Watson's trial Melcher explains that he gave money to Manson because the assembled group "looked hungry." Under Vincent Bugliosi's careful questioning, Melcher powerfully reclaimed the class distinction between himself and the Family: after Bugliosi's prompt ("So you felt sorry for them and you gave Mr. Manson $50"), Melcher replied "Well, sorry, or charit—yeah perhaps sorry."[23] Manson read—or at least presented—the exchange quite differently; as Jeff Guinn explains, Manson presented the exchange to his followers as representing some sort of advance contract.[24]

The Manson Family's interaction with the new elite of Los Angeles can be best understood as a failed set of experiments aimed at erasing profound differences in class status and access to cultural capital. Most of these interactions went well beyond the simple power dynamics built into Terry Melcher's almost-articulation of the word "charity." But the Manson Family were certainly *being* creepy crawled just as intensively as they were creepy crawling. While the historical record is fairly clear about what Charles Manson wanted to get from Wilson, Melcher, Jakobson, Hopper and so on, what is less clear in the whole affair is just what Melcher et al. wanted from Manson.

Melcher was not completely done with Manson in April of 1969. He went back to the ranch in June with musician and engineer Mike Deasy, who, according to both Ed Sanders and recent Manson biographer Jeff Guinn, had some experience doing field recordings of Native Americans; by Deasy's own account he had *hopes* of recording some Native Americans.[25] Jerry Cole, a member of the Los Angeles assemblage of session musicians known as the Wrecking Crew, remembers Terry Melcher getting the tapes to him, asking him to "chart it up" and then organize a session—which, Cole says, ended up including legendary drummer Hal Blaine, guitarist Tommy Tedesco and other members of the Crew—to turn the rough demo into a finished track.[26] This was Melcher's standard method—to employ the best available professional musicians to play behind appealing vocal talent. Manson, alas, did not have the chops of the Byrds and Melcher finally had to break the news to him that he did not think he could do justice to these tracks.

Terry Melcher was, on paper at least, a good pick for Manson to focus his efforts on. The rock critic Dave Marsh has called Melcher the "most underrated Hollywood [music] producer of the sixties."[27] Much of Terry Melcher's career in the 1960s was lived right on the hinge of corporate culture and counterculture. He was a professional and, by most accounts, quite accomplished producer. When it came time to record "Tambourine Man" with the Byrds in 1965, Melcher did not let most of the band in the studio to play their instruments—he brought in members of the Wrecking Crew in to lay down the track. This work with the Byrds represented a breakthrough moment for Melcher and for the band. Most notably, he produced their folk-rock versions of Bob Dylan's "Mr. Tambourine Man" and Pete Seeger's "Turn, Turn, Turn." It is worth pausing over these two songs for a moment to think about Melcher's role here as a cultural intermediary—as one of the key industry figures working to translate counterculture musical contributions into a broadly popular form: both "Tambourine Man" and "Turn, Turn, Turn" went to number one on the Billboard charts. Melcher was a highly sophisticated musical, cultural, and business figure. He understood the hip cachet the Byrds brought to the table, and believed that to best capitalize on their bright vocal sound (and McGuinn's chiming twelve-string guitar) he needed to bring in the Wrecking Crew to do the work of building a solid, professional track.

In studying the mutual creepy crawl at work in the meeting of Melcher, Wilson, and Jakobson with the Manson Family, it is important to read Melcher's testimony—his literal trial testimony, the songs he wrote, the reminiscences he would later share—with a critical eye. Terry Melcher spent years after the Tate killings trying to make sense of what *he* had done and what was done to him. In an interview with the BBC Melcher tried to sort out his relationship to the "disenfranchised" young people he met at Spahn Ranch: "All right," he claims to have felt when he met Manson's Family, "this is what is going on today."[28] At Tex Watson's trial in 1971 Melcher resisted briefly when Watson's counsel tried to pin him down as to whether he classified Watson as a "hippie" as opposed to a "straight" when he first met him. Melcher briefly tried to claim that this sort of categorization was foreign to him, but finally acknowledged that he understood what "hippie" meant and that Watson was one.[29] Melcher frequently played the ingénue—perhaps no surprise given his home training as Doris Day's son!—when it came to explaining his relationship to Charles Manson and his followers.

What Melcher's faux-innocent recollection ("All right . . . this is what's going on today") obscures is that some of the most powerful figures in the Los Angeles music and film business in the 1960s were complexly tied up with—and in fact partly defined by—a more marginal group of scene-makers who might variously be identified as "fans," "groupies," and "dancers." It is in this arena that we find a major truth about the relationship of the Manson Family and the Los Angeles popular-culture elite of the late 1960s. At bottom, Charles Manson believed that he was operating in a kind of radical meritocracy that would provide opportunity even for a marginal figure like him. (His DIY approach certainly appealed to the generation of punk rockers in LA and elsewhere who would adopt Manson as something like a patron saint in the late 1970s and early 1980s.)

The Golden Penetrators, on the other hand, operating with a stunning arrogance (let's index this as "male privilege" and "class privilege" for now) and blithe disregard for the ardent efforts of Manson to break into their professional circles, operated from the premise that they could take whatever they wanted from Manson and his "girls" and remain safe as milk. Ed Sanders has, as I have already noted, argued that when "Manson plugged into the restless world of successful rock musicians" he found his movements constrained by the fact that this world was largely populated by "interlocking circles of young sons and daughters of figures in the motion picture and music industries."[30] Terry Melcher was the son of Doris Day and trumpeter Al Jorden (and stepson of film producer Marty Melcher), and Candice Bergen was the daughter of ventriloquist Edgar Bergen and model Frances Westerman. The pre-Tate/Polanski renters at 10050 Cielo Drive were at the very inner circle of this Los Angeles nobility.

Hungry Freaks

Along with the significant details of how Terry Melcher, Dennis Wilson, and Gregg Jakobson interacted with the Manson Family in their "private" lives (a dune buggy ride at Spahn ranch for Melcher? A present of Beach Boys' gold records given to Manson by Wilson? Melcher loaning his fancy car and gas credit cards to Family members? The regular and meaningful contact Jakobson had with the Family?) all three were—with varying degrees of commitment and consistency—willing to trade on the power they derived from their professional status to organize their contact with Manson and his followers.[1] The Golden Penetrators tried to slot the Manson Family into two available categories—"groupies" and "freaks"—which had been well-established on the rock-and-roll scene by the late 1960s. (Cathy Gillies, before her membership in the Family, had been an avid follower of Buffalo Springfield.)[2] What makes the story of the Manson Family particularly interesting is that these roles proved too constricting for the "fans"; while the Golden Penetrators were acting from a script that had been well-established, in and beyond Los Angeles for a number of years, the members of the Manson Family were improvising; insisting, in short, on telling their own story.

Female "groupies" were widely understood by male musicians and film-industry figures to be a side benefit of their positions. There are obvious ethical and legal considerations to take into account in any discussion of young groupies and their relationship to relatively powerful male figures. The first and most important question has to do with matters of consent. Without traveling too far afield into legal and cultural arguments about age, agency, and rape, it is crucial to notice that the relationship of virtually every girl who became a part of the Manson Family and then made available to the Golden Penetrators, and various other men in the Los Angeles popular culture ecosystem, was defined by the power realities of age difference. The extreme examples (sixteen-year-old Ruth Anne Moorehouse going off with the Family, ultimately with the blessing of her father; thirteen-year-old Dianne Lake leaving Wavy Gravy's Hog Farm commune, also with her parents' permission, to begin traveling on her own) remind us of how radically key cultural terms—"family," "consent," and "parent," just for starters— were being renegotiated in this moment. It is important that we not shy away from acknowledging that what *we* call statutory rape was a constitutive part of this "new" culture in Los Angeles.

The Manson girls and other groupies of the late 1960s were not simply the prey of controlling and vicious men. The most well-known groupies in the Laurel Canyon and Sunset Strip scene were undoubtedly the women who comprised GTO (Girls Together Outrageously). With Frank Zappa's Laurel Canyon Log Cabin as their home base, and at least two of the group serving as childcare providers for Dweezil and Moon Unit Zappa, the GTOs embodied a freewheeling raunchiness. Zappa seems to have treated them as an anthropological curiosity at best, even recording an album with them, *Permanent Damage*, which was the second release on his companion labels Bizarre and Straight. (The debut recording was the infamous *An Evening with Wild Man Fischer*, a record that made hay out of the mental illness of its subject.) In his usual above-it-all and slightly cruel manner, Zappa remembers the GTOs group with boldfaced mockery, as being "totally dedicated and devoted to every aspect of rock and roll—especially the part about guys in bands who had Big Weenies."[3] It is possible that the "Big Weenies" part is just a sly joke on Zappa's part, a reference to the GTOs' association with Cynthia Plaster Caster, who gained some notoriety in the late 1960s for her practice of casting the penises of famous musicians. But at least lurking in the margins of Zappa's remembrance is the indication that the emerging leaders of the Los Angeles music and film scene understood, as David Toop has so cogently summarized, that in this scene "male creativity" would be supported by "female servitude."[4]

New codes of behavior were being worked out by what we can nominally call "performers" on the one hand, and "audiences" on the other. In the canyons of Los Angeles (mostly Laurel, but also Topanga and Benedict) and the clubs of Sunset Strip there was some significant cultural work being done beginning in the mid-1960s that resulted in a redrawing of the borders that previously had clearly marked off the territories of artists and audiences. Central to this process were the "freak dancers" who appeared first as an adjunct to the Byrds' stage performances at the Whisky. The "freak dancers" were organized around Vito Paulekas, a key member of the Laurel Canyon counterculture, who among other things was part of an early 1960s Southern California social world that, as Rachel Rubin explains, became the origin point of the Renaissance Faire.[5] Terry Melcher met Paulekas in 1960 when Paulekas was the proprietor of an art studio that Melcher and some of his high school friends would visit—largely, as Melcher explained, because Paulekas had nude models there.[6] The importance of Paulekas to this scene should not be underestimated: as Barry Miles puts it, Paulekas and his troupe (including his wife Szou and his friend Carl Franzoni—a.k.a. "Captain Fuck") were "the first hippies in Hollywood, perhaps the first hippies anywhere."[7] One of the major innovations of Paulekas and his group was to refer to themselves, proudly, as freaks. This group of dancers would appear regularly with the Byrds, whenever that group played at the Whisky, and they even accompanied the group on tour. Later, according to Barry Miles, they also accompanied Frank Zappa and the Mothers of Invention, even though "Zappa's music was never as danceable as the Byrds and required a lot more concentration."[8] Zappa was clear on the significance of Vito's freak dancers to the success of the Mothers' performance: "As soon as they arrived they would make things happen, because they were dancing in a way nobody had seen before, screaming and yelling out on the floor and doing all kinds of weird things. They were dressed in a way nobody could believe, and they gave life to everything that was going on."[9]

Vito and his freaks "lived a semi-communal life and engaged in sex orgies and free-form dancing whenever they could." Paulekas was much older than most of his freak colleagues (already in his fifties by the mid-1960s) and with Captain Fuck he acted as what Barry Miles calls a "sexual predator" who would focus "his attention upon the teenage girls who hung around the dance troupe at concerts."[10] About Franzoni, Zappa said simply that "Carl doesn't get along with people who don't fuck him."[11] In retrospect, Los Angeles music producer and impresario Lou Adler described Paulekas and his troupe as being like "a nonviolent Manson situation, a little cult."[12]

While "hippie" has been defined, diagnosed, contextualized, buried, and reanimated, its close cousin, "freak" (which is what Vito and his troupe called themselves), has received considerably less attention. Ultimately, part of what made the Manson Family so unsettling to the cultural leaders of Los Angeles is that they seemed, at first, to be modeled on just the kind of safe freaks they had been surrounded by for some years. Michael Walker is correct to note that Manson set himself up in the Los Angeles music world as parallel to other freak cliques. But while Frank Zappa's group of freaks was more or less headquartered at the Log Cabin, and Vito Paulekas and his freak dancers were mostly to be found at the Whisky, Manson's freaks *seeped*: they broke through walls, and later through windows, at 10050 Cielo Drive.[13] One of their great sins in the eyes of the musicians and film people with whom they interacted is that they did not seem to understand the rights and responsibilities of ownership. Brian Wilson of the Beach Boys summarized the troubling freakiness of the Manson Family by saying that they "had weird names, they were dirty, they showed little respect for our property."[14]

Rachel Adams has written helpfully about the changing meanings of "freak" in the course of American history, and her work can help us understand how Manson and his Family were mistakenly (and tragically) misread by their contacts in the canyons and on the Strip as representing another relatively benign tribe of freaks, right alongside Vito and his dancers, Ken Kesey and his Merry Pranksters, Zappa and the Mothers (and the GTOs). Adams explains that the twentieth-century history of "freak" begins in the sideshow (whose "scary" and "deformed" characters were enshrined in Tod Browning's 1932 movie *Freaks*). After World War II the word was applied more broadly to any sort of "nonconformity such as sexual perversion or communist sympathies."[15] Adams elaborates, "As hippies morphed into freaks and the Greatest Show on Earth moved out of the circus tent and into the streets, the meaning of *freak* exploded exponentially." A "freak" sea change ensued in the late 1960s, according to Adams, as a "youthful counterculture . . . made freakishness a valued sign of rebellion." This bubbled up to leaders of the counterculture (especially Abbie Hoffman and Jerry Rubin, Adams claims) who used "flamboyant . . . strategies of resistance" organized around "the figure of the freak, whose performative antics transform the serious business of courtrooms, schools, and streets into sideshows."[16]

Attempts to promote "freak" as an honored identity were not without challenges: the very familiarity of "speed freak" or "Jesus freak" as negative characterization alerts us to this reality. Just before the countercultural reformation of "freak" really took hold, Bob Dylan had already begun to destabilize it. In his 1965 song "Ballad of a Thin Man" Dylan included a verse that explicitly challenged audience members to consider the possibility that the performer (i.e., "the geek") considers the spectator to be a freak. Here, Dylan dramatically opens questions surrounding the relative "freakiness" of performers and audience members; just when you think it is safe to gawk at the spectacle, the performer holds up a mirror so you can see how grotesque you look.[17] (Manson himself knew that after his arrest he was being framed as the bad kind of "freak." Explaining that he was living in something like a "television cell," the prisoner complained that for prison employees, some of whom brought "their sons in on the week-ends to take a look" at him, he had become a grotesque sideshow attraction.)[18]

Though it would be foolish to extract a one-dimensional meaning from Dylan's hyped-up surrealism, it does seem clear that the song is demanding that listeners consider just what they think they know for sure about freaks. This is one of two songs on *Highway 61 Revisited* featuring "How does it feel" as a key phrase. The first one, on the record's opening song ("Like a Rolling Stone"), is an accusation directed at one character; "Ballad of a Thin Man" (which closes Side One of the LP) redeploys the phrase so it can serve as a rhetorical question and in the process broaden the singer's address. No one hearing the song can pretend it is about somebody else. In any event, by 1968, Tom Wolfe was writing of how "freak" had become a keyword for the hippies in the Haight-Ashbury. Freak, according to Wolfe, referred to "style and obsessions"; it was used as a simple descriptive, as in "Stewart Brand is an Indian freak." It was not, Wolfe emphasized, a "negative word."[19]

Frank Zappa was the most important "theorist" of the freak in mid-to-late 1960s. His debut release with the Mothers in 1966 (now renamed the Mothers of Invention) was called *Freak Out!* Its opening song, "Hungry Freaks, Daddy" articulated the cultural battle over the word "freak" itself. According to the liner notes of *Freak Out!*, this song was written for "Carl Orestes Franzoni" who is "freaky down to his toenails. Someday he will live next door to you and your lawn will die." The notes for this song go on to implore the reader and listener to "Drop out of school before your mind rots from exposure to our mediocre educational system. Forget about the Senior Prom and go to the library."[20]

The chorus of the song establishes that the "freaks" in question are the "left behinds of the Great Society." Musically it is defined at first by what sounds like a kazoo, but according to the liner notes must either be "tweezers" or a "bobby pin" (or an uncredited kazoo!). It is a freaky song, with freaky instrumentation. The lead vocal is doubled, and is comprised of an angry-sounding recitation by Zappa and Ray Collins. From the first verse on, Zappa makes it clear that mainstream culture is empty and dead. The emergence of the questing freaks of the title stands as the country's only hope of redemption. The "voice" of the song is, clearly, in sympathy with the "left behinds"—uninterested in participating in the rampant consumerism of the American dream.

The music of *Freak Out!* was packaged as a double gatefold LP and it is important to pay attention to the appearance of the record along with the music inside. All of the music of *Freak Out!* is framed by the record's cartoon cover art and the manifesto of sorts that Zappa includes with the liner notes. The manifesto makes clear how individual transformation can lead to social change:

> On a personal level, *Freaking Out* is a process whereby an individual casts off outmoded and restricting standards of thinking, dress, and social etiquette in order to express CREATIVELY his relationship to his immediate environment and the social structure as a whole. Less perceptive individuals have referred to us who have chosen this way of thinking and FEELING as *"Freaks,"* hence the term: *Freaking Out.*

Zappa is acknowledging here that in his moment "freak"—as noun or verb—is generally understood to have strongly negative connotations while hinting at the radical potential of reclaiming the word—and the behaviors associated with it— as a badge of social resistance:

> On a collective level, when any number of *"Freaks"* gather and express themselves through music or dance, for example, it is generally referred to as a *FREAK OUT.* The participants, already emancipated from our national *social slavery*, dressed in their most inspired apparel, realize as a group whatever potential they possess for free expression.
>
> We would like to encourage everyone who HEARS this music to join us . . . become a member of the The United Mutations . . . *FREAK OUT.*"

The serious purpose of Zappa's *Freak Out!* was leavened with plenty of parody. On the record jacket itself potential freaks were offered help on their journey with the image of a map to "Freak-Out Hot Spots," which would lead them to freak nightclubs, restaurants, "and many more interesting places," and which would also give information on "where the heat has been busting frequently with tips on safety in police-terror situations." These liner notes promise that a full version of the map—in "magnificent color (mostly black)"—could be had for a dollar. Zappa's tongue-in-cheek consumerist anti-consumerism was itself a "freak" act.[21] Not everyone in Zappa's orbit embraced his freak politics, of course. Don Van Vliet, leader of Captain Beefheart's Magic Band, was particularly upset by what he perceived as attempts by Zappa (serving as his producer) to make him "into a horrible freak."[22]

The *Freak Out!* sleeve also features names of artists who had become important to Zappa's development; these people were listed under the heading "These People Have Contributed Materially in Many Ways to Make Our Music What it is. Please Do Not Hold it Against Them." Later, Zappa would say that the whole package was meant to be "as accessible as possible to the people who wanted to take the time to make it accessible. That list of names in there, if anybody were to research it, would probably help them a great deal." Musician and producer Don Was, who bought the record in the summer of 1966, says the package worked just so for him: this was, he remembers, the "first time I heard of Charles Ives, Willie Dixon, Lawrence Ferlinghetti and Eric Dolphy." Intent on joining the "freak" movement, Was says that he and a friend left Michigan in the summer of 1966 and "took a trip to LA . . . just to check out all the locations that Frank listed as freak out hot spots. When we finally reached the hallowed portals of Ben Franks restaurant on Sunset, we felt like we'd become part of a movement—even if it was 10 a.m., and there wasn't a freak in sight!"[23]

"Freak" lived as an important social category for quite some time. As Rachel Adams explains, the "young people of the 1960s voluntarily adopted the name *freak* as a banner of rebellion against the authority of parents, schools, government" and "rebellious young people embraced freakiness as a sign of social dissidence."[24] Jimi Hendrix waved his freak flag in "If 6 Was 9," a song he first released in 1967, but which also made an impact in 1969 as part of the *Easy Rider* soundtrack. One of the signal achievements in the world of visual popular culture in the late 1960s, Gilbert Shelton's *Fabulous Furry Freak Brothers* (which debuted in 1968), established that "freak" had developed a countercultural cachet well beyond Zappa's Los Angeles circle. The word remained ripe with energy as the decade turned: on the one hand we find David Crosby singing about why he decided not to get a haircut and turning the (non)event into a freak's declaration of independence from "straight" norms; out on the more political edge of the counterculture, "freak" was being drafted into active duty by the radical Weather Underground, which, in its very first of a series of communiques declared categorically that "Freaks are revolutionaries and revolutionaries are freaks."[25] This political declaration, circulated in 1970, is one indication of how fully the name and role of the "freak" had been transformed by the activity of the 1960s counterculture to become a sign of thoughtful and energetic insurgency.

Of course "freakiness" was quickly coopted. For some early adopters, "freak" performance all too easily slid into a sort of empty self-display and self-indulgence, a cheap collation of thrift-store knick-knacks and hallucinogens. No one was more quickly and fully disappointed by how "freak" could be diluted than Zappa himself. In the summer of 1966, the Mothers were involved with a number of events in Los Angeles that Zappa hoped would help carry his arguments about the "freak out" to an even larger group of young people. These young people had been coming under increasing fire from the police (at the behest of the merchants of the Sunset Strip) largely because they loitered quite a bit—blocking the sidewalks—and bought very little. Zappa tried to articulate how this anti-consumerist orientation should not simply be chalked up to relative poverty, but could be situated at the heart of the "freak" challenge to the dominant culture. In August of 1966, Zappa and the Mothers performed to a huge audience at "Freak Out! Son of GUAMBO" at the Shrine Exposition. GUAMBO had been an earlier show, organized to celebrate the second anniversary of the *Los Angeles Free Press*, a major vehicle of the countercultural ethos in the city. After the success of the August show, the Mothers were booked to headline a repeat performance on September 17. In advance of this show Zappa paid to publish a four-page insert in the *Free Press*. It was made up of photo collages and encouraging text, meant to help his young fans see "through the lies of modern consumer society."[26] A week later Zappa took out another advertisement, and by this point his tone (and the presentation) had already radically changed. Now, Zappa is "hectoring," reminding the audience for the Mothers that there is a "danger" in the "'Freak Out' becoming an excuse instead of a reason. An excuse implies an end, a reason a beginning." "Freaking Out," Zappa reinforces, "should presuppose an active freedom . . . liberation from the control of some other person or persons." Zappa finishes his *Free Press* freak manifesto with a warning: "What WE must try to do then, is not only comment satirically on what's wrong, but try to CHANGE what's wrong."[27]

Zappa did not stop here, instead engaging for the next few months in culture spats that essentially revolved around his sense that other people (including Vito Paulekas, and Carl Franzoni, "Captain Fuck" himself) were trying to cash in on Zappa's "freak out" innovations. Of course, as Barry Miles points out, Paulekas had been holding proto–freak outs on his own for some time. But, as I have been trying to suggest, one major story to trace as we try to follow the Manson Family's creepy crawl over the Strip and through the canyons, is how much the landscape was already primed, by the time they arrived, for a battle royale where the prize would be male-freak supremacy (with all the rights and responsibilities that entailed). There were many ways that the Manson Family appeared as just a slightly more extreme version of the tribes that had been established in the mid-to-late 1960s in Los Angeles, which "centered on charismatic men inside or on the fringes of the music industry."[28] Vito Paulekas, with his retinue of female and a few male acolytes (including Kim Fowley) was the leader of one such tribe; Frank Zappa, with his Mothers, his

GTOs, and his Mothers' Auxiliary (including Paulekas) and others who blew in and out of the Log Cabin was another. Musician Bobby Beausoleil, on a smaller scale, was developing just such a entourage when he first came in contact with Charles Manson, and some have explained the rapid development of the Manson Family as something like a merger of these two bands of freaks.

The line between "cult," "freak family," and "band" became increasingly hard to draw in the last few years of the 1960s. Manson was clearly on the cult side of the ledger, as were Father Yod, leader of the Source Family (also in Los Angeles, and with musician Sky Saxon of the Seeds as one of its key figures), and the Lyman Family. Lyman is often treated as a sort of sub-Manson cult leader—possibly because he did not seem to direct his followers, explicitly, to kill. Armed robbery, maybe; murder, no. But Lyman accessed a kind of cultural power that Manson never developed.

On the "band" side of the equation, we can certainly comfortably place Zappa's Log Cabin, the Grateful Dead (with its group house at 710 Ashbury Street in San Francisco), Captain Beefheart's Magic Band, and Quicksilver Messenger Service. Historians have not been able to resist the Manson Family analogy when discussing the complex work–life arrangements developed by these acts. Harvey Kubernik, for instance, describes Quicksilver Messenger Service as living one version of the hippie dream at "a commune in Marin County where all manner of musicians, old ladies with babies, dope dealers, and human driftwood coalesced into a barely functioning whole. It wasn't exactly the Spahn Ranch, but it bordered on the hairy edge of calamity."[29] It has become even more commonplace to describe the late 1960s existence of the Magic Band with language inspired by the cultural creepy crawl of the Manson Family. One friend of Don Van Vliet (a.k.a. Captain Beefheart) describes the Magic Band's experiment in communal living as "positively Manson-esque" and notes that while "Don was taking vitamins and eating well," the remainder of the band were maintained on "a barely liveable diet." Additionally, the "ongoing regime of control," established by Van Vliet (as with

Manson's strategy) relied at least in part on the strategic use of hallucinogens.[30]

This communal experiment culminated in the appearance of the record *Trout Mask Replica*, released just a few months before the Tate-LaBianca killings. Guitarist Bill Harkleroad (known in the Magic Band context as Zoot Horn Rollo) recounts that this period of the group's life was marked by "brainwashing sessions" during which Van Vliet "turned on one of the group and systematically criticized him to break him down." This period in the Magic Band's history is summarized by Harkleroad as being characterized by a "Mansonish Gestalt Therapy kind of thing."[31] Manson rarely seems to have used such direct means, favoring more of a theatrical and allegorical approach to attacking the ultimately constricting boundaries of "ego." As Gregg Jakobson put it at the Tex Watson trial (skittering dangerously on the edge of breaking into the opening lines of "I Am the Walrus"), the "overriding philosophy" was that "he is me and I am him and I am you and you are me."[32]

When Charles Manson and his Family let their "freak flag fly" it was recognized by a surprisingly large number of powerful industry figures as an appealing invitation, a gesture of peace and goodwill, and an emblem of alliance. "Freak" was a key word, a densely packed concept, central to the Los Angeles counterculture's sense of its own identity as anti-establishment; for a time Charles Manson was able to wield his own freakiness as a calling card, a high sign that he flashed that helped him gain entrée to the clubs, recording studios, and private homes of Los Angeles. How *did* Charles Manson install himself as a "freak"? The dance floor was a major venue for him to establish his freakiness. By the time of Manson's arrival on the scene, Los Angeles rock-and-roll performers and audiences were already well prepared—by Vito Paulekas and his troupe, among others—to understand dancing as a site of important social activity. In his recent biography of Charles Manson, Jeff Guinn makes the smart decision to open his entire book with a description of Manson accompanying Dennis Wilson (along with the other two Golden Penetrators) to the Whisky in 1968. While the three other men made their way to a reserved table, Manson peeled off and headed to the dance floor. In one of his more fanciful passages, Guinn imagines that Jakobson, Melcher, and Wilson let him go—fully expecting to see Manson receive his "comeuppance" on the dance floor and return quickly to their table. But then Manson, a "whirling dervish," springs into action and takes over the floor; while all three of the celebrities had seen Manson dominate smaller-scale social events before, this was unexpected. Jakobson summarizes this surprising evening by saying this is when he and his compatriots realized, for the first time, that "Anytime, anywhere Charlie wanted to be the center of attention, he could be."[33] A new Vito (with more than a little bit of Captain Fuck rolled in, of course) had arrived!

While dance-floor theatrics were never a major part of Charles Manson's repertoire, this appearance at the Whisky along with his ability to regularly hold the floor (at Wilson's house first, and then later at Spahn Ranch) as a solid, improvising musician were crucial to establishing his freak credentials. Paul Watkins, a one-time Family member, is one of the few people besides Neil Young to credit the freaky power of Manson's music-making. In his memoir, published ten years after the murders, Watkins spends considerable space trying to capture the functional vigor of Manson's jam sessions:

> Those who have written about Manson have always implied that drugs and sex were his primary means of programming the Family. But music was perhaps even more influential. No other art form better expresses the nuances of the soul. While Charlie was never a great instrumentalist, his voice was strong and he had a good range. He could wail, croon, and get funky. . . . He got it moving by making up songs, singing nonsense verses with uncanny timing. I felt completely relaxed and into it. When he suddenly began a new verse, then hesitated halfway through it, I obeyed an impulse and sang the rest of it.[34]

Much of what Watkins says about Manson's freaky and powerful music making could be drawn from the most conventional narratives of a certain strand of California's countercultural music culture—the Northern California kind, that is. Here Watkins emphasizes the spontaneous, the communal, and the everyday, the significance of individual and group improvisation over the Los Angeles scene's increasing emphasis on the rehearsed and polished.

Paul Watkins's thoughtful evaluation of Manson's freak improvisations could have been drawn from any one of literally dozens of accounts of the Grateful Dead. Carole Brightman, in her book *Sweet Chaos: The Grateful Dead's American Adventure*, boils down the role of improvisation to the Dead's music with the observation that it represented "chaos accepted and embraced."[35] Avoiding the "slick" approach of Los Angeles professionals, Manson deployed the freak strategy of improvisation to signal that he was operating in a musical democracy—that his music was meant to convene not "fans" but co-creators. Watkins is aware of how Manson's work as a performing artist involved walking on a tightrope. On the one hand his singing and playing inspired devotion on the part of his female followers. Describing young Ruth Anne Moorehouse (Ouisch), Watkins writes of how she watched Manson, "her eyes wide, her mouth slightly ajar. She reminded me of a teenager watching Elvis Presley in his prime. All eyes, in fact, were riveted to Charlie." On the other hand, Manson was careful not to let his performances create too much distance between performer and audience or to emphasize technical accomplishment over "feeling": "Though Charlie was always the lead vocalist, everyone got involved in the music. . . . Nothing brings people closer together than their own voices in song."[36]

Manson's appearance on the Los Angeles freak scene was an important continuation of the détente of Northern and Southern California that the Monterey Pop Festival had first brokered. Of course, Manson himself (after his release from Terminal Island in 1967, during the "Summer of Love") followed a path that took him from the Haight-Ashbury to Southern California in an old school

bus the Family had painted black—possibly a parody of the multicolored bus Ken Kesey's Merry Pranksters took on their trips.
More important than his physical journey from North to South,
however, is the way that Manson brought elements of Northern
California's musical culture to Los Angeles: the open-ended
jam, the shaggy communalism, and the belief that music could
be a vehicle for spiritual growth were all hallmarks of the "San
Francisco Sound," which Manson helped introduce to Dennis
Wilson, Gregg Jakobson, and many others who engaged with
the Family in the last two years of the 1960s. At just the moment
when Wilson's brother Brian was making deep investments in the
notion that the art of the Beach Boys would be a studio art, relying
not only on the professional musicians of the Wrecking Crew but
also on an assumption that the studio itself had to be approached
as if it were a sort of meta-instrument, Dennis Wilson was acting out a small-scale rebellion through his embrace of Manson's
folk-oriented, extemporaneous creations.

Manson and the Family would not have been able to infiltrate
the freak scene of Los Angeles if they had not also *looked* the part.
Manson and his Family obviously did look like freaks. They wore
the right clothes (or *didn't* wear the right clothes, as the occasion required) and the right accessories, their hair was freaky, and
their talk was freaky. On *Freak Out!* Frank Zappa had included
throwing off "outmoded and restricted standards of . . . dress" as
part of the necessary reinvention of the "freak" who is trying to
alter "his [sic] relationship to his immediate environment and the
social structure as a whole."[37] With the requisite long hair on men
and the leather thong around Manson's neck and the girls—when
clad—wearing the kind of second-hand hippie finery that was first
sold at Szou Paulekas's "Freak Boutique" (located above Vito's clay
studio), the Family made a visual claim to territory on the Strip, in
Laurel Canyon, and in Dennis Wilson's home. Even the renaming
of the tribe (Gypsy, Katie, Ouisch, Squeaky, Snake, and so on) had
its parallels in other freak "families."[38]

There is a particularly poignant moment that comes in just
about every retelling of the night of the murder at 10050 Cielo

Drive, which finds Abigail Folger looking up, smiling and waving at Susan Atkins as Atkins passed by the room Folger was reading in. Built into these accounts is the implicit claim that Atkins looked like she belonged in this swinging Benedict Canyon pad. Virtually everywhere that Manson and his Family went in and around Los Angeles in 1968 and 1969 they were welcomed as friends and lovers, brothers and sisters. While many notable figures back-pedaled from the Family as news of the arrests broke, filmmaker John Waters remembers thinking that they "looked just like my friends at the time"; Waters goes on to admit that Tex Watson reminded him of "Jimmy, the frat-boy-gone-bad pot dealer I had the hots for in Catholic high school, the guy who sold me my first joint."[39]

The Manson Family's freak bona fides were also, no doubt, underscored by their manifest anti-consumerist stance. From their thrift-store visual palette to their reclamation of usable food through regular trips to dumpsters outside of supermarkets, the Manson Family presented a sharp alternative to the material traps of hip capitalism so firmly in place by the late 1960s. (This political aspect of the creepy crawl would, finally, find expression in 2004 in the German film *The Edukators*.) It is worth repeating here that the Family's calling card was the creepy crawl—breaking and entering into a private home, rearranging furniture, perhaps having a quick snack, and then leaving without, usually, taking anything. The creepy crawl represented the upsetting flipside of dumpster diving. If the Manson Family was able to develop a sustainable model of food production by making something out of nothing (i.e., meals from what most Americans would call garbage), it was also intent on underscoring the emptiness at the heart of rampant materialism by leaving "valuable" objects behind when they were ripe for the picking. Paul Watkins offers a strong case for understanding Manson's surprising level of influence over Dennis Wilson as originating in his ability to prey on Wilson's confusion at being "an all-American middle-class surfer kid who had suddenly made it rich and didn't know quite how to handle it": "Dennis sure as hell had it made . . . the classic Spanish-style Hollywood mansion, complete with manicured lawns, vibrant recently cultivated rose gardens, and an enormous kidney-shaped swimming pool. The inside was no less lavish: furnished to the hilt with antiques, original French paintings, Persian rugs and countless mementos and photos of the Beach Boys' international acclaim in the record industry."[40] Wilson also had fancy cars, including a red Ferrari, which was totaled by Watkins and Steve ("Clem") Grogan.

Wilson was a "prime target for the Family," Watkins writes. Manson "self-righteously played the role of Robin Hood, taking from the rich, namely Dennis, to give to the poor, namely Charlie. He really went to work on Dennis, made him feel guilty for possessing so much wealth, urged him to renounce it in exchange for a simple communal life based on love: Charlie's love."[41] Of all the Beach Boys, Dennis Wilson seems to have been the only one with consistent aspirations to freakiness; Mike Love always made following the Maharishi and taking hallucinogens look like right-wing frat boy behaviors. Rachel Adams has argued that for many countercultural freaks in the 1960s, it was possible to "profess" radicalism without introducing "progressive solutions to the social order they condemned" and while also remaining "ignorant of the contradictions in their own attitudes."[42] Wilson does seem to have developed some sense of his own "contradictions"—largely under Manson's direction. The freak dancing of Vito Paulekas and his troupe (filmed evidence of which can be found in the 1968 documentary *You Are What You Eat*) was predicated on the premise of letting go, tapping into the unconscious, merging with other people, and working without a script. Manson's freak achievement, especially vis-à-vis his exploitation of Dennis Wilson, was to create the illusion he was improvising, working for some collective good, all while he was running a long con. Manson himself was more than happy to abscond with goodies from Wilson's mansion, including "most of his wardrobe" and "all of his gold records"—which he would later hand out "in the streets of Hollywood to passersby, just to blow their minds"—at the same time he worked to convince Wilson this was all part of a program of self-actualization. Manson challenged Wilson to think about the empty symbolism of gold records: "What did they mean to the spiritual man? What did they represent other than the epitome of American capitalism?"[43] Wilson had plenty of ground to travel; Paul Watkins claims that when the Beach Boy first came into contact with the Manson Family he "came on like a polished playboy bachelor—glib, loose-jointed, and hip."[44]

For a time, Charles Manson was able to deploy the recognizable signs of the "freak" to penetrate the world of Dennis Wilson, Terry Melcher, and Gregg Jakobson. He danced at the Whisky, lived at Dennis Wilson's house, recorded at Brian Wilson's home studio. But for all of his ambition, Manson was not prepared to make it as a popular artist. If Manson was any kind of artist, he was the kind that we generally understand as a "naïve" or "outsider" artist. This is not to suggest that Manson and his Family did not commit a considerable amount of energy (and money) to its musical project. Paul Watkins explains in his memoir that the Family practiced its music daily, and invested a large amount of money in "new sound equipment" and instruments: "Through Dennis and Greg [sic] we lined up recording sessions at Brian Wilson's studio. But none of them went well. Charlie liked to improvise, even during live recordings, and it just didn't work. Invariably our best sessions were outside the studio, in a relaxed environment."[45] It is clear that Manson was made remarkably uncomfortable by the professional demands of making music in a recording studio. When Manson was interviewed for *Rolling Stone*'s cover story on June 25, 1970, he admitted that he was never able to get comfortable enough to perform well in the recording studio: "I never really dug recording, you know, all those things pointing at you. You get into the studio, and it's hard to sing into microphones. [He clutches his pencil rigidly, like a mike.] Giant phallic symbols pointing at you. All my latent tendencies. [He starts laughing and making sucking sounds. He is actually blowing the pencil!] My relationship to music is completely subliminal, it just flows through me."[46]

"Flow" might have been a reasonable organizing principle for the freak dancers sponsored by the Byrds and the Mothers, and Frank Zappa may have been comfortable releasing the music of Wild Man Fischer—thus putting the "sideshow" back in contemporary attempts to redefine "freak" with a positive spin. But Manson could never find the proper sponsor with the consistent interest, industry savvy, and musical skill to help him fly his freak flag in an organized way. On some level what Manson most notably lacked was a "company freak." In her essay on the "company freak" (also known as the "house hippie"), scholar Devon Powers has written persuasively of men like Billy James, Jim Fouratt, and Danny Fields, who were basically hired by record companies as mediators, charged with translating the new musical forms and social stances into marketable products. But Powers wants us to notice that these men did not simply "bridge" two distinct cultures—they forged "a common culture . . . an environment in which rock music, the capital of major labels, and the individuals who transacted that relationship made sense together." What was most important about the company freak was his "performative role"—the way he claimed "institutional and social space" through his own acts of communication and his own forging of professional and personal relationships.[47] For a time it looked like Phil Kaufman would play this role for Manson. But he simply did not have the industry juice to help Manson break into the big league. Manson thought he was auditioning various men—Kaufman, Melcher, Wilson—to serve as his "company freak," but it turned out that none of them really wanted the job. As a result Manson was left to his own devices, and his own devices were not nearly up to the task of breaking him into the music business.

The Bad Fathers
of the Feast

The death of this tentative arrangement that brought entertainment industry celebrities so close to everyday people was hastened, for sure, by the killings at 10050 Cielo Drive. Michael Walker has nicely summed up the immediate Laurel Canyon reaction to the murders: "The next day, across Laurel Canyon, you could practically hear bolts snapping into place behind doors that for the past five years had gone unlocked day and night."[1] Phil Proctor, of the Firesign Theatre comedy group, remembers his sense that now parties at Jeanne Martin's house felt "filtered," as if references were now being checked.[2] One film journalist notes that the "intimidating automatic gates that had heretofore been beneath contempt in the Age of Aquarius became de rigueur."[3] The mainstream press acknowledged this new reality; the San Francisco *Chronicle* ran an article soon after the arrests with a headline that read "Manson Arrest Reaction: The 'War on the Longhairs'" and which went on to detail all the ways that hippies were now coming under intensified suspicion.[4] Sally Stevens, a Los Angeles record-company executive, explains that everyone "thought at first it was a big dope dealer who was revenging himself on people. There was one guy, a boyfriend of Cass Elliot's, everyone thought it was him, and he'd fled for Algiers or something."[5]

Key players in the music business developed a remarkably consistent and inflated rhetoric about the killings—especially during the period of immediate fallout when the "Melcher hypothesis" was still in play. An oft-repeated anecdote about the aftermath of the Tate murders holds that Stephen Stills "ran around shrieking, 'They're killing everybody with estates.'"[6] At the same time a communal game developed that Peter Biskind has called the "I-almost-got-killed bandwagon."[7] Dennis Doherty of the Mamas and the Papas, with some exasperation, confirms that he knew large handfuls of people who claimed they were supposed to be at 10050 Cielo Drive—that they had been invited over that night but decided at the last minute not to go.[8] Biskind reminds us of the complex webs connecting up the victims at Cielo Drive to various players in the New Hollywood: "No one was untouched. Everybody knew them. They had their hair done by Sebring . . . or had been invited up that night and begged off because they were too tired, too stoned, or had something better to do."[9] The realities of these multiple connections particularly obsessed Roman Polanski, husband of Sharon Tate, who launched an informal investigation of his own, once he returned from London to Los Angeles after the murders. John Phillips has recounted that Polanski dusted Phillips's garage for fingerprints, and later directly questioned Phillips as to whether he was the killer; Phillips understood Polanski worried he might have been motivated by revenge after Polanski had sex with Phillips's estranged wife, Michelle. In fact, production designer Richard Sylbert (who worked on *Rosemary's Baby* with Polanski) explains that the director suspected a number of his friends because he had either "fucked their girlfriends or their wives."[10]

The novelist Robert Stone, in his memoir *Prime Green*, is especially eloquent about the tumult in Los Angeles in the days and weeks after the murders: "It was saturnalia time in Hollywood, a very grim feast of the meaningless. The youngsters disappeared from the boulevard as though the bad father of the feast had eaten them." The frenzy included a lashing out and a turning inwards.[11] Stone argues here that a major change followed the murders at Cielo Drive; never, he writes, "did the lights go on so fast and the glitz come off the columns and the glass balls shatter as in the wake of a couple of murders."[12] Stone is clear in his claim that the killing of Sharon Tate, Jay Sebring, Voytek Frykowski, and Abigail Folger (but not so much Steven Parent who, as John Phillips says, "was a single man none of us knew") also had a fatal effect on the loosely organized, but real, alliance of Los Angeles industry insiders, camp followers, and unaffiliated freaks.[13] There "was a whole lot of shaving going on in Los Angeles," Stone writes: "Good-humored tolerance of the neo-bohemian scene was suspended."[14]

In subtle fashion Stone works here to unsettle the world-weary "oh-how-dreadful-to-be-murdered-now-be-a-darling-and-hand-me-a-cigarette-won't-you" paradigm established by Joan Didion in her essay "The White Album." Recall that Didion's central claim in this essay is that when news of the Tate murders broke, the truly terrifying thing was that "no one was surprised." But the agitation all over Los Angeles gives the lie to Didion's above-it-all formulation. John Phillips remembers how "paranoia swept through Beverly Hills and Bel Air. . . . There were bizarre theories that attempted to link the murders to LSD and Satanic rites, kinky and deadly sexual perversions, and somehow to Polanski's own penchant for violence in movies."[15] Robert Stone remembers the wild theorizing too—including that Nixon had organized all this bloodshed, somehow, to "embarrass the antiwar movement. A well-known person offered a theory that naval intelligence had killed the victims."[16] (It is possible that Stone is mixing up dates here and is here thinking of radio personality Mae Brussell, who began promoting her very complex naval intelligence theory in 1971.) Stone remembers the days after the murders as being drenched in fear. As the novelist fancifully puts it, when "the bearded trolls and their consorts were run out of town, fear remained. People hired body guards. At one house (I swear) the protection would follow a swimmer doing laps up and down the length of the swimming pool."[17] The Manson Family had creepy crawled all over the terrain of the Los Angeles area and it was going to take some time and quite a bit of effort to make the scene feel secure again.

The indictment of Manson and members of his Family in December of 1969 were, if anything, even more devastating to the music community in Los Angeles than the murders themselves had been. The developing possibility that the "guy with the long hair and the beard could turn out to be the devil was really a nightmare."[18] In the wake of the arrests and indictments the Los Angeles music community worked assiduously to erase any impression that Manson was one of them—a professional musician. *Rolling Stone* magazine checked with the president of the musicians' local in Los Angeles who said "he had checked his union's records and that Manson definitely was not a musician."[19] In a more diffuse way, the hip and powerful cultural elite of Los Angeles expressed their panic at having been so intimately tied up with the mastermind behind these mass killings. In his book *Bitter Carnival*, literary critic Michael André Bernstein has written of how dramatically Manson's arrest acted as a tragic "warning sign of just how high the cost of 'breaking down' the footlights" had become.[20] Richard Schechner's immersive theater projects, *Commune* and *Dionysus in 69*, opened up the question (in the context of the Tate-LaBianca murders) of what it meant to erase the boundaries that usually separate audience and performers. These theatrical responses launched by Schechner and his troupe gained meaning from the wider context—all those dramatic everyday meditations on impurity and hysterical efforts to draw clear boundaries of class and vocation, and to rationalize what had gone wrong in Los Angeles. In a 1974 interview with *Rolling Stone*, Terry Melcher recounted that it had been clear to him that the media was going to try to script the Cielo Drive murders and the December indictments as a "New Hollywood/hippie/drug shakedown." Melcher suggested that the events of the second half of 1969 "really turned a lot of people against each other. I noticed that a few people became afraid of me. I know I became afraid of everyone else."[21]

The indictment of Manson and his Family members put a very definite punctuation mark on all the speculation that had occupied the Los Angeles entertainment world since the murders.

There were, of course, the early attempts to situate Manson as some kind of countercultural hero. But for the most part, all the evidence connecting Manson and his Family to the larger world of popular artists in Los Angeles was deeply upsetting. This was not, as Peter Biskind acutely reminds us, death by "pigs" (as *Bonnie and Clyde, The Wild Bunch, Butch Cassidy* and *Easy Rider* had fantasized it.")[22] There was going to be, it soon became clear, a sort of "correction" of the cultural marketplace as the news of the "hippie guru" circulated. Additionally, and as many other commentators have noted, the cultural confusion caused by Manson's indictment in early December was intensified by the tragic free concert headlined by the Rolling Stones at the Altamont Freeway not even a week later. The painful social truths exposed by the Hells Angels' murder of Meredith Hunter, an African American audience member, was captured on film by the makers of *Gimme Shelter*. This chilling moment is joined by a bizarre inability on the part of a few key performers to demonstrate that they understood just how fully the imagined audience/Angels/performers alliance was disintegrating. The filmmakers responsible for *Gimme Shelter* (the Maysles Brothers and Charlotte Zwerin) managed to smuggle a surprising amount of critical material into the movie—perhaps none as devastating as the single word ("bummer") uttered by the Grateful Dead's Jerry Garcia after another musician informs him of the brewing violence. In the same vignette, Phil Lesh, the bassist for the Grateful Dead, just cannot seem to stop smiling.

The anti-hippie backlash came quickly and reached the music world of Los Angeles as something of a calamity. Session musician Randy Cierley (who also recorded under the name Randy Sterling, with Cher, Neil Diamond, Frank Zappa and many, many others) remembers worrying about the revelation that this had been the work of a "failed musician." Cierley felt clear that whatever else resulted from the arrests, this was going to "hurt longhairs."[23] The coverage in the mainstream press confirmed that the arrests and indictment of the Family members would feed into a narrative of the dangers of countercultural living. *Life* magazine's

December 19 issue, with a tight shot of Manson's face—eyes whited out to make him look demonic—and the headline "The Love and Terror Cult" (subhead: "The Dark Edge of Hippie Life") contributed to the quickly evolving notion that the violence of the past few months had to be understood as part of the inevitable wreckage caused by the social and cultural insurgency of the younger generation. It would not take long for pulp fiction and film to jump on this particular dogpile. One industry insider, reflecting on the meaning of the arrests for the evolving "neo-bohemian" scene in Los Angeles, claimed that this series of events "just destroyed us. . . . I mean everyone was looking at everyone else, not quite sure who was in that house and who knew about it. And then no one trusted hippies anymore. . . . Everybody went behind closed doors."[24] Producer Jack Nitzsche put things even more frankly: "Then it quickly became, 'No more fucking hippies hitchhiking.' Rule number one: that shit is over. 'No I don't want to buy a *Free Press* newspaper from you.'"[25] (One interesting renunciation of this distancing comes with the 1975 film *Rafferty and the Gold Dust Twins*, which reimagines hitchhiking as a way to build family. Screenwriter John Kaye, whom we will meet in the final section of this book, has claimed that the idea for the book came to him after he picked up two members of the Family in Los Angeles. Somewhat spooked by the X marks on their foreheads and their intimidating silence, Kaye claims to have engaged in an "act of creative transmutation and joyful surprise" to bring this story to life in a form that was "both whimsical and serious." His story gains resonance, of course, given the presence of Papa John Phillips's teenaged daughter Mackenzie playing the younger of the "twins.")[26] Buck Henry, who was centrally situated in the New Hollywood, argues that the crime at Cielo Drive "affected everybody's work, it affected the way people thought about other people."[27] Writing from the other coast in the *East Village Other*, Allen Katzman suggested that the murders had brought the "community of moviedom to a point of psychotic silence."[28] A major effect of the killings was to draw a much firmer border between the freaks and the famous.

After Manson's arrest the music of Laurel Canyon and much of the rest of white Los Angeles turned away, somewhat, from social engagement. The newer music emphasized the centrality of private personal experience in the wake of a sense of countercultural failure. We should take note of Joni Mitchell's trajectory from the late 1960s through the early 1970s, and particularly her adoption of the politically passive, valedictory stance in her 1971 song "California," wherein the singer acknowledges that fighting for peace was just a passing fantasy. The distance traveled in this California/Manson art might be measured in the move (as rock critic Robert Christgau put it) between Mitchell's 1969 record *Clouds* to her 1970 release *Ladies of the Canyon:* recognizing Mitchell's new reliance on keyboards, after the acoustic guitar–based palette of *Clouds*, Christgau described the trajectory as a shift from "the open air to the drawing room."[29] That drawing room imagined by Christgau was in the Laurel Canyon house where Mitchell lived with Graham Nash. The real anthem of this move from open air to drawing room is not a Mitchell song, but Nash's composition "Our House" (released on Crosby, Stills, Nash and Young's *Déjà Vu* in 1970). The political communion at the heart of so much countercultural subversion of public, white mainstream American culture is gone, replaced here by the pleasures of private romantic love and an invitation to play for an audience of one. Graham Nash and others have actually underscored this turn to the "power of the personal" as a victory of individual vision in response to the "failure of the collective."[30]

While the popular arts would continue to host a conversation about public and private, about what was normal and what was "freaky" (particularly in the Black music of the mid-to-late 1970s), the central cleansing drama of the post-arrest period took place in the courtroom. Recall Rachel Adams's claim that one central element of the "freak" challenge to straight culture was to "perform" outlandish acts in sites usually reserved for serious business. The political aim of the strategy was to upend the authority usually taken for granted in the assigned space. In the case of courtroom dramas, the goal of such acting out is usually quite clear—it is meant to call into question who is judging whom. Manson's performance at his trial demonstrated without question that the defendant was hoping to turn the court into his own sideshow. Much of the early drama at the trial circled around the question of whether Manson would be authorized to act as his own counsel. Judge Charles Older—with a name and bearing sent directly from central casting—refused Manson's request to represent himself but "allowed" him to choose Irving Kanarek, a remarkably anarchic performer in his own right, as his lawyer. In the courtroom dialogue Manson and Older engaged in, Manson repeated that his first choice was to serve as his own counsel, but that his "second alternative is to cause you as much trouble as possible."[31] Manson engaged in all kinds of theatrics. First he got into character by carving the infamous X on his forehead; he broke out to sing "The Old Gray Mare" at one point; he held up a copy of the *Los Angeles Times* with the headline that President Nixon had declared "Manson Guilty"; he used his co-defendants as a Greek Chorus of sorts, commenting on the matters at hand; he made scary eyes at witnesses and he jumped over the defense table and leaped up to try to attack Judge Older with a pencil.

Manson never took the stand himself—which might have been a bad decision in terms of how fully he could "freak out" in court—but he did deliver a statement during which he played a number of different roles. One significant role Manson took on was as simple and humble naif: "I never went to school, so I never growed up in the respect to learn to read and write so I have stayed in jail and I have stayed stupid, I have stayed a child while I have watched your world grow up. . . . Hippie cult leader . . . that is your words. I am a dumb country boy. . . . I went to jail when I was eight years old and I got out when I was thirty-two. I have never adjusted to your free world. I am still that stupid, corn-picking country boy that I have always been."[32] Manson's efforts were not inconsequential, but ultimately they were neutralized by the prosecutor's success in rendering Manson as a fringe figure—not a norm-challenging freak, but as a slightly pathetic striver who did not have the talent or cultural capital to help him earn the mainstream success he so desperately craved. In essence, what Bugliosi constructed for the jury was a Manson tale that explained away his capers as the desperate efforts of a "failed musician" who could not make it in a more conventional way. As early as the December 5 Grand Jury hearing Bugliosi was using Melcher and Jakobson to begin building this characterization.

At the first trial (of Manson himself, Susan Atkins, Patricia Krenwinkel, and Leslie Van Houten) in 1970 and at Tex Watson's trial in 1971, Prosecutor Vincent Bugliosi collaborated with some key members of the new Los Angeles cultural leadership to publicly purge Manson from the music scene he had broken into so dramatically. If Manson had rearranged some of the furniture of the Los Angeles's cultural scene, then it was going to be Bugliosi's job to get the house back in order. The Golden Penetrators had a particularly crucial role to play, from the convening of the original Grand Jury, through the long trial of Manson and the girls, and the later trial of Tex Watson. The purifying rituals that took place in the context of these courtroom dramas had a few key components. First, the trinity of the Golden Penetrators came to at least an implicit agreement that Gregg Jakobson would do most of the heavy lifting when it came to explaining how Manson had come to be such a central part of the Los Angeles music scene. This was the first move in depreciating Manson's cultural assets. Much of Bugliosi's courtroom portrait of Manson would rely on a complicated math: the prosecutor needed to present the leader of this family as totally in control of his small kingdom, but off the rails with respect to understanding his place in the wider culture— mildly delusional but not totally insane. Bugliosi used Manson's attempts to break into the music business to help establish that Manson was operating from organized, if deeply daft, motivations. Also important at the trial was that the Family as a unit needed to be constructed as an anthropological curiosity—certainly worth paying attention to (and perhaps even worth "recording") but not to be mistaken for peers or potential colleagues. Implicit in all this, too, was an argument that this Family sure did not look like *your* family. Finally, Bugliosi—with the help of his key witnesses—would need to help the jury understand what it meant to be a professional musician in Los Angeles in 1968 and 1969 in order to make clear how little Manson had in common with the *real* musicians with whom he came in contact.

Even the most cursory reading of the trial records reveals this interesting fact about Dennis Wilson: The Beach Boy did not sing. During the discovery period before the first trial, according to Vincent Bugliosi, Wilson initially "claimed to know nothing of importance." Ultimately Wilson agreed to "level" with Bugliosi but held fast to his refusal to testify. Ed Sanders suggests in the *Los Angeles Free Press* that Wilson had, in early interviews with Bugliosi, taken a decidedly "mishiga" approach and was making it clear to the prosecutor that he would act crazy on the stand if forced to testify.[33] By his own admission Wilson would not testify because he was scared—and by most accounts the musician had reason to worry.[34] In addition to creepy crawling Wilson's house, Manson also directly threatened to hurt Wilson's son.[35] Dennis Wilson's intimate involvement with the Family left him vulnerable to its threats—Manson and his followers certainly knew where Wilson lived. The time the Family spent at Wilson's Sunset Boulevard home was crucial to its overall growth and to its access to some of the most powerful figures in the film and musical worlds of Los Angeles. During this Sunset Boulevard spring, the Family doubled in number and gained some key male members, including Tex Watson, Paul Watkins, and Brooks Poston. These few months also resulted in the Family developing its "star map" of Los Angeles; through Wilson they met Jakobson, Melcher, and Rudi Altobelli, an agent for a number of Hollywood figures and owner of 10050 Cielo Drive.[36]

Wilson was also something of a believer. He appears, actually, to have been more convinced by Manson's philosophy than by Manson's music. When Terry Melcher finally ended his radio silence in 1974 to speak with *Rolling Stone* (as part of a promotional effort on behalf of his first solo record), he noted that Dennis Wilson thought Manson was "some kind of guru."[37]

Melcher may not, however, have been forthcoming about his own seduction by Manson. According to Rudi Altobelli (who lived in a guest house on the Cielo Drive grounds), "Terry and Gregg Jakobson were always talking about Manson and his philosophy."[38] Altobelli thought that the two were, possibly, trying to get him interested in taking Manson on as a client.[39] For his part, Dennis Wilson seems to have been happy to share his home, his cars, his wardrobe, and more with Manson and the Family. Wilson obviously enjoyed the relationships he forged with the women of the Family, but he also seems to have embraced the spiritual connection he felt with Manson. This was not the first time Wilson threw his lot in with a charismatic spiritual leader. A year earlier Wilson had concluded the same thing about the Maharishi Mahesh Yogi (also the Beatles' guru for a brief time) that he later felt about Manson, and he encouraged his bandmates to engage with the holy man's teachings.[40] But the key difference separating his dalliance with the Maharishi and his involvement with Manson was that even as Wilson acted as an acolyte to both, it was only with Manson that Wilson could so completely exercise class privilege. After developing a deep and meaningful relationship with the Family leader and aspiring musician, Wilson was able to cut ties completely, to construct an impermeable boundary between himself and Charles Manson. It was an open secret in 1969 that "Never Learn Not to Love," at the very least, had its roots in Manson's "Cease to Exist." After Manson was arrested, Lynnette "Squeaky" Fromme showed up at Gregg Jakobson's house demanding money for the composition, which was not forthcoming.[41] Whether his relationship with Manson is construed as a business matter or a social relationship, Wilson's privilege enabled him to make this problem go away. The Beach Boys did not pay royalties to Manson and Wilson did not have to testify about his relationship to Manson at the trial. While the whole episode may have left enduring marks on Wilson's emotional landscape, as some have suggested, the Beach Boys' drummer was able, more or less, to hit a rim shot and move on.

In 1976 Wilson said definitively, if not particularly clearly, that he would not talk about Manson: "I think of Roman and all those wonderful people who had a beautiful family and they fucking had their tits cut off. I want to benefit from that?"[42] A year later Wilson revisited his categorical refusal to talk, telling the editor of a Beach Boys' fanzine that he knew "why Charles Manson did what he did. Someday I'll tell the world. I'll write a book and explain why he did it." That book did not get written.[43]

For his part, Terry Melcher simply created as much distance as he could between himself and Manson, particularly in the testimony he gave at Manson's trial. He did this, as I suggested above, by treating the Family as worthy (maybe) of a type of quasi-anthropological interest and by emphasizing that what *he* was—a professional producer and musician—had little in common with the sit-around-the-fire-and-sing rituals of Manson and his followers. In Melcher's testimony Manson emerges as admirably charismatic (i.e., somehow he was able to control all these women) but not as a talented performer or competent social actor likely to make it in the complex Los Angeles music industry.

The testimony offered by Melcher at the trial showed a Manson as almost completely guileless when it came to his understanding of the "real" world of the music business. Under Vincent Bugliosi's careful questioning, Melcher made it plain that Manson had been engaged in some magical thinking with respect to getting recorded and getting paid; what Melcher needed to explain to the aspiring musician was that "money derived from the sale of records were paid to the artists on a royalty basis, you know, which companies have different pay periods of six months or something like that and, you know, you don't get a record and get paid for it. You make a record and then if it sells you get paid a certain percentage of the sale." Melcher presented all this to the jury as a cut-and-dried matter—strictly business, nothing personal—but of course, he was not telling the truth. Offering contracts with advance money attached (sometimes held against future earnings) was standard industry practice at this point—I will just mention Los Angeles's Buffalo Springfield and San Francisco's Quicksilver Messenger Service as acts that received considerable money up front. But Melcher held steady here under Bugliosi's questioning:

Q. Was Mr. Manson interested in getting money immediately, is that what he told you?

A. Yes.

Q. And you explained to him under the royalty process that it took time to get money, is that correct?

A. Yes.

From here Melcher worked with Bugliosi to establish that every bit of his conversation with Manson was in the form of "general advice"; at no time did he make a promise or offer.[44] It is also worth noting that notwithstanding some problems Doris Day had vis-à-vis her husband Martin Melcher's mismanagement of her money (Martin Melcher died in 1968), Terry Melcher himself did not seem inordinately concerned with resources. John York, who was briefly a member of the Byrds after Chris Hillman left the band, recalls that he "enjoyed working with Terry" but noted that the producer "had this annoying thing of being a guy who didn't have to ever worry about time or money."[45]

Melcher's efforts to distance himself from Manson began right with the Grand Jury that was convened soon after his arrest. Melcher explained that "the type of music they were doing and the whole setting itself" was peculiar for "the pop music business. Melcher then spoke of his friend, Mike Deasy, who had that remote recording unit and planned to "spend a summer traveling around the country trying to record various Indian tribes doing native songs." Melcher recounted telling Deasy that the Family "seemed to be something like an Indian tribe, they sat around and all sang together, and all participated, that perhaps that might be they type of thing he was interested in."[46] The record producer, according to his account, also told Manson about Deasy, promoting the latter as interested in "un-Hollywood or un–New York music, you know, things that came out of the roots of something . . . all the things that the word ethnic implies, you know, is what he was interested in recording."[47]

Melcher's account in court deserves some scrutiny. His fantasy—perhaps inspired by the popularity of *National Geographic* magazine—established a few important premises about Manson and his Family. The most significant claim here, as I have been suggesting, is that his testimony reads Manson *out* of the ranks of professional (or potentially professional) musicians. What the record will show, from this moment forward, is that Manson and his followers might hold some interest as the *object* of a professional musician's interest—in this case, Melcher's friend Mike Deasy—but there was never any chance that they would occupy the subject position. Deasy may have been serious about this mission Melcher described, but Melcher could not help but communicate to Manson that no one in Los Angeles took him seriously as a musician. To Melcher, Manson and the Family were folkloric, an oddity, something that might be colonized and put on display. But Manson was not going to get paid.

The countercultural embrace of Native Americans in this era has been well documented. In 1967 the Human Be-In in San Francisco's Golden Gate Park was advertised as a "Gathering of the Tribes." Many of the participants would clothe themselves in what they understood to be garb associated with Native Americans. The "Indian" connection was made even more explicit by a poster created by Rick Griffin for the event, which advertised the event as a "Pow Wow." Griffin's poster featured an Indian, on horseback, holding a hollow-body (unplugged) electric guitar. Griffin's Indian is silent and picturesque, functioning as a symbol of the tribes being convened in San Francisco. As with the infamous television ad featuring the "crying Indian" Iron Eyes Cody that would debut in 1971, the Native American is a container for white fantasies of silent nobility. In the case of the Gathering of the Tribes, the speaking would be done by all those listed individually around the sides of the poster—Allen Ginsberg, Timothy Leary, and so on. When Terry Melcher went to Spahn to audition the Manson

Family he essentially saw Manson and an undifferentiated mass of women: "There were forty or fifty, it's hard to say exactly, they were everywhere."[48] The Manson Family, the "hippie cult," comes to visibility in Melcher's testimony in much the same way. Melcher admits that they held some interest for him (though this is immediately deflected onto Mike Deasy) as a "tribe" but not as *actors* on the scene.

Terry Melcher's use of "Indian tribe" in connection with the Family also invokes earlier usages—George Catlin's nineteenth-century portraits of "vanishing" Americans, some New Deal photography, and, perhaps most directly, the countless Western movies that had been filmed at Spahn Ranch.

Here is Gay Talese, writing in *Esquire* in 1970, about the ranch:

> The row of empty buildings extending along the dirt road toward Spahn's shack—decaying structures with faded signs marking them as a saloon, a barber shop, a café, a jail, and a carriage house—all were constructed many years ago as Hollywood settings for cowboy brawls and Indian ambushes, and among the many actors who performed in them, or in front of them, were Tom Mix and Johnny Mack Brown, Hoot Gibson, Wallace Beery, and The Cisco Kid.[49]

Spahn Ranch was in terrible shape by the time the Manson Family came to squat there. It was rarely used as a film set anymore and in its latter days was used only for the occasional Marlboro commercial. The ranch also served as backdrop for the softcore Cowboys-and-Indians movie *The Ramrodder*, which was released in 1969 and included appearances by Family member Catherine "Gypsy" Share and Bobby Beausoleil.[50]

Tommy Udo has correctly observed that in just a very few years Charles Manson was able to make "an astonishing number of contacts in the film, music, and entertainment industries."[51] But even more quickly than Manson was able to insinuate himself into the lives of the Los Angeles elite, he was thoroughly expelled—first by the testimony of Terry Melcher at the Grand Jury hearing and then by the aggressive closing of ranks enacted by the same entertainment-industry figures who had taken such pleasure from mixing it up with the Family. Despite the "moral and metaphysical aftershocks" from the murders, Peter Biskind is right to focus on how quickly "Hollywood returned to normal." If the Manson episode represented some kind of "sign," it was a sign that most in Hollywood were "too busy making movies, doing drugs, having sex, and spending money to heed."[52]

Terry Melcher acknowledged at Manson's trial that he knew the suspect and had met him to audition him a number of times (Gregg Jakobson urged him to do this "around 100 times," Melcher says); the producer first tried to claim that he "wasn't really in the recording business very actively at that point. I was, you know, moving into, like a TV sort of area, and I wasn't doing any recording at all." That is not true, of course: after a hiatus of a few years Melcher had returned to work with the Byrds to produce their record *Ballad of Easy Rider*, released in November 1969. Melcher also insisted at Manson's trial and at Tex Watson's trial that he found little merit in Manson's music. When Prosecutor Vincent Bugliosi asked Melcher if he was impressed with Manson's performance, he called Manson's voice "average" and said "I wasn't too impressed by the songs. I was impressed by the whole scene." When Bugliosi asked Melcher to clarify that latter remark, Melcher said straightforwardly "Jesus is there anyone who is not impressed by it?" The judge struck this from the record, but with this final comment Melcher made it clear that he liked *something* besides the music out at Spahn Ranch.[53]

The crisis of his association with the Manson Family seems to have stayed with Terry Melcher well up through the 1970s and left clear traces on the two solo records he released in that decade. In 1970, when Melcher testified at the main Manson Family trial, he used the opportunity of appearing as a witness—a reluctant witness, to be sure—not only to disentangle himself from the "hippie cult" but also to create space between himself and the other two Golden Penetrators, Dennis Wilson and Gregg Jakobson. In 1970

Melcher would not even acknowledge the reality of his relationship with the Beach Boy. Bugliosi tried to explore this with Melcher:

Q. You are a friend of Mr. Wilson?
A. I have known him for about ten years.

Q. Okay. Have you had any business association with him?
A. No.[54]

By 1971, at the Tex Watson trial, Melcher seems to have loosened up somewhat and was singing quite a different song. During this appearance, when Bugliosi asks Melcher where he met Manson he responds "At the home of a friend of mine named Dennis Wilson." Bugliosi follows up to clarify Wilson's identity ("Is Dennis Wilson a drummer for the Beach Boys recording group?") and asks whether he is a friend of Melcher: "He has been for a long, long time."[55]

Melcher was much more equivocal when it came to defining his relationship to Gregg Jakobson; Jakobson was, essentially, being set up to take the hit for the Golden Penetrators. On some level this seems to reflect his greater intimacy with Manson and the rest of the Family, but there is also a status issue here. Jakobson did not have the same small-f family status Melcher accessed through his mother and Wilson enjoyed with his brothers to protect him from the creepy stain of the Family. In his testimony, Melcher seems to have steadily pushed Jakobson out of his inner circle. In his Grand Jury testimony Melcher referred to a "friend of mine named Gregg Jakobson, who at one time had worked for me . . . in the capacity as a talent scout."[56] At the actual trial of Manson, Melcher first responded to Vincent Bugliosi's question about his relationship with Jakobson by saying, "We have a lot of mutual acquaintances; and I think for about one year he worked for me as some sort of, I guess, talent scout, you might call it, looking for songwriters or recording groups and the like."[57] On cross-examination by Paul Fitzgerald, Melcher acknowledged Jakobson as also a "close personal friend."[58] By 1971, Jakobson is demoted in Melcher's testimony; now he is characterized by the producer as having been "in my employ as a talent scout . . . although he wasn't in my employ at the time . . . he took me to Spahn Ranch." As Melcher was presenting things, when it came to engaging with Manson, Jakobson was freelancing.[59]

Jakobson did not simply consent to Melcher's denial of him. At the trial, Jakobson claimed, in response to a prompt from Bugliosi, that he worked consistently for Melcher: "My title was . . . vice-president," Jakobson claimed. When Bugliosi asked for clarification ("vice-president in charge of talent"?) Jakobson explained that there was no additional title—just "vice-president": "I was the only one at the time."[60] While there is more than a little pathos in Jakobson's failed attempt at self-aggrandizement (he seems to have been "Gregg Jakobson, Vice-President of the Golden Penetrators") Jakobson did successfully establish that if he was going to be able to act as the representative of the Los Angeles musical elite it was because he was so centrally positioned—whatever his title—in the arena of music production. Jakobson's testimony at the 1970 Manson et al. trial and at Tex Watson's 1971 trial at once put Manson at the heart of Los Angeles's musical and social life in the last two years of the 1960s while also underscoring that Manson was of interest as raw material and not finished product. Jakobson, according to his own account, found the Family to be something along the lines of "scenic." Jakobson acknowledged that he spent quite a bit of time in recording studios with Manson and says plainly that Manson wrote the song that would become the Beach Boys' "Never Learn Not to Love." But he emphasized above all that he was trying to drum up interest in making a documentary film about the Family. Jakobson created a setting for the anthropological possibilities suggested by Melcher's testimony, explaining that often when he was at Spahn Ranch, he thought of how "nice" it would be for the film: "I stood there on the field out in the back of the ranch with the motorcycles and the girls and the guys and the horses and the trucks and the brown grass and the green trees and the blue sky and the stream would have made a very nice picture for other people to see."[61] Jakobson imagined that with the Family as subject he could midwife a rebirth of Spahn Ranch ("Spahn's Ranch" as the Family seems to have referred to it) as a working film set. This did not happen: the Ranch burned down in 1970.

Family Affairs

The Manson murders were some kind of catastrophe for musical Los Angeles and the New Hollywood. Of course there was the personal pain: the loss of Sharon Tate for her husband and her friends in the film and music industries; Terry Melcher's deep psychological misery; and John Phillips's having to feel a little uncomfortable around Roman Polanski for a little while. But the popular rhetoric surrounding the Manson case suggests another order of magnitude altogether. It regularly (still) causes observers to make the most remarkable claims about its impact. Greil Marcus is always a trustworthy source of hyperbole and he does not disappoint here: "The specter of the Manson slaughter hung over every Hollywood icon, hanger-on, or rock 'n' roll musician, as if it were L.A.'s Vietnam."[1] Leaving aside the "every" as too easy of a target to go after, what can we make of Marcus's claim that this was "L.A.'s Vietnam"? Presumably Marcus's equation is "Manson is to Los Angeles as the American war in Vietnam is to the people of Vietnam" and that, of course, will not do. The Manson murders did have a profound impact on the music and film communities in and around Los Angeles but it is important to resist the sort of mystifications offered by Greil Marcus and Van Dyke Parks, the important Los Angeles music figure and Beach Boys' collaborator who has argued that the 1969 murders somehow represented a "collective sin" and led to a necessary reevaluation of the "idealism that had gotten us to this point."[2] This is an interesting claim to parse: if "this point" refers to murders of well-off, glamorous, Hollywood figures, by people who had very much been in their orbit for the past year or so, then the "idealism" Van Dyke Parks is throwing under the bus is really just the short-term open-door policy of rich people who decided for a brief time that it would be fun to let the freaks in.

John and Michelle Phillips hosted an infamous New Year's Eve party at their Bel Air mansion as 1967 became 1968. By some accounts (including Michelle Phillips's own), nine hundred people showed up, and Ed Sanders says that Charles Manson was one of them; John Phillips himself has crowed that he and Michelle invited all of their "Hollywood friends, plus the cast of the new L.A. production of *Hair*."[3] Here we find a wonderful snapshot of what Tex Watson called "phony Hollywood hippies" (the Mamas and the Papas and their "Hollywood friends") meeting up with "hippies" from the musical stage—many of whom, according to a thrilled John Phillips, came in costume (i.e., naked). *Hair* had opened on Broadway in the spring of 1968 and in Los Angeles that fall. It represents one more relatively significant piece of evidence as to how easily mainstream institutions of popular culture—in this case Broadway and the Los Angeles music industry—incorporated the social challenges of the counterculture.

The musical of *Hair* itself made a major splash—as antiwar statement and as engine of pop hits. Most significant by far was the 1969 medley of "Aquarius/Let the Sunshine In" released by the 5th Dimension—a Black pop vocal group who first charted in 1967 with a cover of the Mamas and the Papas "Go Where You Wanna Go." The 5th Dimension was thoroughly a product of the Los Angeles professional music scene, signed to Johnny Rivers's Soul City label and produced by Bones Howe (who had engineered many of the major hits released by the Mamas and the Papas); these records featured the contributions of the Wrecking Crew, including Terry Melcher's friend Mike Deasy, who played guitar on a number of the 5th Dimension albums.[4]

The album packaging continued the process of muting whatever social protest might have been built into the original performance of the song onstage. If the song contained a list of a few hints of antiwar (well, pro-peace at any rate) sentiment, the

5th Dimension LP package turns the whole proposition into a matter of goofy style and astrology. Photographs of each of the five singers dominate the inside of the gatefold LP package. The astrological sign of each is given (both women, Marilyn McCoo and Florence LaRue, are actually Aquarians!) and the fashion choices range from Carnaby Street-on-a-very-light-dose-of-acid for the women to sophisticated Player (Ron Townson has a pipe.) for the men. Art director Ron Wolin very carefully deploys elements of psychedelic visual arts—multicolored letters in the title, kaleidoscope effects—without tipping into the overtly trippy.[5]

This is a long way from the purposefully chaotic inner gatefold of Frank Zappa's *Freak Out!* Zappa's liner notes encourage his (implicitly male) readers and listeners to consider how they can join his movement and become "emancipated from our national social slavery"; the 5th Dimension record, from the glamorous wardrobe and beatific smiles on the faces of the singers, to the information for the group's "International Fan Club," suggests a clear demarcation between performers and audiences. While Charles Manson may have put feelers out to Zappa's Laurel Canyon scene through Bobby Beausoleil, it was the much straighter musical world of the Mamas and the Papas and the 5th Dimension to which he aspired and energetically attempted to crash. The world of Mike Deasy and Bones Howe overlapped with John Phillips, Terry Melcher, and Dennis Wilson (and Dennis Hopper): this was a social milieu defined by professional class allegiance. Critics and historians are correct to note that the Tate-LaBianca murders shook up this population of people working in the music and film industries—but the events of August 1969 and the ensuing trials did not add up to "Vietnam." The landscape was not devastated, the murders were not mass, the people were not terrorized. The days of the nine-hundred-guest New Year's Eve party (freaks welcome!) might have come to an end, but business was, more or less, as usual.

The most obvious immediate effect of the Manson murders—after the bolts were locked, the bodyguards hired, and the guns bought—is that the elite of Hollywood and Los Angeles's music industry came to a fuller understanding of themselves as socially distinct from Vito Paulekas, from the girls who the Mamas and the Papas sang about in "Twelve Thirty (Young Girls Are Coming to the Canyon)" in 1967, from Charles Manson and the Family. Those girls who were so appealing in 1967—the narrators of the Mamas and Papas' song, trained in East Coast reserve and repression, still cannot help but interact with them—are invisible to the singer of "Our House" who can only see one woman and is driven to beseech her to play her music all through the night—but only for him. The secure private home has replaced the dream of porous boundaries. The freaks have been sent on their way.

There is a fabulously campy 1971 movie, *The Love-Thrill Murders,* inspired by the Manson Family murders, which includes an orgy scene during which the freaks turn on the straights: "You had fun with us freaks," one of them says, "now it's our turn." This is paranoid pulp cinema, of course (and its central message has been repeated ad nauseum from the day after the Tate murders to our own time, pretty much). But it is only separated from the analysis of Joan Didion and Greil Marcus by its mode of address. While Charles Manson seems briefly to have held Dennis Wilson and Gregg Jakobson (and maybe Terry Melcher) in his thrall, he was never able to develop the sustained power that he craved and that Mel Lyman enjoyed in the Fort Hill commune in Boston and that Father Yod developed in Los Angeles and then Hawaii. Some—including Peter Maas in a 1970 *Ladies Home Journal* article—claimed that Manson recognized that music had failed him as a route to power: "How are you going to get the establishment?" Maas claims Manson said. "You can't sing to them. I tried that."[6]

It is worth noting here that Charles Manson is undoubtedly using "establishment" here to refer to people like Terry Melcher and Dennis Wilson, powerful figures in the music world of Los Angeles who may have enjoyed the frisson of danger or wildness provided by Manson and the Family, but who had no compunction about expelling them from the Garden. In public, especially at the trials, Terry Melcher claimed that he did not particularly take note of social differences separating various populations in Los Angeles. This became especially clear during Tex Watson's trial, when defense lawyer Maxwell Keith asked Melcher to try to describe what impression Watson made on him when they first met, in 1968: "Do you remember anything about his physical appearance . . . ? Did he look like a hippie or did he look straight?" To this direct question Melcher acknowledged that if he "had to choose between his having appeared as a hippie or as a straight, as you put it, I would say a hippie." Melcher went on to confirm that Watson's hair was long—about as long as Melcher's, and that he wore blue jeans ("I presume so. That's what most young people wear."). Keith goes on to ascertain that Watson was certainly not wearing a business suit, but that Melcher "wouldn't classify him as a hippie," just because "he didn't wear a coat and tie." To this Melcher tried to open a little rhetorical space by arguing, "I don't classify anybody as a hippie, sir." This line of questioning trailed off before Melcher could say whether he considered himself a straight or a hippie, with the music producer attempting, once more, to claim, "I don't know how to classify."[7]

But Terry Melcher knew how to classify: he knew that he was not a hippie himself. Ed Sanders correctly notes that Manson had focused on the children of famous people in Los Angeles "in order to scarf up free credit cards, money, hospitality, fame-grope, connections and most important, acceptance and adulation." Sanders also noted that these "children or relatives of entertainment personalities . . . often form close associations with one another."[8] These children—the son of Doris Day, the daughters of Dean Martin, Edgar Bergen, Angela Lansbury, and Lou Costello, and so on—may have done some drugs and consorted with some figures from the margins, but they ultimately were able to close the curtain when they chose. The Family, as Manson himself so eloquently put it at his trial, was populated by "people you did not want, people that were alongside the road, that their parents did not want."[9] Terry Melcher and Dennis Wilson are the powerful couple at the center of this experiment in social interaction—the

Daisy and Tom Buchanan of *The Great Manson*: "They were care-less people . . . they smashed up things and creatures and then retreated back to their money or their vast carelessness . . . and let other people clean up the mess they had made." Their behavior in relation to the Manson Family underscores that Maxwell Keith was on the right track when he enlisted Terry Melcher to help him draw the line between "straights" and "hippies." In late-1960s Los Angeles living as a "rich hippie" may not have been strictly impossible, but it was a tough act to pull off consistently. And Melcher and Wilson were certainly happy to have others clean up their mess—Melcher with his dumping of his Manson prob-lem onto Gregg Jakobson, and Wilson with the deputizing of his manager to evict Manson and the Family from his Malibu home. Thomas Pynchon captures this moment of rejection efficiently in his Manson-drenched novel *Inherent Vice*, in which his character Doc Sportello says that what he has been "noticing since Charlie Manson got popped is a lot less eye contact from the straight world. You folks all used to be like a crowd at the zoo—'Oh, look, the male one is carrying the baby and the female one is paying for the groceries,' sorta thing, but now it's like, 'Pretend they're not even there, 'cause maybe they'll mass murder our ass.'"[10]

John Phillips's first solo record, *John, the Wolfking of L.A.*, was one of the first major pieces of Los Angeles art to enact that desire for distance from such marginal figures as the men and women who constituted the Manson Family. As product, Phillips's record represents a sort of muscle-flexing of Los Angeles musical power—produced by Lou Adler, it features not only the usual suspects (members of the Wrecking Crew) but also Elvis Presley's guitarist, James Burton. The record does not shy from hard tales—"Topanga" is a sketch of the ravages of Phillips's drug addiction—but makes its impact, above all, as a bit of reportage from Los Angeles's musical aristocracy: the entire record is keyed, unironically, around the the idea that the elite of Malibu have got life pretty much all figured out.

The musical palette is organized to communicate "sincerity." This effect is accomplished mostly through the regular deployment of gospel-style piano (Larry Knechtel of the Wrecking Crew) and background vocals (Darlene Love, Jean King and Fanita James) and two different steel-guitar players—Buddy Emmons, the premier steel player of the post–World War II Nashville music scene, and Red Rhodes, a Los Angeles mainstay. That "sincerity" is used to frame not only the love stories ("April Anne," "Someone's Sleeping") but also one tale ("Drums") about the people who stole a set of thirty-dollar Blackbird drums from the singer's car. The singer is flabbergasted—though an earlier song found the narrator going up to Topanga to meet his own dealer—that such people exist. He makes a point of suggesting that the thieves (does he have film of the robbery?) have converted musical instruments into injectable drugs. The emotional distance between the troubled protagonist of "Topanga" and the belittled drug users of "Drums" neatly encapsulates the us-and-them dynamics of post-arrest Los Angeles.

Terry Melcher did not make his own debut solo album until 1974, but he did get involved with another "family" almost immediately after his experience with the Manson group. In 1970 Melcher brokered an agreement between John Phillips and Sly Stone (of Sly and the Family Stone) to have Stone move into the Bel Air mansion that Phillips and his wife Michelle had previously lived in. Stone was particularly happy to have a house with a recording studio built in. He was beginning work on the record that would, in 1971, be released with the title *There's a Riot Goin' On*. Embodying the more general retreat from the communal and collective, Stone's work at this time was done independently, largely through overdubbing; the fierce and passionate group work of Sly and the Family Stone (narrated in its own 1968 hit "Dance to the Music") is here replaced by layer after layer of Stone's own voice. (Family saxophone player Jerry Martini has explained that this was the era he called "guns and dogs," going on to note that this was "an insane time. That's when Terry Melcher, Doris Day's son, sleazebag motherfucker, was around . . . very bad person.")[11] There is a privatization in Stone's music in this era that is in keeping with the Los Angeles elite's turn away from the possibilities and dangers of the open-door era.

Two regular guests to the Bel Air house in 1970 and 1971 were Bobby Womack and Jim Ford, both of whom, by most accounts, also played on *Riot*, though the LP has no credits. Ford would later write "Harry Hippie" for Womack, allegedly inspired by stories about Womack's own brother, but important here for how it cruelly dismisses poor hippies. On some level, "Harry Hippie" seems like a dark answer song to the Hollies' 1969 hit, "He Ain't Heavy, He's My Brother." The relatively high diction of the verses of the Hollies' song and its ennobling message is met in "Harry Hippie" by offhanded indifference: Harry Hippie is mostly content to sleep, walk around, and sing to himself, and maybe—in a pinch—sell a few copies of the Los Angeles alternative weekly paper as he makes his way down Sunset Strip. The song's narration (supported by Womack's dig-deep soul vocals and terse guitar lines) appears rational and, in a strange twist, socially responsible. Ultimately "Harry Hippie" prepares listeners to sympathize with the singer's cruel disavowal of Harry: he will not be carried by the narrator. As the song comes to an end, Womack's narrator invites the listeners to join in the cruelty by singing along. In the great gospel and soul tradition the prescribed "response" of the audience is built into the "call" of the singer.

This quick tour of post-Manson, Los Angeles–based works by John Phillips, Sly Stone, and Bobby Womack is meant only to give a brief indication of how the profound creepy crawl performed by the Manson Family was neutralized by a sort of music-industry backlash organized around drawing clear demarcations between the freaks and the hippies on the one hand, and the entertainment-industry elite on the other. Of course this was neither a linear nor a systematic "movement"—there was no manifesto or action plan. The retreat to "Our House" was part of an anxiety-driven and unruly set of cultural assumptions and articulations. There were of course, numerous challenges to the music industry's denial and rejection of the freak, including Steely Dan's remarkably empathetic "Charlie Freak," released on 1974's *Pretzel Logic*—the group's first record to feature major contributions from Los Angeles session musicians (who did their work at Cherokee Studios in Chatsworth, not far from Spahn Ranch). The song's narrator tells the tragic story of a character who dies from an overdose after he sells a gold ring—the only thing he owns of value—in order to get some money to buy drugs. Where the narrator of "Harry Hippie" can barely stand to look at the title character, "Charlie Freak" ends with a communion of sorts. The narrator of the song hears the news and rushes to the morgue to return the ring to Charlie's finger and carry the body to its final resting place.

It is not as if members of various countercultures gave up on "freak": Ed Sanders's multidecade mission to untangle the Manson Family from the Los Angeles counterculture was very much inspired by his displeasure with how "violence was encroaching on the domain of the freak-out."[12] Sanders noticed immediately that mainstream coverage of the Tate-LaBianca murders and the arrests of Manson and the other members of the Family had a distinctly "anticounterculture and antihippie flavor, as if the Mansonites, by their single set of transgressions . . . had been the real funeral of Hippie."[13] The patently "fake freak" language Sanders peppers throughout *The Family* (most frequently "oo-ee-oo") was one tactic the author used to underscore the inauthentic character of the Manson Family's freakdom. Rather than retreat or turn away from the freak, Sanders, covering the trial for the *Free Press*, enacted a freak reclamation project. Likewise, when David Dalton and David Felton incorporated their June 25, 1970, *Rolling Stone* cover story on Manson into a 1972 book they included the phrase "acid fascism" in the subtitle, in an attempt to mark off Manson and his Family from other counterculture radicals and seekers.

Of course "freak" reappeared in full force in American dance music culture beginning in the mid-1970s—now as an index of a vague but clearly celebratory attitude toward insurgent sexualities in disco, funk, and then hip-hop music.[14] The peak year for this reappropriation of "freak" was probably 1978—it brought not only Chic's "Le Freak," but also "freak" songs by Isaac Hayes, Timmy Thomas, the Michael Zager Band, the band Phreek itself, and many others. This wave of freakiness seems to have been kicked off in 1974 when T. K. Records' house band, Miami, released an LP called *Freak Party* (which featured parts 1 and 2 of "Freak Party" as well as "Freak on Down My Way") and when Betty Davis issued her song "He Was a Big Freak," (which features a turquoise whip). There is no one single or simple "freak" story to be reconstructed from the dozens of popular song usages, but their presence helps us resist the doomy end-of-the-sixties rhetoric that has too often accompanied accounts of the Manson Family and its legacies. One obvious point to make here is that Black popular culture seems to have been relatively untouched by the hand-wringing over freakiness that plagued white Americans in the wake of the the Family arrests and trials.

Nile Rodgers of Chic has written passionately about disco utopianism as an improvement on hippie expressive culture. Here he describes a friend and her dance partners: "Karen and her stylish comrades all danced their curvy asses off. For them, the movement, in every sense of the word, was as open and communal as the forces driving the hippies of my youth. . . . I'd say they were even more expressive, political, and communal than the hippies before them, because they bonded through their bodies, through dance."[15] Rodgers is perhaps overstating the radical break represented by the disco dancers and ignores their roots in the freak dancing of Vito Paulekas and his troupe. Nonetheless, his claim is a good reminder of how powerful the dance floor "freak out" remained even in the late 1970s. The Family's creepy crawl over and through Los Angeles was real and had a major impact on the film and music cultures of its time and place, but it did not put some kind of definitive and magical punctuation mark on the "sixties." The summer of 1969 was the summer of the Tate-LaBianca murders, but it was also the summer of the Stonewall Riots in New York. A retreat from "freak" culture by a Papa, a Beach Boy and the son of Doris Day did not spell the end of the counterculture, the sixties, or anything, really.

Perhaps it was true that after the murders you could hear bolts locking into place and Stephen Stills running around shrieking in Laurel Canyon. Terry Melcher had not even lived in Laurel

Canyon, of course; Cielo Drive was in Benedict Canyon. But battle lines were being drawn all over Los Angeles and not just in the canyons. The promise of the idyllic private home (a backlash surely against the communal innovations of the 1960s, already parodied in 1969's *Easy Rider*'s "simple food for our simple taste" commune scene) would appear, briefly, as a remedy for the social chaos thrown into stark relief by the Manson case. It would take a few years for the powerful people at the center of Los Angeles's culture industries to hit the reset button that would allow them to retreat back into the comforts of their privileged social, economic, and domestic arrangements. It is telling, and still a little bit surprising, that the single most important actor in this process was Vincent Bugliosi, whose true-crime book *Helter Skelter* was at the center of a far-reaching cultural conversation held in the 1970s about criminality, families, artistic ability, sexuality, drugs, and so much more.

*

Part III

Creepy Crawling Truth: Charles Manson and Our Crime Tales

*

The Bug vs. the Fug

In 1988, the Irish rock band U2 opened their double-live LP and film *Rattle and Hum* with a version of "Helter Skelter." Introducing the song to the crowd, the band's ever-understated lead singer Bono announced, "This is a song Charles Manson stole from the Beatles. We're stealing it back." The claim here is simple and clear and more than a little misleading. Charles Manson never "owned" the brand on Helter Skelter; prosecutor Vincent Bugliosi (known to the Family as "the Bug") has cornered that market ever since he obtained convictions of Manson, Leslie Van Houten, Patricia Krenwinkel, and Susan Atkins in 1971. Helter Skelter was the motive Bugliosi insisted upon at the trial even though—as he has explained numerous times in numerous venues—prosecutors do not even have to prove motive, they only have to demonstrate beyond any reasonable doubt that the person charged with a particular crime in fact was responsible for that offense.

In legal terms, as numerous observers have pointed out, Helter Skelter was gravy: Bugliosi did not need to prove motive to obtain convictions. Much more important is how Helter Skelter has become a cultural and economic phenomenon—the cornerstone of Vincent Bugliosi's true-crime empire. U2's Bono may have thought he was taking aim at big game on *Rattle and Hum*, but really he missed the target completely. To be sure, Charles Manson was obsessed with the Beatles' 1969 double album as a whole and the song "Helter Skelter" in particular. He did, according to all credible testimony, project a wide range of disorganized but fiercely held beliefs onto this shambling collection of songs. To put it in the psychological vernacular, when Manson put on the White Album, he "heard voices." Manson thought the Beatles were communicating directly with him and that belief, of course, might be taken as a sign (one among many) that he was mentally ill. It is standard in the study of popular music to assume that artists are not in complete control of the meanings of their work: "what if rock stars don't know what their own songs are about?" is how music critic Rob Sheffield has recently made this challenge.[1] The marginalization of Manson's reading of the White Album has been shaped by a prosecutor who had a whole lot riding on making Manson's basic approach to music fandom appear insane. But critics and historians of our own time have successfully argued with Bugliosi's dismissal of Manson as a listener. The literary critic Michael André Bernstein rejects Manson's approach to the White Album as a "paranoiac over-interpretation of a few lyrics," but I prefer the argument of another literary critic, Nicholas Bromell, who has slyly suggested that what Manson heard in this album was "what every attentive Beatles fan found there: a message, an authorization, an affirmation of one's understanding of the '60s."[2] (I should also note that Manson was not the only one to torture hidden meanings out of the White Album; "Revolution 9," with its putative secret message—"Turn me on, dead man"—is, of course, the locus classicus for the idea that playing a record backwards would reveal dark secrets. "Manson was insane," Bromell concludes, but "he was also representative.")

Devin McKinney has taken this approach even further, suggesting that there is nothing delusional about the broad contours of Manson's reading of the White Album. As McKinney puts it, the White Album "is also a Black album: haunted by race." Trying to put the record back in the actual context of its making, McKinney provocatively claims that "Black rage and Black music are in the air these songs breathe." McKinney refuses the simple corrective claim that the song "Helter Skelter" itself was about a big slide; the performance of it—the "chainsaw" guitars and hysterical vocal—index an anarchic cultural moment.[3]

Perhaps a more efficient way of getting at the argument I am trying to hint at here is to describe a picture Family member Leslie Van Houten drew of the jury during her trial. I am not interested in the art so much as the caption, which read "All the Lonely People Judgment."[4] Van Houten here was applying what she had learned from the Beatles' 1966 song "Eleanor Rigby" in a manner that many in the surrounding culture would have considered measured and appropriate. She is expressing something like sympathy for what she imagines to be the barren lives of the jury members—even as she creepy crawls them a bit by labeling each figure by name.

The Manson Family's attraction to the Beatles was a completely conventional stance. But Deputy District Attorney Bugliosi, coming into the Manson trial with a 103–1 record in felony jury trials (by his own accounting in *Helter Skelter*, the book), needed to construct a Manson who was exceptional—not representative. Bugliosi did just this at Manson's carnival of a trial in 1970. But this was just a start; Bugliosi never took very long breaks from acting as hype man for Manson. And Manson never stopped being willing to participate in Bugliosi's plotting of his role. He, like Norma Desmond, the main character of *Sunset Boulevard*, is pretty much always ready for his close-up.

Manson's conviction for his role in the Tate-LaBianca murders was delivered in early 1971. Over the next five years or so Bugliosi continued to prosecute him—in public appearances, documentary films, and most significant by far, in the book and televised versions of *Helter Skelter*. These two immensely appealing texts promoted a "true" crime narrative which suggested that the horrifying threat of Manson and his Family had been contained—mostly by the good work of an energetic prosecutor and (some) police officers. That is what *Helter Skelter* is *about*—the narrating of Bugliosi's victory over Manson; but it *does* something much different. Because Bugliosi is so interested in demonstrating just what a big thing it is he accomplished, he cannot help but depict Manson as embodying as much bad stuff as he could bring to mind. As scholar Jean Murley has smartly pointed out,

Bugliosi and Gentry structure this book so that its multiple story lines would be sure to "attract and repel" numerous distinct audiences. There is red meat here for law-and-order types and for countercultural insurgents to chew on, compelling stories for frightened parents and questing youth.[5] Bugliosi's desire to turn the Tate-LaBianca murders into the *most* bizarre crime ever, to have Manson stand as the *worst* bogeyman of all time means that he cannot really offer readers anything like closure in *Helter Skelter*. The legal process has ended, but (as we can now see) Manson and the Family creepy crawled right off these pages and continued rearranging American furniture. In memoirs and manifestos, televised interviews and publicity stunts, the Family has always performed as formidable cultural actors. Bugliosi certainly never seemed to mind not having the stage to himself, as long as he kept getting called to relitigate the case on television news every August. Putting Manson in jail was one thing, but it is in *Helter Skelter* that Bugliosi did his much more significant cultural work (with major assists from Ed Sanders and too many others to name): he turned Manson into a celebrity whose popularity would never really dim.

The main thrust of the Helter Skelter story organized and circulated by Bugliosi is familiar and requires only the briefest summary. After all, *Helter Skelter*, co-written by Bugliosi and Curt Gentry, is generally credited as being the best-selling true-crime book in publishing history. The title of the book, as Jean Murley has explained, has essentially become synonymous with "Manson phenomenon." Murley also very helpfully summarizes that it was Bugliosi's book (along with the television miniseries developed from it) that converted Charles Manson from being a person into the "personality" he has remained since then. Reviving old ideas about the demonic nature of criminals, Bugliosi energetically embraced the possibilities offered by true crime to turn a criminal into a celebrity.[6]

According to Bugliosi's book, Manson was motivated by his belief that an apocalyptic race war was imminent. This end-of-days conflict would nearly destroy the white population, but the victorious Black population would find that they did not know how to run things, and would come looking for Manson (squirreled away in the desert) to take over the reins of power. The wheel of history turned too slowly and Manson grew impatient; he began to wonder if African Americans would ever take the violent initiative that he had predicted. Thus, he ordered his followers to commit the murders in the hopes that a well-placed hint or two (most notably Rosemary LaBianca's wallet being placed in the toilet tank of a gas station in what Manson thought was a Black neighborhood) would be a sufficient catalyst for hostilities to break out. At the second crime scene, the LaBianca house in Los Feliz, Family member Patricia Krenwinkel even wrote the name of the plan ("Healter Skelter" in her slight misspelling) in blood on the refrigerator. Gregg Jakobson and others offered clear testimony in 1970 that Helter Skelter was an important part of Manson's worldview. But it was Vincent Bugliosi who insisted at the trial and in the larger cultural arenas he operated in that Helter Skelter was the Family's engine, its ultimate reason for being, its alpha and omega.

How can we understand Vincent Bugliosi's success at selling *Helter Skelter* as motive, book, career? This work of understanding his cultural victory requires a few parallel inquiries, all set in the years from 1969 (the murders, the arrests, the Grand Jury) through 1976 (the airing of the miniseries). The first task is to offer a quick overview of how Vincent Bugliosi literally prosecuted Helter Skelter. Here we will need to pay special attention to how Bugliosi, Curt Gentry, and the makers of the televised version of the book shaped the case into the now-familiar form of "true crime." John Harrison has aptly called Charles Manson "paperback's first true crime hero," arguing that Manson could "be considered the catalyst" for the "thriving market for true crime paperbacks" on the contemporary scene.[7] Vincent Bugliosi's construction of himself as a trustworthy representative of the straight world—as a modern folk hero of sorts—will be at the heart of my investigation of *Helter Skelter*. But I also want to give the proper attention to the context Bugliosi's rhetorical victory was set in.

Bugliosi was, for instance, in dialogue with Ed Sanders, author of *The Family* (published in three editions from 1971 to 2002) who first covered the Manson affair for the *Los Angeles Free Press*.

Ed Sanders, the radical poet, member of the countercultural rock group the Fugs, and founder of the journal *Fuck You*, has been shadowing Bugliosi from almost the moment that the deputy district attorney was assigned to the case. It is too one-dimensional to suggest that Sanders has acted as the countercultural foil to Bugliosi's straight man, but from his early *Free Press* work in 1970 to his most recent writings on the case, Sanders has refused the crazy math of Helter Skelter in favor of a much more richly contextualized analysis of the case.

Sanders has nothing like Bugliosi's reach, but his work in the Freep (as the *Los Angeles Free Press* was commonly called), in *The Family*, and elsewhere serves as an important reminder that the dominance of Bugliosi's *Helter Skelter* should not deceive us into thinking that the prosecutor's work has gone unchallenged. So, while the "true crime" accomplishment of Bugliosi's efforts in the courtroom, in his book, and in the miniseries will be carefully investigated, Helter Skelter needs to be returned to its original setting. Ed Sanders's challenges to Bugliosi will sit at the center of this exploration, but I want to reintroduce the multiple voices angling to be heard in the aftermath of Manson's arrest and the trials of the Family. From "legitimate" journalists to representatives of the underground press, to pulp writers and B-movie producers, to members of the Family itself, there is a dense thicket of claims about Manson and his followers that need to be considered. Helter Skelter was—and remains—a claim, a proposition, a hypothesis. As a basic explanatory template Helter Skelter has, of course, won the day, even as it has been challenged by Sanders, Family members, and various scholars and journalists. The remaining work is to figure out how this victory was accomplished and what competing narratives it elbowed out of the cultural and political marketplace. And ultimately, we need to begin to understand why Bugliosi's triumph has ultimately *not* been successful in shutting down the creepy crawl that Manson and his followers have enacted and inspired from 1969 down to our own time.

The installation of Helter Skelter as "true" by Vincent Bugliosi and his supporters has helped to shape not only the contours of nonfiction crime writing, but larger discussions of the counterculture of the late 1960s and early 1970s. Helter Skelter, as prosecutorial narrative, as "true crime" book, and as television miniseries, has continued to exert remarkable power in cultural conversations about marginality, murder, and collective guilt. While "true crime" can seem to promise straightforward solutions to complex problems ("placing a boundary around something knowable," as Jean Murley puts it),[8] *Helter Skelter* offers some compelling evidence for how this hybrid form—an innovative mix of police procedural, courtroom drama, and popular sociology—not to mention amateur musicology—can disturb certainties even as it can organize chaos. Murley has made a good case that *Helter Skelter* is the book that "bestowed autonomous genre-status" on true crime.[9] But what this means may not be as straightforward as it first appears. I am thinking here of cultural critic Mark Seltzer's maxim that "true crime" is "crime fact that looks like crime fiction."[10] Modern true crime, as Jean Murley explains, also tends to offer up copious detail on the "contexts of murder, simultaneous distancing from and identification with the killer, four-part narrative structure of crime-backgrounds-trial-puishment, the creation of narrative tension and interest . . . a narrator insider . . . and an overriding sense of the inevitability of evil."[11]

Crime fiction can take many different forms, but the important role models for Bugliosi come from nineteenth-century "mysteries of the city"—those delectably dirty novels of urban underworlds filled with constant violence and hot, weird sex. *Helter Skelter* might have helped to "dignify" true crime as a mainstream proposition, but that does not mean that it bypasses the pleasures of perversity built into precursor forms. The purple prose of Bugliosi and Gentry comes from the nineteenth-century Gothic as does the book's sense of untamed, inherent evil and its opposite number, upstanding righteousness. Murley has made a compelling case that a large proportion of the most significant American true crime books from the mid-1960s through the 1970s were sited in the West. The mysteries of the city were rewritten as tales of the West, and a huge number of social anxieties about life in that region were processed in this genre of books that pretended to be about just the facts.[12] But as literary scholars long ago recognized about the Gothic novels of the nineteenth century, part of the fun for readers is being given the opportunity to immerse themselves in a world that, supposedly, has nothing in common with their own lives. Fears about cults, communes, youth experimentation with drugs and sex could be delightfully entertained in the pages of *Helter Skelter* and then safely sequestered as the evildoers are locked up in the back end of the true crime book. *Helter Skelter*, as Jean Murley has rightly explained, mostly serves a function that might be summarized as "I told you so." But that disciplinary conclusion is not achieved before Bugliosi indulges plenty of his readers' worst nightmares or fondest fantasies.[13]

It is very difficult to communicate how imperfectly the usual words ("trial," say, or "testimony") fit the proceedings that traveled under the name *The People of the State of California vs. Charles Manson, Susan Atkins, Leslie Van Houten, Patricia Krenwinkel*. While Manson himself is usually rightfully plotted at the center of the carnival of events in Judge Older's courtroom, we must also consider the truly astounding role played by Manson's lawyer Irving Kanarek. The byzantine set of courtroom activity that essentially stripped Manson of his right to defend himself is outside of my concerns here, but it should be noted that Kanarek was not exactly Manson's first choice.[14] "Dilatory" is the adjective that Bugliosi uses in *Helter Skelter* to try to indicate what he had heard about Kanarek before the Manson trial. But even a cursory reading of the trial record makes it clear that "dilatory" suggests a methodology at once too passive and too organized to capture Kanarek's approach. The number and nature of Kanarek's objections are legion: "[T]he prejudicial value far outweighs the probative value" was just the chorus of an epic ballad of sidebars,

requests for mistrial, stalling tactics, and other verbal challenges thrown up by the remarkably inventive lawyer. That Bugliosi was able to fashion something like a coherent case over the nine-and-a-half-month-long trial is a testament to the deputy district attorney's focus and patience. Kanarek was found in contempt of court four times during the trial—the first time for interrupting too much.

By way of illustrating the challenges Kanarek posed to the logical unfolding of Vincent Bugliosi's Helter Skelter script, let me introduce Linda Kasabian, a one-time Family member who turned state's evidence in exchange for immunity. After Susan Atkins renounced her Grand Jury testimony (and forfeited the deal she had made with the prosecution to avoid the death penalty), Linda Kasabian became the linchpin of the prosecution's case. While Kasabian had been with the Family for only a brief time, she had been exposed to all the key elements of Charles Manson's racial belief system and was ready to report fully about them under Bugliosi's direction. But on July 27, 1970, before Kasabian could begin testifying (just after the bailiff instructed her to raise her right hand) defense attorney Kanarek was up on his feet with this: "Object, your Honor, on the grounds this witness is incompetent and she is insane."[15] Of course Kanarek was admonished by the judge and the jury was instructed to disregard his comments. The conversation about Kasabian's competence was continued at the bench, with all lawyers and Judge Older conferring. Patricia Krenwinkel's lawyer Paul Fitzgerald summarized defense counsel's objection to Kasabian's appearance: Kasabian, due to her "prolonged illegal use of LSD is a person of unsound mind, is mentally ill, is insane, is unable to differentiate between truth and falsity, right and wrong, good or bad, fantasy and reality."[16]

Kanarek began his cross-examination of Linda Kasabian with the (seemingly genuine) suggestion that she have sodium pentothal administered to her in the hopes that this would ensure that she tell the truth. From here Kanarek's main tactic in impugning Kasabian's sanity and veracity was to question her at length about her LSD use. In the fog thrown up by the defense attorney

in his attempt to use Kasabian's approximately fifty admitted LSD trips to undercut her reliability, Kanarek outdid himself with this: "Well, will you tell us what did you think of, say, on your 23rd trip?"[17] Kasabian, of course, could not answer; she did promise to try to remember as the trial continued.

In the book *Helter Skelter*, Bugliosi skates over the extreme difficulty he had producing the central narrative he was intent on constructing. While Helter Skelter in its basic vernacular meaning and in the Manson application signifies wild chaos, Bugliosi is intent on reproducing the unfolding of the prosecution's case as logical, coherent, and clear. In *Helter Skelter*, Bugliosi gives little detailed information about Kasabian's testimony. Admitting that he moved as quickly as possible through the orgy issue, Bugliosi explains that he turned to other matters: "Helter Skelter, the black-white war, Manson's belief that the Beatles were communicating with him through the lyrics of their songs, his announcement, late on the afternoon of August 8, 1969, that 'Now is the time for Helter Skelter.'"[18] The prosecutor introduced the race-war motive in his opening statement and managed to have a number of key witnesses—Kasabian and talent scout Gregg Jakobson perhaps most powerfully—attest to its centrality in Manson's philosophy. Gregg Jakobson, as always during the trial, was more than willing to acknowledge his own intimacy with Manson and his deep knowledge about Manson's motives. Jakobson testified that Manson believed in an "imminent" race war and recounted Manson's acknowledgment that he needed to help to set off the Helter Skelter cascade. Additionally, as Jakobson explained, African Americans would emerge victorious from this cataclysmic conflict but would prove unable to lead their own new society and would come find Manson and the Family in the desert and beg the cult leader to take the reins. Jakobson also offered testimony with respect to Manson's faith that the Beatles were "prophets and they were prophesying Helter Skelter. . . . They were the leaders of the movement."[19] At the trial Bugliosi took incredible care to parse the lyrics of the White Album with Jakobson's help. Bugliosi has argued in numerous venues that he knew that he needed to find

a "crazy" motive to explain these crazy crimes. With the help of Jakobson and a few other witnesses, Bugliosi was able, ultimately, to tell a "true" story to the jury—about rock and roll, an apocalyptic battle, and mind control—which turned out to be more compelling than other motives floating around, most notably the initially dominant "revenge on Terry Melcher" and the truly compelling Bobby Beausoleil–inspired "love of brother" explanations.

These other two alternative explanatory frameworks have had major support from the time of the crimes onward, but they bring with them much less occasion for larger social investigation and critique than does the Helter Skelter motive. In other words, to make a case that Manson ordered the killings at Cielo and Waverly Drives because he was angry at Terry Melcher for refusing to sign him to a record contract would have required an accompanying portrait of Manson as weak, untalented, pathetic, and narcissistic: one more Los Angeles failure. The "love of brother" Beausoleil narrative is organized around a sense of Manson and the Family as, above all else, a criminal enterprise—tied up with biker gangs and petty "business" matters. This motive builds on a sense of Manson as "institutionalized," unable to make it in the straight world and comfortable only around other lawbreakers. Neither alternative motive would have easily opened up on to the broader social questions Bugliosi wanted to litigate, nor would they allow Bugliosi to create a sense of Manson as a frightening bogeyman. (It is the latter achievement, by the way, that Bugliosi has relitigated repeatedly since the trial ended. In an afterword to the twenty-fifth anniversary edition of *Helter Skelter* for instance, Bugliosi more or less rejects the notion that the trial carried any major social weight. Rather than join the Didionesque "end of the '60s" camp, Bugliosi encourages his readers to understand our continuing obsession with Manson as simply a cut-and-dried product of the fact that this was "the most bizarre mass murder case in the recorded annals of crime" and "people are magnetically fascinated by things that are strange and bizarre." Good lawyer, bad historian.)[20]

The Helter Skelter scenario opened up an impressive array of questions about American political, social, and cultural life in the moment. Of course Vincent Bugliosi was stitching together the explanatory power of Helter Skelter not to endorse Charles Manson's worldview, but to contribute to a picture of a criminal who had no grip on reality. Just as Terry Melcher and Gregg Jakobson's testimony about Manson's musical ability would ultimately support a characterization of him as unable to understand the difference between his social interactions with music-industry figures and his actual talent and prospects, so too did the information provided by Jakobson, Linda Kasabian, and others about Manson's phantasmagorical Helter Skelter script paint the defendant as woefully unable to "read" the world around him. When Manson told the court "I don't read or write real good and I've stayed like a little kid," he likely thought he was mobilizing sympathy for his case. But it was just this inability to "read" that Bugliosi would use as evidence that Manson was not able to make his way as a rational actor in the complex world of making meaning.[21]

Bugliosi's story of racial strife discredited not only Manson and the Family, but also the increasingly radical action of the Black Panthers and other insurgent groups. Manson himself had only a tenuous grasp on what a Black Panther was; he did not seem to know who Huey Newton was.[22] But much more important than the cult leader's understanding of the racial landscape was how the prosecutor used this opportunity to tar the entire counterculture. I have already noted that Bobby Beausoleil has argued that Bugliosi's analysis of the case seems to have been a blatant attempt to undercut the political and cultural achievements of the counterculture. Beausoleil was not alone in this belief and was joined by a variety of commentators from late in 1969 through the early 1970s.

As early as 1971 radio personality Mae Brussell was promoting the notion that Manson was a "patsy" for powerful forces looking to blunt the impact of the countercultural insurgency of the 1960s. In our time Brussell would likely be defined (and marginalized) as a conspiracy theorist. Her fondness for magical, meaningful coincidences makes it hard to credit much of what she says. Brussell makes quite a bit, for instance, out of a claim that Lawrence Schiller, the person most responsible for circulating

Susan Atkins's claim that Manson had controlled the minds and actions of his followers, was the same Lawrence Schiller who got Jack Ruby to say that he was acting alone in killing Lee Harvey Oswald. Brussell's real smoking gun in her Manson case, though, is LSD: If Manson was using the drug as his chemical agent of control, she suggests, it is important to ask where the LSD came from. Here Brussell is tapping into a broader argument that many have made about the journey of LSD from government labs to city streets and college campuses. The notion that the government was organized enough to place the drug directly in Manson's hands, trusting that this would sow chaos in the counterculture is hard to credit.[23] But Brussell's larger point (not hard to credit given what we later came to know about MK-ULTRA, the CIA's human subject program) is that the American government did investigate using LSD as a tool of mind control beginning in the 1950s. In Brussell's terrifying vision, LSD is simply the weapon. The object was to exploit Manson's own anti-Black racism to target the Black Panthers and other radical African American groups.

Bugliosi, of course, had no interest in promoting such a wide-lens political vision: he was representing the state, after all. With contributions from Linda Kasabian ("a real flower child" as Vincent Bugliosi's prosecutorial teammate Aaron Stovitz, violating a gag order, told *Rolling Stone*)[24] and others at the Family's trial, the state was able to introduce this focus on potential racialized violence as the product of a sick mind living in a sick society. The Watts riots, incited by police violence against a Black motorist, were only a few years in the past and government surveillance and persecution of Black Panthers and other Black radicals and activists was intensifying; a shootout at UCLA in January of 1969 between two Black Power groups, which had been very much stage-managed by the FBI (and which led to the deaths of Bunchy Carter and John Huggins) was certainly present in the minds of the many people circling around the Manson trial who were concerned about racial violence in Los Angeles. And the arrest of Manson and his followers in early December jostled on the front page of countless newspapers with headlines about the police assassination of two

Chicago Black Panthers, Mark Clark and Fred Hampton. (Here's how the Madison, Wisconsin, *Times* titled the two stories: "Illinois Black Panther Party Chairman Killed By Police" and "Leader of Hippie Cult Emerges as Key Slaying Figure.")[25]

Bugliosi's trial focus on Helter Skelter threw Manson's supposed obsession with "imminent" race war into the same conceptual bag as bottomless pits in the desert, wild sex orgies, (mis)readings of the Bible and the Beatles, and near-constant use of psychedelic drugs. This was the truth according to Vincent Bugliosi and it was the truth accepted by the jury when it brought back its guilty verdicts early in 1971. In one sense the collective storytelling organized by Bugliosi at the trial and beyond was a useful corrective to other attempts to reduce the murders to a hand-wringing story about why the Laurel Canyon (and Pacific Palisades) elite should have seen this coming and needed to start locking their doors to keep out the countercultural riffraff. Bugliosi swung a much wider gate open with his Helter Skelter proposition; as Bobby Beausoleil, Ed Sanders, and many others have pointed out, this mostly provided entrance to people intent on using the Tate-LaBianca murders as an opportunity to undermine a variety of countercultural aims.

It took some time for Vincent Bugliosi to organize the Helter Skelter narrative. He was appointed to the case in November of 1969 and Manson was arrested in early December. The trial began in the summer of 1970. The period from late 1969 to mid-1970 was full of competing theories and attempts at mobilizing the crimes and the arrests. Popular explanations ranged from the aforementioned "Grudge Against Doris Day's Son Linked to Tate Slayings" (in the *Los Angeles Times*) to various versions of "Scientology Leader Denies Manson 'Family' Connection" (it was the Process Church he was connected to, according to the public relations director for the Scientologists), to the commentary by local news commentator Piers Anderton on KNBC-TV, which held that the murders were an "inevitable end-product of the hippie culture"—a predictable outcome for a culture so committed to "doing your own thing" and letting "it all hang out."[26]

Vincent Bugliosi was not the first to reach a wide public with an "inside" account of the Tate-LaBianca murders. By far the most important first contribution to this collective chronicle was the "confession" of Susan Atkins—published in the *Los Angeles Times* on Sunday, December 14 (as well as in many other newspapers in the United States and beyond), and then in book form in January of 1970. The circumstances surrounding Atkins's narrative of the events of August 8 and 9 are sketchy—in both major senses of the word. To begin, it is not at all clear what part Atkins (a.k.a. Sadie Mae Glutz) played in the writing of "Susan Atkins' Story of 2 Nights of Murder": while the long article was rooted in information she had provided to the Grand Jury and the District Attorney's office, it was the brainchild of Lawrence Schiller, who brokered a deal with Atkins's lawyer to have Jerry Cohen, on leave from his regular job at the *Los Angeles Times*, ghostwrite the account. Schiller seems to have been in charge of selling the rights to English and German news outlets.[27] How the *Los Angeles Times* came into possession of a copy of the manuscript is a hotly debated point. Suffice to say that mutual accusations flew among Richard Caballero, Atkins's lawyer, and Schiller. (When David Dalton and David Felton got around to the question of Atkins's published confession in their June 1970 *Rolling Stone* cover story on the case, they wrote, soberly, that representatives of the *Los Angeles Times* told the truth when they insisted no money had changed hands. "[T]he *Times* people didn't buy the confession," according to Dalton and Felton, "they wrote it. Word for word.")[28]

Regardless of the questions surrounding the manuscript's mysterious origins and circulation, it is most noteworthy in retrospect for its silence on the racial apocalypse motive. The primary goal of this work—in addition to providing crime details of compelling voyeuristic value—was to establish that Manson directed all of this violent activity. "Charlie had control over everybody," Atkins avers: "I never questioned what Charlie said. I just did it."[29] The "Susan Atkins" (well, actually, the Sadie Mae Glutz) presented here is told explicitly by Manson's deputy-in-charge, Tex Watson, that they are going to Cielo Drive "to instill fear into Terry Melcher because Terry had given his word on a few things and never came through with them. So Charlie wanted to put some fear into him, let him know that what Charlie said was the way it is." Among other things, the Atkins "confession" raises the interesting possibility that not every member of the Family alleged to have been involved with the Tate-LaBianca murders had the same understanding of why it was necessary to journey to Cielo and Waverly Drives on the nights of August 8 and 9, 1969. And just to make sure that Atkins had no credibility whatsoever, the "confession" ends with Atkins saying that she needs to stop reflecting on the mayhem—it has exhausted her. Also, according to the accused murderer, her lawyer was coming soon, and bringing with him "a dish of vanilla ice cream": "Vanilla ice cream really blows my mind."[30]

When Schiller's book, *The Killing of Sharon Tate with the Exclusive Story of the Crime by Susan Atkins (Confessed Participant in the Murder of Sharon Tate)* appeared, Sadie Mae Glutz's confession had been demoted to the back half. The first part of the book, presumably written by journalist Jerry Cohen (Schiller occupied an interesting position in the 1960s and 1970s as something other than an author—he was more of a curator or event-planner of books) was taken up with faux-sociological inquiries into the broader implications of the murder: "Did eight persons die horribly because of the Family's antecedents in the hippie movement?" The book strikes something of a jeering tone as it outlines the imagined reception of the murders and arrests for the large percentage of observers. The authors nod to "members of the silent majority"—the demographic category identified by President Richard Nixon in a November 1969 speech—who found the "solution to the Tate case" (the arrest of Manson and associates) to be "secretly satisfying."[31] Putting the events in the context of a film genre that would, before long, find much to borrow from the Manson murders, *The Killing of Sharon Tate* proposed that as "in the horror-film battles" in which, for instance, Frankenstein encountered the Wolf Man, it was a case of the hippies meet the Beautiful People. The middle class watched, relieved, happy to be spectators, as two out-groups fell upon the other.[32] Leaving aside the question of how the "Beautiful People" could be construed as any sort of "out-group," this book promotes a delectable vision of murder as corrective action—a painful but necessary restoration of the social order. Insofar as the book is interested in particular motives for the crimes, its heart seems to be with a blame-the-victim suggestion that the real target may have been "Polish playboy" Voytek Frykowski, who had been running with a much-too-rough crowd of drug dealers.[33]

Once Sadie Mae Glutz is introduced as a speaking subject (about midway through the book), it is hard to get past her "confession" that, as I recounted in Part One, she knew that her father "wanted to have an affair" with her.[34] After she admits that she "actually did want to have an affair with him" as well, it becomes clear that Sadie Mae Glutz's role in the book's moral universe is to shock its readers and remind American families to clean up their own backyards before they spend too much time worrying about murderous hippies.[35] *The Killing of Sharon Tate* has little to say about race relations, outside of Sadie Mae Glutz's rather offhanded contention that Charlie "reacts to Black people, digs them" because he had spent so much time around them during his prison years.[36]

Perhaps the most puzzling early entry in the Manson true-crime sweepstakes was George Bishop's *Witness to Evil* (also known as *The Trial of Charles Manson*), which is remarkably free of any point of view—aside that is, from the sexism and racism dripping off of so many of its pages. Among other memorable turns of phrase, Bishop refers to Sharon Tate's domestic servant Winifred Chapman as a "sepia Camille" and wonders if it is hard to understand what the defense attorney Daye Shinn—"a natural-born United States citizen of Korean ancestry"—says in court, not only because he speaks "chop-chop English" but also, perhaps, because of the "unfathomable reasoning processes of the Asiatic mind."[37] Bishop's rhetoric is similarly distasteful with respect to gender politics: we are told that "Miss Bijou Nolan" who had worked with defense attorney Paul Fitzgerald earlier in his career has "one of the finest pair of legs in the history of public defense."[38] Prosecution witness Ronnie Howard was, according to Bishop, "an early thirties brunette in good shape despite considerable mileage."[39] (This might be an appropriate moment for me to note that in the huge welter of nonfiction historical narratives and cultural analyses produced about the Manson Family since 1969—aside from first person accounts by key figures involved in the case—a truly astonishing proportion has been written by men. Except for Joan Didion's crucial "White Album" essay, Karlene Faith's underappreciated book on Leslie Van Houten, and Karina Longworth's multipart podcast, male authors have dominated the arena. Uneasily, I take my place.)

Witness to Evil makes it clear that if it has any particular point to make it is to remind readers that it is time to fight back against the forces of anarchy represented by Manson, the Family, and—this is important—Manson's lawyer Irving Kanarek. The book includes a modicum of parental, straight-culture tsk-tsking: the foreword, after all, is written by Art Linkletter, who connects up the murders and his daughter Diane's recent death, which was officially ruled a suicide but consistently described by the television personality as the result of a "bad trip." Bishop himself is fairly desultory about prosecuting his case, noting only that we all ought to figure out what part LSD played in the murders because we "don't want carloads of people riding around in every city and town" targeting "you or me as random murder victims."[40]

Bishop seems to have been a daily spectator at the trial (hence the "witness" of the title). What remains most valuable about his book is that it makes a good, clear case for what Bugliosi achieved during the many months of the trial. While Manson was the big fish Bugliosi ultimately needed to land, he had plenty else to wrestle with—mostly the demons of disorder also known as the defense team. Two of the defense lawyers were later barred from practicing law in California (for reasons unrelated to the Tate-LaBianca trial); another member of the team, Ronald Hughes, disappeared during a trial recess under very mysterious circumstances and was later found dead. The cheese who stood alone was Paul Fitzgerald—representing Patricia Krenwinkel—who by all accounts did a decent job. Bishop has fun making fun of the defense team, at one point even suggesting that some of their tactics were "so gauche" that it might seem as if one was a used-car salesman and one the manager of a rock band. Punch line? One of them (Shinn) had, according to Bishop, been a used-car salesman in the past; and one (Hughes) had previously managed a rock group known as the United States Government! The team was strengthened after tragedy befell Hughes, and Maxwell Keith was named by the court to replace him. Keith, as newspapers around the country reported, was known as the "Ivy League Hillbilly" for what was described as his combination of "country boy mien and erudite mind."[41]

The king of this crazy court was Irving Kanarek, and George Bishop really wanted his readers to understand that this man represented, on some level, not just Manson, but also those terrifying forces of cultural anarchy that had come to be adjudicated in Judge Older's courtroom. Accounts of Kanarek's performance in the courtroom tend to lazily follow Bugliosi's lead and organize around keywords like the previously mentioned "dilatory" and "obstructionist." But Kanarek was consciously and consistently anti-authoritarian, and his main target was Vincent Bugliosi. Before the trial proper even got underway, the prosecutor was seeking relief from what he perceived as Kanarek's purposeful abuse. Among other things, Bugliosi explained to the judge that the defense attorney was mispronouncing his last name (as BUG-li-o-si instead of Boo-lee-o-si) in order to try to "get to" the prosecuting attorney. After a quick lesson in Italian pronunciation ("You can forget about the 'G'"), Bugliosi requested that the judge instruct Kanarek "to make an effort." This pretrial colloquy seems to have made little impression on Kanarek: on day forty-two of the trial Bugliosi stopped the proceedings to complain to the judge about Kanarek putting the "G" back in: "The 'G' is silent, sir."[42] (These narcissistic interruptions are fascinating in large part because of how they interfere with the heroic narrative Bugliosi would construct of himself in interviews, documentaries, and above all, in his own book. *Helter Skelter* would be packaged in

1974 with a subtitle promising that it presented the "true story of the Manson murders," but in this book by Bishop, as in the reporting by Theo Wilson and others, we get important reminders that the veneration of Vincent Buglioisi has mostly been authored by Vincent Bugliosi.)

At the trial Irving Kanarek did not seem to have a unified plan of action. More than anything he seemed to be want to upset the workings of the judicial machinery at every turn. His challenges were existential, really. Kanarek's individual objections and delaying tactics could certainly seem jejeune when read out of context, but his challenges added up to a profound question about what it means to be a speaking subject. Manson himself spoke movingly of having no voice in the proceedings, and Kanarek did all he could to make sure that Bugliosi's narration would not completely dominate the proceedings. Kanarek also had his moments of compelling rhetoric, as when he insisted to the jury in his closing argument that they must respect Manson's homegrown spirituality because, after all, a man "can be a church inside his own body."[43]

According to Bishop, Charles Manson had a vision, to be sure, but it was "disjointed." Bishop will not acknowledge that Manson's inarticulateness is largely a result of his disempowerment—in the courtroom, of course, but really for all of his life. Bishop suggests that Manson could tailor aspects of his "demented doctrine" to willing audience members but that he could "not put the whole thing together." It was Bugliosi who was able to stitch the amorphous bits of Manson-wisdom into a unified worldview; with his "organized, reasoning mind," the prosecutor was able to present to the jury the apocalyptic philosophy that he claimed animated all of Manson's crimes—the Helter Skelter that would later give his own book on the trial its iconic title. In his most efficient and profound declaration, Bishop suggests that it "was quite possible that Bugliosi believed in Helter Skelter more than did Manson!"[44]

Most of *Witness to Evil* is taken up with a plodding narration of the trial's daily happenings. A much more interesting book, by far, is *5 to Die*, written by Ivor Davis, a British journalist who, while earlier working for Reuters, had traveled with the Beatles and Jerry LeBlanc. Like Schiller's book, *5 to Die* was rushed into print in January of 1970. Schiller's book was published (as Vincent Bugliosi points out in *Helter Skelter*) by New American Library—which was owned by the same parent company that "also owns the *Los Angeles Times*."[45] *5 to Die* was issued by Holloway House, an independent Los Angeles publishing concern owned by two Jewish men, Ralph Weinstock and Bentley Morris, which had been, as Justin Gifford explains, a "niche publisher of adult magazines and erotic paperbacks," until it turned, after the 1965 Watts Riots, toward marketing to an audience of "Black working-class consumers." By the late 1960s Holloway House had become "the premier publisher of underground Black literature by publishing Iceberg Slim's *Pimp: The Story of My Life*" and later added Donald Goines (and the magazine *Players*, often referred to as the "Black Playboy") to its roster.[46]

  5 to Die is an odd hybrid. Davis tried to flog a reprint of the book on the fortieth anniversary of the case as a serious work of investigative journalism; his promotional materials include an anecdote about a fortuitous meeting he had with Aaron Stovitz (co-prosecutor on the case with Bugliosi until he was pulled for refusing to honor the judge's gag order) years after the trial, during which Stovitz told him that *5 to Die* had provided the state with the "blueprint" they would use to obtain convictions of Manson and the other defendants. The authors of *5 to Die* do seem to have had access to some Family members, but the book is most noteworthy for how awkwardly it combines very sharp social criticism with pulpy descriptions of the victims at Cielo Drive (which included more than a hint that these victims were not completely innocent) and the deliciously perverse sexual life of the Manson Family.

  Here is "Votyck Frokowsky" (the transliterated spelling of his name would not settle into stable form for some time) according to Davis and LeBlanc: "a big, bold, full-fleshed man who lived in a grand manner. He was full of life and he worshipped life, enjoyed every minute of it to the hilt. His voice was big, his gestures were large and his actions were sweeping . . . when he drank, he drank a lot, when he loved, he loved fully . . . he believed he was immortal like all people do, and he believed that he would die young, too, and saw no conflict in that because he lived for the moment."[47] Living large seems to have included taking a whole lot of LSD, the authors suggest, as they acknowledge that "no one"—not even their almost-omniscient selves—"will ever know what hallucinations might have scrambled through his mind that night as he lay on the deep-upholstered brown sofa in the living room."[48] The big Polish man's girlfriend, Abigail Folger, comes in for similar treatment. "Gibby," the heiress, "had a firm lip and cool, intelligent eyes that some might mistake for the mark of hardness, but when her face lit up with a smile of pleasure . . . she was all woman, soft and fragile." The authors worry about her tendency to socialize with hippies, and raise the possibility that she came in contact with Manson in the Haight-Ashbury.[49]

While the romance-novel noir of these descriptions is predictable enough, the book takes an especially dark turn when it comes to describing the general level of alleged debauchery at Cielo Drive: "Wild drug trips, gang bangs, ritualistic witchcraft practices, sadism, blindfolds and diamond encrusted whips."[50] (True-crime scholar David Schmid reminds us that "blaming the victim" is a hallmark of true-crime work on women killed by serial murderers.)[51] The evolving true-crime genre here takes a wild detour into nineteenth-century Gothic. All Davis and LeBlanc's version of the Tate murders needs is a secret passageway or two, a perverse monk, and a confidence man (oh, actually it has that) and it would be ready for primetime (in 1845 or so). Obsessive focus on ghastly murders and the ensuing trials often contains more than a hint of the pornographic. The Tate murders—the death-scene photographs of the partly clothed doomed "starlet," the developing narratives of Manson Family orgies, and the investigative/speculative details about what the "beautiful people" people did behind closed doors—provide a sumptuous feast for the eyes of titillated readers. Well before Bugliosi could rationalize the "true-crime" tale at the trial and in his published and broadcast work, many others rushed in to construct a dark caricature of contemporary social life. Bodies are in motion, seemingly firm boundaries are being breached, films may or may not be available. It would be hard to say if Davis and LeBlanc are more intrigued by the sex lives of the rich and famous or the sex lives of the Manson Family. (On the latter front, they recount a wonderfully implausible story about an undercover police officer who had, before the arrests, infiltrated Family life at Spahn Ranch—with "shaggy hair" and "fragmentary beard." The police officer faces an impasse when the cult leader requires that he go through the usual orgy-as-initiation process. The lawman, as Ed Sanders would likely put it, decided to "get after it").[52]

Perhaps the winner (loser?) in the "blame the victim" sweepstakes came in a chapter of *The Beautiful People: The Pacesetters of the New Morality*, written by J. D. Russell, and full of the sort of juicy details familiar to readers of *Confidential*. Given her work as a Hollywood actor, Tate was a fairly familiar face to consumers of magazines with names like *Raw Flix* (not to mention *Playboy*, which had a feature on Tate in 1967). The chapter in *The Beautiful People* acts as a useful summary of tabloid interest in Tate after her death. Most central here is what the murders brought to light about the "dark side" of Hollywood: "The growing drug-dazed Cult of the Kink was slammed forcibly into the limelight with the grisly, macabre murders of actress Sharon Tate and four others."[53] Cielo Drive, we are no longer surprised to learn, had been the site of "wildly freaked-out drug parties with weird sexual overtones." If there is a dash of social commentary in *The Beautiful People*, it has to do with the promiscuous mixing that had become the norm in the New Hollywood. These people moved across many "castes"—having dinner one night with Garson Kanin, "rubbing shoulders with the likes of Arthur Rubinstein" but also interested in socializing with the "wild younger set."[54] Even that level of commentary is absent from Gay Talese's article "Charles Manson's Home on the Range," published in *Esquire* in March 1970. Talese, you might recall, could not seem to take his eyes off the dry humping of two of the Ranch's residents long enough to say anything analytical.

Of these pulpy immediate accounts, it would seem that Ivor Davis and Jerry LeBlanc's *5 to Die* would be as easy to dismiss as *The Beautiful People* or "Charles Manson's Home on the Range" if it pursued a simple agenda of arousal. But as with the prose of nineteenth-century American Gothic literature, LeBlanc and Davis combine (as Leslie Fiedler said of George Lippard, author of *The Quaker City* [1845]) "sex, horror, and advanced social thought." "Pornography," as Fiedler put it in his analysis of Lippard, "is justified as muckraking."[55] In Davis and LeBlanc the sexualized descriptions of violence seem to tip into self-parody. The authors understand they are in the business of titillation. Moreover they know that their role in the backlash is to make sure to indict the sketchy victims along with the frightful villains. The book does not hold back when it comes to full-out horror. This is most evident in their narration of the death of Donald "Shorty" Shea, a ranch hand at Spahn's. Shea's final moments, according to *5 to Die*, featured members of the Family simultaneously "sticking knives into him" and "stimulating his penis." With a wink to the reader, the authors provide a "money shot": at "just the moment of climax, they chopped his head off with a machete." In case this is not clear enough, Davis and LeBlanc emphasize that this must "have been a sight," as Shea's head came off at one end while his penis was "spitting away at the other."[56]

The Tate murders and details of Family life provided (minimally) fact-based opportunities to project potentially shameful fantasies onto safely distant characters—members of the elite creative class and figures from a marginal "hippie cult." Both Ed Sanders's *The Family* and Vincent Bugliosi's *Helter Skelter* (with dramatically different affect) promoted a true-crime modality—that powerful form still with us today—relentlessly focused on discovering and recounting the "facts." But Davis and LeBlanc's book inhabits a much less settled form than "true crime." These authors make it clear that unlike Bugliosi they do not intend to reassure readers or tie up loose ends. Numerous scholars in African American studies have explained how narratives written by escaped slaves served multiple objectives: abolitionist rhetoric

and prurient thrill were not casual or accidental narrative partners, but complementary elements in a carefully designed social
text. Before *Helter Skelter* was able to establish its norms for an
"appropriate" way to talk about the case and its many tentacles,
the Tate-LaBianca murders energized a broad and robust cultural
conversation about class, sexuality, gender roles, and much more.

Ivor Davis and Jerry LeBlanc used the affair to launch some
devastating—and still startlingly useful—social critique. While
the authors of *5 to Die* shed no tears for the accused cult leader,
they insist that Charles Manson also has to be understood as a
"one-man indictment of America's penal institutions." This "guru,"
they explain, "stands as a monument to the failure of welfare, the
police, the courts and the prison system of America to divert
a scrawny kid from the road mapped out before him in all its
shocking inevitability—a road beginning in squalor and headed
for destruction via neglect, dissatisfaction and alienation."[57] In
addition to putting Manson on this path of personal doom, life in
prison, according to Davis and LeBlanc, also exposed the "slight"
guru to "strange religious sects and the occult, mesmerism and
scientology, that controversial pseudo Freudian religion." While
stopping short of launching a defense brief on Manson's behalf, the
authors here return him to context—the prison—most responsible for his acculturation. If Manson was able to turn his followers
into "robots" after a "sort of Manchurian Candidate conditioning"
it was a result of his own training in various prisons.[58]

This emerging narrative of Manson's "institutionalized" character was underscored by Alvin "Creepy" Karpis (late of Ma
Barker's gang and a prison-house associate of Manson earlier in the
decade) and by a writer for the *Los Angeles Free Press*, in January
of 1970, who reminded readers that Manson was not a product
of hippie culture, but rather "the product of a violent, uncaring
society and of brutal, oppressive penal institutions." Toward the
end of 1970, John Lennon joined this opinion, in a *Rolling Stone*
interview during which he argued that Manson "is a child of the
state, made by us."[59] In our time no one has made this argument
more forcefully than rapper Killer Mike, who samples a Manson

interview to powerful effect in his song "Belly of the Beast." With a Jonah-inspired title that also makes obvious reference to Jack Henry Abbott's 1981 prison memoir and perhaps to a speech issued by South Africa's African National Congress in 1980, Killer Mike (with Manson's help) makes a clear case that the main work of the prison is to institutionalize and brutalize. The rhetorical question repeated at the song's end ("do you know what you're creating when you send the boys to the belly of Satan?") makes plain the argument that the state holds the ultimate responsibility for making career criminals like Manson.

5 to Die's other major analytical intervention comes with the authors' attempt to offer a thumbnail social history of Inyo County, the home of Barker Ranch—where much of the Family fled to in the wake of the August 1969 murders. In a cutting aside, the authors note that law-enforcement had, just before the Manson Family arrests, been taken up with sorting through the recently discovered remains of a plane crash. This, they note, is "the biggest story" in Inyo County since "the early nineteen-forties," which saw "an influx of Japanese" who would soon be imprisoned "in barbed wire camps."[60] While the Family understood Barker Ranch to be safely removed from Los Angeles, the authors of 5 to Die use this vignette to explain how the once-remote region has come to be defined by Los Angeles people. Davis and LeBlanc describe a region that "lives on tourists, hunters, fishermen, skiers—and thirst of Los Angeles." Not only were outsiders exploiting Inyo County assets in situ, but the city was now regularly drawing resources away from the area. "[T]he whole county is practically owned by Los Angeles, bought lock stock and barrel for an elaborate aqueduct to bring water" from the mountains to "the metropolitan area, but in effect stifling all local industry and growth. There are small towns, and smaller ones, and ghost towns."[61] This is no longer a journalistic narrative solely concerned with murder victims and their killers—it is ethnic history, environmental history, political and economic history. 5 to Die is a contribution to the literature of the Manson Family creepy crawl that reminds us that the case provided plenty of room—at least until Vincent

Bugliosi and his team streamlined the story—for multifarious critical and historical investigations.

David Dalton and David Felton proposed to the readers of *Rolling Stone* in the cover story of its June 25, 1970, issue that the "question that seemed to split underground editorial minds more than any other was simply: Is Manson a hippie or isn't he?" Dalton and Felton were purposefully reducing a whole complex of pre-trial investigations into this simple formulation. It was not only the "underground editorial minds" that had become obsessed with this question. The *New York Times* was a relatively early (and earnest) participant in the conversation, with a December 15, 1969, story on page one, titled "The Hippie Mystique." The title is some kind of failed gloss on Betty Friedan's *The Feminine Mystique*, published six years earlier. The whole point of Friedan's use of "mystique" (with its echo of the key Marxist term "mystification") is that prescribed gender behaviors were seductive to women exactly because there was so little public opposition to the notion that these social constructions were, in fact, natural outgrowths of biological sex. But Roberts's article, like so much mainstream media work in the immediate aftermath of Manson's arrest, had to acknowledge that the "longhairs" had been coming under attack for some time. "The Hippie Mystique"—title notwithstanding—actually takes pains to explain that Manson is not a hippie; the accused had "rejected" the label and furthermore (according to an unnamed psychiatrist serving as a source for Roberts) hippies stress the "beatific" while Manson is all about the "demonic."[62]

If the *New York Times*'s reporter struggled, with apparent sincerity, to sort out the realities of Family life from the more general hippie ethos ("essentially anarchistic"), *Life* magazine was much more interested in using Manson's arrest and his obvious "non-hippie" modalities as an excuse to work on the sex/horror axis. The cover of the December 19, 1969, issue is now one of the more familiar images surrounding the case. The story is presented under the title "The Love and Terror Cult" and it does not take long for the magazine's writers to make clear that they will be scripting this as something like a horror movie, subgenre zombie. Davis and LeBlanc, too, had called the Family "an army of modern day slaves and zombies." While later cultural representations of the Family would lean toward vampires and cannibals (as with 1971's film *I Drink Your Blood*, which invokes both), in the immediate aftermath of the crime "zombie" was the preferred image. The *Life* story is invested, perhaps above all else, in warning about how older men like Manson might take advantage of the free-love ethos of the larger hippie movement. "The Love and Terror Cult" works a groove that would become central to Ed Sanders's approach to the Family (anticipating Sanders's focus on the "valley of thousands of plump white rabbits surrounded by wounded coyotes"), but from a position of patronizing disgust, rather than Sanders's in-group concern. Manson and many others like him ("criminals and ex-cons") have "discovered a new sort of refuge in the last couple of years: they grow hair, assume beads and sandals, and sink—carnivores moving in with vegetarians—into the life of hippie colonies from the East Village to Big Sur."[63]

"The Love and Terror Cult" articulates a moral panic about hippie life that serves, above all else, as a warning to parents to keep a close watch on their children. Revelations about the Tate-LaBianca murders, and this "love and terror cult" accused of committing these crimes, "struck innumerable Americans as an inexplicable controversion of everything they wanted to believe . . . about their children." While the article's headline uses the word "and" to join "love" with "terror," the body of the piece makes it clear that this is really about love (sex, really) *as* terror. The one real journalistic coup in the article is a sidebar that features input from Manson's parole office and, much more significantly, Dr. David E. Smith, of the Haight-Ashbury Free Medical Clinic, who had come into regular contact with the Family during its San Francisco sojourn (and co-wrote the essay about their living arrangements with Alan J. Rose). The careful work Smith and Rose published was intent on placing not only the Family, but also the larger culture under the microscope. "The final and most interesting questions," Smith and Rose argue, "relate to why this alternative communal life style holds such an attraction for thousands of adolescents and young adults. Why, for example, were these young girls so attracted and captivated by a disturbed person such as Manson? What is happening within the framework of the dominant culture and its monogamous, nuclear family units, that so many youths must feel compelled not simply to rebel but totally reject traditional life styles?"[64] But in *Life*'s sidebar, not surprisingly, the thoughtful San Francisco doctor has his work reduced to another exhibit in the developing effort to expel Manson and the Family from the counterculture: the Family "was unlike any other commune I've known. They called themselves a family, but most family communes are monogamous sexually."[65]

Life's Manson is almost supernaturally powerful; he comes to his power over young women through "day-long sexual marathons." In *Life*'s portrait the saga of the Manson Family reads as if it belongs to the tradition of the American captivity narrative—one of the oldest and most significant forms of processing gender relations. The original captivity narrative chronicled the alleged kidnapping and "conversion" of white women, often very young, by Native American men. *Life* is plying not "true crime" here, but another sort of (sex) crime narrative, one whose origins stretch back earlier than the founding of the republic and which has continued to bear fruit in modern narratives of American white women—Jessica Lynch above all—captured during the "War on Terror."[66] *Life* establishes a template that would be copied by so many others, including Bugliosi. Manson is the "Indian" in this scenario, only recently released from captivity himself, and now applying the mind-control techniques he learned in prison to exploit vulnerable young women. Here Manson is not the countercultural insurgent of the February 9, 1970, issue of *Tuesday's Child*—the infamous Manson "Man of the Year" cover—or Bernadette Dohrn's "The Weathermen Dig Charles Manson." This is Charlie as Svengali, the hypnotic outsider controlling young women.[67] While George du Maurier original novelistic depiction of Svengali in *Trilby* (1894) (and various film adaptations) depicted the controlling older man as frighteningly Jewish, by the

1960s the characterization was more or less mainstreamed and was commonly used to describe the relationship of powerful figures in the music business to the talent they produced, managed, and so on. The portrait of Manson as all-powerful, hypnotic man offered by *Life* and other mainstream media outlets makes it more possible to understand a bizarre interruption in *5 to Die*: in the photographic insert in the book, the authors break from the pictures of the crime scene, key players in the drama and so on, to invite readers to study and notice the similarity in facing pictures of Manson and John Barrymore, playing Svengali in a 1931 film version of Eliot's novel.

John Waters' *Playdate* (2006) Silicone, human and synthetic hair, cotton flannel and polar fleece, Manson: 19 x 14 x 11 inches, Jackson: 15 x 13 x 27 inches, Edition of 5, Courtesy Marianne Boesky Gallery, New York

The women of the Family worked for years on the vest that told their story. *Sue Terry/Los Angeles Public Library.*

Charles Manson, in the vest, on his way to court. *Michael Haering/Los Angeles Public Library.*

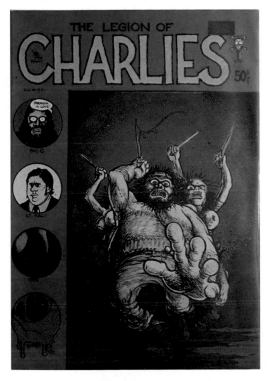

Left: The 1971 comic book that insisted on the Manson/Lieutenant William Calley link.
Below: Apocalyptic cover of Neil Young's *On the Beach* (1974).

Manson helping to move product for Rise records.

An example of Raymond Pettibon's work for Black Flag in the early 1980s.

Raymond Pettibon, *No Title (The family dog)*, 1990, Pen and ink on paper, 14 x 11 inches (35.6 x 27.9 cm), © Raymond Pettibon, Courtesy Regen Projects, Los Angeles.

Christopher Wool's *HELTER HELTER*. Untitled, 1988, Enamel and flashe on aluminum, 96 x 60 inches, (243.8 x 152.4 cm), © Christopher Wool; Courtesy of the artist and Luhring Augustine, New York.

Negativland's *Helter Stupid* (1989).

Derek Erdman's *Charles Manson in a Cubs Hat*
(2008), courtesy of the artist.

Banksy's Manson
(2005).

Joachim Koester's Barker Ranch series, #2 (2008).

Koester's Barker Ranch series, #4 (2008). From a series of four selenium toned silver gelatin prints, each 44 x 58, 3, courtesy Galleri Nicolai Wallner

strategy, and so on, than the mainstream press was. A large part of this had to do with simple matters of will and column inches. As early as January 1970, the alternative paper was devoting a great deal of space to considerations of Manson's changing legal strategy given the emergence of Susan Atkins's recent confession. One in-depth article appeared side-by-side with a cut-out coupon for a promotional LP put out by Frank Zappa's Bizarre/Straight record labels (with contributions by the GTOs, Captain Beefheart, and Wild Man Fischer) and addressed "Dear Establishment Freaks." Everything about the *Free Press*—from ad copy to font type to the very matter of journalistic real estate committed to the impending trial—signaled that the arrest of Manson and his followers was of great importance to members of the counterculture, whether Manson turned out to be a hippie or not.[5]

The *Free Press* articles are worth pausing over because they may well represent a relatively isolated effort to imagine Manson as an individual—rather than the symbol he would become for so many commentators. What is perhaps noteworthy for later readers of Ed Sanders's book *The Family*, is how sympathetic Sanders is—at least at first—to Manson and his followers. This framework of sympathy was established by the Freep before Sanders arrived on the scene; in an early major article on Manson, the *Free Press*'s correspondent—almost certainly thinking of the infamous *Life* magazine cover—makes special mention of the "gentle cast" of Manson's eyes. (A year later Yippie leader Jerry Rubin would publish *We Are Everywhere*, in which he would recount how he "fell in love" with Manson's "sparkling eyes" and "cherub face" when he first saw him on television).[6] It is impossible to know, of course, how much Michael Hannon's "direct" quotations of Manson are, in fact, direct, but it is clear that his work was aimed at reintroducing Manson to *Free Press* readers as at once a countercultural rebel and a vulnerable outsider. After recounting his distrust of lawyers ("The second lawyer came in here and he wanted to incorporate me"), Manson, in a set of winter 1970 interviews, works with Hannon to present himself as a sort of working-class hero: "My philosophy comes from underneath the boots and sticks and clubs they beat people with who come from the wrong side of the tracks."[7] As for the media obsession with the circumstances of his own birth, Manson told Hannon that the newspapers refer to his mother as a "whore, but she was really just like the flower children. I was born from love."[8]

Hannon's sympathetic two-part interview in the *Free Press* was, over the course of 1970, joined by an abundance of other supporting materials. In March, for instance, Manson's entire "pro per" statement (essentially the case that he should be allowed to serve as his own lawyer) was printed in the Freep—full as it was of wonderfully implausible demands. The Freep also printed highly stylized drawings of Manson, poetry and prose written by the prisoner (and supporting documents written by the Family), and advertisements and coupons for his music and writing. But it was Ed Sanders's bitter, comic, and outraged writing on the trial that was the heart of the *Free Press* coverage of Manson's trial. While Sanders's general stylistic attack (the "cheap head prose" dismissed by a later critic) will be familiar, what is jarring is how completely Sanders's anti-government and anti-bourgeois orientation had prepared him to find Manson and his followers worthy of sympathetic attention, and how willing Sanders was to use the Manson case to launch a variety of radical critiques of political and social business-as-usual.[9]

Ed Sanders hit the pages of the Freep in May of 1970 and his first target was the police; *Rolling Stone*'s June 25, 1970, piece was correct to note that much of the seemingly "pro-Manson" coverage in the underground press was really more aptly described as "anti-cop."[10] In Sanders's first article (cheekily titled "Back at the Ranch") the police are described as an occupying force, constantly raiding the ranch without search warrants, looking for "runaways, for murder information, and one suspects, for thrills." Sanders is clearly wary of the worshipful stance taken by the women at Spahn toward their jailed leader, but is also concerned about how the imagined (male) (sexist) readers of the Freep might be projecting their desires onto these besieged figures. Sanders calls these readers into being only to then warn them not to "go out to the Spahn

Movie Ranch hoping that you're going to be sucked off by naked girls with LSD smeared on their lips riding machine gun mounted dune buggies, buddy."[11]

Later, in a 1975 lecture and 1976 written manifesto, Sanders would codify much of his work as belonging to a domain he called "investigative poetry": "the poets are/marching again/upon the hills/of history" Sanders announced, arguing that it was the task of the history-writing poet to be "uncompromising, "revolutionary," "seditious," and "absolute."[12] While Sanders's *Free Press* articles are not "poetry" in any standard definition of the term, they are full of figurative language, appeals to sound as well as sense, and dazzlingly allusive elements. And given the dominant media culture's rush to convict Manson well before his trial, there is much about this work that could be considered "uncompromising" if not, in fact, "revolutionary."

The work Sanders published "about" Manson *is* about Manson and many other pressing social concerns as well. In "Back at the Ranch" Sanders meditates on what keeps the Family together, even with their leader in jail and even with almost constant police harassment. His conclusion, quite surprisingly, is music. Having visited the ranch and observed the social function of music-making among the remaining Family members, Sanders files this report:

[T] he songs of Charles Manson, especially as interpreted by the Family every night at the Spahn Ranch group sings, are often moving and sometimes beautiful. A lot of it is better than what you pay six dollars for at the Fillmore. About one week at Johnny-On-The-Spot Rehearsal Studios and a good engineer would enable the friends of Manson to leave groups like Crosby-Stills eating gravel. To the friends of Manson, it's the music they perform together that sustains a life style surrounded by hostile police, buzzing helicopters, bulldozers, and the constant intrusion of crew-cut tourists and reporters from *Paris Match*, *The National Enquirer*, *Stern*, *Time*, *Ladies Home Journal*, and *The Russian Journal of Astrophysics*.[13]

Sanders trods some heavy terrain here. First there is his wonderful sideswipe at David Crosby and Stephen Stills; perhaps Sanders shared Terry Melcher's sense that Crosby, who "broke up the Byrds and joined Buffalo Springfield, and broke them up," was "worse for the good feelings" of the hippie era "than Manson was." More significant, of course, is Sanders's embedded contention that collective, not-for-profit music-making can be a force of social cohesion and mutual support.[14]

Sanders went even further with his appreciation of the music of these "friends of Manson." "No one can prevent its beauty," he wrote, nor "its revolutionary implications": "For if the high school kids of the United States ever start singing together, adios oil slick."[15] Sanders is saying (at least) two fascinating things here. The first, and more obvious, has to do with music itself—and the kind of "slick" production that the Los Angeles music industry was known for—as opposed to the rawer, less polished sound of the Bay Area, for instance. Having just taken a whack at David Crosby and Stephen Stills (but mysteriously leaving Graham Nash alone), Sanders seems to be indicting the "plastic" music of Los Angeles more broadly.

If "oil slick" can be read as a reference to the overly smooth music of Crosby, Stills, and their followers, it also must be interpreted as "oil slick." The worst oil spill in United States history—not surpassed until the Exxon Valdez accident of 1989—resulted from a "blowout" off the coast of Santa Barbara in late January 1969. This environmental tragedy, "five miles off the coast from the aptly named small coastal community of Summerland," was covered in painful detail in the mainstream and alternative press—from *Life* to *Ramparts*. The spill devastated the area's animal life and also led to a remarkable amount of local and national activism. Geographers Keith Clarke and Jeffrey Hemphill, of the University of California, Santa Barbara, trace an impressive number of substantial developments in the environmental movement (including the beginning of UCSB's own environmental studies major) to the spill. A little more than a year after Southern California's ecological disaster, Sanders is invoking Union Oil's spill to make a (hyperbolic) claim about the power of communal song to effect social change.[16]

Sanders would change his own tune about the Manson Family over the course of the trial and his additional research for his book. But for now I want to savor this moment of appreciation for the music the Family made at Spahn Ranch. A few months before Sanders published this appreciation, the Freep ran a poignant story under the headline "Media Ignore Manson Music." This story, by Dave Mason (apparently not the same Dave Mason of the British rock band Traffic, who in 1971 would record an LP with Cass Elliot of the Mamas and the Papas) offered a sharp critique of members of the media who visited Spahn Ranch to take part in what, essentially, was supposed to be a release party for Manson's LP *Lie*.[17] The event had to be postponed once, because of the demands of Manson's legal situation (this was in the midst of wrangling having to do with Manson's pro per status), and when it did take place, only Paul Watkins and Brenda McCann were available to represent the Family; its usual spokesperson, Lynnette Fromme, was "downtown trying to see Charlie." Mason uses the occasion of the record's release to excoriate other members of the media who attended the press conference but then filed stories that had nothing to do with the release of Manson's music. While those journalists were not at all averse to "exploiting" Manson's "police . . . made image" in order to "sell advertising," they proved unwilling to take seriously the media critique expressed by the *Lie* cover (helpfully explained to Mason by the record's producer, Phil Kaufman) and especially intent on silencing Manson's voice and vision as captured by the album's songs. This, to Mason, was especially egregious given Judge William Keene's recent decision to revoke Manson's pro per status.[18] In addition to this critical article by Mason, the *Free Press* made space in the same issue for a large coupon/advertisement promoting the record.

Half a year later, Sanders invoked the California oil slick again, but this time with an additional sharp political argument in the mix. In a piece whose manifest content was an account of a visit Sanders made to visit Bobby Beausoleil at San Quentin ("It

seemed incongruous to be discussing Frank Zappa with a condemned man on Death Row"), the *Free Press* correspondent takes
time out to consider how the Manson trial serves the interests of
the dominant culture:

> Manson is an alcoholic editor's dream come true—an over-
> sexed, acid-gobbling, long-haired, nearly middle-aged,
> song-singing, devil-worshipping, bastard son of a teen-
> age prostitute who thinks he's Jesus and who formerly was
> arrested for white slavery. With people like Manson on the
> front page, you don't have to do any serious investigative
> reporting. And the authorities can shoot as many Mexican-
> Americans as they want. And the real criminals, the crim-
> inals with the computers and the oil slicks, walk around
> worshipped.[19]

In addition to the obvious "Bread and Circuses" critique of the
social function of the courtroom drama for the media, Sanders is
also using the case to bring attention to a different August crime
than the one Manson was on trial for—the murder of Los Angeles
journalist Ruben Salazar, on August 29, 1970. Ruben Salazar, as
Hector Tobar has explained, was a columnist for the *Los Angeles
Times* and "also news director at KMEX, L.A.'s pioneering Spanish-
language television station. He was the city's leading Latino media
voice, and he had been critical of police abuse." On August 29,
Salazar was covering the National Chicano Moratorium march
in East Los Angeles—a protest against the Vietnam War and the
disproportionate number of Mexican Americans who had died in
that conflict. Salazar was killed that evening, in the Silver Dollar
Bar, when a deputy from the Los Angeles Sheriff's Department
shot a tear gas projectile that pierced Salazar's skull.[20]

Sanders's brief mention of Salazar's murder (chronicled,
famously, by Hunter S. Thompson's "Strange Rumblings in
Aztlan," published in *Rolling Stone* the following April) is one
more reminder that the poet was using his perch at the *Los Angeles
Free Press* not only to narrate the wild action of the Manson trial

itself. The work Sanders would ultimately publish in book form as *The Family* is relentless in its offering of "facts." When Robert Christgau reviewed *The Family* glowingly for the *New York Times* he called attention to its "data-mania" and avoidance of the literary artifice of the New Journalism—"no fabricated immediacy, no reconstructed dialogue, no arty pace."[21] Sanders's prime directive by the time of *The Family* (certainly influenced by his sense that he would be talking to a much broader audience than the readership of the *Free Press*) was to distinguish Manson's criminally antisocial activities from the consciously rebellious modes of countercultural life. It is not hard to understand Sanders's strategic decision to step back from the broader social commentary of the *Free Press* series in favor of the gonzo just-the-facts-ma'am approach of *The Family*, but this also meant a substantial loss for what "truths" could be processed in Manson "true crime" literature. One of the real contributions Sanders made when he joined the *Free Press* as its special "Manson correspondent" was that he understood he could at once provide an in-depth account of the legal issues playing out in the courtroom while also using the case as a mirror, a cudgel, and a stack of Marshall amps. What was perhaps most impressive about Sanders's Manson series is how hard he worked to domesticate the courtroom. In other words, one of Sanders's central objectives in this journalistic work was to illustrate that the cultural space of the trial was not "pure" but held concentrated doses of the corruption and violence which defined the larger culture. This came most clear in Sanders's linkage of the death penalty in play in Judge Older's courtroom and the death being wrought by American forces in Vietnam.

In mid-August, 1970, Sanders filed a long article that ranged from sharp critique of Linda Kasabian's immunity deal, description of a few hot rumors being passed among journalists (did Jay Sebring cut the hair of the LaBiancas' daughter?), and a brief overview of the poetics and politics of "Irving Kanarek jokes" being told in the Hall of Justice. But the article takes a sharp turn in its last two paragraphs. Here Sanders, possibly responding to criticism of his coverage of the case up until this point ("Those who have accused me of making a hero out of Charles Manson can go make motions of unification with a weather balloon") issues something like a manifesto:

> This trial, this case, these defendants, these prosecutors, this system of capital punishment, this prison system . . . bring into sharp focus everything that ails this mammal society of humans called America. I could write a hundred pages about what it's like to die in the gas chamber, with the exact rituals of lung snuff, defecation of the person gassed, the whole barbaric dungeonistic spectacle of capital punishment. Or I could write a thousand pages detailing the dreadful massacres inflicted upon those suffering victims now overtaken to the earth, those seven souls . . . .
>
> This country which perfected the concept of the "free-fire zone" in wars against the Orient, this country which finds free fire zones and the spirit of the fragmentation bomb suffused upon the well kept lawns of the homeland, this country is in trouble. It is time to stop the fires of cruelty that Mr. Salter spoke up against in arguing against the death penalty for Bob Beausoleil. It is time to stop. Later for the code of Hammurabi. Later for cyanide. Later for barbarism. Get out of Vietnam. Get out of encroachment, get out of the gas chamber, get out of the temple of human hamburger.[22]

In January 1971, Sanders would put an even sharper point on his anti–death penalty position in an article the *Free Press* titled "Five Poignant Points to Ponder"—a sort of summary of the trial as the case was sent to the jury. Here Sanders invokes what had become a familiar objection to the prosecution of Manson: not that he was "innocent," but rather that it was unfairly selective of the government to hold Manson accountable for his crime if it was going to be unwilling to try other products of its institutional indoctrination: "[I]f you kill Manson you have to kill Calley." With this Sanders is invoking the American army lieutenant who directed the My Lai massacre of March 1968; these crimes did not come fully to light until November of 1969. Calley's trial, which began in November 1970, raised questions of individual culpability in the context of chain-of-command responsibilities.[23]

Ed Sanders had as little patience for claims that Calley was simply "following orders" as he did for the prosecutorial claim that Manson telling his female followers to "do something witchy" constituted a directive not only to murder Sharon Tate and her friends but to write words in blood and all the rest. The Manson/ Calley connection that Sanders emphasized was energized in late March of 1971: on March 29 Manson was sentenced to death and Calley was convicted (and then sentenced to life in prison on March 31) and numerous newspapers had the stories jostling each other on the front page.

So it is no surprise that Ed Sanders had plenty of company in 1971 and after when it came to bringing Manson and Calley into conversation. Journalist and activist Paul Krassner recalls in his memoir that he spoke on his radio show (on KSFX in San Francisco) about similarities between Manson and Calley— describing Manson as an "individualized version of the state."[24] The alternative press was full of Manson/Calley features. Marvin Garson's San Francisco *Good Times* (successor to the San Francisco *Express Times*) published an early April front page article by Yippie and antiwar activist Stew Albert that challenged powerful figures of the establishment to accept Manson and Calley as products of their own handiwork. Do not "feel superior to these two orphans," Albert directed, "to whom you denied both your love and your wealth, and yet thought you were their father."[25] In New York, Allen Katzman was prosecuting a similar case in the the *East Village Other* suggesting that if "Sharon Tate and her friends were slanty-eyed 'gooks' and lived in Viet Nam, Manson and his followers would have been following orders and therefore immune to the Ten Commandments."[26] Bobby Beausoleil made an even broader point to John Gilmore, during a jailhouse interview soon after his conviction. "When you talk of killing innocent people, what about the truly innocent and humble people of the villages who are living from day to day, planting their rice and raising their children in peace? And then this mechanical Godzilla sends airplanes over there and drops bombs on their home, defoliates their land and kills their children."[27]

The crimes of these two "institutionalized" men (Manson as a product of the prison system, Calley through the military) were put most literally into dialogue in a play written by Andrew Dallmeyer, which arranges to have the two men sitting in a prison cell together, discussing the contradictions of living in a society that first trains men to kill and then punishes them for successfully fulfilling its prescriptions. Much more in Sanders's gonzo vein were graphic works that appeared in 1971 in comic book and magazine form. First up was a simulated boxing match between Calley and Manson organized in the pages of *National Lampoon* (in its August 1971 "Bummer" issue). With a composite of Calley and *Mad* magazine's Alfred E. Neuman on the cover— and Neuman's usual "What, me worry?" morphed into "What, My Lai?"—*National Lampoon*'s feature was narrated by Howard Cosell and offered pre-fight interviews and a round-by-round analysis of the match. Calley ultimately wins (after some crucial intervention from President Nixon) but not before Manson predicts, Muhammad Ali-style, that the day of the fight will be "the helter-skelter date, when I'll be the No. 1 welterweight."[28]

The release of this issue of *National Lampoon* more or less coincided with the publication of the comic book *A Legion of Charlies*, which was written by Tom Veitch and illustrated by Gregg Irons. The title joke was rooted in the fact that William Calley was a member of "Charlie" Company. *Legion of Charlies* has been heroically summarized by M. Steven Fox on his website:

Legion of Charlies . . . incorporates Manson's power to control the minds of others into a story about Calley coming to San Francisco after his release from prison. In the story, Calley is named Rusty Kali [yes, it's a bad Hindu-pantheon joke], and he suffers from severe post-traumatic stress disorder, promptly killing a prostitute he has bedded on his first day in the city. After returning to the streets, Kali drops some acid and has a vision about Manson, which changes him into a mindless puppet and "dedicated follower of the word of Charlie!"

Simultaneously, hundreds of other Vietnam veterans across the country undergo the same transformation, inciting a mass migration of Charlie-zombies to a remote retreat in the mountains of Utah. The Legion of Charlies is born on this mountain and they celebrate with a frenzied riot that includes cannibalism as spiritual communion. According to the gospel of Charlie as espoused by Kali, members of the legion can acquire another person's power just by eating them. Led by Kali, the Legion of Charlies begin a trek around the world, devouring political leaders (such as Spiro Agnew and Chairman Mao) and assuming their powers.

This lethal turn of events does not go unnoticed by President Nixon, who invites the Legion of Charlies to New York for a meeting. But Nixon's secret purpose for meeting the Charlies is to seize them and take control of the powers they've ingested. Unfortunately for Tricky Dick, the spirit of Charlie possesses more celestial power than he ever expected![29]

Legion of Charlies joined Sanders and so many others on the political and cultural Left in arguing that Manson and Calley need to be understood as Frankenstein monsters and their crimes had to be traced back to their roots in the programming done by the institutions of the dominant culture.

If *National Lampoon* and *Legion of Charlies* represented the "low" culture avant-garde construction of the "true crimes" of Manson and Calley, then surely the emblematic work of the "high" culture avant-garde was *Commune*, a theater happening first presented in December 1970 by Richard Schechner's Performance Group. *Commune* played for over two years, as theater historian Esther Sundell Lichti has explained, "in one form or another . . . both at The Performing Garage and on tour." As Lichti makes clear in her work on *Commune*, the piece "began with an exploration of the idea of community, in both its real and mythic senses."

Commune was developed as a collective workshop experience "to which all members contributed thoughts, ideas, and materials" and ultimately revolved around "two events: the murder of Sharon Tate by the Manson Family, and the massacre of Vietnamese civilians in My Lai by American soldiers."[30] Schechner, a major figure in avant-garde New York drama and theater education, has made it plain that the crimes of Charles Manson and William Calley were construed by the company as constituting "rather identical incidents of national policy."[31] This consonance is underscored in the performance in such a way as to make audience members consider their own complicity as well. Patrons entering the theater space were asked to give up their shoes; these shoes are later worn by actors portraying the Manson Family killers as they commit their crimes at Cielo Drive (all of which unfolds as "Calley" is describing his own crimes).[32]

In the years immediately following the Tate-LaBianca murders it was a common feature of commentary on Manson to suggest that the "true crime" at issue here (as with the My Lai massacres) was how murderers are produced by the American military and prison complexes. This was not always a particularly nuanced rhetoric: much of it seems to be inspired by the Rolling Stones' key "insight" in their 1968 song "Sympathy for the Devil" that all of us were somehow responsible for the killing of John and Robert Kennedy. Vincent Bugliosi would argue against this cultural tendency in his prosecution and, with much broader social impact, in the true crime book he ultimately wrote with Curt Gentry. But it flattens out the meanings of the Manson case to ignore this earlier attempt—haphazard, undigested, and unsustained, ultimately, as it was—to rehumanize Manson (de-demonize him?) by stitching him back into a recognizable web of social relations. Manson himself joined the argument at his trial. "We train them to kill," he said, "and they go over and kill, and we prosecute them and put them in jail because they kill."[33]

Hippie Ugly! Hippie Shit! Toothpaste Good!

It was Ed Sanders who launched the most sustained challenge to the Bad Man narrative constructed by the prosecution in the Manson case. The "truth" in the serialized "true crime" Ed Sanders produced for the *Los Angeles Free Press* has very little to do with the investigative police work and courtroom drama that would form the heart of Vincent Bugliosi's *Helter Skelter*. Rather, Ed Sanders used the trial of Charles Manson to prosecute his own case in the *Los Angeles Free Press* about the murderous contradictions at the heart of United States domestic and foreign policy in 1969 and 1970. Rather than cede to the aggressive "end of the sixties" rhetoric developing around the murders and the trial, Sanders advances an alternate politics that uses the trial to propose a number of crucial areas in which the cultural and political meanings of the sixties itself was being put on trial along with Manson and his followers. With perhaps greater consistency and more intensity than any other published commentator, Ed Sanders worked to demonstrate how Manson was being used as a sign of all of the "excesses" of the counterculture: "Manson fuck much. Guilt! Manson live commune. Guilt! Manson LSD. Guilt! . . . Hippie Dirty! Hippy Whore! Hippie Ugly! Hippie Shit! Toothpaste Good!"[1]

When he was able to ramp down his purposefully extravagant prose a tiny bit, Sanders was also able to explain how Manson's "true crime" was set into starker relief by the prosecution's strategy of using Linda Kasabian—the star of the state's case—as the "good" hippie counterpart to Manson. Sanders noticed fairly quickly how Kasabian was being used by her prosecutorial and journalistic supporters as what original case prosecutor Aaron Stovitz called a "true flower child" who had unwittingly fallen under the influence of Manson. In the summer of 1970 Sanders speculated that Kasabian was essentially becoming an object of what Tom Wolfe, in that same moment, was defining as "radical chic" (though really "liberal chic" in this case). Though born in 1939, Sanders was really more of a late-model fifties radical/beatnik than a hippie, and his feelings about Kasabian were colored no doubt by his sense that she was a turncoat—naming names in order to spare herself.

Sanders was especially incensed at the role played by New Journalist Joan Didion who, according to his description, was preparing a version of Kasabian's "flower strewn life story" for publication and would likely "appear on Johnny Carson" before long.[2] The Kasabian book never did appear, though Didion ultimately incorporated some of this material into *The White Album*, a key text in establishing the Manson case as the "end of the sixties." By her own admission, Didion joined Vincent Bugliosi in making sure that Linda Kasabian looked the part she was attempting to play at the trial. As Didion explains, she was enlisted by Kasabian to shop for the dress that this "flower child" would wear as she began her testimony at Manson's trial: "I went to the Magnin-Hi Shop on the third floor of I. Magnin in Beverly Hills and picked out, at Linda's request, the dress in which she began her testimony about the murders at Sharon Tate Polanski's house on Cielo Drive. 'Size 9 Petite,' her instructions read. 'Mini but not extremely mini. In velvet if possible. Emerald green or gold. Or: A Mexican peasant-styled dress, smocked or embroidered.'"[3] There was some urgency to Didion's errand, as the journalist explains, because Bugliosi had vetoed Kasabian's original wardrobe choice, "a long white homespun shift" because—according to the prosecutor-cum-fashion-consultant—long "is for evening."[4] While the prosecutor was rejecting the dress Kasabian wanted to wear to court, a number of the other Manson women continued to work on their own piece of "homespun"—the vest they had been making Manson for the past couple of years. In *Rolling Stone*'s June 25, 1970, cover story, Family member Sandra Good explained that various women had been "working on this for two years . . . adding things, sewing on patches. It's for Charlie to wear in court."[5] Paul Watkins explains that from the day he first joined the Family he noticed that "there were always girls working on Charlie's ceremonial vest—a vest embroidered by hand in every imaginable color, a vest begun the day the Family was started by Charlie's first female follower, Mary Brunner. During the Summer of Love it was embroidered with flowers . . . then little scenes were added depicting the Family's odyssey across the country, and finally, their arrival at Spahn's. There were scenes of making love, riding horses, smoking dope, dancing, making music, going to the desert."[6] Watkins is eloquent in his description of the vest's function as a counterhistory of the Family and its times, a chronicle meant to challenge the official story of the Manson Family being constructed by Vincent Bugliosi and his witnesses in court: "In time the vest became a vibrant, living chronicle of events within the Family, all the way through the period of Helter-Skelter, the murders and the trials. Over a two-year span more than fifteen girls worked on the vest continually—sometimes twenty-four hours at a stretch. It looked like a medieval tapestry depicting a legend or a myth. During the trials, after the girls cut their hair, great locks of it were sewn into the fabric."[7] *Rolling Stone* certainly understood the significance of the vest. In its cover story on the Family and the case in June of 1970, the first two pages include pictures first of Manson wearing the vest, and then a close up of the back of the vest itself. In *Manson*, the 1973 documentary on the Family directed by Robert Hendrickson and Laurence Merrick, one of the women says simply of the vest, "It's our story."

A competition of stories (one produced by the prosecution, one by the defense) is, of course, the basic structuring reality of trials in the judicial system of the United States. While the Manson Family women attempted to mount an effort to shape opinion outside the courtroom—on the sidewalks of Los Angeles, in the underground media—they had virtually no power to shape what actually happened inside the Hall of Justice. Sanders takes note of the fact that Manson had something like a "P.R. apparatus" that "reached out to the media tirelessly. Family members wrote letters, approached editors, visited newspapers" and managed to "get some sympathy"—including quite a bit from Ed Sanders himself. Sanders had some complicated work to do: he was committed to establishing the culpability of Manson and the Family in the murders, but he also wanted to demonstrate that the coverage of the arrests in the mainstream media had a distinctly "anticounterculture and antihippie flavor, as if the Mansonites, by their single set of transgressions" had represented the "real funeral of Hippie."[8]

But of course the Family was not able to have much effect on the actual workings of the justice system. Their elaborate, coded vest story would have no bearing on the proceedings in Judge Older's courtroom and their songs would not be heard by many. The Family's lack of access to power was certainly apparent to Ed Sanders, but this reality did not necessarily make his work any simpler. Sanders, as American Studies scholar Thomas Myers has carefully explained, found himself in a particularly fraught position when it came to sharing his voluminous research findings on the case. Myers makes a convincing case that Sanders worried about the relationship of his work over the course of the 1960s to the frightening realities presented by Manson and his followers. Noting that Sanders's primary vehicle of expression was not only called *Fuck You/A Magazine of the Arts* but that it promised in its motto a "Total Assault on the Culture," Myers explains that Sanders was aghast at the frequent depiction of Manson as a key figure of the counterculture—both by the underground press and radical activists (looking for political meaning in the murders he allegedly directed) and by the "establishment" (pointing to him as the logical apotheosis of the excesses of the counterculture). Quoting George Butterick on the possibility that Sanders may have been worried that somehow his oppositional words "had spilled over into unanticipated reality," Myers concludes that the pacifist poet and musician committed himself to fighting against the way the Manson Family represented the "larger appropriation . . . of the very cultural program to which his life . . . had been dedicated."[9]

This all is useful if overstated. There is really no evidence that Sanders took the Manson case quite this personally. While it took Sanders half a year or so to get clear on the fact that Manson simply was a bad guy who "welded together" a group of hippies and turned them into a "war-like clan," after that point he was hellbent on exposing the "acid fascism" (as David Dalton and David Felton of *Rolling Stone* would call it) energizing Manson's power in the freak world of late 1960s Los Angeles.[10] Robert Christgau, in his *New York Times* review of *The Family*, was (marginally) less fanciful than Myers in his explanation of Sanders's compulsion to get involved with the Manson case:

> Like Manson, Sanders was into sex, dope, the occult and the downfall of straight society. Both his Fugs monologues and Shards of God were full of references to jelly orgies, titanic mindwarps and arcane rituals. Of course, many of these references were ironic, overstated metaphors that weren't intended literally. But metaphors have content—Sanders really does believe in expanded sexuality, sacramental and recreational psychedelics, and non-rationalistic modes of knowing—and irony is a sophisticated tool. What could Sanders do when a would-be groupie actually brought a jar of jelly to a Fugs concert—send her back for the Skippy? Such misunderstandings are inevitable when avant-gardism is transformed into a mass movement. This is a liability that long-haired criminals like Charlie Manson and who knows how many other punk charismatics can exploit.[11]

Christgau, perhaps writing out of his own cultural closeness to Sanders's milieu (as an emerging East Village rock critic traveling in some overlapping professional and personal circles) slightly skews the weight of the biographical case. Sanders never demonstrates much in the way of self-doubt or concern that his own art or political practices were being put on trial. Rather, his approach is more that of a bohemian gatekeeper. Sanders used his relative power as a countercultural artist and activist (as opposed to the

potential suspect of Myers's and Christgau's descriptions) to figure out if any of the "Mansonites" should be allowed to come over
to his freaky side of the velvet rope.

Sanders explains in the introduction to a revised edition of *The
Family* that as he began to research the case he became increasingly distressed "over what these people and their connective
groups had done and were still doing."[12] While Sanders was not
going to accept the caricature of Manson as natural evolution of
the counterculture, he was even less likely to accept the simplistic
solved "picture puzzle," as Thomas Myers calls it, presented at the
trial by Vincent Bugliosi.[13] Even before the trial began, Sanders
was questioning the approach to the crimes being promoted by
the prosecution: "What is lacking if the defendants are guilty," he
wrote in May 1970, "is a motive. No one in the media has really
swallowed the whole Helter Skelter routine." In the book version
of *The Family*, Sanders was even more succinct in his evaluation
of the Helter Skelter theory, using his signature nonsense insult:
"oo-ee-oo."[14] That said, Sanders was making it clear by the time he
first published *The Family* in 1971 (before Tex Watson had even
gone on trial) that he was on a mission, helping to rid California of
the "curse of ritual sacrifice, Helter Skelter and satanism."[15]

In order to contest the neat package Bugliosi and his team produced at the trial, Sanders embarked on what he learned from his
mentor, the poet Charles Olson, to call a "saturation job." Olson
first developed this idea in a letter to the poet Ed Dorn, and later
revised it for publication:

"Best thing to do is to dig one thing or place or man until you
yourself know more abt [sic] that than is possible to any other
man. It doesn't matter whether it's Barbed Wire or Pemmican or
Paterson or Iowa. But exhaust it. Saturate it. Beat it."[16] Sanders
was, to put it mildly, a participant-observer when it came to doing
the work of investigating the Family. He explains that on occasion his research "required the adoption of a persona to secure
data, as when I posed as a New York pornography dealer with
Andy Warhol out-takes for sale during an elaborate two-month
caper in which I attempted to purchase certain famous porn-films

of Manson and the Family and citizens of Hollywood." At other times, Sanders found himself impersonating "a Satanist," as well as a "dope-tranced psychopath."[17] Thomas Myers says that in his researching of *The Family*, Sanders converted himself into equal parts "countercultural Continental Op [from Dashiell Hammett's detective fiction] and Emersonian transparent eyeball."[18]

Myers's phrase is evocative, but it captures none of the manic intensity of Sanders's work—either in terms of the exhaustive efforts he made to find out everything he possibly could about the Manson Family and all its tentacles, or about the sometimes exhausting form his writing ultimately took in *The Family*. Here Robert Christgau's review is helpful—particularly his coinage of the phrase "data-mania." As Christgau observes, Sanders "refuses to philosophize, psychoanalyze or make excuses": "'The Family' is nothing more than a chronological arrangement of . . . facts, apparently written direct from the files, rapidly. . . . There is no theorizing, and no new journalism either—no fabricated immediacy, no reconstructed dialogue, no arty pace."[19] (It is instructive to compare Christgau's description of Sanders's work to John Gilmore's account of his own approach in writing true crime books—including his 1971 Manson book, *The Garbage People*. Gilmore, originally trained as a method actor, described his research as growing from that early teaching: "I wasn't a reporter, a chronicler. I was the artist, and these experiences and encounters were as paints, hues, tones, values and varnishes I was laying across a space to form a vibrating picture, mirroring the human experience."[20])

The Family is neither the neo-noir of Thomas Myers's description nor the rawboned documentary Robert Christgau reads it as. Although the word would not come into widespread general critical usage until a few years after *The Family* was published, it seems clear now that Sanders was working the same artistic vein as the visual artists called "hyperrealists" in this moment. What Ed Sanders shared with the hyperrealists—Duane Hanson (*Supermarket Shopper*, in 1970 and *Woman Eating*, 1971), Audrey Flack (*Farb Family*, 1970) and Chuck Close (*Nat*, 1971) in sculpture and painting, but also John Cassavetes (*Husbands*, 1970) in film—was the ability to pull off the sleight of hand through which a radical challenge to dominant politics, aesthetics, and ways of thinking cloaks itself in the neutral garb of documentary precision. Perhaps my favorite hypperrealist moment in *The Family* comes when Sanders gives his readers directions—really clear directions—to "Devil's Hole," the putative entrance to the bottomless pit in Nevada where Manson, allegedly, told his followers they would live while the race war was playing out above ground:

> One such entrance to The Hole was thought to be the so-called Devil's Hole in the northwest triangular corner of the Death Valley National Monument where the monument extends briefly into Nevada. Devil's Hole, fenced off from potential visitors, is a baleful pit full of water, and inhabited by blind fish, according to the Family. A couple of skin divers had drowned several years previous trying to touch bottom.
>
> For anyone interested, to get to Devil's Hole you proceed to Death Valley on Route 127. Then drive north to a town called Death Valley Junction. Hang a right there and proceed to Ash Meadows Rancho. Then grab a northish country road across the California–Nevada Line to the Hole.[21]

There are facts aplenty in *The Family*, but they don't exist in an artless vacuum. What Sanders achieves in *The Family* is a gonzo version of what Clifford Geertz called "thick description"—the anthropological practice of paying attention to context, listening to "native informants," staying focused on webs of social discourse, and remaining attentive to details with meticulous care.[22] The inclusion of geolocators in the pages of *The Family*, along with the book's media criticism, agitprop, legal and rhetorical analysis, anti-Satanist rants, and so on, makes it plain that Sanders is not the "transparent eyeball" of Thomas Myers's description. His work is highly stylized political journalism and history. It masks itself as an objective and chronological account of the crimes, investigations, trials, and aftermath, but also manages to incorporate a huge amount of social critique, much of which has to do with the corruption of the American legal and judicial systems.

The main tool of Sanders's cinematic book is the extreme close-up: Tex Watson's stash of powdered amphetamine is in a Gerber's baby food jar; the Family listens to the Beatles' record *Abbey Road* on a "battery-operated" portable turntable; one of the Beach Boys' gold records ends up "in the hands of George Spahn's brother."[23] If the book has a breathless, "and then, and then, and then" feel and this relatively linear organization makes it read like documentary, it is important not to underplay how explicitly the book presents a hyperreal vision of multiple overlapping presents. The seeming clarity of *The Family* is a willful act of writerly misdirection; it is Sanders's main method for establishing his rhetorical credentials as he takes on the mainstream press, Vincent Bugliosi, Richard Nixon, and the rest of the establishment.

In his work for the *Free Press* and then on what became *The Family*, Ed Sanders was flying two flags. He was working diligently to explain just what kind of freak Charles Manson was and, in doing so, create plenty of daylight in between Manson and the rest of the tribes constituting the counterculture. But he was also attacking Vincent Bugliosi's claims of being omniscient and evenhanded. While Sanders let his apparently single-minded data curation do most of the arguing for him, *Rolling Stone*'s David Dalton and David Felton were much more up-front in their analysis of how hard it was to argue with the dominant culture, even quoting social philosopher Norman O. Brown: "[L]egalistic rationalism does not get away from magic," but "on the contrary, it makes the magical effects so permanent and so pervasive that we do not notice them at all."[24] Dalton and Felton go on to argue that contemporary citizens are "under a spell" and that "the courts, the government have mesmerized us with documents, facts, fetishes to keep our minds off what is really happening."[25] But where Sanders regularly suggests that the "magic" of judicial protocols could only be mobilized by the state, Dalton and Felton theorized quite differently in the *Rolling Stone* cover article; to them the messiness of the Manson case (just what crime was Charlie really being accused of, anyway?) was going to make it impossible for the trial to do its work of "assigning blame" for a "single, separate crime . . . with a single, obvious motive."[26] Manson, they believed, would be able to "manipulate" the system more or less by being his own unpredictable self. Sanders was less sanguine about the power of Manson, his Family, and his legal team to combat the awesome force of the state. Sanders understanding of the situation proved much closer to the actual result.

Manson and his counsel were certainly able to disrupt the regular workings of the courtroom, but ultimately it was Vincent Bugliosi who controlled the narrative, garnered a conviction, and—as Sanders would see things—protected the moneyed and powerful interests of Hollywood. By late 1970 Sanders was using his space in the *Free Press* to launch a full-bore critique of the trial and the evidence it revealed about the corrupt workings of the police and the prosecutor's office. Sanders was particularly incensed that Terry Melcher and Dennis Wilson were being shielded from having to reckon with the consequences of their various entanglements with the Manson Family. While Sanders does not accuse the two (or Gregg Jakobson) of any crimes per se, the Freep journalist was determined to explain to his readers just how partial the "truths" revealed at the trial were. In an article published in October 1970 with the headline "Manson & the missing groin clink" and the subhead "Where oh where is Dennis Wilson," Sanders speculated that Terry Melcher would get away with simply testifying that he never did help Jakobson make that documentary about Manson. Sanders noted that Melcher would definitely not say anything at the trial about the underage Ouisch. As for the Beach Boy, Sanders claimed that Wilson had been acting crazy whenever "questioned by authorities" and it was plain that Irving Kanarek would not be able to get Wilson to testify at the trial with respect to the "surprising list of famous starlets, children of entertainment giants, and people with hot careers—all with whom Manson clinked groins."[27]

This web of "indiscriminate apertural-appendage conjugation," as Sanders later called it in *The Family*, would not make an appearance at the trial because Vincent Bugliosi did not want it to.[28] Sanders's work for the *Free Press* and then in *The Family* was very much organized around the notion that Manson and his Family were intimately tied up with various overlapping communities in and around Los Angeles. Sanders's early sense was that "dope traffic" was going to turn out to be the key to understanding the series of events leading to the eventual murders at Cielo and Waverly Drive. By the time he published *The Family* Sanders was also convinced that various non-traditional religious practices (i.e., "Satanism") played a major role in the process by which the Family went completely off the rails. To Sanders, Manson's "true crime" was using his leverage in the counterculture to wreak great damage and bring disrepute onto hippies and other bohemians. Drugs and "outsider" religious organizations kept Manson more or less in the general swim of things in California in the late 1960s; a theory of race war pushed him fairly far beyond the boundaries of relevance.

But acknowledging that Manson had insinuated himself socially and sexually into the elite circles of Los Angeles's film and music industry would work against the truth Bugliosi wanted to establish—that Manson was a completely marginal and delusional figure, plotting Helter Skelter as revenge for a lifetime of feeling disempowered. Ed Sanders argued in his *Free Press* series that no serious journalists bought Bugliosi's Helter Skelter theory to explain the crimes. He also mocked the input of Brooks Poston, a close Family compatriot of Manson, who could allegedly put himself into a trance state at will and who testified that the cult leader had directed these killings in order to somehow "trigger off the destruction of the United States by Black militants": "I mean, come off it," is Sanders's response.[29] (Bugliosi, in what was likely a fit of triumphalism, given that his version won the day, quotes defense attorney Irving Kanarek's dismissal of Helter Skelter in his closing argument. Kanarek wondered if the jury was "to believe that by means of a wallet found in a toilet tank Mr. Manson intended to start a race war."[30])

As late as his 1992 parole hearing Manson himself was still challenging the Helter Skelter theory: "[A]s far as lining up someone for some kind of Helter Skelter trip, you know, that's the district attorney's motive. That's the only thing he could find for a motive to throw up on top of all that confusion he had." Manson went on to instruct the parole board that Helter Skelter was not a theory of race war, but "was a song and . . . a nightclub—we opened a little after-hours nightclub to make some money and play some music and do some dancing and singing and play some stuff to make some money for dune buggies to go out in the desert. And we called the club Helter Skelter."[31]

What virtually none of the true-crime writers has wanted to acknowledge is how *not* crazy it would be to worry about interracial violence, particularly in Los Angeles, and particularly in 1969. I need only mention the mayoral election of that year, which pit the candidate of the white establishment, Sam Yorty, against the insurgent African American candidate, Tom Bradley. Bradley ran far ahead of Yorty in the April primary, but Yorty (carrying water for the FBI's COINTELPRO) very successfully raised concerns that Bradley was putting together a threatening coalition of Black Power advocates and radical leftists. Paul Mazursky's strange film *Alex in Wonderland*, released in 1970, approaches the question of Black revolution as a matter of some moment, but very few narratives of the Los Angeles scene—and the Manson Family more particularly—take seriously how deeply so many residents of Los Angeles were worrying about race relations in 1969. In the Manson context it is, somewhat surprisingly, only the television series *Aquarius* that puts Black Panther Bunchy Carter right at the center of things in Los Angeles.

A Newcomer, an Intruder

It is interesting to think about Charles Manson's post hoc explanations of the remarkably unthreatening way in which Helter Skelter circulated in his Family. It is interesting to think about Ed Sanders's claim that no journalist observing the trial gave any credence to the theory of Helter Skelter promoted by the prosecution. It is also interesting to consider the claims made in the foreword to a revised edition of John Gilmore's 1971 *Garbage People* (1995), which pretends that this volume has acted as a "spectral 'third' title" along with *Helter Skelter* and *The Family* in defining the true crime Manson landscape. Here the publisher makes the mathematically neat but historically indefensible claim that *Garbage People* has made an impact as the midpoint on a line graph stretching from Bugliosi ("Mr. Straight, ready to cash in on all the gore") to Ed Sanders (trying to "restore the good name of peace-loving flower children around the world from the stain of guilt by association").[1]

If there is indeed a spectral third title, it is not *Garbage People* but rather the film documentary *Manson* by Robert Hendrickson and Laurence Merrick, first screened in 1973, but which did not get much of showing until 1976. Jean Murley has written eloquently about this movie and is especially convincing about its status as a major product of what we might call the latency period of Manson narratives. As Murley puts it, this film was made between 1969 and 1972, before Manson had been frozen in place as a "cultural signifier of mayhem and subversion." Unlike so many later narratives, *Manson* allows Family members to have a voice—through direct testimony, but also via the documentary's ethnographic richness. In the movie we see the women of the Family engaged in what is obviously meaningful activity, from embroidering Manson's vest, to scrounging for food and having group sex, to sitting in protest outside the Hall of Justice in Los Angeles. The film, which features music made by Family members Brooks Poston and Paul Watkins, is, as Murley claims, "[q]uiet, balanced, and small." Abjuring the sensationalism that would characterize so many later narratives of Family life (and which, in fact, characterized Sanders's book), Hendrickson and Merrick instead focus their attention on the Family as text—they capture the rituals and organizing principles of everyday life—while also paying careful attention to the historical context framing the Manson phenomenon. The filmmakers try to make sure that their viewers will read the life of the Family in the context of "violent street rebellion, the Vietnam war, and race riots."[2]

The *Manson* film has had an occult presence, at best, reemerging from legal limbo every so often to remind viewers that Bugliosi's Helter Skelter narrative is neither inevitable nor exclusive. One of the best things about *Manson*, the documentary, as Jean Murley has emphasized, is that it does not reenact the murders, abjuring whatever pleasures that action might have afforded to viewers.[3] Instead, the movie acts, *avant la lettre*, as a corrective to the dozens of cultural productions—most notably Bugliosi's book and the television miniseries based on it—that treated the killings themselves as the required money shot. But whatever *Manson* (or *The Family* or *Garbage People*) accomplished, it is foolish to suggest that any other text can compete with *Helter Skelter* when it comes to analytical or marketplace domination. That Bugliosi's "Mr. Straight" persona was fairly widely challenged in the early to mid-1970s is largely irrelevant to his accomplishments at the trial and in the print and televised versions of *Helter Skelter*.

It is not really possible to separate the presence of Charles Manson in the historical record and popular consciousness from the work done by Vincent Bugliosi and his co-writer Curt Gentry. The book established its claim to dominance almost immediately upon publication. If anything like a consensus developed about Bugliosi's work in the wake of its release, it basically took the form of a grudging respect—this was an important subject but not much of an actual book. The *New York Times* actually evinced more than a little bit of discomfort in its review of *Helter Skelter*; while the account is generally favorable, the review carries a dismissive subtitle—"Manson Meets the Bug" (the "Bug" was a nickname promoted by the women of the Family during the trial and supported by defense attorney Irving Kanarek's frequent mispronunciations)—and a sardonic tone. Additionally the *Times* devoted relatively few column inches to what the paper must have recognized was a fairly major publishing event. What is most interesting about the review is how fully it articulated the idea that both Charles Manson and Vincent Bugliosi practiced the hard sell. This represents an interesting moment in the cultural processing of the Tate-LaBianca murders. In a sense it is the last time that anyone with a central place in mainstream culture would treat the Helter Skelter theory as anything other than the simple truth about this case. "The entire notion" of these murders being committed in order to set off a race war, according to reviewer Michael Rogers, was "quirky, inconsistent and psychotic." It remains something of a mystery, he goes on to write, that Manson was able to "sell it to his unimaginative, middle-class band of runaways. And it's as much an accomplishment on Bugliosi's part that he unraveled the whole twisted ideological package. But most to the prosecutor's credit is that he managed to turn around and sell it himself to an unimaginative middle-class jury. In that courtroom feat, more than any other, Charles Manson truly met his match in Vincent Bugliosi."[4]

In Rogers's apt rendering, Helter Skelter comes to light not as an interpretive given, but instead as a theatrical contest. Rogers's intervention would have little impact, of course. Bugliosi's version of events would soon become entrenched as conventional wisdom for explaining the Manson Family. Still, Rogers's claim is interesting for the position it takes on the persuasive abilities of powerful men: the jury, in this reviewer's account, is made up, essentially, of the parents of the young people who constituted the Family. The implicit (and somewhat surprising) claim here is that it is not particularly hard to control the minds of "middle-class" people—whether teenage runaways or full-grown members of a jury.

In his review Rogers also correctly noted that Bugliosi's achievement was not only in *Helter Skelter*'s substance—its explanation of Manson's motive—but also in its tone. The book's success, as Rogers explained, was rooted very much in its ability to create a narrative voice that captured the easy authority of the prosecutor. The prose of *Helter Skelter*, as Rogers put it, is "methodical, tight, occasionally ironical and rising to emotional pitch only on rare occasion. And even when Bugliosi raises his voice, one still senses the calculated flavor of a closing argument to the jury."[5] In *Helter Skelter*, as Rogers's review suggests, Bugliosi is not only doing the important work of (re)litigating the case—he is also demonstrating how a proper middle-class father instructs his charges.

Bugliosi's appearances on local media during the trial made it clear that he was more than willing, and quite able, to represent navy-blue-suited rationality. It is worth remembering that Bugliosi and Manson were exact contemporaries—they were born just three months apart from each other in 1934. In addition to obtaining convictions, another main task for the prosecutor (inside and outside the Hall of Justice) was to present a comforting visual and auditory antidote to Manson with respect to what thirty-five looked like in California in 1969. Bugliosi's work (in the court of public opinion anyway) was made easier by the fact that the defense team did not exactly present a formidable opposition. Bugliosi consistently dominated Los Angeles television news coverage, with little challenge from anyone on the defense team. The local media could not get enough of Bugliosi during the trial—he looked good, but not too good, and he spoke well. Next to Bugliosi, members of the defense team looked socially marginal. The cameras lingered on the defendants' lawyers only long enough to show audiences a sketchy shyster (Irving Kanarek), a baffled if amiable young hippie (Ronald Hughes) and an above-it-all cosmopolitan (Daye Shinn, rarely filmed or photographed without a grin on his face or cigarette in hand, seeming to be on the lookout for his missing cocktail). Bugliosi's performances in public, on the other hand, revealed a relatively young man—with a reassuringly receding hairline signaling gravitas—more than able to take on the mantle of reassuring authority.

There are, of course, challenging stories about Bugliosi that have been circulating at least since the time of *Helter Skelter's* publication. In our own time it has become simple to access these counternarratives—both about his work as prosecutor and about his personal life. On the latter front, a simple web search of "Bugliosi" along with the keywords "milkman" and "mistress" reveals that there is a solid core of Manson-case enthusiasts who have devoted quite a bit of energy to researching questions widely publicized by George Denny III in 1974 about the prosecutor's personal rectitude. Denny first crossed paths with Bugliosi in his role as lawyer for Manson Family member Bruce Davis in the trial for the murder of Spahn Ranch laborer Donald "Shorty" Shea. But for years after this, Denny had something of a side career as a thorn in Bugliosi's side. His well-publicized attacks on Bugliosi reached its peak in 1974 during the time Bugliosi was unsuccessfully running for attorney general of California. Denny (working on behalf of William Norris, Bugliosi's Democratic primary opponent) held a press conference on the eve of the election to detail his accusations. According to Denny's statement, Bugliosi had harassed (and then paid off) his family's milkman in 1969 after developing an obsessional fear that the milkman was the actual father of his child. Bugliosi's deviations from his "Mr. Straight" persona continued in 1973 when, according to some accounts, he beat Virginia Caldwell, a woman he allegedly had a sexual relationship with, after she refused his demand to have an abortion. If Bugliosi was going to serve his role successfully he would need to keep his own expressions of violence and experiments in sexual liberation under wraps.[6]

These questions about Bugliosi's personal rectitude dissolved in the narrative power of *Helter Skelter*. The prosecutor was one of the two most important "characters" in the Manson case, and he makes sure to narrate the story in a way that makes this clear. Defense attorney Paul Fitzgerald's oft-repeated quip about the lack of evidence the state was bringing into the courtroom ("All the prosecution has are two fingerprints and Vince Bugliosi") was an early articulation of what would collectively become a fairly wide-scale cultural practice. If Helter Skelter came to be understood as something like potential social chaos, then its opposite number—and vanquisher—was certainly Vincent Bugliosi.[7]

Bugliosi needed Manson. Or to put this another way, Bugliosi needed *a* Manson that he could make work for him. Cultural critic Rob Sheffield has written recently that Bugliosi felt compelled to move Tex Watson from the center of the crime story he was authoring, even though Watson "might seem more like the leading man—he was there both nights, did the actual killings, etc." But as Sheffield puts it, Watson was "all wrong for the part. He had short hair and boy-next-door looks—a high school football hero, for crissakes."[8] If Watson was "all wrong," then Manson was all right: he was "a longhair, wild-eyed cartoon villain" who fit the "auteur" role perfectly and was more than willing to "embrace" the celebrity that came with his arrest and trial.[9] From here Sheffield joins the George Bishop tradition of suggesting that Manson himself was not quite up to the task Bugliosi required of him by stitching him into this starring role, but I think like so many others Sheffield underestimates Manson's game-playing skills. And, as I will discuss in the final section of this book, Manson himself has turned out to be such a compelling character that the voice he worried about "losing" in the courtroom has never been very successfully silenced. Manson and his Family cohort have always managed to creepy crawl out from the disciplining pages of books by Bugliosi, Sanders, and others, and have found ways to tell their own stories and to participate in making themselves available to all manner of creative artists. The central point here is simple: However we want to tell the story of the Tate-LaBianca murders, we seem to always have to put Charles Manson and Vincent Bugliosi at the center and in an incredibly intimate relationship with each other. Bobby Beausoleil has summarized all this as efficiently as anyone. About Manson and Bugliosi he has said, simply, "[T]here was a romance there."[10]

Bugliosi and Gentry introduce the prosecutor with considerable fanfare in *Helter Skelter*—but not until Part Three of the book. This is where Bugliosi makes the move to position himself at the center of a chronicle that, until this point, has been a fairly standard police procedural—with the major caveat that it is a police procedural about what a terrible job the police were doing. Here the authors insert a strange note, addressed more or less directly to "the reader," who has already become, through the first third of the book "an insider in a sense highly unusual in a murder case." At this point, Bugliosi explains, the reader must be prepared to meet the prosecutor—"a newcomer, an intruder"; having been content to act as offscreen director up until now, Bugliosi (in a ridiculously anticlimactic "reveal") strides on stage as the star of the show! There is little doubt that the choice of the word "intruder" here is purposeful. Bugliosi, with no cape or tights, is the superhero who will set right all the chaos set in motion by the Family creepy crawls. His appearance is a sign that the creepy crawl has ended. But the fears inspired by Manson cannot be put to rest until Bugliosi changes into his superhero clothes; as David Schmid has put it, there is a "disarming absence of modesty" about Bugliosi. "Garbed in the cloak of the people's champion," Schmid continues, Bugliosi establishes himself over the many pages of *Helter Skelter* as a powerful enough figure to get in the ring and grapple successfully with the cult leader.[11]

Bugliosi's readers cannot possibly miss what a big deal he is when he hits the stage. This "sudden switch from an unseen background narrator to a very personal account is bound to be a surprise," Bugliosi suggests, and then goes on to reason that the "best way to soften" the blow is to introduce himself. In addition to informing the reader of his stunning win-loss record (104 felony jury trials, and "only one loss"), Bugliosi also provides the important information that he has acted as technical advisor and script editor for "two pilot films" of *The D.A.*—a series made by Jack Webb, of *Dragnet* fame. According to Bugliosi, the star of the show, Robert Conrad, "patterned his part after the young prosecutor."[12]

The shift in narration turns out to be something of an anti-climax. Bugliosi's function is to restore order, and *Helter Skelter* is nothing if not orderly. There is no "oo-ee" in *Helter Skelter*, no "snuff buffs" coming to watch the trial. Bugliosi and Gentry want neither to compete with the "nonfiction novel" version of true crime that Truman Capote talked so much about in the second half of the 1960s, nor the fevered hyperrealism of Ed Sanders. This entry in the true-crime genre has more than one case to prosecute—the one against Manson and his Family, of course, but also against the Los Angeles Police Department and a smaller-stakes one against Polanski and Tate—and does so with an abundance of detail and a shortage of narrative charisma. By the time *Helter Skelter* was published Bugliosi had already made his case and now seems only to want to memorialize that achievement—and settle a few scores.

Christopher Lehmann-Haupt captures the flatness of *Helter Skelter* in his *New York Times* review, noting that once Bugliosi has made his claim about motive the book "doesn't seem to have much point any more." The reviewer goes on "to wonder about his ulterior motives for continuing, and to suspect him variously of pandering to commerce, of trumpeting his ego, of plumping for law and order and even of running for political office." None of these critical punches lands very hard. Of course the prosecutor believes in law and order and wants to make money, and he did run for higher office. But Lehmann-Haupt's review does capture a certain surprising aimlessness to Bugliosi's book. This did not keep it from becoming a runaway bestseller, of course, as well as serving as the basis of the hugely influential television movie released in 1976.[13] The book, as Jean Murley has pointed out, benefits from Bugliosi's ability to take advantage of a "burgeoning paperback market." It was a selection of the Book-of-the-Month club and the *Playboy* Book Club and was also helpfully condensed (in *Book Digest*) and serialized (in the *New York Times*).[14]

But what does *Helter Skelter* do? On some level its main function is to promote the mythology of Manson's unified purpose that Bugliosi developed at the trial. *Helter Skelter* lacks the hallucinatory hyperrealism of Sanders's *Family*, but it does share that book's basic strategy of cramming in as much detail as possible. For his part, Christopher Lehmann-Haupt noted that while Bugliosi hints in the book that a trial lawyer cannot risk overwhelming the jury with too much detail, in his book he does not "give the same consideration to his readers."[15] Sanders creates webs of meaning based on making cultural, political, and social connections that at times seem to exist only in his own head. Bugliosi, on the other hand, offers up a dogged "linear chronology" that situates the case in a narrow groove. Bugliosi is one of two main "characters" in the story, we learn virtually nothing about him. "Married. Two Children" is about all Bugliosi tells readers to give a sense of who he is as a person. In the broadest sense the two major chroniclers of Manson, Bugliosi and Ed Sanders, were both embedded as participant-observers with their subjects, but Bugliosi's careful distancing of himself from the Family serves to remind readers that he remained untouched by whatever appeal (political, musical, sexual, etc.) the Family might have carried. Sanders could not make the same claim in *The Family* and nor does he want to. When Sanders mentions his family, he gives them names—he discusses staying in a hotel with his wife Miriam and daughter Deirdre in Los Angeles as he prepares to take a "tour of Mansonland" with Abbie Hoffman and Phil Ochs.[16]

Bugliosi was certainly operating from a very clear understanding of the zero-sum stakes of the American adversarial system. In *We Are Everywhere,* Jerry Rubin writes of the theatrical framework of American trials: "both sides," he writes, "put on a play and create a myth for the jury. Two versions of history. Two theatrical performances. The jury then goes into the jury room and decides what play feels more real to them."[17] Convicted Family associate Bobby Beausoleil went even further with this approach in an interview he gave to John Gilmore in the early 1970s. Beausoleil suggested to Gilmore that through "a big trial that judicial machine can make a million dollars. So they play this big game of theatrics and drag the thing out as long as they can." Beausoleil underscored not only the profit-making impulse stitched into the "adversarial" system but also reminded his interviewer that the "public defender and the prosecutor have offices next door to each other, and they get their pay from the same window."[18]

Such matters were far beyond the prosecutor's ken. Bugliosi's plodding realism (as opposed to Irving Kanarek's Theater-of-the-Absurd) won the day, of course, and it is equanimity, above all, that Bugliosi wants to project in *Helter Skelter*. Over the hundreds and hundreds of pages of this true-crime saga, readers never see a tear in the fabric of the prosecutor's case—not even a seam, really. There is little here that would support Family member Sandy Good's contention that outside the courthouse Bugliosi threatened her. That Bugliosi—if he actually existed—does not appear on the pages of *Helter Skelter*.

Not Just the Facts, Ma'am

P erhaps the best way to call attention to the relentlessness of *Helter Skelter*'s fealty to the constraints of the police and legal procedural forms is to discuss two times Bugliosi and his co-author break free of them in order to include what might initially seem like tangents. It is crucial that Bugliosi not veer too far away from his clear commitment to "objectivity" over the course of *Helter Skelter*. What David Schmid has written of the "nonfiction novel" developed by Truman Capote and others in the 1960s is equally true of Bugliosi's true-crime tale: the claims to "objectivity" are carried in part by "authorial invisibility" even as the author gives up "none of his control over the shaping and presenting of events."[1]

Both of the ruptures in *Helter Skelter* break from the standard template in order to prosecute (at least by implication) a norm-setting agenda. The first break comes early in the book, in a discussion of the possibility that the Tate killings were inspired by a "drug burn or freakout."[2] While Bugliosi quickly dropped this investigative thread, many others—including Family associate Bobby Beausoleil—have called attention to the evidence connecting Sharon Tate and her friends at Cielo Drive to the drug underworld of Los Angeles.[3] In his discussion of four men implicated by this early investigative work, Bugliosi notes that their names have been changed "for legal reasons" in *Helter Skelter*.[4] After introducing the four suspects and noting his use of pseudonyms in this section, Bugliosi then goes on to explain that "Wilson, Pickett, Madigan, and a fourth man . . . were frequent visitors to the Cielo residence." With this out-of-the blue reference to soul singer Wilson Pickett (a presence on the rhythm-and-blues charts and, occasionally, on the pop charts during the second half of the 1960s), Bugliosi makes a seemingly pointless pun in a book otherwise short on digressions, laugh lines, or really many elements of what might be called creative writing.

In addition to his regular appearance near the top of the rhythm-and-blues charts beginning in 1963, and his steady incursions on the pop music charts, Wilson Pickett was also consolidating his persona in 1967 and 1968—a persona captured by the titles of two of the albums he released in those years—*The Wicked Pickett* and *The Midnight Mover*. Pickett's adoption of the Bad Man pose in the late 1960s had roots, of course, in more than a hundred years of African American cultural productions, from post-slavery folktales, rhyming verbal performances of rebelliousness and protest, and blues songs. Pickett's own cover version of the core African American crime story "Stagger Lee" in 1968 served as one declaration that he was trying on the mask such songs made available.

In this "Wilson, Pickett" moment *Helter Skelter* swerves from a brief, and ultimately irrelevant, summary of the activity of a few (presumably white) drug dealers in the Tate-Frykowski circles, to an invocation of the Midnight Mover. (That song could be described as a Creepy Crawling Blues; it literally features a main character who is sneaking in and out of homes in the dark of night.) For a book that takes place in Los Angeles in the 1960s, there are hardly any Black people present. Given Bugliosi's insistence on the racial paranoia at the heart of Manson's cracked Helter Skelter vision, the true crime narrative itself suggests that the cult leader did not encounter many African Americans in his peripatetic Los Angeles life.

One of the few Black men to feature at all in Bugliosi's true-crime tale is Bernard Crowe, a.k.a. "Lotsapoppa." Manson may have believed that Lotsapoppa, a well-known drug dealer, was also a Black Panther, and at least briefly believed that he had killed Crowe during an altercation over drugs and money: in fact, he only wounded him. (I cannot resist mentioning that another "Lotsa Poppa" broke into limited public consciousness in the 1960s. This "Lotsa Poppa" was an Atlanta-area soul singer who had a regional hit with a cover of "I Found a Love," originally recorded by Wilson Pickett's group the Falcons, and re-recorded as a solo song by Pickett himself in 1967.)[5]

The appearance of "Wilson, Pickett" as half of the list of drug dealers considered as suspects in the early days of the Tate-LaBianca investigation cannot help but serve as a racialization of drug use and drug sales. Bugliosi's book is ultimately about the "frightening" claim that too many social boundaries were being breached in Los Angeles (white/black, celebrity/civilian, rich hippie/poor hippie, street culture/private life) in the era of the Manson Family's rise to visibility; projecting creepy-crawling evil onto recognizable Others (hippies, Black people, Hollywood stars) became a central part of Bugliosi's courtroom and true-crime strategies. Where Ed Sanders takes as a given that the Tate-LaBianca murders had to be plotted on a very busy map of cultural meetings, Bugliosi frames this reality as the germ of horror.

The next break in *Helter Skelter* also comes relatively early in the book when Bugliosi takes some time out to give some background on Roman Polanski. After a concise description of his film career and his relationship with Sharon Tate, Bugliosi moves on to a brief summary of the numerous "non-friends" who had negative things to say about the Polish film director: "One, referring to the fact that Polanski (like Manson) was just over five feet tall, called him 'the original five-foot Pole you wouldn't want to touch anyone with.'"[6]

If it is not immediately clear why Bugliosi wants to recount this syntactically tortured and not so funny remark, this break in the narrative opens up an episodic case made by the prosecutor over the course of the book having to do with the shortness of the men at the center of the case. Just after the "five-foot Pole" quip, Bugliosi suggests that whether "one was captivated by his gaminlike charm or repelled by his arrogance," Polanski "appeared to touch off strong emotions in nearly everyone whom he met." (Translation: Audrey Hepburn or Napoleon? You decide!)[7] While *gamin* is the masculine form of the French noun meaning "street urchin" or "waif," by the time Polanski rose to fame the word was much more familiar in American popular culture in its feminine form (*gamine*) and was used almost exclusively to refer to female screen actors. Calling Polanski *gaminlike* was, then, a way to call into question how well he measured up to standard visions of American masculinity.

This concern with Polanski's size turns out not to be an isolated moment in *Helter Skelter*. While it is not surprising for a prosecutor to recount forensic details, Bugliosi seems particularly intent on establishing the vertical challenges of a few key players in the case. Danny DeCarlo, treasurer of the Straight Satans motorcycle club, is identified as being only 5' 4" tall—although Bugliosi does spare a moment to mention that DeCarlo was known as Donkey Dan— not small in all respects, as it turns out. Bugliosi also mentions that Jay Sebring was 5' 6" and apparently liked to tie up women and beat them. But the most diminutive of all was Manson himself: "I hadn't realized how small he was. He was just five feet two . . . . I could not believe that this little guy had done all the things it was said he had."[8] Deana Martin, daughter of Dean Martin and close friend of Terry Melcher, describes Manson as having been "very small" and looking like "every other hippie on Sunset."[9] Bugliosi emphasized his "surprise" at Manson's size throughout his post-trial career; in one interview he reveals that he felt "shocked how little he was. He was scruffy, with long, scraggly hair, and kind of hunchbacked. I thought, 'He doesn't look imposing.' But I'd already learned enough about him to know that it would be a great error on my part to underestimate him."[10] Cultural historian Jeffrey Sconce has explained that a major effort was made in the mainstream media to cut Manson down to size, with repeated references to the cult leader as "pint-sized" and "diminutive."[11]

In Bugliosi's rendering Manson comes to light as a troll— small, ugly, and yet somehow possessed of great power. (It might be worth mentioning here that there is nothing objectively "true" about the prosecutor's articulation of Manson's appearance. Compare Bugliosi's description of the convicted criminal to that offered by artist Raymond Pettibon, who has used Manson's image repeatedly in his work: "Here was this charismatic, good-looking guy whose followers might be your own daughters.")[12] Bugliosi could not allow for the possibility that part of Manson's appeal to the young women who constituted the bulk of his Family's membership was simply that he was physically attractive. Bugliosi's burden in *Helter Skelter* is to make clear that Manson's power was disturbingly nonstandard—it was, in fact, occult and pathological. Paul Watkins, often described as Manson's "second in command," had a much different reading of Manson's stature. Watkins argued that Manson gravitated to "Little Paul" as a result of the "definite camaraderie" that arises among small men. According to Watkins, being "five-foot-five in a macho world of six-footers was never easy. It's a bit like being a racial minority."[13] Where Bugliosi could see only deviance (and childishness—"this little guy") in Manson's physical self, Watkins finds the origin of Manson's empathetic outreach and powerful charisma.

Once we accept the (obvious) premise that true-crime books are not *only* true, it becomes much easier to see how invested these books are not only in narrating details of the crime(s) in question, but also in prosecuting various other cultural concerns. Feminist sociologist Karlene Faith has been particularly sharp in her critique on this front. According to Faith, *Helter Skelter* was "a bestseller, and is still in print today, replete with inaccuracies due to the defendants' false testimony in court and their own propagation of sensationalized myths."[14] *Helter Skelter*, like so many true-crime books, invites readers to enjoy the thrill of "actual" crime-scene spectacle and investigative puzzles while also presenting a carefully crafted tale that moves with the inevitability of myth. The characters are simply drawn, representing basic types rather than fully dimensional human actors. While Vincent Bugliosi invoked fictional Los Angeles detective Joe Friday (from the television show *Dragnet*) to suggest that his co-writer Curt Gentry helped him to organize the material of the Tate-LaBianca murders and ensuing trials into a "just-the-facts" chronicle, it is important to remember that the selection and organization of those "facts" is at the heart of the process by which readers constitute particular meanings out of narratives.[15] If Ed Sanders and other insurgent figures were interested in banishing Manson from the counterculture, Bugliosi's job was to expel him from mainstream culture. The seemingly irrelevant details about the size of Manson (and Polanski and Sebring and DeCarlo) act as a reminder that these are men on the fringe—perhaps powerful in one sense or another (Polanski's cultural cachet, Manson's personal magnetism, and so on)—but not fit for a place in conventional society. Choosing between Bugliosi and Sanders is something like choosing between allopathic and homeopathic remedies: do you want someone very distant from the accused to neutralize the fears they inspire or do you want someone in their world to inoculate you against them with a little bit of freaky medicine?

Bugliosi's attempts to marginalize Manson (in the arena of pre-trial public relations, at the trial itself, and in post-trial accounts—*Helter Skelter*, above all) should not be understood as simple cruelty or as triumphalist crowing. One important task Bugliosi had to accomplish in his work as the voice of the People of the State of California was to "cultivate" Manson as a scapegoat and make him available as a container for a considerable measure of free-floating social anxiety about the counterculture. The work of sociologists of the 1960s and early 1970s on deviance (especially that done by Howard Becker and Kai Erickson) makes clear that "outsiders"—as Becker called them—are created by their host culture and are not simply revealed as having some inherent defect. Deviants, in short, are made and not born.[16]

It is not difficult to see that Bugliosi was invested in demonstrating that Manson and his codefendants did not simply do bad things but embodied profound deviations from key mainstream conceptions of family, gender, love, adulthood, sexuality, and so on. Where Sanders's agonized text is meant to anatomize just how Manson perverted countercultural practices for his own benefit,

Bugliosi's work was much less nuanced: counterculture bad, law and order good.

A central part of Bugliosi's mission—in court and on the page—was to neutralize the countercultural threats posed by the Family. Bugliosi's emphasis on the stature of key male figures in the case served as one strategy he deployed to undercut the potentially frightening power Manson exercised. Joined with this was Bugliosi's relentless efforts to infantilize the young women who circulated in Manson's orbit. Describing the Family women again and again as "girls" (or "little girls") acted as Bugliosi's attempt to render Squeaky, Sadie, and the rest as neither terrifying nor sexually alluring. In *Helter Skelter* Bugliosi writes that although Squeaky Fromme and Sandy Good were both in their twenties, there was a "little-girl quality to them, as if they hadn't aged but had been retarded at a certain stage in their childhood. Little girls playing little-girl games." Elsewhere in the book he refers to Leslie Van Houten's "little-girl cuteness" and cites jailhouse informant Virginia Graham's sense that Susan Atkins appeared to be a "little girl lost." Finally, Bugliosi also makes a point of suggesting that "for some reason" Manson seemed to attract only "flat-chested girls."[17] George Bishop, in his quickie true-crime book *Witness to Evil*, also spares a moment to discuss the breasts of the Family's women, but in the service of a much more complex argument than Bugliosi would ever launch. Noting somewhat cruelly that these "girls" tended to be "moderately endowed both intellectually and physically," Bishop then turns the camera on the "middle-aged observer" of the trial (himself? All the older men in the courtroom?) who was likely to "mistake vacuity for cuteness and nubility for sensuality."[18]

Concerning a very different context (Atlanta in the Progressive Era) the historian Nancy MacLean has written about the practice of referring to young women as "girls." MacLean explains that this practice grows from a fantasy promoted by powerful people about how long young women can occupy the safe space of childhood.[19] Central to Vincent Bugliosi's work in court and on the pages of his authoritative true-crime account of Manson and the Family is an attempt to press "reset" on the gender console. Bugliosi needed the jury (and then his readers) to understand Manson as some kind of crime family Godfather, a patriarchal agent who was completely able to program the behavior of his female followers. Mario Puzo's *Godfather* novel, released in the same year as the Tate-LaBianca murders, sold some nine million copies in the first two years after its initial printing. Francis Ford Coppola's film version of Puzo's book did more business at the box office than any other movie released in 1972. *The Godfather*—in print and on-screen—posited a world in which women barely existed. One of the few women who exerts anything like agency over the course of the epic is the outlier (i.e., non-Italian) Kay Adams.

If *The Godfather* represents part of a cultural backlash against the insurgency of women's liberation and other countercultural movements, then so too does Bugliosi's true-crime book act as a sort of course correction. True-crime narratives frequently involve reenactments of some type. Errol Morris's near-obsessional forensic work in his 2012 book on the Jeffrey MacDonald case is just one recent example of true crime's burden. Bugliosi's task in the courtroom, in press briefings, and ultimately in *Helter Skelter*, however, was not simply to recount the "facts" of the case, but perhaps even more significantly, to embody the proper workings of white-male agency. However scandalous Bugliosi may have been in his maelstrom of a private life, no matter how intemperately he may have spoken to Sandra Good outside the courthouse, no matter how completely he alienated a large number of police detectives and members of the press corps covering the case, Bugliosi kept his eye on the people who mattered: first, the jury hearing the case against Manson and his co-defendants, and then the reading and viewing audiences who would continue—by the millions—to validate what one observer has aptly enough labeled Bugliosi's "myth-building, crazyass" approach to explaining the motive in the crimes.[20]

Central to Bugliosi's success at reinforcing his own power was his reassuring affect. One of the major crises fueled by the

Tate-LaBianca murders and subsequent trials had to do with the way this helter-skelter violence seemed to reveal a horrifying transference of loyalty enacted by the Manson girls from parental authority to the not-quite peer authority of Charles Manson. Manson was older than all of his followers, but only months apart from Bugliosi. Bugliosi's central goal was to convince the jury that he, the prosecutor, could be trusted to put everything back together again that Manson had broken.

Bugliosi did not have much of a fan club during the investigation or trial. Theo Wilson, who covered the trial for the *New York Daily News*, later described in detail how deep the enmity toward Bugliosi ran among the journalists at the courthouse. As Wilson recounts, the esprit de corps that developed in the trial trenches did not extend to Bugliosi. "The prosecutor had . . . irritated some of the reporters," she writes, "by telling them how to write their stories, and berating them for not recognizing the importance of his work in the courtroom."[21]

Bugliosi also managed to create deep animosity between himself and the Los Angeles Police Department. The frame established by Bugliosi around his discovery of the Helter Skelter motive is that only the prosecutor had the broad vision and courage to figure out what was really going on here. Helter Skelter described not only the chaos that would ensue once Manson and the Family kicked off the world-historic racial uprising but also the status of the investigation until Bugliosi got involved. Even as late as the publication of the book *Helter Skelter*, Bugliosi was still prosecuting his case against the detectives assigned to the Tate murder, who, by his account, almost completely bungled the investigation. Forty years after the crime, one of the LAPD detectives, Mike McGann, felt called upon to defend the work he and his colleagues had done: "I have nothing but respect for Bugliosi as a lawyer, but his attitude pissed me off. He didn't solve the case. We solved the case. We brought the case to the district attorney's office in a pretty good package. He found more evidence, but that's what he's supposed to do."[22] It is worth noting that Bugliosi was not the only one criticizing the LAPD; Theo Wilson agrees that the "police work on the case was so bad that evidence was being found by TV reporters and other civilians, including a precious little kid who found one of the Family's guns near his house."[23] Jim Knipfel has written sharply of how the television miniseries version of *Helter Skelter* emphasized the "morons and muttonheads" vision of the LAPD first offered by Bugliosi and Gentry in their book: "I'm actually shocked they'd paint the LAPD as a bunch of incompetent boobs, but they did."[24]

But Bugliosi was not critical of all the police work—just that done by the Los Angeles Police Department on the Tate case. The LaBianca investigation, for jurisdictional reason, was led by the Los Angeles Sheriff's Office (LASO) instead of the LAPD and Bugliosi found much to admire in their work. This is not surprising, given that the LASO detectives shared much with the prosecutor himself. As Bugliosi tells it, the LaBianca detectives were "generally younger" and "better educated" than those working on the Cielo Drive murders. They also combined an inclination to use "modern investigative techniques" such as pro forma fingerprint runs and abundant polygraph tests, along with a willingness to consider "far out theories" (including the meanings of the bloody writings at the Waverly Drive home of the LaBiancas). Most gratifying to Bugliosi is that the LASO detectives took note of the similarities between the word "rise" found on the front door and the use of the word "arise" in the current Beatles' song "Blackbird." The LASO detectives also noted that the same album that included "Blackbird" also had songs called "Piggies" and "Helter Skelter."[25]

Bugliosi uses the pages of *Helter Skelter*, in short, to continue to prosecute his case against the Manson Family (and their alleged Bugliosi-scripted motivation) but also to make an argument about how the forces invested with power by the establishment would need to respond to this frightening new world of crime and disorder. Relatively early in *Helter Skelter*, Bugliosi offers a key of sorts for the reading of his own work: "Given Roman Polanski's affinity for the macabre; rumors of Sebring's sexual peculiarities; the presence of both Miss Tate and her former lover at the death scene while her husband was away; the 'anything goes' image of the Hollywood jet set; drugs; and the sudden clamp on police leaks, almost any kind of plot could be fashioned."[26] Fashioning a "plot" is always the prosecutor's burden in the courtroom. Bugliosi, it is clear, shouldered this mantle with impressive gusto and sustained creative energy. While Irving Kanarek's behavior as defense attorney during the trial has often been dismissed as simple and desperate obstructionism, it is worth thinking about his tactics as part of a consciously wrought strategy to interrupt the methodical unfolding of Bugliosi's master narrative. Kanarek failed to succeed in this effort, of course, as have most attempts to chip away at the prosecutor and author's confident tale-telling. Kanarek's one bravura courtroom move was his decision to simply rest without launching a defense case. He believed (or at least acted as if) the jury would share his belief that the prosecution had only inadmissible hearsay to offer in its case against Charles Manson.

Kanarek's post-Manson career took a much different path from Bugliosi's—it included a very public breakdown in the Torrance, California, district attorney's office in 1989, and a subsequent disbarment in 1991. Kanarek has surfaced occasionally—most poignantly during his "Motel 6" years of the 1990s—during which he publicized his efforts to be readmitted to the California bar.[27] Even as Kanarek attempted to call attention to his own plight, including his sense that his defense of Jimmy Lee Smith (one of the "Onion Field" killers, convicted of killing a Los Angeles police officer) led to his own persecution at the hands of LAPD, the lawyer never fully stopped promoting his brief on behalf of Manson. But the defense attorney's proposition that Manson was not only "legally innocent" but also "actually innocent" has never gained much traction even as it rests on a basic truth of the case—that Charles Manson did not kill anyone at Cielo Drive or Waverly Drive.[28] What Kanarek consistently fails to take into account (or purposefully ignores) is that the offenses imputed to Manson by the prosecution were at once much less concrete and much more pervasive than the simple charge of murder. Manson was essentially accused by Bugliosi of felonious misuse of male power in the process of promoting a crackpot vision of racial violence at the End of Days.

It is significant that Bugliosi titled his book *Helter Skelter* and not *Slaughter in Los Angeles* or *The Tate-LaBianca Murders* (though he does allow for *The True Story of the Manson Murders* as his subtitle). Before Bugliosi and Gentry published *Helter Skelter* in 1974, the other major books on the case—*The Family* above all, but also *The Garbage People*—used their titles to signal something about the perversion of countercultural communalism embodied by Manson and his followers; in essence these titles invite readers into a completed drama. The aims are quite distinct, to be sure. Gilmore wanted to point at the Family's social marginalization and desperation while Sanders aimed to use his main title to call attention—strangely enough, for him, in an understated way—to how Manson exploited the collective to carry out some very concrete aims (have sex, sell drugs, promote Satanism). In both of these cases the true-crime titles are meant to indicate something collective and relatively stable—a set of social arrangements organized by Manson and his followers to establish their place in the larger culture. My own title, of course, is meant to call attention to an ongoing process—a continuing challenge to mainstream cultural norms, institutions, and protocols.

But Bugliosi's *Helter Skelter* signals what might have happened had the prosecutor not done his work so successfully. *Helter Skelter* is a cautionary tale about hierarchies of power, organized around a nightmare vision of the breakdown of patriarchal authority. Bugliosi's performance in *Helter Skelter* served as smug punctuation on an intragenerational skirmish he had already won in 1970. In a courtroom overseen by Judge Older (who had nearly twenty years on Manson and Bugliosi), the prosecutor enacted a reassuring demonstration that the men of his generation were ready to take charge—having dispatched the insurgent Charles Manson and his deviant and criminal Family. Bugliosi was doing important cultural work here, joining Joan Didion (also born in

1934) in acknowledging that things had gone frighteningly off-course in Los Angeles in the past few years. Manson's crimes, as outlined by Bugliosi, were multitudinous: "Manson fuck much," as Ed Sanders put it, and so on. Manson was himself aware of what he was being charged with, and attempted to refute the claims in his November 1970 speech to the court:

> These children that come at you with knives, they are your children. You taught them. I didn't teach them. I just tried to help them stand up. Most of the people at the ranch that you call The Family were just people that you did not want, people that were alongside the road, that their parents had kicked them out or they did not want to go to Juvenile Hall, so I did the best I could and I took them up on my garbage dump and I told them that in love there is no wrong . . . . I was working at cleaning up my house, something that Nixon should have been doing. He should have been on the side of the road, picking up his children, but he wasn't. He was in the White House, sending them off to war.[29]

Manson's attempt here to dress himself in the garb of the caring patriarch could not contend with Bugliosi's successful construction of the defendant as an abusive and exploitative father.

A year later, in 1971, David Bowie would release his song "Changes," with its bracing echo of Manson's formulation. In Bowie's songs, the radical children have not been kicked out— just spit on. (In "Oh! You Pretty Things," the next song on *Hunky Dory*, Bowie returns again to these same children who are driving their parents crazy) With its stuttered enunciation of the title word instructing listeners to meditate on the roots of "Changes" in the Who's hit 1965 song "My Generation," Bowie's image of countercultural youth being spat upon represented a brave, if generally unnoticed, reversal of the powerful claim then emerging about antiwar protesters spitting on returning veterans from Vietnam. The appearance of the "spitting image," as sociologist

Jerry Lembcke has called it, framed a moment when the much-discussed generation gap was being rearticulated and processed as peer conflict.[30]

That peer conflict was put on dramatic display during the Tate-LaBianca investigation and even more starkly in the courtroom script enacted by Vincent Bugliosi and Charles Manson. Working under the approving eyes of Judge Older, the prosecutor easily outmaneuvered the accused and convinced the jury that incipient Family induced chaos required swift and decisive corrective action. Vincent Bugliosi and Charles Manson were mismatched combatants. With his UCLA law pedigree and institutional leverage, the prosecutor was able to use his bully pulpit not only to convict Manson but also to expel him from the center of the cultures—mainstream and counter—he had so successfully creepy crawled for the past couple of years. Manson seems to have been aware that he was being neutralized in the courtroom. After being denied the right to represent himself, the defendant told Michael Hannon of the *Free Press* that he "never said" he was "capable of being a lawyer": "I just didn't want to lose my voice."[31] Manson attempted throughout the trial—with his flashing of the famous Nixon headline, his run at Judge Older, and his various efforts to use his eyes and body language to communicate with other people in the court—to stay visible and audible (and to try to get a mistrial declared). But Bugliosi did not find it difficult, ultimately, to convince the jury that his crime story should be credited, and that Manson (not to mention Polanski and the other suspicious short men of Los Angeles) needed to be quarantined from the mainstream—at least rhetorically.

If the actual and symbolic rearrangements of furniture enacted by the Family during their creepy crawl represented symptoms of a frightful cultural ailment, then Bugliosi's bedlam-conjuring vision of Helter Skelter served at the trial, in print, and on screen, as the remedy. As a declaration of Bugliosi's power to put things right in Los Angeles and beyond, Helter Skelter served as a relatively successful short-term strategy: the prosecutor convinced the jury and the author sold a huge number of books. But *Helter*

Skelter could not ultimately act as anything like a final punctuation on the upheaval wrought by the Family (or to put it more precisely, the upheaval laid at the Family's door). Bugliosi could not put the stopper back in this jug. Manson and his girls have proven to be far too interesting, far too unruly, to be bound inside the covers of "true crime." From the time of the crimes to our own time, the Family's overflow has been consistent, seeping into and helping to define our film, our music, our visual art, our fiction, our material culture, and our drama.

*

Part IV

Creepy Crawling Art: Charles Manson in Our Minds

*

Blood in a
Swimming Pool

The visual artist Raymond Pettibon has this to say about why Charles Manson has appeared so often in his own work: "Manson is a kind of shorthand. I guess . . . you could create your own character like Manson, invent your own cult leader, and invent activities and stuff around him. But Manson already comes with all that baggage so he's really useful."[1] On some level Pettibon's claim reads as a simple restatement of Voltaire's oft-quoted maxim that if god did not exist, it would be necessary to invent him. But Pettibon's use of "shorthand" and "useful" warn against such a simplistic interpretation. Since December of 1969 Manson has permeated the visual, aural, and textual vocabularies of American vernacular and high art. He has functioned as a hint, a name conjuring up a web of associations, a part representing the whole. For decades now, Manson and his Family have demonstrated a remarkable level of "usefulness"; they have creepy crawled across the landscape of American fiction, horror film, indie rock, painting and installation art, animated and live-action television, comic books, T-shirts, and all manner of Internet cultural productions.

Artists across genre and across time have found ways to make use of Manson and the Family. While it is tempting to make some broad declarations to try to get a handle on all this ("There is no American horror film in the 1970s without Manson!" "Manson matters more to indie rock of the late 1980s than to any other genre!"), it is perhaps better to admit that Manson's creepy-crawling ubiquity is going to make neat categorization and clear chronology difficult. While we can certainly identify key moments when the Manson Family held particular power over the cultural imaginary of the United States, the real story here is that Manson has never left our minds for long. And there is no reason to think his death will change that. If 1974 must be taken seriously as a crowning year for Manson art, so must 1989. And 2016 shaped up to form a fairly dramatic spike on the graph of Manson creation as well.

Manson and his Family, their crimes, and the basic challenges they made to conventional morality and social arrangements have served as a remarkably rich pool of inspiration for artists high, low, and in-between for more than forty years now. I cannot pretend to capture much more than a representative sample of the Manson-inspired art of our time. From the horror movie borrowings to the punk rock and hip hop shout-outs, the pulp magazine and fiction references, and the crucial role the cult leader has played as inspiration and subject matter for photographers, painters, and other visual artists, Manson has never left us for more than an instant. The cultural action here has to do with history, social arrangements, changing landscapes: how *these* people came to live in *this* way at *this* time. And what does their example mean for the rest of us? For more than forty years now Manson has served as a cultural Rorschach test; invocations and versions of him are multiple, contradictory, and unpredictable. To understand how deeply Manson has served as an artistic and cultural touchstone since 1969, it is important to consider the broadest possible range of artifacts, from the most "serious" visual arts presented in a gallery context and "high" literary novels, to the most ephemeral articulations of Internet culture.

"Manson" (as subject, as accent, as punctuation) has been a major source of input for the arts over the course of four decades so far. Perhaps the central burden "Manson" has shouldered is as vehicle of passive resistance—not the "No! in thunder" that

Herman Melville ascribed to Nathaniel Hawthorne, and which American critics from Leslie Fiedler to Pauline Kael (in writing about 1974's *Godfather II*) to rock critic Greil Marcus have identified as a central burden of American literature, and film, but the less celebrated tradition of Herman Melville's Bartleby, who "would prefer not to." Faith Franckenstein, a member of the Lyman Family of Boston, argued that her group was not concerned with whether Manson was guilty or not: "He made a gesture against all the things we do not believe in."[2] Bringing Manson to the table, more often than not, has been a way to refuse the deceptive promises of American success and comfort.

The cultural power of Manson has not been consistent, linear, or organized. Manson art is not the work of a coherent movement; there is no manifesto, no positive program. But there is a swath of American art created in the wake of the Tate-LaBianca murders that includes not only the most obvious true crime works and prison conversion narratives, but also American splatter films of the 1970s, the early work of John Waters, and the California folk and country-rock music of the 1970s that emphasized individual feelings of dread and the privileging of personal experience over broader cultural concerns.

There have been historical moments when Manson art erupted into special significance and carried a particularly noteworthy level of cultural baggage. 1974 was the first of those moments, both for works directly about Manson and for works shaped by the influence of the Family. This was the year of Bugliosi's *Helter Skelter*, of course, as well as numerous other major works marbled with Manson: Roman Polanski's *Chinatown*, John Waters's *Female Trouble*, Tobe Hooper's *Texas Chainsaw Massacre*, Neil Young's "Revolution Blues," and Robert Stone's *Dog Soldiers*.

Zachary Lazar refers to the stories he plumbs in *Sway*—the interconnected lives of the Rolling Stones and their entourage, experimental filmmaker Kenneth Anger, Bobby Beausoleil, and Charles Manson—as "contemporary folklore." As with other folkloric motifs, themes, and characters, the material offered up by the Manson Family is ductile and usually articulated in the subjunctive mood; Manson art tends to suggest "what if" possibilities rather than "must be" conclusions.³ While there have been, of course, numerous realist narratives inspired by Manson and his followers (the *Helter Skelter* book and miniseries are likely the most influential here) most "Manson art" is organized around feeling rather than argument; hints, winks, and feints, rather than linear narration. There is also a minor tradition of meta-Manson art, which itself reflects on the ubiquity of Manson in artistic expression. Here, for instance, we find Leonard Cohen's post–Cold War song, "The Future," (1992) which evokes the barren cultural landscape of its moment by making reference to all of the failed writers who think they can upset cultural norms by imitating Manson.

Perhaps most explicit in its attempt to comment on the omnipresence of Manson imagery itself is street artist Banksy's portrait of Charles Manson hitchhiking while holding a sign that reads, simply, "Anywhere." Originally located on a corner wall near the Archway tube station in London, Banksy's work denotes something about Manson as an actual figure. He is wearing his prison uniform and chain, and is looking to pick up any ride he can get. He might have ended up in your town in 1967 when he was released from prison! (Except he didn't. Unless he did.) The real power of Banksy's image and text, given his characteristic stencil presentation on a public wall, comes on the level of suggestion—that Manson's iconic power has remarkable spatial reach and cultural depth. Banksy's Manson, with his too-smudged-to-read prison number, his "anywhere" sign, and his surprising resemblance to the Che Guevara of T-shirt fame, is not an easy image to interpret—maybe a heroic revolutionary, maybe a scary serial killer, maybe just the No Name Maddox of his birth certificate. This is, in essence, Banksy's visual translation of Mojo Nixon's 1987 song "Elvis Is Everywhere," which at once insists upon and undercuts the power of the star's cultural presence. For all of the fun Mojo Nixon has with Elvis, the payoff is always the same— Elvis is the King.⁴

Bansky's consequential revision—trading "everywhere" for "anywhere"—acts as a reminder that Manson's assault on the culture was less frontal, less direct, than was the triumph of Elvis Presley. When Andy Warhol silk-screened eight Elvises in 1963, he borrowed an image of the singer and actor taken from the movie *Flaming Star*, which has the King pointing his gun right at us. Banksy's Manson, on the other hand, makes his impact by stealth—the "anywhere" tag is a reminder of how terrifying the creepy crawl really is. Manson and his minions might in fact be anywhere—in the music the children are listening to, in the blood on the walls of too many horror movies to count, in your house while you sleep. While those responsible for these Los Angeles murders of 1969 might have been put behind bars, in some more diffuse culture sense the killer is still on the road.

Manson art *travels*. It moves from genre to genre, jumps around in time and space, and climbs up and down from pulp to highbrow with stops at all the levels in between. Even a simple (and very partial) roll call of artists who have in some way participated in making "Manson art" tells a story of remarkable cultural breadth and investment: Banksy, Leonard Cohen, Zachary Lazar, N.W.A., Thomas Pynchon, Sonic Youth, Paul Schrader, John Cale, Raymond Pettibon, Joan Didion, Devendra Banhart, John Waters, Joe Coleman, the Ramones, Akrobatik, Steven Soderbergh, Lana Del Rey, Joyce Carol Oates, Jim Carroll, Richard Schechner, Eminem, Brian De Palma, the Lemonheads, Wes Craven, Lil' Kim, the Pixies, Don McLean, John Moran, Cady Noland, Neil Young, James Ellroy, Death Grips, Jerzy Kosinski, the Flaming Lips, Stephen Sondheim, Killer Mike, Joachim Koester, Nine Inch Nails, Trey Parker and Matt Stone, Negativland. In Mexican professional wrestling (Lucha Libre) there are at least three distinct figures using the cult leader's name—Charly Manson, Charly Manson, Jr., and mini-Charly Manson.

Drive-by citations of Manson often seem slight, but still manage to be saturated with class and regional bias (recall comedian Robin Williams's oft-repeated line about people who live below the "Manson-Nixon line").[5] Sometimes invocations of the demon Manson do not seem to add up to much at all. For instance in the first season of *American Horror Story*, a television anthology series, a number of Manson "signs" are deployed, none more obvious than the fact that it features a main character in Southern California named Tate Langdon (yes, that gets the first six letters of "Tate-LaBianca" doesn't it?); in case we don't get the scary joke of his name right away, we also find him whispering "Helter Skelter" just after planning a murder. As the series progressed and a robust fan culture developed around the show, its producers encouraged speculation about whether an entire upcoming season would be devoted to Manson and his Family.[6]

The artists listed above—and others I did not mention who "use" Manson—work in opera, horror film, rap, television animation, reggae, literary and genre fiction, immersive theater, various subgenres of indie and punk rock, musical theater, photography, and in what the Internet Movie Database dubs "Hippie Exploitation and Manson Family Inspired Films." They are cultural traditionalists and cut-and-paste renegades. They are avatars of the avant-garde and creators of kitsch (and in the case of at least one—John Waters—both). They invoke Manson to reanimate old ideas about "the end of the sixties" and to challenge received notions about whether there ever was such a thing as the "sixties" that could have a distinct beginning or end point. The creators of Manson art treat the cult leader and his Family with derision and with respect. If Manson has served as a tool for countless artists since 1969, then it's as a hammer—used equally to break and to build. The art world's Manson is sometimes the applecart and sometimes what tips the applecart over.

Before we get any further into the terrain of Manson art, I need to make it clear that the cult leader has been particularly overrepresented in a few genres of popular music including heavy metal, hip hop, and various subgenres generally discussed under the more general rubric of hardcore (including horror hardcore). My list above of artists engaging with Manson Family lore and sounds would be truly unwieldy if I tried to include all relevant actors. The use of Charles Manson and the Family in popular music falls into a few major categories: drive-by invocations of his name as efficient intensifier (of horror, domination, and so on), samples of his many jailhouse interviews, lyrical or musical references to actual Manson Family recordings, chronicles of the actual events of 1969, and jokes. Hip-hop shout-outs to Manson regularly use the cult leader as a hashtag of sorts to index masculine power—usually either in the rapper's ability to control women or triumph over other rappers. We find such application of Manson's name in Lil Wayne's "Trap House," Das Efx's "Here It Is," N.W.A.'s "Straight Outta Compton," Akinyele's "Messin' with My Cru," and even the Fresh Prince's "Trapped on the Dance Floor." In some ways the video for Lana Del Rey's "Freak" treads similar shout-out ground, including as it does an appearance by Father John Misty doing a sort of vague Manson impression. After collecting Manson references in the hip-hop sphere for some years, I can report that one of the only truly surprising conclusions I have come to is that the Wu-Tang Clan appears *not* to have made lyrical reference to the cult leader; it is comforting to discover that at least one member (Raekwon) has done so on a solo project, one (Method Man) has appeared on a track with the Manson-inspired duo Heltah Skeltah, and the Clan's official website does boast a fairly lively "Charles Manson Appreciation Thread." (Of course no act has been as dogged in its use of Mansonabilia as the Memphis collective that imaginatively named itself Manson Family. The Manson Family has one record called *Heltah Skeltah* and one called *Blood on the Wall*.)

The interviews Manson has given over the decades have also provided a rich body of material, not only in hip hop but in heavy metal and hardcore as well. Here I will mention Jedi Mind Tricks, Dragonland, and Flatbush Zombies to represent the many artists who make this move. Particularly popular on this front are samples of Manson dramatic monologue that includes the lines "I make the money / I roll the nickels / The game is mine" (reproduced in Death Grips's "Beware" for instance). Manson's "maybe I should have killed four, five hundred" speech also appears in popular song relatively often. It is common when discussing the use of sampling in hip hop and other forms of contemporary music to emphasize that this form of quotation can carry a whole range of possible meanings and can be used for a variety of artistic purposes, and the Manson samples are no exception. Often he is made to sound flat-out crazy and is used to intensify a tale of danger or terror. But here and there the speech samples make Manson sound thoughtful, funny, and even prophetic.

References to, and samples of, actual Manson musical productions are less common but bespeak what is perhaps a deeper engagement with the history in question. Here I am thinking of the double-dipping Denver rap group Krookid Hooks, who not only title their song "Love and Terror" (a reference to both the *Life* magazine cover about the Family and the Manson Family record released in 1970) but also includes a sample of the Family singing "I'll Never Say Never to Always." The mentions and samples of Manson music act as a sort of cultural high-sign, an expression meant to connect artist and audience through their shared obsession with the case. Songs by the Flaming Lips, Throbbing Gristle, and the Brian Jonestown Massacre that invoke Manson's music make no sense unless we assume that listeners will, on some level, *get* the references to "Cease to Exist," "Arkansas," and so on. And in the case of Brian Jonestown Massacre, of course, listeners also have to appreciate the extracurricular frisson built into the phenomenon of this band named for *one* California cult leader revisiting the music of *another* California cult leader.

Even more arcane lyrical references to the murders and life with the Family go well beyond the plausibly visible high-sign into the realm of the cryptograph. When mathcore band Car Bomb works a mention of Roman Polanski's film *The Pianist* into a song called "Cielo Drive" or metal act Superjoint Ritual (with Hank Williams III on bass) includes a reference to Manson's slippies-hippies distinction into its song "Creepy Crawl," it is clear that we are being asked to recognize relatively deep Manson lore.[7] This is artistic work created by Manson Family insiders for other insiders; among other goals, the work seems organized around creating something like a musical language of recognition—a sort of Manson vernacular. This deep lore is certainly hovering in the background of rapper Nicki Minaj's character "Roman Zolanski"—an alter-ego whose development has unfolded in various songs of hers (and on the records of other artists including Kanye West). Perhaps the funniest moment in this ongoing tale comes in the song "Stupid Hoe" when the rapper, in character as the gay man Roman Zolanski, insists that there is no connection between Zolanski and Polanski. And speaking of deep lore, it seems not coincidental that a television program debuting in 1976 that featured an "invisible boss"—an older and powerful man giving orders to three young women working as private investigators—was called *Charlie's Angels*. As psychiatrist Clara Livesey has written, the basic premise of the show "seems like a parody . . . of the other Charlie."[8]

Playwright Erik Forrest Jackson working with the Theatre Couture company in the mid-1990s noticed the "preponderance" of Charlies on the scene in the late 1960s and 1970s and so created a theater piece that involved the Angels' Charlie, Manson, the Star-Kist Tuna, Revlon's Charlie perfume, and more. (Conspiracy theorists will want to take note of the fact that on the television show one of the Angels was played, in a later season, by Shelly Hack, who was best known for being the advertising "face" of Revlon's perfume.) Jackson's *Charlie!* was a surprise hit, drawing "listening room" only crowds for months and garnering a positive review from Ben Brantley at *The New York Times*. After the initial run and a change in venues, the creators received a cease-and-desist order from Columbia TriStar, who controlled the rights to *Charlie's Angels* and who were likely displeased by the drag aspect of the show (it featured Sherry Vine, Justin Vivian Bond, and Candis Cayne, among others) and by its conclusion that the "Charlie" giving the three detectives their orders by remote control was Manson himself.

The show was, on the face of it, a raucous entertainment. It is full of sly puns and plenty of very broad winks from the performers to the audience, community-building rooted in shared popular cultural reference points. The actors were in glamorous gowns and upheld the drag tradition of calling attention to surfaces and offering what seemed to be ephemeral moments of pleasure. But there was, as Jackson has explained, some serious business going just below the surface of the hilarity. Jackson's script was intended as a feminist provocation and tool of empowerment, an effort, essentially to defuse the power of these particular icons of the patriarchy as well as the less visible but no less pernicious effects of corporation like Revlon, who profit largely through the marketing of narrow ideals of female beauty. Theatre Couture's camp performance of *Charlie!* draws on the assumption that the juxtaposition between the hilarity of the performance and the quite serious content lurking just below the surfaces would be accessible to audiences who were meant to take in the play's claims about male dominance in the counterculture and the corporate commodification of women.

Charlie! was serious play. It was a instance of what I am calling "deep Manson lore," which has to be distinguished from the frequent use of horrifying details—especially in music—of the case in what might be called (after film critic David Edelstein's coinage) "musical torture porn." These songs obsessively focus on Sharon Tate's body, blood, and fetus and operate in an explicitly misogynist context. Without endorsing the position taken by the family of Sharon Tate that virtually any artistic representation of her life or death is on the face of it exploitative, it is clear that musical reenactments of her murder (by Righteous Pigs and others) bring little to the conversation apart from a sort of sophomoric shock-the-squares agenda. Ultimately the joke songs that mention Manson carry much more artistic weight—largely because they tend to serve as metacommentary on overinvestment in Manson as a figure of horror. At least two of these songs (the Mr. T Experience's "Even Hitler Had a Girlfriend" and the Angry Samoans "They Saved Hitler's Cock") up the rhetorical ante with invocations of the Führer. My larger point is that the landscape of Manson art is defined both by thematically and generically organized *collections* of popular artistic expression and by individual works of greater depth and breadth.

Bridging the gap between these poles of artistic activity is the post-Manson life of the song "Helter Skelter," which I mentioned briefly in connection with U2's version of it at the start of the previous section. I will only discuss the song briefly here, not because it does not merit sustained attention but because that work has largely been done already by Gerald Carlin and Mark Jones in an essay they published in 2012. In their careful genealogy of the continued life of this song (in cover versions, samples, lyrical references, and so on), Carlin and Jones demonstrate that by the mid-1970s or so it was impossible to perform "Helter Skelter" "without Manson's shadow falling over its performance or reception; in the battle for the legacy of the 1960s countercultural project, 'Helter Skelter' had become ammunition."[9] From a 1970s cover version by the Ramrods, a Detroit rock band who performed it together with the Who's "My Generation" and the Stooges' "Search and Destroy" (thus, according to Carlin and Jones, retroactively placing it "into a genealogy of youth rebellion and punk attitude"), to Mighty Sphincter's mid-1980s deathrock version, to the regular sampling of it in more recent days, "Helter Skelter" has carried a remarkable amount of cultural baggage. One synth-goth band not only covered the song, but ended its performance with a sample of the Family itself singing "I'll Never Say Never to Always."[10] In short, when U2's Bono accused Charles Manson of "stealing" "Helter Skelter" from the Beatles, he neglected to mention how much help the cult leader had! Manson art depends on Charlie and the Family, but most of its work has been done outside their control.

One recent major example of Manson art, the thirteen-episode first season of the television show *Aquarius* (2015) represents perhaps the most promiscuous deployment of Charles Manson to date. Manson does not build Stonehenge in *Aquarius*, but he does live at the heart of a web connecting up a truly astounding range of political, cultural, and community actors in and around 1960s Los Angeles. *Aquarius* rereads Manson's time in Los Angeles as a postscript or aftershock. The series begins in 1967, from the premise that if Manson ended up playing such a major role in Southern California life in 1969, then he must have begun to make his presence felt much earlier. *Aquarius* is, to put the matter in the vernacular, a hot mess—but it is a meaningful hot mess. This television series attempts to measure just how much ground Manson and his Family creepy crawled over beginning in the second half of the 1960s. *Aquarius* wants above all to frame Manson (as defense lawyer Paul Fitzgerald put it) as "some sort of right-wing hippie."[11] If Fitzgerald's description (an analogue to the "acid fascism" framed out by David Dalton and David Felton) has a baffled tone of unforeseen discovery, *Aquarius* quite audaciously makes "right-wing hippie" a literal fact: the origin story of *Aquarius* is organized around the revelation that Manson has for years been in bed with Ken Karn (the "KK" of his name meant to evoke both the KKK and "RR"—Ronald Reagan), a Republican lawyer and fundraiser who hopes to take a position as California finance chief for Nixon's 1968 campaign. Virtually all of the action involving Manson in this show traces back to Manson's late 1950s relationship with Karn, which apparently stretched the definition of attorney–client privilege to include lots of desperate sex.

Contemporary reviews of *Aquarius* tended to miss the point of the show's breadth. June Thomas, writing in *Slate*, argues that there is "something cheap about using a monster like Manson as the big bad on a police procedural. Well, it's sort of Manson . . . . Our charismatic creep is Marlie Chanson, just a random 33-year-old who, like Manson, had by this point spent more than half his life behind bars."[12] But *Aquarius* shows little interest in hewing to Manson's own story; as lead actor Gethin Anthony put it, "We're not presenting a biography . . . . [W]e're presenting a paradigm."[13] (And it is probably just as well that the show does not attempt biography, given that the executive producer and writer of the show, John McNamara, claims to have done extensive research in order to create the show, and has learned that Manson is "not from Mars. He's not from Hell. He's a guy from Oklahoma, but, boy, did he make some bad, bad choices." Bad choices, sure. Oklahoma? Not so much.)[14] The "paradigm" presented by *Aquarius* is another expression of the "contemporary folklore" identified by Zachary Lazar as central to his own Manson project. In *Aquarius* Manson is the "rough beast" of Yeats's "Second Coming," a poem on so many commentators' minds as 1967's Summer of Love gave way to the wreckage of the last few years of the decade.

In the show Manson is the hub of a crazy wheel whose spokes radiate out from him into the national Republican party, the gay-rights movement, the Vietnam War and the antiwar activism of veterans, the Black Panther Party, the Chicano movement (with the late-in-the-first season appearance of the journalist and activist Ruben Salazar), the hip capitalism under development in Los Angeles in the second half of the 1960s, the multifocal movement for sexual liberation, religious nonconformism, the rearguard activism of the real-estate industry attempting to sustain residential segregation, and psychedelic experimentation. John McNamara has been clear about the animus energizing his show: "Usually stories about the '60s take the point of view of the radical left . . . . I've never seen a guy with a crew cut in a modern retelling of that era. So, that was the POV, and that was the entire reason to do the show."[15] McNamara claims to be a follower of the end-of-the-sixties narrative developed by Joan Didion and her followers—"I believe that Manson single-handedly destroyed the '60s. Tate LaBianca was the end of the '60s. It turned everything wonderful or explosive or radical or new or amazing into death, paranoia and murder."[16]

The series may ultimately come to support McNamara's overcooked end-of-the-sixties rhetoric, but the Manson art of its first season has a much less trite story to tell—a story that is essentially about Manson as a *creator* of what we conventionally refer to as "the sixties." The key year in the series is 1959; this is when Manson seems to have made first contact with right-wing lawyers Ken Karn (a repressed gay man) and Hal Banyin (a not-so repressed fetishistic torturer of sex workers). What Manson provides both men, as *Aquarius* frames the back story, is a way to express their unconventional sexualities in a relatively safe way. On the literal level, Manson is a pimp and these two men are johns. But *Aquarius* has a broader story to tell about how purveyors such as Manson and strip-club owner Lucille Gladner endeavor to support the work of Karn and Banyin, powerful social actors. The key establishment figures of *Aquarius* are rising stars of California's neoconservative revolution; the spirit of Ronald Reagan, who took over the California governor's office in 1967 (the same year the series begins) hovers over much of the action in *Aquarius.* Reagan does not get name-checked until the fourth episode of the first season of *Aquarius,* but his anti-youth, anti–African American, pro–private property, pro-law-and-order tactics define *Aquarius*'s Los Angeles.

Historian Eric Avila has written of the rise of Southern California's conservatism of the second half of the twentieth century as an expression of "countersubversive" backlash "that targeted civil rights crusaders, feminists, antiwar demonstrators, and gay activists as culpable for the social ills and economic malaise wrought by economic restructuring, deindustrialization, and the dismantling of the welfare state."[17] While viewers are invited to see Karn and Banyin as familiar-enough villains, it is their relationship with Manson that moves them from garden-variety bad guys to truly terrifying agents of destruction. The relationship of the Republican power brokers to the ex-con is intimate, but unstable. *Aquarius* certainly does not encourage viewers to think that the three can form anything like a sustained alliance. This is, after all, a police procedural, and there is little doubt that the "good" white cops—Sam Hodiak, the World War II veteran and father of a son gone AWOL from Vietnam; Brian Chafe, working undercover as a hippie (Manson's double, in this respect) and living as the husband of a Black woman; and Charmain Tully, the newbie who is sure she can keep up with the boys in the station—will form the shaky blue line holding back the forces of anarchy. Hodiak is particularly important because he can understand and "speak" the languages of a diverse range of Southern California constituencies. How surprised radical Black Panther Bunchy Carter looks when Hodiak completes his quotation of Trotsky's maxim "You might not be interested in the dialectic, but the dialectic is interested in you." That said, *Aquarius* makes clear that the Anglo-power that would come to define the Reagan Revolution, with its emphasis (as Avila puts it) on "patriarchy" and "privatization" is most fully embodied by Karn and Manson, not by the self-described "mongrel" Hodiak, who had a Jewish parent![18] *Aquarius* does not have a clear point of view about Manson's role in the political and cultural life of Southern California in the 1960s. It does, however, have a relatively clear case to make about how Manson's imprisonment in the 1950s and 1960s prepared him to understand how institutions work, and manipulate them to his own benefit. In a melodramatic moment of confrontation Hal Banyin tells Ken Karn that "Charlie gives us what we both need." The point of this purple declaration is that it is true—Manson helps the two men live the idea that their desires should define the world around them.

White male desire is at the heart of many of the retellings of the Manson story under consideration here. In his novel *Inherent Vice* Thomas Pynchon has his character Shasta accuse Doc of being attracted to the promise of male dominance presented by Manson: "Submissive, brainwashed, horny little teeners . . . who do exactly what you want before you even know what that is. You don't even have to say a word out loud, they get it all by ESP."[19] *Aquarius* reminds us that Manson's pathological vision of white-male triumphalism is a demonic twin to what Eric Avila has explained as core work of Southern California's mainstream culture—the culture of Walt Disney and his sanitized theme park in Anaheim, of the removal of Chicanos from Chavez Ravine to make way for Dodger Stadium, of the highway construction that, among other things, would expedite the travel of newly suburban white people to Dodger Stadium (and other urban attractions).

While *Aquarius* has relatively little interest in Manson's actual biography and often seems to go out of its way to get things wrong—why call what is obviously Spahn Ranch by the name of a different Family crash pad, the Spiral Staircase?—it has an appropriate investment (expressed visually and aurally) in depicting the racial segregation undergirding the postwar developments that defined life in Southern California. Avila's book demonstrates persuasively that white flight could not have been achieved without the concentrated will and investment of government, private industry (including Hollywood, professional sports, and real estate interests) and countless individual citizens. *Aquarius* can only hint at all this, but its relatively early invocation of Nixon and Reagan, its bizarre subplot about a Cuban American police officer who has been "passing" as white, and its painful segregating of the music on the soundtrack (Black music when Hodiak goes to South Central to pay a visit to the Black Panthers, seemingly random Spanish-language music when drug kingpin Guapo is onscreen, and so on) indicates that the creators of the show are purposefully emphasizing the forces of separation in late 1960s Los Angeles culture. When Elliot Hillman, a record-company executive, visits the Family on the ranch, he tells Charlie, "This thing you got going on out here. It's bigger than songs. It's a worldview." It is obvious that Hillman is trying to *manage* Manson here—out of his fear of violence and his hope for some more of that Family free love— but it is equally obvious that the makers of *Aquarius* are using Hillman to express the show's truth: Manson does have a worldview, and it is consonant in many ways with that of Ken Karn and the national Republican figures for whom he works.

It would be overblown to make these large claims for one network television show if not for how regularly Manson art has been asked to carry such heavy cultural baggage. Manson art, to borrow the name of a key Rolling Stones album of the second half of the 1960s, is the art of *Aftermath*. It is the art of what novelist Dana Spiotta has called a "cracked Southern California creepiness," a landscape of almost-abandoned Western movie sets, bleached bones in the desert, of the eruption of the irrational after the moment of intense crisis.[20] In the aftermath, as readers and viewers and listeners, we are left with the challenges presented by encrusted layers of meaning. The cultural conversations inspired by the case cannot be easily contained by clear-cut interpretive frameworks or definitive rubrics.

The tour of Manson art I offer makes no claims of being comprehensive or even systematic. The premise of any such study (if it is to be trusted) must be that Manson art is so large you can't get over it and so wide that you can't get around it. As Pynchon has written, the influence of Charles Manson and his Family, and the havoc they caused, "spreads, like blood in a swimming pool, till it occupies all the volume of the day."[21] Historian Rick Perlstein has argued suggestively that if one wanted to rename the politically and culturally charged United States of this era, one way to do so that would capture the apocalyptic rhetoric defining the life of the nation in the late 1960s and early 1970s would be to call it "Nixonland." But "Mansonland" would also do, wouldn't it?

They Are Still among Us

The major goal of Vincent Bugliosi's *Helter Skelter* was to declare the Manson case closed. That is a truism, of course. With notable exceptions that only prove the rule, the central impulse of true-crime writing is to solve the crime and expel the criminal from the body politic. Bugliosi's sales and his harder-to-measure but no less significant cultural influence suggest that *Helter Skelter* did its work successfully. Bugliosi offers a true-crime master class in this book, which includes a "plausible" motive, a stable of bad guys put behind bars, and the expression of powerful consensus that the thrilling and threatening social mixing defining Los Angeles in the late 1960s had gone too far. Bugliosi is the good father to Manson's anarchic "Uncle Sugar" (as Kenneth Anger called him in *Hollywood Babylon*), setting things right in Southern California as he reasserts the proper workings of patriarchal authority. True crime is a formalist art—it is rare for a true-crime book to deny its readers the pleasures of procedural certitude. When a true-crime book *complicates* the case in question, rather than simply resolving it (as with Errol Morris's *Wilderness of Error*, a sort of meditation on true crime, rather than a true-crime book itself), the repudiation of convention is likely to be foregrounded as a titillating challenge to genre expectations.

In general, though, the true-crime accomplishment of Bugliosi's investigative and courtroom drama *Helter Skelter* is to establish Manson and his Family as scapegoats who can then be fully neutralized. *Helter Skelter* accomplishes the central task of true crime non-fiction—it announces (as Gerald Ford also said in 1974, in his inaugural address) that "our long national nightmare is over." The conventional true crime work include no portentous afterwords, no "remains to be seen" implications stitched in, no dark inferences to be drawn about what the future might hold. True crime tends to work in favor of the status quo; the form belongs to police officers, prosecutors, and journalists. The compulsive focus of the true-crime book is to demonstrate that all has been set right.

But there is a considerable subset of fictional Manson stories that compete fairly directly with true crime's reassurances. If one of the blessings offered by standard true-crime work is its certitude, the mainstream of Manson art has largely consisted of attempts—by gallery artists and pulp-fiction writers, popular musicians and filmmakers—to point out that the applecart has not been set right. Vincent Bugliosi may have succeeded in locking up Charles Manson (and a handful of Family members), but his work at the trial, in the book, and in the television movie, seems to lack force when plotted against the hydra-headed creature of Manson art. This branch of Manson art is largely comprised of *hauntings*—often in the form of fictional visitations by putative Manson offspring, as well as by forgotten followers, or dangerous copycats. At times the haunting is less literal, and takes place on the level of feeling. This Manson art, what I am naming as "They Are Still among Us," seems to borrow from various horror-movie tropes ("You can't kill what is already dead"? "They're back"? "Seed of Chucky"?) as it carries a resolutely concrete message about the persistence of deviance, the incompleteness of Bugliosi's prosecution, the enormity of the sickness present in Southern California in the late 1960s, and the impossibility of "curing" it by locking up a few relatively powerless "slippies."

Much of this rhetorical zombie action is found in crime fiction—the darker id put into regular dialogue with the superego of true crime's nonfiction. This fiction is, for the most part, weird and unruly. It rarely focuses on Manson himself as a "character" or even as engine of main plots, but rather posits the unsettling premise that Manson and his Family have continued to creepy crawl over the landscape of Southern California and other parts of the United States, or that there are countless Manson-inspired or Manson-like killers on the loose. Often these Manson references work on the level of what I have been calling the "shout-out"; they help establish context and gravity without necessarily making any claim to operating as an independent expression."[1]

Take a recent example, Andrew Gross's 2011 crime novel, *Eyes Wide Open*. With its immediate titular evocation of Stanley Kubrick's 1999 film *Eyes Wide Shut* and its concern with the sexual rites of a secret society, Gross signals to readers that he may indeed be bringing them onto the landscape of the creepy crawl. The main contemporary plot in the novel has to do with the tragic death of Westchester doctor Jay Erlich's nephew, Evan, in California. Evan lived unhappily with mental illness for years, and his death is quickly ruled a suicide. But when Erlich arrives in California to support his ne'er-do-well brother, Charlie, he quickly comes to believe that Evan's death is somehow tied to his father's connection to a murderous cult leader decades earlier. It is in the narrating of this backstory that Gross borrows liberally from the history of Manson and his Family. Gross's cult leader is Richard Houvanian, coincidentally Armenian, and with a dream of popular-music stardom that will strike even the most casual Manson case observer as familiar. Houvanian develops a set of readings of popular songs (particularly by the Byrds and the Doors) that support his own apocalyptic vision; the Doors' "Riders on the Storm" becomes Houvanian's ur-text, a song performed by Jim Morrison's group to communicate with the cult leader and offer support for his apocalyptic vision.[2]

Living at "Riorden Ranch"—Spahn here displaced to Big Sur (using some geographical sleight of hand to throw us off the trail!)—Houvanian and his family indulge in wild drug-use and sexual experimentation, until the owner of the ranch makes a move to evict the commune. In August of 1973 members of the Family "ritualistically" slaughtered Riorden and five guests at his house, and then moved on to the home of Sally and George Forniciari to kill them (Look! The second set of murders are of a couple with an Italian last name!). The chests of the victims were smeared with bloody words including "Judas," "whore," and "betrayer." The Manson material is blatant enough, even as Gross makes peremptory efforts to mask his source material. (One can imagine the dark nights of the soul the author spent trying to figure out how to reconfigure the character of Tex Watson before landing on the ingenious solution of renaming him "Tel." Gross's only real competition here comes from literary novelist Madison Smartt Bell whose cult leader does not want to say "creepy crawl" to his followers so he says, "Go slither.")[3]

Gross seems to be following Raymond Pettibon's dictum that since Manson is already *there*, you might as well use him. (The recent movie *California Scheming* (2014) seems similarly happy to use whatever it needs of Manson—and of course the Mamas and the Papas for its title—to advance its contemporary plot. In this teen potboiler, Chloe has a picture of Manson on the wall, coerces friends to go on a creepy crawl, and organizes a night of terror, but the references to the convicted cult leader have virtually no substance and work exclusively in the area of character development. Chloe's obsession is a quick way to establish that she is a sociopath.) Given the pro forma usages of *Eyes Wide Open*, it comes as something of a surprise to discover that for Gross the Manson-frame is personal. Gross's father lived at the top of Benedict Canyon, and at one point hosted fifteen-year-old Andrew, visiting from New York. "My dad moved out to L.A. in the '60s and my older brother [who gets transformed into the major character "Charlie" in *Eyes Wide Open*], a wayward spirit trying to become a musician, was out there as well, and uh … took up residence on the Spahn Ranch, where Manson lived. The two of them came up to my father's place one day and tried to sell him on anteing up for a demo." According to Gross, Michael Gross and Manson were joined by an "over-selling sidekick who called himself a rock producer and may well have been Terry Melcher." (Nope: Maybe Gregg Jakobson.) There is little point in trying to hunt down the accuracy of the author's historical scholarship. What matters is that Andrew Gross drew from the Manson tale when he needed an efficient way to establish sustained horror in his crime thriller.[4]

What *is* interesting in *Eyes Wide Open* is Gross's decision to have his cult leader articulate the terrifying possibility that he and his followers will be back. In the place of Manson's relatively philosophical and mournful courtroom speech at his trial, Gross uses this moment in his book to proffer a warning: "Watch," the cult leader tells the assembled, "no one knows when the master will choose to come back." Houvanian puts a point on his creepy-crawl rhetoric with the suggestion that he might return while the non-specific "you" are asleep.[5]

It turns out that Houvanian has maintained control over at least some of his followers and has been controlling them from inside of his prison cell. The real point, of course, is that Houvanian no longer has much work to do: the initial "infection" took hold decades ago and his followers will never be cleansed of his influence. While this variant of Manson art can, on occasion, seem to follow the contours of the zombie film, it sometimes seems closer to the "contagion" subgenre, with the consistent implication that there is a little Manson in, if not everybody, enough people to be a menace.

In an essay on "Hip Pocket Sleaze," John Harrison has helpfully explained how quickly publishers and film studios began to churn out pulp stories drawing on the Manson Family as a ready-made horror package: "From skid row film producers to sleazy underground paperback publishers, the sensational aspects of the savage killings committed by members of the Manson Family— from its celebrity victims and the shattering of the 'peace and love' illusion to the LSD orgies and charisma of the Family's leader, Charles Manson—were a potent melting pot of ingredients ripe for exploitation." Harrison argues that movies "like *The Love-Thrill Murders* (1971), *I Drink Your Blood* (1971) and *The Deathmaster* (1972) were clearly inspired by the Manson case and kept audiences in grindhouses and drive-ins entertained with lurid tales of violent, doped-up hippies on a murderous rampage."[6]

Joining the "mainstream books" that "appeared covering almost every aspect of the Manson case and subsequent trial (and helping to create and define the popular true crime literary genre in the process)" publishers also circulated "fictional pot-boilers which used the news headlines as merely a springboard for an adventure far more raunchy and gaudy." Part of the point of this horror film and fiction was to allow audiences the titil-lation of safely experiencing Manson-inspired terror, and then to neutralize the threat as quickly and decisively as possible. The cult leader in Ray Stanley's *The Hippy Cult Murders* (1970), after indulging himself in all kinds of terrifying rituals of sex and violence is, by novel's end, dispatched with "swift and sav-age justice."[7] This early generation of Manson art, obviously, had more than one function. It was sexually titillating, it marginal-ized youth cultures, and it threw a big bear hug around cops. But what it promised above all was fast resolution—terror coming out of nowhere followed by bad guys getting their comeuppance like lightning.

But these simple pleasures of pulp fiction could not be sus-tained. The ongoing tale of Manson art reveals a much different moral, one that requires audiences to acknowledge that they are *in* the story—that stories of the Manson Family are stories of their own time, their own place. The most perfunctory versions of this story tell us that either Manson's *Family* (i.e., his communal fam-ily of choice) or Manson's *family* (i.e., his biological offspring) are creepy crawling our landscape.

The 2007 film *Gimme Skelter*, for instance, is organized around the character Philip Valentine, who grew up in foster care believ-ing that he is truly the son of Charles Manson. (There is some consensus that the first "real" Manson Family baby was Michael Valentine, born to Mary Brunner and named for the main char-acter of Robert Heinlein's 1961 novel *Stranger in a Strange Land*.) *Gimme Skelter*—whose title, it probably goes without saying, brings together the Beatles and the Rolling Stones and Manson in a great/horrible pun only notable for how long it took someone to make it—tracks this Valentine as he leads a murderous gang through its paces. The Manson scenario is half-hearted. Time is spent in the desert and the group members get instructed to do "something witchy" in connection with their crimes. The animus for all of this, the film finally informs us, is that Valentine wants to rack up a higher kill count than his murderous father in order to get some much-desired attention from him. It is a strange Oedipal twist *Gimme Skelter* delivers—"Father, I want to kill (more people than) you"—but still it underscores the availability of Manson as a sign of ongoing cultural horror.

The "Son of Manson" artistic thread has a tale to tell about a certain level of cultural disquiet related directly to the sexual activity of Family members during the heyday of Manson in Southern California, and about the unwillingness (or inability) of the Manson Family to assign children to nuclear family formations. In short, these genre films and novels organized around Manson children reveal not only a concern with Manson's diffuse cultural influence, but also about the possibility that even as his body is locked up, his "blood" might be running through the land. Crime-fiction writer Michael Perry explores this notion in his 1994 book *Skelter*, a follow-up to a 1992 book he wrote, which imagines that serial killer Ted Bundy did *not* die in the electric chair and is still himself on a rampage. This truly strange book features a cult-leader wannabe who calls himself "J'osuf" and an acolyte named Trumbo who ultimately learns that his own "real" father is Charles Manson. Trumbo learns this from Manson himself, who also promises not to reveal this truth to anyone else: "I don't want you having the baggage I had to carry around—reform school, jail, trouble every minute of my life."[8]

These fictional narratives of Manson parentage are framed in the larger culture by numerous attempts—mostly in Internet news outlets—to answer some variant of the question "Where Are Manson's Children Now?" These pieces all tend to ask three basic questions—Is s/he really Charles Manson's kid? How scarred is s/he by this fact? And how dangerous? These works demonstrate little inclination to plumb the larger implications of Manson's family/Family.

More ambitious work has mostly been carried forward by artists interested in cultural legacies of the Manson Family's creepy crawl rather than in relatively foursquare questions about actual paternity. A number of crime fiction writers have traced the impact of Manson-aftershocks, including major figures such as T. Jefferson Parker in *California Girl* (2004) and Jeffrey Deaver in *The Sleeping Doll* (2007), the latter of which centers on a criminal who is referred to as "Son of Manson" but bears no direct connection to the cult leader. William Harrington also teases out the continuing influence of Manson on his followers in a very strange hybrid work titled *Columbo: The Helter Skelter Murders,* which operates from the principle that the titular detective (spun-off from the television show of the same name) was involved in the original Tate-LaBianca investigation and is still trying to tie up loose ends from the case. Manson seems to be continuing to direct the activities of his followers, perhaps including a recent murder with requisite blood-writing on the wall. This slightly demented book arranges to have Columbo visit Manson in jail as he tries to collect information about the criminal plans of still-faithful Family members who, according to Columbo (channeling Damon Runyon, it seems), have names like The Kid, Bum Rapp, Squatty, Boobs, and Puss Dogood. This approach also structures Nicholas Sarazen's *Family Reunion* (1990), which revolves around an investigative journalist who pieces together a narrative about the possible threats posed by former Family members.

It is interesting to consider two issues of Marvel Comics' *Punisher* from the late 1980s that intervene quite remarkably in the ongoing evolution of this "still among us" trope. In October and November of 1988, the Punisher, a Vietnam Veteran, decides that he can no longer abide the fact that Manson (here "Samson") escaped the death penalty. It is Manson himself who still walks among us! While there is some evidence to suggest that Punisher belongs to a distinct trajectory of "crazed returning vet" narratives, these comic books ultimately encourage readers to understand any of his behavioral deviations from the norm as the product of his otherwise healthy and deep patriotism. The Manson character here is frighteningly powerful. Punisher has his Vietnam bona fides, to be sure, but Samson has that swastika on his forehead—the symbol seems to grow at times and the comic artists call attention to it by sometimes turning the bad guy's eyebrows into arrows pointing at it. And Samson has the potent long hair of his biblical namesake, even when he is in jail.

These two issues of *Punisher* take pains to elaborate on the initial Vietnam reference. Taking a little bit of historical license, *Punisher*'s writer has Samson's crimes take place on the same day that William Calley is convicted for his Vietnam murders. When it comes time to kill the Squeaky Fromme character, Punisher pushes her from a helicopter. When Punisher needs help settling all of his scores, he appeals to an old buddy from Nam, who is more than willing to join this new campaign. In many ways *Punisher* fits a film template that historian Lary May has described in convincing detail.

These movies—perhaps most notably the *Dirty Harry* and *Death Wish* franchises and then later some Chuck Norris films and the *Rambo* series—"emerged in the 1970s and lasted . . . until the early 1990s" and gave "vivid expression to the political backlash unfolding at the time against the social movements and cultural upheavals of the 1960s."[9] The protagonist of these films, as May explains, is usually a disgruntled police officer or military person; the challenges of American life, particularly in the city, are explicitly described as a "war." *Punisher* has particular echoes of Charles Bronson's character in *Death Wish*—both vigilantes spring into action after acts of horrific violence are committed against their families in New York's Central Park. (May reminds us too that the bad guy in *Death Wish III* looked like Manson and shared some of his mannerisms.) The stakes are high in these films and the "cheers for the righteous detective or vigilante" in movie theaters showing them represented a sort of wish fulfillment through which the loss of the Vietnam War and the disorder on the home front are set right.

Read in this light, *Punisher*'s right-wing politics becomes more legible. *Punisher*'s creators seem quite purposefully stitching him into this anti-counterculture, pro-establishment cultural movement. Punisher is not just mad about the crimes committed by Samson and his followers, but he hates their whole damn creepy crawling "hippie pranksters" mode (and yes, *Punisher* does take this whack at Ken Kesey and *his* followers). While the kind-of-Manson-kind-of-Patty-Hearst "Liberation Army" depicted here claims to be making war on "rich capitalist pigs," Punisher can see through the rhetoric in order to take measure of "the usual collection of drug abusers and career criminals hiding behind a cloak of political involvement." By the time the "Samson" storyline reaches its conclusion, as Samson's followers begin to morph from scary hippies to scary punks, readers will not be surprised to see the jacked-up Punisher completely dominating the bad guy (who, in a neat twist, is depicted as tall). Having been paralyzed in the struggle, Samson begs Punisher to kill him, and the hero obliges. They walk among us no longer, at least not in the Marvel universe.

The "walk among us" trope has figured not only in genre fiction and comic books, but "high" literary fiction as well. Most recently Madison Smartt Bell has brought together the Tate-LaBianca tragedy and the 9/11 attacks in his book *The Color of Night* (2011). The main character begins to relive old experiences from her time with the Family (here called "The People") as a result of seeing footage of the twin towers falling on television. Michael Lindgren correctly points out that Bell seems to be making some broad and unsupportable claims about the relationship between the violent tragedies of the late 1960s in the United States and the devastation of September 11th. Bell has ambitious (self-indulgent?) mythology-inspired aims in *The Color of Night*, and has explained that the female characters are to be read as Maenads—the female followers of Dionysus. Bell is interested in exploring the relationship between terror and ecstasy and does so in about as coherent a form as that goal suggests. (He also does not seem to know—or does not want to acknowledge—that Richard Schechner and the Performance Group got to this idea with *Dionysus in '69* a long time ago.) This book has the predictable Manson allusions (Family members are given new names—Creamy, Crunchy, and Stitch, women are instructed to do witchy things after their crimes, members are told to "slither"—that is, creepy crawl, and so on) and the now-familiar implication that Bugliosi did not complete the work of shutting the Family down. *The Color of Night*, in fact, draws on Bell's interest in mythology and in spirit possession to plot the 1969 crimes as simply one point on the timeless graph of violent frenzy. Bell's work is explicitly anti-historical—evil is a root force in the world and it erupts into violence when the stars align.[10]

John Kaye's *The Dead Circus* (2002) stands as perhaps the most satisfying literary refutation of the common practice of mystification of Manson that is given voice in Madison Smartt Bell's book (and elsewhere). Beginning with two invented pieces of documentary evidence, Kaye establishes immediately that Manson's legacy will have to be traced on an actual landscape of social relations. After presenting an excerpt from a newspaper article about the 1985 murder of Eddie Cornell, with a quotation from a police detective who (apropos of nothing else, so far) denies that this murder had anything to do with the Manson case, Kaye then offers up a long quotation, allegedly drawn from "unpublished prison notebooks" written by Manson: "I am, just a child with salt and cinders underneath his skin, a chooser not a beggar . . . . I'm safe here in this cellblock . . . . But you're not safe out there, because your hearts are locked against the children who cried out for help, who left you with the silence of an empty bedroom, their clothes in their closets and their schoolbooks still on the shelves, the air crackling with their anger." "They are waking up now in dead alleys or climbing out of ditches," this fictional Manson continues, convincingly, "and soon they will be loose and running, half-starved and forgotten, crossing and recrossing this fouled country, waiting until the winds calm and the flames die out before they decide to come home." Finally, Manson warns, "that, my friends, is when you get to face the truth."[11]

Like the pulp novelists, Kaye also describes Family members who are still among us (the book features a major character named Alice who was a significant player in Family life), but his chronicling of the current day activities of Manson women is not the important story in *The Dead Circus*. To be sure, Kaye is scrupulous in his attention to detail—both in historically sourced actual detail and in his outright fictional creations, which often have an uncannily documentary feel. *The Dead Circus* acts as a sort of primer to the dark byways of Southern California life (and especially the music industry) from the mid-1960s through the 1980s. It jumps off from the story of Bobby Fuller, the Los Angeles rocker who died in Hollywood in 1966 under strange and still unsolved circumstances. Kaye has few peers when it comes to describing the Family and its murderous work. He is especially interested in tracing out the legacy of the abuse many of the women in the Family suffered, and suggests that Manson too was the victim of sexual abuse (by a stepfather) as a child. The historical accuracy is less important than the attempt Kaye makes to plot the members of the Family into a convincing chronicle of suffering and victimization: "We were girls who were tender, with hurt places," one fictional Manson woman explains. "We were all just gullible girls with separate selves," she says, "part of a creepy chain of hope that carried the wrong message."[12]

The Dead Circus is organized around Gene Burk, a Los Angeles cop in the 1960s, now retired and focusing on his record collecting. Burk's hobby is not a tangential bit of characterization. Through his activities readers come to learn that that Kaye's real aim in the book is to prosecute all of us for consuming—consistently and pruriently—the details and material culture of the Manson case. *The Dead Circus* is what we might call a metanarrative; it is a book about collecting (stories, songs, films, and so on) and about how collectors—and readers and listeners and viewers—can become a part of the stories they collect. It is, in short, a book about how all of us create Manson. Kaye's book is, it seems, the work of someone deeply invested in the world of popular music collecting (or at least someone willing to do lots of research before writing his novel): an early plot thread has to do with a rare 45 Gene Burk wants to buy of "Big Boy Pants," a (fictional) song by the (real) Juvenairs, who were the predecessor group to Danny and the

Juniors (also real). Later in the book, Burk negotiates for a photograph reportedly taken during an early (fictional) Linda Ronstadt recording session, during which Ricky Nelson played guitar and sang, alongside Family member Cathy "Gypsy" Share, who also sang backup. The dealer who offers the picture to Burk refers to it as "Ozzie and Harriet meet Charles Manson."[13]

The book's statement of purpose comes in passages that reveal where it got its title:

> Beginning in the late 1970s, the underground market for pictures and artifacts associated with the Manson murders had been growing steadily, not only in the U.S. but worldwide. This fact had not gone unnoticed by Charles Manson or those members of his family who still remained loyal to him while he was incarcerated. In 1981, for example, a welder from Traverse City, Michigan, paid $500 for a pair of soiled panties owned by Patricia Krenwinkel; and six months later, he paid another $750 for the Kinks concert-logo T-shirt that Clem Grogan was photographed wearing outside the downtown courthouse in Los Angeles, where Charlie was on trial.[14]

This disorganized market of collectors was somewhat rationalized in the early 1980s, when a "magazine devoted to Mansonabilia began to appear on newsstands in Los Angeles, New York, and several other cities. It was called *The Dead Circus*, and, in the premiere issue, there was a full-page ad offering a color photograph of Charlie sporting a full erection." After a "prominent art dealer in Philadelphia" pays $10,000 for the picture, it turns out to "be a fake." It is actually a picture taken at Woodstock, of a "sandal maker from Taos, New Mexico." Manson's appropriate response to this entire turn of events is to muse that now "at least I know how much my pecker is worth."[15]

The discovery of this morbid market for Mansonabilia gets the attention of Manson himself, who has, for years, been quietly sitting on the knowledge that he has control of the single most desirable collector's item of all: six canisters of 16 millimeter film that capture the Manson Family in its heyday—with a particular focus on their orgies with music- and film-world celebrities, and possibly with some film shot inside Sharon Tate's house on the night of the murders. Here John Kaye seems to be inviting readers to think about Don DeLillo's novel, *Running Dog* (1978), which is organized around an international collectors' search for a pornographic film shot in Hitler's bunker. In that novel, too, there is a magazine that gives the book its title. The real goal of Kaye's book is to indict readers (and of course, himself) as co-conspirators in the fetishizing of Charles Manson and the Family. When Manson more-or-less rhetorically asks a neighbor of his in prison what "would be the ultimate possession" if you "really wanted to own a piece of the Manson family legend," Kaye is provoking the reader: while he has already planted clues about what Manson might be hinting at, he also knows that each of us will, in this moment, imagine our own vision of the most desirable Manson collector's item.[16]

Earlier in the novel Kaye had already explored in a quite literal way how the Manson Family violence can serve as a form of pornography for viewers. Gene Burk learns this when he visits the House of Love, a brothel that is on the corner of Hollywood Boulevard and Las Palmas—on exactly the site where his own father ran a twenty-four-hour newsstand from the late 1940s through the early 1970s. At the House of Love, a sex worker tells Burk, there is a "Manson suite." At the Manson suite a cast of actors "re-creates the murder . . . . Everything is performed according to the trial transcript. The dialogue, the floor plan. It's all exactly the way it was." Kaye's barely hidden challenge has to do with why so many of us have become such willing audiences for such ritual performances.[17]

Burk ultimately gets deeply involved with a "forgotten" member of the Manson Family, a woman named Alice who has been living a relatively marginal existence since the time of the killings. Alice's name is certainly meant to invoke the complexities of Wonderland, not only the fantasy world created by Lewis Carroll, which was such a crucial text for members of the late 1960s counterculture, but also Wonderland Avenue in Laurel Canyon, site of four horrifying murders in 1981 often compared to the Tate-LaBianca killings for sheer bloodiness. What is most important about this Alice is that she has access to the grail—the films that have been obsessively discussed, searched for, and not found since 1969. Alice may still "walk among us"—*The Dead Circus* operates firmly in this tradition of Manson art—but Kaye's argument in introducing it is to suggest that it might be time for all of us to renounce our willingness to engage with the Manson Family as entertainment, arousal, a good time.

It would be virtually impossible to list all of the articulations of popular and "high" art of the past few decades that indulge in the type of crudely voyeuristic Manson-collecting Kaye is targeting here. Perhaps we can draft Tony O'Neill's sophomoric 2010 novel *Sick City* (it's title "daringly" borrowed from a Manson song) to stand as a representative of this deep well of material. This sub–William Burroughs romp through the dark underbelly of Los Angeles shares *The Dead Circus*'s interest in possible Tate-related film, but here the aim is not to offer a critique of the exploitative economy of collectors but to shock the bourgeoisie. Or somebody. O'Neill's novel also has a hot-property piece of film—a party scene from the late 1960s, with "some pretty big people. Steve McQueen was there. Sharon. Roman Polanski. Lee Van Cleef. Mama Cass." Sharon Tate is the ultimate sex object at this party: "They all fuck her. Steve McQueen fucks her, and then he rolls off her, and Yul Brynner has a go. Mama fuckin' Cass is naked and eating her pussy, while someone is screwing her from behind." The two men who are discussing this potentially valuable film agree that if they could get their hands on it to sell, it would be like having "the Holy Grail, or the Shroud of fuckin' Turin."[18]

Contrary to the witless and incendiary grotesqueness of O'Neill's novel, Kaye takes care to construct a scenario of punishing self-critique and renunciation. Alice's definitive gesture is to walk out into the desert, toward Barker Ranch, and burn the reels of film that have been in her care. As the film smolders, Alice "said their names out loud: Sharon Tate, Jay Sebring,

Abigail Folger, Voytek Frykowski, and Steve Parent, the five who died at 10050 Cielo Drive on August 9, 1969." As Gene and Alice walk away from the site of the destruction, in "the absolute stillness of the moment, he felt something that passed for peace, and a voice inside him spoke with fierce clarity: *Keep me in your heart. That's all I ask*."[19] It is not clear whether the voice belongs to Burk's own lover, tragically killed in an airplane accident, or to Sharon Tate's fetus who, according to Alice, just wanted "a name and a birthdate and a mother to sing him a lullaby."[20] This rather mushy New Age conclusion to the burning ceremony cannot mask Kaye's quite sharp critical analysis, an interpretation that emphasizes how important consumer behaviors (collecting, reading, watching, and so on) have been to the maintenance of Charles Manson's power. Kaye suggests in *The Dead Circus* that the actual presence of Manson Family members on the contemporary scene is a minor detail, essentially the answer to a trivia question or an online quiz. The central cultural dilemma facing those of us who want to engage with the legacy of the Manson Family, Kaye suggests, is how to do so without being economically exploitative, culturally sensationalist, or just plain gross. (Time to announce this: my own older child said to me, when I was a few years into the research process for this book, "It is really time for you to start writing. Otherwise this is all just a very weird hobby.") Whether we think of ourselves as living in the true-crime domain of Vincent Bugliosi's *Helter Skelter*, or the (mostly) pulp world of those "live among us" tales, Kaye insists that we must investigate our own obsessive interest in keeping the Manson story alive.

Gene Burk, for his part, is ready to put not only Manson behind him, but also the collecting that has structured his retirement: "That's it," Burk tells his brother, "I'm done. No more collecting."[21] Putting on his own version of the "Big Boy Pants" that the Juvenairs sang about in the song Burk considered buying earlier in the novel, Gene Burk here acknowledges that his investment in the Manson case has not primarily been about tying up loose ends from his days as a detective. He has been *collecting* Manson for his own private purposes, in an obsessive attempt to redefine himself after he has given up his job and lost his lover. As music journalist Amanda Petrusich has helpfully summarized, "[C]ollectors customize an identity via the serialization of objects."[22] The appeal of collecting Manson, as John Kaye makes clear, comes with the special offer it makes to grant mastery to the collector over the the irrational and the downright messy. John Kaye's Gene Burk stands as a reproach to all of those (all of us) who embrace Manson as a private obsession—a route to control whatever dark forces we struggle with, forces that can be conveniently projected onto this one man.

He's a Magic Man

Keeping Manson and his Family alive in our movies and fiction, our music and visual art, has contributed to the development of a form that builds on an important American dark art, what we might now call a slow-motion Gothic. The historian Karen Halttunen has written cogently about the complex challenges we face when we try to figure out what to "do" with murderers in our midst. According to Halttunen, the "most important cultural work" of crime narratives has been to construct the criminal as "a moral monster from whom readers were instructed to shrink, with a sense of *horror* that confirmed their own 'normalcy' in the face of the morally alien, and with a sense of *mystery* that testified to their own inability to even conceive of such an aberrant act." But what Halttunen calls our "ambivalent engagement" with killers is not so simple to master; as she puts it, our "fascination with the 'monster' betrays our uneasy sense that our intense interest implicates us, if only as voyeurs, in the crime."[1]

The "secret films" at the heart of the novels by John Kaye and Tony O'Neill certainly serve as good reminders of how a cultural investment with high-profile murderers can be transformed into acts of exploitative viewing. But the "zombie" plot in Manson art—the compulsively repeated notion that Manson's children or members of his Family are at large wreaking havoc—argues in favor of our watchful stance. Simon Wells is correct to suggest that Charles Manson (and, I would add, his Family) long ago transcended the concrete facts of their lives and crimes and "morphed into a popular metaphor for unbridled horror."[2] At the heart of the Manson Family terror is the simple fact that they fit in with various emerging and powerful social groupings in Los Angeles. They fit in on the Sunset Strip, in Laurel Canyon, and even at fancy Hollywood parties. The dark shadow accompanying the "live among us" plot grows from a blame-the-victim implication that Sharon Tate and her friends somehow brought this all on themselves. The modern penny dreadfuls were full of this suggestion: "Somewhere along the line," *Movie Life Yearbook* suggested in 1969, Sharon Tate "may have begun to lose sight of her real self." Tate's death, according to this line of (un)reasoning, may have been caused by her "lack of selectivity in choosing her friends and her great need to have as many of them as possible" in order to compensate for the "false and one-dimensional image Hollywood had created for her."[3] In November of 1970, a pulp magazine called *Movie Mirror* suggested that Manson and Tate were twins of a sort, both pursuing "glamour in separate ways" but inevitably meeting in a "horrible culmination of all that has been kept secret in Hollywood." *Modern Screen* asked the core question fairly directly: "What went on at the 'swinging' party that led to mass murder!"[4] If Manson and his Family could so fully infiltrate the inner sanctum of Hollywood and Los Angeles's popular music culture, then why should we have any expectation that they would be ejected simply because a few of their members were put on trial and in jail?

It would be foolish to deny that Manson's primary function in expressive culture has been as a sign of horror, a dark exclamation point on the cultural formation we generally refer to as the sixties. John Moran, composer of an opera inspired by the Family's activities, has captured this belief system efficiently. "He really did close the '60s,'" Moran has suggested. "Until the murders, psychedelia had been associated with the idea of love. After Manson and because of the way the media portrayed him, psychedelia became associated with flipping out and violence and fear."[5] Tommy Udo has rightly noted that "horror films post-Manson betray the real anxieties of the public in a way that a factual film or documentary could not."[6] The list of Manson-inspired (or Manson-inflected) horror films in the immediate wake of the killings and trials is impressive, and includes not only *Texas Chainsaw Massacre* (1974) and Wes Craven's *Last House on the Left* (1972), but numerous less well-remembered films, ranging from *I Drink Your Blood* (1971), in which the band of hippies is literally rabid, and *The Other Side of Madness* (1972), also known as *The Helter Skelter Murders*.

In his book *Subversive Horror Cinema* Jon Towlson helpfully summarizes the ways that the Manson Family's cultural creepy crawl helped define the vocabulary of horror films of the 1970s. These films (most notably *Last House on the Left* and *Texas Chainsaw Massacre*) portrayed the "American counterculture during this period as extremely dark." The films served as an articulation of the popular idea that "even peace-loving hippies harbored antisocial, violent impulses." The "dark counterculture" of these horror films present a landscape on which "rape, murder and sadism have replaced peace and love as the alternative to bourgeois social norms."[7]

In this light, the actual references to the Manson murders in *Last House on the Left*, or various other horror films of the 1970s, are probably less consequential than is their general vision of an anarchy loosed on the American scene by a counterculture whose murderous members cannot be easily distinguished from the positive forces of what soul singer Otis Redding, at the Monterey Pop festival, called the "love crowd." David Ray Carter, writing about *Texas Chainsaw Massacre* (released in 1974, the same year as Bugliosi's true-crime bible), argues that American audiences would have been very likely to read the film in the context of Manson: "The film was released three years after Charles Manson and his 'family' were convicted," he writes, and "it would be difficult to imagine that audiences viewing the film in 1974 would not make a correlation between the film and the Manson family."[8] Much of the landscape of horror film post-1970 is shaped by Manson Family themes and images; John Cline and Robert G. Weiner have suggested that numerous films in this era articulated

Manson-related social fears, particularly having to do with "home invasion" or the breaching of private space on the one hand, and with cults and threatening subcultures on the other.[9] The "Manson framing" that gives outline to so many horror movies of the 1970s and beyond usually works as a sort of cultural quarantine. Manson has been invoked consistently and terrifyingly in this "contemporary folklore." But even as we applaud these rituals of expulsion—presumably taking comfort in these stories in which Manson and his Family emerge on our landscape only to be mocked, neutralized, killed—we have also developed a fairly solid culture of appreciation surrounding the cult leader and his followers.

To be sure there are no major components of pro-Manson sentiment circulating in literary, film, or visual cultures. There is no body of culturally significant work we could call "Mansonist" or "Mansonical." There are, of course, Family members who have created exculpatory "non-fiction" chronicles about their own lives and involvement with Manson, and there are celebratory images and stories created by latter-day followers, many of whom travel with Manson under the environmentalist ATWA (Air, Trees, Water, All the Way Alive) banner. But these works are parochial and rarely enter into substantial cultural conversations outside of their own very tight circles of production and reception. With few exceptions (Paul Watkins's co-written memoir comes to mind) these are works that mean to settle scores and preach to the converted with little investment in artistic strategy.

Even as Vincent Bugliosi and so many others, including Manson himself, have worked assiduously to write this charismatic figure out of the mainstream of American cultural life (as uneducated, short, a "hillbilly," a deviant, and so on on) his talismanic power has never waned since 1969. Jeffrey Sconce, who has aptly called Manson the "psychopath of choice" for successive generations of journalists looking for a good story, notes that "Manson's notoriety is not based on a simple arithmetic of atrocity, his evil residing somewhere other than in a mere body count." Manson's hold on the collective imagination of Americans, as

Sconce puts it, grows from a complex calculus of sex, gender, and power; Sconce provocatively suggests that what might provoke "outrage" in public discussion of Manson "can often serve as fuel for fantasy in private thought." The guilt of Manson and his followers, Sconce notes, was never as interesting to observers as was the question of how to understand the "real" relationship that connected Manson to his Family.[10] It is no surprise, then, to find that outside of Bugliosi and a few others, there has been relatively little attention paid to the courtroom trials of Manson and the Family. Our interest in Manson has been much more about how he lives in our world, rather than how he lives in his.

Consider a rumor about the song "Magic Man" by Canadian rock group Heart, led by sisters Ann and Nancy Wilson. Jeffrey Sconce explains that for a few years in the mid-1970s, a story circulated that the song was not only about the cult leader but that "profits from the record were being turned over to him."[11] (The secret-message variant of the rumor is, of course, particularly rich given the vibrancy it gains from how it interacts with Bugliosi's vision of Manson as a tragic misreader of the Beatles). Internet message boards and other sites continue to host versions of this rumor; it has traveled at least as far as the Wilson sisters themselves, who felt obliged to address it in their joint autobiography in 2012.

As with so many texts that generate rumors, there is little concrete in "Magic Man" to suggest a Manson connection. But as David Ray Carter argues about *Texas Chainsaw Massacre*, audiences in 1976 were prepared to hear a song about a powerful (possibly older man) controlling a young woman as being inspired by the seemingly hypnotic power Manson held over his female disciples. "Magic Man" is keyed around a competition between a young woman's mother and her suitor, both of whom are clamoring for her to "Come on home, girl." The song has elements that point away from Manson ("Never seen eyes so blue") and elements that point toward Manson—at least in a broad sense ("It seemed like he knew me / He looked right through me" could come out of an autobiography by one of the Manson girls).

It is not, additionally, much of a stretch to hear "Played inside the months of moon / Never think of never" as being rooted in, in some very vague way, in Manson's own "I'll Never Say Never to Always." But of course neither the actual lyrics nor the sound of Heart's song is particularly important to the creation or circulation of this rumor.

Manson's function as culture-generator from the late 1960s until our own time depends on flexibility. While Charles Manson is hardly a blank slate—you cannot simply bounce *anything* off of him—he has been the launch pad for a stunningly broad range of expressive forays. All evidence suggests that however often and in whatever ways the Wilson sisters protest the "incorrect" reading of "Magic Man" there continue to be powerful agents and vehicles of reception (i.e., you, me, and the Internet) continuing to insist on the Manson reading. For what it's worth, Hall and Oates have been similarly plagued by the Patty Hearst reading of their 1977 hit "Rich Girl"!

Waves of Mutilation

If we are going to conduct a serious evaluation of Manson art—works inspired in one way of another by his charismatic leadership, his nonconformism, his scary eyes, the murders he was convicted of directing, the landscapes he and his Family inhabited, and so on—we will have to pause to acknowledge at least briefly that Manson himself was some kind of artist. Numerous observers have emphasized what Bugliosi referred to as the "certain amount of theater" involved in the killings; Ed Sanders called him a "performance killer."[1] But the musical creation that was at the heart of Manson's search for a platform in the last couple years of the 1960s has not been as significant to Manson's celebrity in recent decades as have the ways he has been deployed by and himself manipulated the forces of material culture production. Manson's fame has spread on posters, stickers, T-shirts, and so on. Sites that specialize in such material—supernaught.com and rottencotton.com (and Etsy and eBay, to be honest)—have consistently profited from selling Manson's image. Manson himself got in the game fairly early, offering up a "hand painted prison yard rock" (for $4,500), signed bags of snack food, paintings and sketches, and various pieces of signed ephemera (e.g., Monopoly money). Manson may not have have been able to make much of a mark in the late 1960s as a recording artist, but he did pretty well for himself as a purveyor of visual art and material culture.

The most notorious piece of Manson-related material culture is almost certainly the "Charlie Don't Surf" T-shirt sold by the Lemmons Brothers out of their Riot Gear store in Newport

Beach, California, beginning in the early 1990s. Repurposing a phrase uttered by Robert Duvall's character in Francis Ford Coppola's *Apocalypse Now* (there used as mordant commentary on the racism of American military violence in Vietnam) and then taken up by the Clash as title for a song on their *Sandinista!* album, the T-shirt turns serious critique into sophomoric kitsch. According to their own account the Lemmons Brothers cleared their T-shirt plan with Manson and arranged a royalty deal with him. The money earmarked for Manson ultimately went to the son of Family victim Voytek Frykowski. The Christian fundamentalist brothers claim that they sent their own share of the royalties to the anti-abortion group Operation Rescue. Mike Rubin, writing in *Spin*, has suggested that "Manson's mug" has "creepy-crawled out of the fringes" to become ubiquitous in mainstream culture. Putting an even finer point on Manson's value in the arena of material culture, Rubin argues that "in the world of mass murderer bubble-gum trading cards, Manson is a Mickey Mantle rookie card."[2] Manson has remained a remarkably stable commodity since at least the time of the publication of Bugliosi's *Helter Skelter*. Our cultural investment in Manson imagery has (not surprisingly) been joined at the hip with all manner of successful economic initiatives.

But the more T-shirts we buy, the less, it seems, we want to reckon soberly with Manson's own musical creations. Very few have been willing to wade through the thickets of shocking imagery and biographical static surrounding Manson to engage in this kind of study. Recall how earnest Ed Sanders was, writing in the *Los Angeles Free Press* during the spring of 1970, about establishing Manson's bona fides as a creative force with his insistence that the Family could easily outdo the top level of professional folk-rock musicians. Sanders rhapsodized further about this music, arguing that "No one can prevent its beauty. And its revolutionary implications."[3]

Very few observers have followed Sanders's lead and taken Manson's own music seriously. Scholar Mark Goodall is almost alone in trying to recuperate the Manson as a purveyor of what generally travels under the banner of "outsider" art. Calling Manson "easily as gifted as many more famous artists of the time," and finding parallels between his work and the music of the Velvet Underground and the Incredible String Band, Goodall explains Manson's failure to capitalize on recording opportunities as a positive reminder that the singer was a "free spirit" who was "guided by whim" and could not fit into the constraints of the commercialized world of popular music. Goodall at once wants to locate Manson as a colleague of the "spontaneous" folk singers of the 1950s who emphasized communal creation above all other goals *and* as a sophisticated individual artist who frequently deployed sophisticated musical strategies: "He makes use of the sixth and unresolved major seventh chords that are more commonly found in Latin music." In his close reading of Manson's song "Maiden with Green Eyes," Goodall notes that the song uses a "rhumba rhythm," along with a "medieval narrative sensibility" and the overall tone of "1950s doo wop." Trying to summarize a number of other Manson compositions, Goodall describes a particularly effective melding of "folk protest" and doo-wop characteristics.[4]

British journalist and musician Lewis Parker has been similarly interested in recuperating not only the value of Manson's music, but that of the performances of the Family as well. Parker has written pointed prose about how masterful prosecutor Vincent Bugliosi has been at "controlling the narrative" surrounding Manson. Parker's own contribution has been, in his writing and music (he is member of a Manson cover band), to offer a revisionist take on Manson's art—a take that, notably, revives Ed Sanders's decades-old support of the Family's musicality. While Parker is interested in Manson's own performance, he is especially interested in the music Sanders heard around the campfire at Spahn Ranch, this "ultimate psychedelic music," repackaged most recently as *The Family Jams*. Parker reads this music as part of the revisionist Western insurgency I will discuss in the last few pages of this section: "This is an album that expresses the vast, raw, intoxicating sense of running away, getting away with, and finally being free." Parker makes a fascinating case that the ramshackle, half-cooked feel of the music is purposeful—that it is meant to invoke "open space, a huge trip" at just the moment when Manson and a number of Family members were facing life-long confinement (if not death itself).[5]

The details here are not nearly as significant as the revision-ist approach. What Sanders, Goodall, and Parker remind us (as of course Neil Young and a few others have tried to do) is that Manson first established himself in the culture of Los Angeles as a folk musician of some merit—an "outsider" artist to be sure, but playing in the same game as the more established artists with whom he tried to forge relationships. Zachary Lazar attempts to capture this reality in his novel *Sway*, looking through the eyes of Bobby Beausoleil: "Other people came to Charlie as if he were a visionary, some sort of guru, but to Bobby he was another musi-cian, someone with connections. He knew the Beach Boys, Neil Young, a man named Terry Melcher who produced the Byrds."[6] Lazar, like Goodall, acknowledges that Manson could not (or would not) simply join the commercial enterprise represented by Melcher and his entourage. Manson's artistic attack, as Lazar ren-ders it, embodied a highly conscious and complex awareness of performer and audience: the singer was "giving himself up to the song, but also making fun of the idea of giving himself up to the song, making fun of you for believing it."[7] Like Mark Goodall, Zachary Lazar insists that contemporary audiences take seriously the idea that the music Manson made was an important part of the larger challenges he was making against the mainstream cul-ture he was rubbing so painfully against. Lazar also insists that Manson's rebel stance took form in the songs themselves. This was "unusual music," which took pains to avoid "the simple pen-tatonic scales of blues and rock for the mysterious spirals of the Dorian mode, the Mixolydian mode. The music reflected back a range of tensions in the room, all the social hierarchies that no one wanted to admit existed anymore, drawing them out. It was not aggressive—it had an ethereal, dreamy sound—but it spread a malevolence that came at first as a faint surprise then blossomed into something so familiar that it seemed obvious. It was the music of dim rooms, or red wine in gallon jugs. It was the music of slow violence unfurling."[8]

These attempts to rehabilitate Charles Manson as a significant artist in his own right are valuable scholarly and artistic exercises. But they remain exercises indeed—interesting theoretically but lacking the force to alter the main currents of Manson art. Manson's music, notwithstanding the revisionist efforts of Goodall, Lazar, and a few others, mostly lives as punch line. In our own time Manson's own music is an Internet curiosity even as it remains available in physical format. His *Lie* record, originally produced for release by self-described "Road Mangler Deluxe" Phil Kaufman, was reissued in the 1980s as a bootleg by Welsh label Fierce Recordings. But it is cover versions of Manson songs—primarily by punk, industrial, and heavy-metal bands—that have kept him most fully present as a musical force. Redd Kross, of Hawthorne, California (also home of the Beach Boys), helped kick off the 1980s wave with their record *Born Innocent*—the title a reference to *Exorcist*-star Linda Blair's television movie (1974) about juvenile prison. The LP is drenched in Manson. Most directly it features a version of "Cease to Exist," the original title of the Manson-penned song ultimately released by the Beach Boys as "Never Learn Not to Love." Redd Kross also offers up an original they titled simply "Charlie," which is a sort of punk-rock haiku of the Tate murders keyed around descriptions of Tate's dead body and the fetus inside of her, which is described either as "little" or "widdle"—it's hard to tell. The singalong that follows is much more clear in its incitement to kill piggies. *Born Innocent* also includes a cover of "Look on Up at the Bottom" from 1970's *Beyond the Valley of the Dolls*, a satirical follow-up to Sharon Tate's original *Valley of the Dolls*. *Beyond the Valley of the Dolls*, according to screenwriter Roger Ebert, was partly inspired by the Tate-LaBianca murders. Redd Kross's Jeff McDonald (yes, he has almost the exact same name as the convicted "Green Beret" killer) has, in later days, admitted that the main target of the band's Manson material was his parents. As McDonald writes,

"We used to just tell our parents we were into Charles Manson just to drive them crazy. . . . They were furious we were on the cover of *Flipside* magazine in our garage and we were holding this picture of Charles Manson. . . . We were laughing. They were not happy."[9]

Redd Kross's early 1980s Manson art statements were joined by numerous others in the 1980s and beyond. Boston's Lemonheads released their Manson cover in 1988, with its version of "Home Is Where You're Happy" and liner notes that thanked "Susan, Lynette, Gypsy, Katie, Mary, Sandra, Leslie, Snake, Ouisch, Little Paul, and, of course, Charlie." Bandleader Evan Dando would evince an ongoing interest in figuring out what he could "do" with Manson as source and image. The alternative music culture's fascination with Manson crested in the first half of the 1990s as Brian Warner created a performing persona which was more or less a double cover version: Marilyn Manson. At the same time Guns N' Roses recorded Manson's "Look at Your Game, Girl" (with royalties ultimately going to the son of Voytek Frykowski). The culture of Manson covers was relatively tame, organized as it was around the sophomoric notion that surely *somebody*'s parents could still be upset by a loud and fast version of a Manson song.[10]

This quick summary of revisions of Manson's music in the 1980s and 1990s is meant mostly as a counterpoint to the body of work that has used Manson as a truly generative reference point—a place from which to initiate artistically rich and culturally challenging explorations. In this light it is worth thinking about "Wave of Mutilation," released by the Pixies in 1989. Rather than indulge in the limited act of actually covering a Manson composition, the Pixies instead built a complex allusion into the first line of their song, which first invokes the Beach Boys conversion of Manson's "Cease to exist" into "Cease to resist," and then follows the narrator as he says his farewells and kills himself and his family by navigating their car into the ocean. Lead singer Frank Black (a.k.a. Black Francis) has explained that the first verse of the song is about Japanese businessmen driven to desperation by feelings of shame surrounding business failure; he also acknowledges that the opening line is a joke on the Beach Boys and Charles Manson. As the singer explains it (with some rudimentary level of understanding of actual historical fact), they "hung out all together . . . . And he wrote this song called 'Cease to Exist.' And supposedly the Beach Boys used a lot of his lyrics and gave him a sports car or something. And they had this boys loved girl song where they went 'cease to resist' and changed his lyrics around. They couldn't have 'cease to exist' because it was all powerful suicide stuff.'"[11] The accomplishment here is the invocation of Manson and the Beach Boys in three words to act as a sort of foreshadowing of the deaths to come. In the Pixies' song, the other side of the Pacific Ocean from Southern California represents not the Endless Summer (to borrow the title of a Beach Boys' compilation from 1974) of that band's most optimistic songs, but the destruction following in the wake of Charles Manson's meeting with Dennis Wilson in Los Angeles. "Wave of Mutilation" goes one step beyond the cover image of Neil Young's *On the Beach*: here the car has crashed not on the sand, but in the water.

With their ambitious reference to "Cease to Exist," in "Wave of Mutilation," the Pixies were extending a tradition of Manson art that reached back into the late 1970s, and that had particularly important antecedents in the punk musical and visual culture of Southern California. Here the key figures are the artist Raymond Pettibon and the hardcore punk band Black Flag, led by Pettibon's brother Greg Ginn. Pettibon and Black Flag were connected not only by the family relationship of the two brothers, but also by the important graphic work Pettibon did for the band—a series of flyers that art historian Thomas Crow describes as having been central to the evolving thematic vocabulary of the band—not to mention that Pettibon was responsible for suggesting the name for the band and designing its logo.[12] This is a key moment in the history of Manson art. Mark Jones and Gerry Carlin are surely correct to suggest that this is when Manson's cultural presence was shifting from the "irrecuperable" to the "radical."[13]

Thomas Crow makes a convincing case that Pettibon's work has to be understood as a commentary on all of the Manson art that precedes it: "The imagery and story of Charles Manson's 'family' became a dominant theme across the entire early phase of Pettibon's career—the aspirations of the counter-culture become sordid crime drama."[14] What Crow finds most interesting in this work by Pettibon is that it at once acknowledges the cliché about Manson "ending" the sixties, while also "refusing the complacent conclusions drawn from it."[15] This multimedia, unruly work that Pettibon has done (Mark Goodall suggests we call it his "Book of Manson," after the artist's own film about the Family) aims, as Thomas Crow writes, to "expose the pervasive pleasure aroused by the story" in conventional people who still manage to maintain a "murderous antipathy toward any perceived deviance or moral challenges from outsiders."[16] In his deceptively simple, text-heavy ink drawings, Pettibon repeatedly invites viewers to view scenarios alternatively absurd (there *must* have been a "Family" dog that participated in the free sexual life at Spahn Ranch) and poignant. Pettibon's Manson is arrogant, baffled, martyred. Incorporating Manson as a key term into the visual language of his punk aesthetic, Pettibon makes a case for the cult leader as a master text of the marginal, the off-kilter, the perverse.

In the late 1980s Pettibon released his full-length film, *Judgment Day Theater: The Book of Manson*—perhaps making a polygamy joke with his subtitle. The cast features members of Redd Kross, Black Flag, and other figures from the Southern California punk scene. The tone of the movie is completely deadpan. The actors generally do not try to hide the fact that they are reading lines from cue cards, and when possible they remove whatever affect might naturally emerge in their voices. Many of the lines read by the actors in *Book of Manson* invoke phrases familiar from general usage and from *Helter Skelter*'s account of Family life and the Tate-LaBianca murders. The shopworn feel of much of the dialogue is purposeful. As Thomas Crow writes of Pettibon's ink drawings, the use of clichés is meant at once to acknowledge the power they have for so many audience members *and* as a way to deny the conventional wisdom allegedly built into them. The reinvigorated clichés take on even greater force when Pettibon juxtaposes them with the fresh, absurdist dialogue he has concocted for the script. So, when a character named "Norman Mailer" wanders onto the scene, announces he wants to be Manson's groupie, and then declares "Charlie cuts right to the heart of the essence . . . you've made me point an accusatory finger at my corrupt bourgeois self," it not only sounds ridiculous, but it also serves to undercut empty bromides like "Teach your children" and "You'll never work in this town again." It is also likely meant as a challenge to Mailer's sponsorship of writer Jack Henry Abbott and Mailer's support of Abbott's release from jail; soon after his release, Abbot stabbed a waiter and returned to prison.

Idiocy is the main tonal register of *Book of Manson*: Pettibon's script and the actors' performances seem dopey-on-purpose. A major goal of *Book of Manson*, in short, is to sap Manson's power; no longer seeming capable of disrupting the counterculture, the film and music industry of Los Angeles, or anything else, Manson is revealed in Pettibon's movie as a rather slow-witted stoner. *The Book of Manson* is no fun, but it *is* a stoner film. As with most films of the genre it is relatively static—nothing much *happens* for the bulk of the movie. The jabbery talk that fills *The Book of Manson* is mostly dumb but also wildly referential. Pettibon's Family members seem less like countercultural renegades and more like passive consumers who have been brainwashed by what they have watched on television and listened to on the radio and the stereo. In Pettibon's rather dim and anesthetized version of things, the Manson Family is "us"—the generic audience—strangled into semi-consciousness by the many tentacles of commercial culture.

Raymond Pettibon's portfolio is also full of the poster art he did for his brother's band, which featured Manson as a central element of its visual palette. Black Flag brought Manson on the road with them by naming their first major tour their "Creepy Crawl." Black Flag's bassist has explained that the band got "arcane and emotional value from Manson."[17] Dewar MacLeod has suggested that Black Flag saw touring itself as an alternative to settling into the "safe suburban home" that beckoned in Southern California. Through its own "creepy crawl," he writes, the band aimed to draw an "inscription . . . on the American landscape with the object to leave their mark and move on, not conquer markets or the masses."[18] Members of Black Flag have acknowledged that Pettibon was the driver of this concept. As his brother Greg Ginn puts it, "It was just basically a series of flyers and other stuff, just on the Manson theme, and the various things you can do with that." Bassist Chuck Dukowski adds that the band very much embraced the creepy-crawl concept. As he explains, Black Flag was interested in finding out what would happen if they could make their audiences feel fear: "You threaten a lot of their values, and the potential for something to happen that they don't understand, or they don't have control of in their existing mental framework, makes it useful to throw them off balance and thus open people up."[19]

If Pettibon's film and his graphic work for Black Flag offered up a disorganized sort of media criticism, the most important piece of countercultural Manson art of the late 1980s—Negativland's *Helter Stupid* (1989)—had a much more cogent argument to make about the crimes of the Manson Family and the motive ascribed to Manson by prosecutor and true-crime author Vincent Bugliosi. Let me make two things clear about Negativland's appearance on the cultural landscape of Manson art right away: *Helter Stupid* is a major and thoughtful contribution to the evolution of this body of work *and* it is misleading to speak of *Helter Stupid* as a discrete piece of art—it was more like a gradually unfolding happening. *Helter Stupid* is, to be sure, the name of an LP released by Negativland in 1989 on SST records, a label founded by Greg Ginn of Black Flag. But "Helter Stupid" is also the name we must give to a chaotically deployed series of media events and articulations that took place over several years in the late 1980s, organized (but not completely controlled) by Negativland. As an interviewer for the magazine *Mondo 2000* put it in an introduction to an interview with members of the band, "'Helter Stupid' is not just the audio 'Helter Stupid.' It's also the chronology and it's the essay on the events."[20]

The chronology of *Helter Stupid* is a fascinating expression of what we have commonly come to call "culture jamming" (a phrase whose invention is often credited to Negativland band member Don Joyce). I cannot improve on this useful summary of *Helter Stupid* that came with the record:

10/20/87
Negativland releases their fourth album, *Escape from Noise*, and begin preparations for a national tour. The album includes the cut "Christianity Is Stupid," which features the "found" vocal of Reverend Estus Pirkle from a sermon recorded in 1968.

2/20/88
Story appears in the *New York Times*, national wire services, and radio and TV network news relating the arrest of sixteen-year-old David Brom in the ax murders of his father, mother, sister and brother two days earlier in Rochester, Minnesota. The *NY Times* article mentions that David and his father may have argued over a music tape David had listened to. The Broms are described as a devout Roman Catholic family.

3/10/88
Negativland cancels the tour when it becomes apparent that the tour will lose money. The group decides to send their American label, SST Records, a phony press release for distribution which attributes the cancellation of the tour to pressure from "Federal Official Dick Jordan" who has advised the band not to leave town pending an investigation into the Brom murders. The press release implies that David and his parents had been arguing about Negativland's song "Christianity Is Stupid" just prior to the murders. The *NY Times* article is distributed with the press release.

3/16/88
Negativland receives phone calls from *Rockpool*, *Pulse*, *BAM* magazine, and several other fanzines requesting more

information about the link between Negativland and the Brom murders. The group maintains that the federal interference is indeed real, but declines to elaborate.

3/30/88

In Minnesota, Judge Gerard Ring "gags" media coverage of the David Brom case, pending his decision as to whether David will be tried as a juvenile or an adult. After entering no plea in a pre-trial hearing David Brom undergoes a series of forensic psychiatric tests.

4/20/88

Citing federal restraints against participation in any live promotion dealing with the Brom case, Negativland consents to a telephone interview with *BAM* magazine. When pressed for information by interviewer Steve Stolder, a group member mentions a "bloody cassette tape" in passing.

4/22/88

Judge Ring rules that David Brom be tried as a juvenile. The prosecution appeals.

5/6/88

BAM prints a full-page article on Negativland and the Brom case, despite Stolder's inability to establish the existence of "Federal Authority Dick Jordan" and despite Stolder's phone conversation with James Walsh, the *Rochester Post Bulletin* reporter assigned to the Brom case. In several months of covering the story, Walsh has never heard of Negativland. The article simply restates the "facts" from the Negativland press release with no trace of skepticism.

5/9/88

James Walsh contacts SST Records, requesting more information on the Negativland–Brom connection. SST sends him a copy of the original press release and puts Walsh in telephone contact with the group. Negativland declines to do more than restate the "rumor" that "Christianity Is Stupid" may have caused the argument among the Broms that precipitated the murders. Negativland now begins to draw back from direct stimulation of the media by claiming that a phony lawyer, Hal Stakke, has advised them not to discuss the case with anyone.

?/?/88

Negativland hires a press clipping service to gather copies of all articles pertaining to the Brom case. Articles on Negativland mentioning the Brom link eventually appeared in *Rockpool, Boston Rock, Buttrag, Pulse, San Francisco Chronicle, Pollstar, Cut, Spy, Lyric,* Penthouse's *Hot Talk, Trouser Press Record Guide* and *The Village Voice*.

?/?/88

Tom Krotenmacher, who presents himself as a reporter covering the Brom story for *Rolling Stone*, sees the *Twin Cities Reader* article and calls Negativland seeking an interview. Negativland declines to comment.

5/11//88

After seeing the *BAM* article, a news producer for CBS Television's San Francisco affiliate, KPIX Channel 5, calls Negativland to request a televised interview. Negativland does not decline this opportunity to reach millions with this message. TV reporter Hal Eisner arrives in the KPIX mobile Electronic News Gathering unit. During the interview Negativland maintains the rumored link to the Brom case, but continue to state that they are unable to discuss details of the case. Much of the interview time is spent discussing the American news media, their appetite for the sensational, their tendency to create their own "news," and related topics. All of this discussion is cut from the aired tape. Like all the other reports to date, Channel 5 takes the purported connection for granted, but this time in a sensationalized feature piece emphasizing links between murder and music and including footage of the Brom family being carried from their home in body bags.

5/14/88

After seeing the Channel 5 News lead story, the *San Francisco Chronicle* religion writer calls Negativland requesting an interview. The group again claims they're unable to discuss the case, but do describe various real and imagined effects that the onslaught of publicity has had on the group. The *Chronicle* prints an article restating the proposed connection, but gets many of the "facts" wrong as a result of their dependence on other media stories as their only source material. It's now abundantly clear that the major source for news is other news.

6/3/88

David Brom is transferred to the Oakes Treatment Center for severely emotionally disturbed children and adolescents in Austin, Texas. *The Village Voice* publishes an article on the Negativland–Brom link. Music critic R. J. Smith recounts the original press release's version of the rumored connection with some skepticism. In researching this piece, Smith and *Voice* media critic Jeffrey I. Stokes go so far as to track down a Negativland member at his job for confirmation of the story. The group, by now apprehensive that their monstrous joke may have become completely uncontrollable, refuses to answer questions on the phone, citing previous reporters' editing and distortions of their comments. Negativland does, however, agree to send a prepared written statement. Smith also reports contacting San Francisco FBI spokesman Chuck Latting, who says of Negativland, "To the best of my knowledge, we've not had contact with them."

6/19/88
The *San Francisco Chronicle*'s pop music critic, Joel Selvin, devotes two-thirds of his weekly column to the Negativland–Brom story. The group also declines to be interviewed in this article, and Selvin was sent a copy of the same statement the *Voice* received, which he accurately reproduced: "As to our uncertain association with the Brom case, we think it's foolish and will comment on it no further. For a while, we made comments to the press and found that we were so misquoted and events so misstated to fit the writer's need to grab attention and the editor's need to abbreviate that we will now make no more statements whatsoever. Sensationalism reigns."

8/1/88
Negativland decides to make a somewhat musical depiction of this entire media odyssey. It is begun as a 12-inch single, but quickly expands to a full LP side.

12/9/88
Minnesota Supreme Court rules that Brom be tried as an adult. Arraignment is set for January, 1989. David Brom awaits trial.

Brom was convicted and sentenced to three consecutive life sentences in October of 1989. Negativland continued culture-jamming, perhaps most notoriously with its attack on U2, released in 1992, for which the band was quickly and decisively sued.

The "facts" of the Brom case are not of particular moment in considering the cultural meanings of *Helter Stupid*. There was much talk in the press about how David Brom may have argued with his father about the music he liked to listen to and/or about his own personal punk stylings. Blogger Cory Frye has explained that a fellow student had informed the local sheriff that David Brom had fought with his father about "a tape he had bought" that his father "didn't want him listening to." Furthermore, according to Frye,

"Newspaper accounts made note of the teenager's 'dyed punk hair-cut' as a means to explain the contrast between the pleasant, friendly boy described by peers and neighbors and the desperate fugitive he had become."[21] Negativland was not interested in launching an investigation into the generation gap or the biography of this one family. This is guerrilla cultural criticism aimed, above all, at exposing "the sheer eagerness of the media to believe what seemed like such an obvious falsehood." As Robert Barry has recently reported, one of the members of the band "even stared a TV news anchor in the face and told him it was a hoax" to no avail.[22]

The story concocted by Negativland as a way to draw attention away from the cancellation of the band's tour (due to typical indie band financial exigencies) proved remarkably strong. Band member Mark Hosler has properly noted that what "really made the story work . . . and what gave it legs was that it was tied into the fears about backmasking and hidden messages in rock music." The Bay Area affiliate of CBS news helped promote this angle with its early coverage, as Kembrew McLeod reports: "Topping Nightcast," the story began, "a possible link between murder and music . . . four members of a midwestern family were murdered. The sixteen-year-old son is the prime suspect. Members of the experimental rock group Negativland have been drawn into the case."[23]

Negativland did not explicitly draw on the magical power of Manson until the band released *Helter Stupid* in 1989, but then the occult power of the imprisoned Family leader was evoked with a vengeance. *Helter Stupid*: the title alone cleaves the history of Manson art in two. While after *Helter Stupid* there would continue to be all kinds of efforts to deploy Manson as a Magic Man in artistic form, it would never again be possible to do so without considering the possibility that perhaps too much was being made out of too little. *Helter Stupid* was wonderfully sophomoric in its response to Vincent Bugliosi's overblown claims of certainty about Manson's motive at the trial and in his true-crime book. Helter Skelter? More like Helter Stupid! Negativland could have used other formulations here—the Yinglish "Helter Shmelter" seems one obvious choice (film director Spike Lee made it "Helter

Swelter' in *Do the Right Thing*), or the fake-hard-of-hearing "Helter What?"—but "Helter Stupid" captures a critical position at once critical of Bugliosi's above-it-all certainty about Manson's motive and of the generational peers of Negativland who were having a little too much fun with superficial allusions to Manson and the Family. (Here we might think particularly of the Dickies' 1979 "I'm OK, You're OK" and its couplet that imagines the singer taking Manson's associate Squeaky Fromme on a special date—to the senior prom! Or the Jim Carroll Band's 1980 song "It's Too Late," which opens with a reminder—maybe unnecessary?—that falling in love with Sharon Tate is no longer a viable option. Think how easy it would be to write your own couplet about Family members or their victims.)

The Lemonheads' 1988 Manson cover may have been on the minds of Negativland's members; Sonic Youth's art project/song/video "Death Valley '69" (featuring Lydia Lunch and released on the band's 1985 album *Bad Moon Rising*) certainly would have been. Sonic Youth never said "Helter Skelter" in its song, but it did say Death Valley, it did quote Manson's use of the phrase "coming down" and the word "rise" and mentioned Sadie (the nickname of Susan Atkins). The video is full of monstrous violence and bloody writing on the wall (and the band did hire Raymond Pettibon to do the cover for its 1987 release *Sister*). Sonic Youth did not have much to *say* about Manson or the killings. The band's work in this project is simply to capture some of the sense of doom that so many have said permeated the air of Los Angeles's canyons, over Spahn Ranch, and out to Death Valley's Barker Ranch. Sonic Youth's Kim Gordon, who grew up in Southern California in the 1960s, has written of Los Angeles having "a desolation about it, a disquiet. . . . There was a sense of apocalyptic expanse, of sidewalks and houses centipeding over mountains and going on forever, combined with a shrugging kind of anchorlessness." "Death Valley '69" is not a pro-Manson song, Kim Gordon wants her readers (and Sonic Youth's fans) to know, but simply an effort to capture the ways that Manson's desert came to represent a certain cultural engagement with destruction in the late 1960s.[24]

Sonic Youth's performance of "Death Valley '69" in 1985, especially the elaborate vocal twining of Thurston Moore and Lydia Lunch (who uses her relative affectlessness to echo and then comment upon Moore's lead), is also clearly meant to summon the sound of Los Angeles's seminal punk group X.[25] Led by John Doe and Exene Cervenka, that band—whose dark vocal blend helped signify what critic Greil Marcus has called X's "readiness for violence"—hit the Los Angeles scene in the late 1970s prepared to evoke the apocalyptic vibe Kim Gordon would later describe in her book[26] The band's name, the simple X, may have been inspired, as John Doe says, by his reclamation of a large "X" from the signage at an Ex-Lax building in Brooklyn. That story, with its wicked suggestion of the band coming along to clear out all the clogged cultural shit of the 1970s, is wonderful. It seems just as likely, as Exene Cervenka claims, that the X was mean to cross out the "Christ" in her given first name Christene. But to use an "X" in this way in Los Angeles in the 1970s would have to invoke the Family's tattooing of their foreheads during the 1970 trial, as an announcement (per Manson) that doing so was a sign of having "X-ed" themselves out of the world. The Nation of Islam had, long before Manson made a public splash, innovated the use of the "X" as a sign of the stolen African name and a way to call attention to the renunciation of the slaveholder last names that African Americans had been force to accept.

Negativland's work on *Helter Stupid* serves, simultaneously, as an acknowledgment of the awesome cultural power Charles Manson had accrued in the twenty years since he first came to public awareness, and as an effort to take some of the wind out of the sails of the various efforts that had served to mystify Manson's presence on the American cultural landscape and had bestowed him with something like superpowers. Robert Barry has helpfully explained that the linchpin of Negativland's LP release is "a single 22-minute track mashing up all the various news reports about the incident with clips from one of Lenny Bruce's rants from Religions, Inc., suggestive B-movie dialogue, interviews in which Charles Manson name-checks The Beatles, as well as 'Helter Skelter' itself, along with an extended take from the Reverend Pirkle and perhaps most curiously of all, Bebu Silvetti's 1977 instrumental disco smash 'Lluvia de Primavera.' The result is a complex, multilayered narrative as well as a rich and compelling work of sound art."[27]

It is perhaps somewhat difficult from our contemporary vantage point to appreciate how remarkably challenging Negativland's multimedia project was in terms of its basic form. What Aram Sinnreich has taught us to understand as "configurable culture" was in an early stage of development in 1989—at least in terms of widely available audio art.[28] Robert Barry has correctly noted that while Negativland had few peers in its own heyday," in our time the band's "febrile blend of archive crunching and avant-trolling seems almost commonplace."[29] Negativland's own Mark Hosler has himself argued that in giving lectures to college audiences he used "to have to carefully walk through this argument as to why it was OK for us to quote-unquote 'steal' things and re-use them." Partly due to Negativland's own influence, Hosler was able, after a decade and a half or so, to omit this part of the presentation; modern college students "just know" that the type of cultural work done by Negativland is legitimate.[30]

Individual works of popular culture are unlikely, according to Negativland, to have the sort of direct, operational force that Vincent Bugliosi ascribed to the White Album, or that various media sources ascribed to Negativland's "Christianity Is Stupid," in the wake of the David Brom murders (or that so many projected onto Ozzy Osbourne's "Suicide Solution" and so on). With very careful language—and incendiary verb choice—Cory Frye has underscored how "Negativland strategically stabs the word 'stupid' throughout, to reject hoary theories regarding popular music's role in the instigation of violent crimes."[31] The mashup art of Negativland, on the face of things, rejects linearity, forswears simple answers to complex questions, and demotes logical reasoning in favor of allusion, juxtaposition, and repetition. In *Helter Stupid*, all of the most significant claims are contingent and subject to powerful counterargument. One example: *Helter Stupid* organizes alternating samples of the phrases "too much data" and "we don't have enough data" and the seeming paradox itself has a tale to tell. With this seeming contradiction Negativland invites listeners to think about how abundant media does not equate simply to great wisdom. One conclusion the band reached, as a result of its own manipulation of the media, is that much of what is circulated as news in contemporary culture is neither new, nor verifiably true. Robert Barry has written that Negativland helped stir up a "kind of whirlpool of self-reference where the only sources of information were other news outlets and gaps in logic were glossed over in a haze of fuzzy language."[32]

The band was clear about its intent with the hoax: "Our lie was intended for and directed to the media, and it proved very effective in exposing the unreliable process of cannibalization that passes for 'news.' Negativland chose to exploit the media's appetite for particularly sensational stories by becoming a subject they couldn't resist—the latest version of a ridiculous media cliché that proposes that rock song lyrics instigate murder. Common sense suggests that murderers purchase records that appeal to them, just as they purchase the weapons they use."[33] Stitching together twenty years of cultural investment in the idea that popular music lyrics have direct influence on individual and group behaviors, Negativland created a "monstrous joke" to call attention to the faulty reasoning and unstable projection at the heart of an "idea" whose history might be said to stretch from Charles Manson's alleged misreading of the Beatles to the blaming of Marilyn Manson's music for the Columbine massacre of 1999. The 1980s, as Negativland was well aware, was characterized by its own "Satanic panic" with numerous claims made—in the media, but also in American courtrooms—that secret messages were being encoded, usually through backwards masking, in heavy-metal music. The 1980s claim—essentially a charge lodged that popular musicians were purposely directing vulnerable young people to do harm to themselves or others—flipped Vincent Bugliosi's lesson upside down; Bugliosi's claim, of course, is that the Beatles were innocent, but that Manson's delusional misreading of that band's music led him to direct his followers to kill. But the interviewer for *Mondo 2000* rightly noted that *Helter Stupid*, with its broad sweep, its inclusion of snippets of the song "Helter Skelter," along with snatches of a speech by Manson, up against the Brom-related materials, was a way to "draw everything back to Helter Skelter, and the linking of the Beatles songs to those . . . murders, right up to the current Tipper Gore Mothers-Against-Dirty-Satanic-Rock-Songs situation."[34]

Helter Stupid was an important avant-garde art project that had enormous influence on other artists. Brian Eno (might have) famously claimed that while only thirty thousand people bought the Velvet Underground's first album, each one of them formed a band; something similar might be said about the work done by Negativland on *Helter Stupid*.[35] With *Helter Stupid* Negativland was able to puncture one dominant mythology surrounding Charles Manson—the notion that he exerted a kind of magical power. When Negativland samples Manson himself in *Helter Stupid*, when we finally get to hear Manson bragging about how much worse things would have been at Cielo Drive if he *had* been there, mostly he just seems pitiable: he is bragging about something he *could have* done a long time ago, but that we are pretty sure he did not do. The power in *Helter Stupid* does not belong to Charles Manson or David Brom—it belongs to those who control the means of production. Negativland may have interrupted (or at least called attention) to this reality for the twenty-two minutes of *Helter Stupid*, but as the band knew well, its very well-played hoax could not ultimately compete with the power of the dominant culture's media narratives about Manson, about families, and about the power of popular music. In fact, as the band came to realize, it would not take much time or effort for the mainstream media to stitch Negativland into the Helter Skelter story it had been promoting since 1969.

Other artists have attempted to disrupt the Helter Skelter narrative so powerfully prosecuted by Vincent Bugliosi in court and on the page. Perhaps most notable in the world of "high" art is the untitled word painting created by Christopher Wool in 1988 and most recently sold (in 2006) for well over a million dollars. Wool has been called the "most important painter of his generation" (he was born in 1955) but this painting is deceptively simple on its face. He takes the by-now familiar phrase Helter Skelter and chops it into stenciled pieces. In Wool's hands Helter Skelter becomes the stuttering four-part phrase "Helter Helter":

HEL
TER
HEL
TER

With Wool's work comes the reminder that Bugliosi's Helter Skelter is made up of blocks—almost like children's toys—that can be manipulated by other people who do not share the prosecutor's faith in simple explanatory solutions. Wool's reformulation of the phrase and its "percussive typography" breaks down what Bugliosi has always tried to present as clarity about Manson's inspiration to kill. The court proceedings cannot inoculate observers from the "political anxiety" and "simmering violence" that keep erupting in and around the Manson case.[36]

The avant-garde artistic responses of Wool and Negativland stand as important commentary on, and symptoms of, the Family's ongoing creepy crawl of American culture, but they have not generated anything like the multitudinous responses energized by more lowbrow forms of popular culture. With respect to Charles Manson, the popular music world has been environmentally responsible: songwriters, singers, and performers consistently reduce, reuse, and recycle imagery evoking the Family and its crimes. Much of the activity I have been describing so far has been located in the sphere of punk rock and indie culture, and much of it never moves beyond the "magic" power invoked with shout-outs to the Manson Family and covers of Charles Manson's songs. I do not pretend to have done much more than hint at how fully Manson has saturated youth-oriented popular music. Did I mention the English rock band Kasabian? Or Frank Kozik's use of Manson's eyes for the logo he created for Rise Records?

While the Manson Family has been especially important for (white) indie rockers and avant-garde artists, its presence has been fairly strong in hip-hop culture as well. In addition to the rap duo known as Heltah Skeltah, the underground rapper Chunk Manson, a short-lived rock-rap group known as Spahn Ranch Family, and the Southern rap collective who refer to themselves as the Manson Family, there are countless lyrical references to, and samples of, Charles Manson, at least since 1989 when Ice Cube name-checked Manson in his verse of N.W.A.'s "Straight Outta Compton" in which he establishes his street credibility with a drive-by reference to the cult leader. These citations are mostly in keeping with rap's normative use of hyperbole. Accessing some of Manson's power, rappers from the most mainstream (Eminem, twice), to the more experimental and marginal (Death Grips, whose song "Beware" opens with a long sample of Manson speaking), have found Manson appealing, to say the least. (There was a decent amount of chatter after N.W.A. broke up suggesting that key members Ice Cube and Dr. Dre were working together on a project provisionally titled *Heltah Skeltah*. That record never came to light but former Dr. Dre associate The D.O.C. did release his own *Helter Skelter* in 1996.)

There is also a tiny subgenre of rap music—it really just consists of two brothers, one of whom raps as "Necro" and one as "Ill Bill" (their mother knows them as Ron and Bill Braunstein)—that we have to call Snuff Rap. Necro, in particular, is obsessed with the details of the Tate killings. In his song "Do the Creepy Crawl," Necro creates a montage of actual Manson quotations ("Do something witchy") and hip-hop slang ("Juxed 51 times") along with some truly surprising word-choice (the phrase "fetal sac" does appear). The chorus of "Do the Creepy Crawl" is fairly straightforward: "Stabbing and stabbing and stabbing and . . . Stabbing and stabbing and stabbing and stabbing . . . Stab you to death!" The quasi-pornographic video for "Do the Creepy Crawl" borrows from Jim Van Bebber's *Manson Family Movies* as it provides a visual landscape to match the sex and violence gore of the song. Ill Bill, with his act La Coka Nostra, is interested less in blood and guts and more in revealing the depth of his familiarity with relatively obscure facts of the case. In "Letter to Ouisch," the rapper narrates from the point of view of the cult leader, complimenting his young follower (Ouisch, of course, was the Family name for Ruth Ann Moorehouse) for stopping Barbara Hoyt from testifying at the trial by giving her a massive dose of LSD. These usages of Manson as scare tactic represent the *reductio ad absurdum* of the Magic Man formulation: shouting "Manson" in a crowded cultural marketplace, they hope somebody will run screaming. There is no evidence anyone has paid much attention.

Desperados under the Eaves

For almost fifty years now, Manson has been used as a sign of social refusal, of an unwillingness to conform to cultural norms surrounding appearance, sexuality, work, consumerism, romantic arrangements, and so on. The landscapes inhabited by the Manson Family—the actual geographic landscapes of Los Angeles, Chatsworth, and Death Valley and the cultural geography of *how* they lived—have become templates for a range of artists working in film, sculpture, fiction, photography, and music. But if we are to understand the breadth and depth of Manson's influence on the arts, we must acknowledge that his presence does not always announce itself directly. Indeed, some of the most significant Manson art features what we might, following the lead of cultural studies scholar Michael Denning, refer to as Manson accents rather than Manson Family plots. Our work is to explore how the story of Manson and the Family has inflected all manner of cultural productions even when those works do not announce themselves as Manson-related.[1]

It is interesting in this light to think about *Then It All Came Down*, a musical project launched by JR Robinson with his collective Wrekmeister Harmonies in 2014 in a Chicago cemetery. Robinson's composition borrows its title from an interview Truman Capote did with Bobby Beausoleil in 1973 and ultimately published in his collection *Music for Chameleons* (1980). While

Beausoleil has, on more than one occasion, renounced the accuracy of Capote's work and grieved over what he sees as its negative effect on his life in prison, Robinson finds in it an apt summary of the forces of anarchy and destruction swirling around the Manson Family. Robinson's music (and the accompanying liner notes he wrote) make it clear that he is particularly interested in how English occultist Aleister Crowley's dark magick seeped into the American counterculture of the 1960s.

Robinson works deftly in *Then It All Came Down* to evoke Beausoleil and his historical moment without ever resorting to cheap sound effects or literal textual reference. The musical building blocks in *Then It All Came Down* include black-metal vocals, guitar drones, and beautiful female vocals. Robinson is composing from within a tradition that includes the doomy meditations of Ed Sanders, Truman Capote, and Zachary Lazar, for instance, but not the rational chronicling of Vincent Bugliosi or Jeff Guinn; the music of Wrekmeister Harmonies (whose own name is something of a joke on a Béla Tarr film of almost the same name) is dense, allusive, and full of chaos. Robinson has explained that in his composition he was "trying to communicate the whole story of Beausoleil's involvement in the murders":

> His chugging down the PCH on a bike represented by the hypnotic acoustic guitar, the melodious singing of "the girls" repeating the phrase "beautiful sun" which devolves into the Leviathan growling vocal section introducing the idea of Bobby's murder of the drug dealer, which in turn leads into the "metal section" representing the violence of the Manson situation and the cultural fallout that it incurred. All of this might appear chaotic to a listener. . . . But from my point of view, there was a very direct compositional narrative that sustains itself through the use of a range of (mainly negative) emotions and in the end does resolve that tension in an almost post-apocalyptic way, with the string section again emerging, sounding almost wounded from the entire

experience, as I believe most of America felt at that time, and most definitely Los Angeles.[2]

Then It All Came Down is impressive as composition and as performance, but also, in a more general sense, as rhetorical gesture. Robinson, with his musical collective, enters the arena of Manson art with a score to play but none to settle. Above all, Robinson seems interested in tracing the influence of Aleister Crowley on the American counterculture. As he puts it in the liner notes to *Then It All Came Down*, "there is a direct line" from Crowley's motto "Do What Thou Wilt Shall Be the Whole of the Law" to the hippie credo "do your own thing."[3] In its way Robinson's composition serves a revisionist purpose; its burden is to retell Bobby Beausoleil's dark tale as a central theme in countercultural history, rather than as some perverse deviation from it.

Robinson is not the first to try to revisit the Family's story as a major narrative of countercultural confusion. One of the first major attempts to "communicate the whole story" of the Manson phenomenon came, rather aptly, from Terry Melcher. Terry Melcher released two solo albums in the 1970s and they represent a fascinating attempt to exorcise the demons of the Manson moment. They exist first as novelties—a dare accepted, a borderline freak show, the elephant dancing. He joins such similarly marginal figures as Jack Nitzsche, John Simon, and Kim Fowley, who worked mostly as producers, but ultimately could not resist putting their names on the front of the record as well.

That said, *Terry Melcher*, the record, is rich enough to deserve a close listen. It represents an important crossroads for Los Angeles (and Manson) art. At just the moment that rock critics such as Robert Christgau were beginning to use the phrase "El Lay" to caricature the place as if it were a David Hockney painting come to life, Melcher's solo debut reminds us to resist this flattening of Los Angeles's musical art of the 1970s. The record is a damning and complex memoir—a dark valedictory about the damages wrought by personal privilege and unstable social hierarchies. *Terry Melcher* is, at its heart, a compelling and mournful evocation of the class confusion that ensued in the wake of the Tate-LaBianca murders.

Terry Melcher is at once an expression of Los Angeles mainstream celebrity culture and a withering indictment of it. The music is played by the cream of two overlapping groups of Los Angeles musicians: the studio royalty known as the Wrecking Crew (including Mike Deasy, who, we recall, had plenty of contact via Melcher with the Manson Family) and figures from an insurgent community of country-rock players, including members of the Byrds.

While *Terry Melcher* offers few surprises in terms of its musical palette, it is startling for how much misery Melcher conveys vocally and thematically. According to *Rolling Stone*'s reviewer, Melcher sounds like "he's given up not just on optimism but even on despair."[4] The critic is not exaggerating. This is a serious, self-lacerating piece of popular art that attempts to evaluate the social changes in Los Angeles represented by the Manson Family. These changes seem to have mostly reached this famous son as personal crisis.

The record opens and closes with "sort of" cover songs. It begins with an anguished take on the (usually) uptempo bluegrass song "Roll in My Sweet Baby's Arms," associated most with Flatt and Scruggs. The key lyric in the refrain of this song, usually played at breakneck speed, is "Lay around the shack / till the mail train comes back / And I'll roll in my sweet baby's arms." Melcher's arranges "Roll in My Sweet Baby's Arms" as a midtempo soul number with bloody Memphis-style horns. His version emphasizes alienation—Melcher begins the song with a dark verse ("Where were you last Friday night / While I was lying in jail") that usually does not appear till the back end of the song; at the song's beginning, Melcher's narrator is already suffering for his engagement with the legal system. Where bluegrass versions of "Roll in My Sweet Baby's Arms" usually communicate a devil-may-care refusal to work and celebration of off-the-clock leisure, Melcher's anguished vocal instead delivers an argument *against* the central proposition of the song—that pleasure and relief will always be found in the beloved's embrace.

Terry Melcher ends with a dark rewrite of "Willie and the Hand Jive"—originally done by Los Angeles's own Johnny Otis and released in 1958—that can't help but suggest that the narrator is so broken down that he cannot even figure out how to masturbate on his own. The song is no longer about Way Out Willie and Rockin Millie. It's now about "Way Out Willie and his Mama too" who are on TV (Melcher focused his career after the Manson murders on producing his mother Doris Day's television career). The first thing to notice about "The Old Hand Jive" is that it erases the rhythm at the heart of Otis's original. The Bo Diddley beat Otis worked with—which also, as George Lipsitz has noted, evokes "children's clapping games and rope-jumping rhymes"[5]—is nowhere to be found in the Melcher song. Johnny Otis may not have *meant* for his "hand jive" to be widely understood to be code for "hand job"; then again, maybe he did. But there is no sex, autoerotic or otherwise, in Melcher's version. Whatever sexual energy the singer managed to stitch into his version of "Rolling" has disappeared over the course of the album.

Melcher's next record would be called *Royal Flush.* Its title—with its secondary and tertiary suggestions of being a washout and being embarrassed—featured the song "High Rollers." But *Terry Melcher* is also shot through with gambling men. Among the cover versions Melcher presents here is a truly distraught version of "Just a Season," a song he produced for the Byrds just a few years earlier. Nicking the structuring riff of Joni Mitchell's "Both Sides Now," with hints of the Byrd's "Ballad of Easy Rider" in the lead acoustic guitar, Melcher's arrangement hints at nostalgic regret before we hear even a note of the vocal. The song also borrows Mitchell's catalog-style of lyric writing. In his delivery of the song, Melcher bears down especially hard on a line about fooling gambling men with his face.

When Roger McGuinn sang it with the Byrds, "Just a Season" was just gorgeous—and I mean "just" in two ways. McGuinn delivers the song with his usual unflappable one-two punch: a beautiful reedy voice echoed by his ringing twelve-string guitar line. But Melcher's "Just a Season" trades the twelve-string for the mournful acoustic and McGuinn's boyish tenor for his own very adult and anguished vocal. As with virtually every song on the record Melcher is reminding listeners that he is not all right, that (since his encounter with the Family) he has not been able to get back on his feet again. On this song (as with most of *Terry Melcher*) it is not hard for listeners to tell when it is time to pay attention for real. Melcher lets us know by going up as far in his vocal register as he comfortably can and then jumps off the edge of his normal range into falsetto when he can go no further. He uses this move, for instance, when bragging about fighting bulls without ever getting hurt, and the effect is to throw the boast immediately into doubt.

The song selection itself is interesting. Here "season" summons not the ennobling Ecclesiastical inevitability of "Turn! Turn! Turn!" but rather the humbling existential pointlessness of the rock-and-roll tour. After acknowledging that he had his fun with young female fans, the singer admits that being a star was pretty simple. Melcher makes one significant lyrical change in this song as well. The Byrds sang "mummers shrouds," underscoring that "Just a Season" is, ultimately, a song about being on the road (the mummers are, I suppose, the band). But Melcher, strikingly, changes "mummers" to "murmuring," and in doing so has transformed this song into the soundtrack of his haunting. The dead of his old home at Cielo Drive continue to speak to him and they are not alone.

The gambling the narrator does in "Just a Season" appears too in "These Days," performed on this record as a duet with Melcher's mother, Doris Day. When the singer describes finally giving up gambling, it sounds not so much like the result of a positive resolution but as a diagnosis of the moment when he lost his will to live. Nothing you might know about Day's usual attack will prepare you for the anomie that characterizes her harmony vocal here. Sounding like some arty forgotten godmother of Lana Del Rey, Day joins her son in offering a version of this Jackson Browne song that—amazingly—sounds far more alienated than Nico's original. A few years earlier there was a *very* popular rumor circulating in Los Angeles that proposed that Day was preparing a duet with Sly Stone on her own "Que Sera, Sera." This rumor seems to have been a corollary of an even more pointed rumor that held that Day and Stone were sexually involved (which likely built on another rumor that held that Doris Day and African American baseball player Maury Wills were in a relationship). Terry Melcher had helped install Sly Stone and *his* Family in Papa John Phillips's Bel Air mansion in the early 1970s during the time they were working on *There's a Riot Goin' On*, as I have discussed. At least one observer suggests that Day and Stone did perform an impromptu duet of sorts on "Que Sera, Sera" at her house during this period.[6] But the rumor of the romantic meeting between the older mainstream white woman ("Doris Day" had come, by this point, to be a synonym for "white bread"—her singing of "Hooray for Hollywood" is a pretty funny punchline in Paul Mazursky's 1970 film *Alex in Wonderland*) and the younger countercultural African American man outlines the sort of LA mixing that *Terry Melcher* pulls dramatically back from. Singing in his chains, the famous son invites his mother into the studio to help sing about his social isolation.[7]

The record reaches its strange peak with the "Medley" that brings Melcher's "Halls of Justice," together, oddly, with two Bob Dylan songs. In "Halls of Justice," Melcher finally gives his version of meeting Manson. What the singer believes is going to be a standard audition turns into something much more complex. The shift to "Positively 4th Street" and "Like a Rolling Stone" captures in a very efficient way the dramatic imprint the Manson family made as they creepy crawled not only through the homes of Laurel and other Canyons, but also through the minds of major players in the cultural scene in Los Angeles.

For its part of the medley, "Halls of Justice" has two clear targets. First, Melcher wants to make clear that he got fooled—as anybody would have—by the images of peace and love promoted by the Family. Melcher rewrites the story of his meeting with the Manson Family to stake a claim that the desperately poor commune-dwellers were actually holding the leverage in the encounter—because only they knew they planned to take advantage of the music producer. Melcher takes care of the Manson part of the song fairly efficiently; it takes him about a minute and a half. The singer then turns to Dylan to help him throw stones, first at all of the friends who abandoned him in his time of need in the Hall of Justice, and then at himself for lacking good sense. The Dylan part of the medley kicks off with "Positively 4th Street," and the artist sings only a tiny portion of the original lyric. Melcher uses Dylan's abrasive original text to sing of his disappointment with his absent friends and then introduces what may be a broken quotation of Stephen Stills's "For What It's Worth" to express his displeasure at the zero-sum reality of contemporary social life.

Then Melcher turns to "Like a Rolling Stone." The opening musical and lyrical salvo of "Like a Rolling Stone" is among the most recognizable in rock-and-roll. First comes the shattering drum beat, immediately joined by bass, electric guitar, organ, piano, and tambourine. And then the indelible opening accusation. But Melcher is audacious (or desperate) enough to turn the song inside out. For him the object of disappointment seems to have shifted and the "you" of the first lines is Terry Melcher himself. Melcher cannot even bring himself to sing the phrase about tossing money to poor people on the street—perhaps because it reminded him too much of what he did at Spahn Ranch when he handed Manson fifty dollars. Melcher turns Dylan's "bums" into "bumps and grinds," thus turning the lyric into a more general meditation on his acknowledged inability to read the encounter with Manson correctly. He thought that he was still at the Whisky dancing with the freaks and they thought he was going to give them the keys to the kingdom. This is a stunning moment as *Terry Melcher* comes near to its close.

In this era, in the white folk and rock music of Southern California, only Joni Mitchell matched the effect. I am thinking particularly of her *Court and Spark* LP, released also in 1974, and the devastating scene of the Los Angeles gathering in "People's Parties." The title alone, with its sad echo of Berkeley's People's Park (which is also directly mentioned in the title song) signals that this will be a narrative of countercultural decline. At this party Mitchell's narrator sees Jack the joker, nobody Eddie, and stone-cold Grace, all as miserable as the model who has convinced herself that laughing and crying provide the same catharsis. The narrator frantically tries to lighten up, and the listener can see her lip quiver as her voice shakes on the *u* of "humor." The song ends with the singer bravely wishing she could laugh at all the absurdity on display at the party. Lead voice Joni Mitchell sings this line alone, but only up through "all"; then countless other, multitracked Joni Mitchells come in to sing the same line *with*, *to*, and *at* the narrator. The multiple voices seem sympathetic initially, but very quickly turn doubtful, worried, critical. The lonely chorus ends with Mitchell at the deep end of her range—it is the obverse of Melcher's falsetto usage and it makes clear that there will be no easy resolution to the clueless fumbling the narrator has bemoaned. (In his book on *Court and Spark*, Sean Nelson also makes the intriguing case that the title track is more than a little bit "sinister": it is, after all "a song about a raving hippie with a madman's soul showing up at your door in LA." This, as Nelson puts it, "wasn't exactly a lullaby in the post–Helter Skelter early '70s.")[8]

The popular art of Los Angeles was full of such darkly reflexive work as that offered by Melcher and Mitchell in the mid-1970s, but rarely was it so self-blaming. Randy Newman's "Guilty," also from 1974, comes close to the level of self-loathing and self-recrimination that saturates *Terry Melcher*; War's "Why Can't We Be Friends" (1975) and Warren Zevon's self-titled album (1976) captured some of the mood of disenchantment in putative allies that made Melcher's debut feel so hopeless. But most of the relevant Los Angeles art of the 1970s was more interested in actual or cultural apocalypse as opposed to self-immolation. Steely Dan's *Katy Lied* (1975) opens, as Greil Marcus has noted, with "a (the?) stock market crash" and gets more depressing from there; the 1975 film version of Nathanael West's *Day of the Locust* is organized, of course, around a painting called *The Burning of Los Angeles*.[9] (The Miracles' "City of Angels," from 1975, and Warren Zevon's

"Desperados Under the Eaves," from 1976, worry, respectively, about Los Angeles and California falling or sliding into the sea; Neil Young's simply titled "L.A." (1973) has apocalyptic scenes of erupting volcanoes and earthquakes.) Similarly oriented is "Hotel California" by the Eagles, also from 1975. With a bizarrely faked "Mexican" accent, atmospheric wind effects, and a quick reference to 1969, the Eagles tell of a doomed California landscape haunted by some rough beast, slouching toward Bethlehem. It is a fairly incoherent song, but it too has inspired its own set of Manson-connected rumors.

Zeroville

If "Hotel California" does not mean to access the events of August 1969 directly, it certainly does not mind if listeners descry a bit of Manson in the pseudomystical tale of a place from which you can "check out" but not "leave." While "Hotel California" has rarely been validated as an example of Manson art, Neil Young's "Revolution Blues" (1974) is widely accepted to be "about" the cult leader. Young's biographer claims that in the song the singer adopts a "demented Manson persona," but that is true only in an approximate and fictionalized sense.[1] The generalized anger the narrator expresses, particularly in the song's most infamous couplet (which Neil Young's publishing company has refused to let me quote here), makes a mishmash of the facts of the Manson case. In "Revolution Blues" the killer imagines killing celebrities in a car—and now in Laurel instead of Benedict Canyon—instead of teenager Steven Parent. The song *does* make some literal reference to Family life—the mode of transportation coming into sight is the kind of recreational vehicle with oversized wheels made for use on the beach or in the desert, which seems like like a clear reference to Manson's favorite mode of desert transport. But the point of the song is hardly documentary. It was meant to evoke a mood (Young's own keyword is "spooky") of a Southern California undergoing a siege of creepy crawl. The apocalypse is at hand, and its four horsemen, Young is clear, will be driving what the British call "beach buggies," not horses. Young himself claims the lyrical content of the song so upset David Crosby (who plays rhythm guitar on it) that the latter begged Young not to go forward with it: "That's not funny," Crosby said to Young.[2] As with so many retrospective accounts of Manson and the Family, Neil Young wants to communicate that the cult leader's presence spelled the end of the surf and sun dreams that the Beach Boys had communicated to so many young Americans.

According to Young biographer Jimmy McDonough, the recording of "Revolution Blues" was the "most deranged moment of the *On the Beach* sessions." This is Neil Young in the mid-1970s, so the phrase "most deranged" must be understood also to imply "in heavy traffic." As the band began to play the song, slide guitarist Rusty Kershaw apparently became convinced that the players were not achieving the correct pitch of intensity: "'Look, man, you don't sound like you're tryin' to start a fuckin' revolution. Here's how you start that.'" And then, as Kershaw explains, he began "breakin' a bunch of shit." "That," he concludes, is "a revolution, *muth'* fucker." From there (according to the liner notes that Kershaw himself wrote for *On the Beach*) the sideman "turned into a python" and then into an alligator. Then he ate up the carpet. Then he started to "crawl up towards Neil, which is pretty spooky." Much of this is potentially explained by Kershaw's self-proclaimed use of "honey slides," a combination of fried marijuana and honey.[3]

"Revolution Blues" occupies an interesting place in Neil Young's canon. Young's willingness (unlike just about every other Los Angeles musician of his time) to admit at least a tempered appreciation for Charles Manson's music seems to have supported the strong claims "Revolution Blues" already has to a place in discussions of popular songs connected to the case. The song is certainly beloved of Young devotees. Likewise, the critical response to "Revolution Blues" was strongly and immediately positive; Stephen Holden, writing in *Rolling Stone*, called it, along with "Ambulance Blues" (which could, in a related way, be called the "Patty Hearst song"), one of the album's two masterpieces.[4] But it has not had a particularly dynamic life since 1974. Young has been relatively stingy with respect to live performance of "Revolution Blues." According to one fan site, the singer has only played it thirty-eight times (compared to, just for example, the 750 performances of the equally terrifying "Powderfinger").[5] According to countless Internet commenters, Young dedicated the song to Manson at a 1983 concert in San Francisco.[6] The song has also proven relatively immune to cover versions.

On the Beach was, by design, *about* alienation and meant to be alienating. It is part of what fans and critics have come to refer to as Young's "Ditch Trilogy," along with *Time Fades Away* (1973) and *Tonight's the Night* (1975). The name comes from Young's liner notes to his 1977 collection *Decade.* Here Young wrote of his dismay at the popular acclaim he reaped when "Heart of Gold" hit number one in 1972: "This song put me in the middle of the road. Traveling there soon became a bore so I headed for the ditch. A rougher ride but I met more interesting people there." Taken together, *Time Fades Away, On the Beach*, and *Tonight's the Night* form a remarkable "aftermath" trilogy. The key to them comes on the most upbeat *sounding* song of the three, *On the Beach*'s "Walk On," which promises (or warns?) that the usual escapist vehicles—drugs, personal eccentricity—will not inoculate the population of Los Angeles against the infringement of the real world.

While I am devoting most of my attention here to *On the Beach*, and "Revolution Blues" in particular, it would be a mistake to take that record out of its "Ditch Trilogy" context when thinking about Neil Young's place in the history of Manson art. The three are drenched in dread and paranoia. Perhaps most terrifying is the sense given by the Ditch Trilogy that all previously trustworthy systems of knowledge and belief have broken down. Emblematic here is the stunning self-referential admission in "Ambulance Blues" that even the most familiar reference point for the artist—rock and roll itself—has lost its explanatory power. *Tonight's the Night* has a clearer story to tell than the other two albums in the Ditch Trilogy. Most tragically it tells the story of Bruce Berry, a member of Young's road crew, and Danny Whitten, a member of his band, both of whom died from drug overdoses. *Time Fades Away* and *On the Beach* capture Young's desire to have his music represent the hazy, confusing atmosphere of post-Manson Los

Angeles by operating in a dense and allusive mode. While working with a fairly broad palette, Young and his supporting players purposefully avoid the comparatively simple folk-rock of *Harvest*, the predecessor to the Ditch Trilogy.

Some things do emerge clearly over the course of the records, most notably that the Ditch Trilogy is meant to act as Young's great refusal, his own "No! in thunder." The LA of the Ditch Trilogy is a poisoned landscape; moments of tenderness, of authentic human connection, or sincere generosity are most noticeable for their absence on these three records. *Time Fades Away* ends with a song called "Last Dance," the final two minutes of which basically feature Young wailing the word "no" over and over again. I should mention that *Time Fades Away* is a live record (and the record that Young has, at least once, referred to as his worst).

On the Beach is what comes *after* the Last Dance. The record cover shows Young staring out at the ocean, having just walked away from the scene of a terrible accident: a car has crashed into the beach (having fallen from the sky, apparently) and is three-quarters submerged. James Reich has written brilliantly of the cover art, a work created by Gary Burden and lettered by the poster artist Rick Griffin, who had earlier done the classic image for the 1967 Be-In held in San Francisco and the Grateful Dead's *Aoxomoxoa* (1969). Reich reminds us that the title and cover imagery cannot help but evoke Nevil Shute's 1957 atomic apocalypse novel (and ensuing 1959 film) of the same name. Shute's title came in turn from T. S. Eliot's "Hollow Men," which Shute used to provide an epigraph— including "This is how the world ends / Not with a bang but a whimper"—for his book. The surrealism of Young's cover art has roots, as Reich argues, in Dali's *The Persistence of Memory* (1931), but also enjoyed an amazing synergy with two works of the same moment, David Pelham's cover art for a paperback reissue of J. G. Ballard's *The Drought* (April 1974; originally 1964), which also features a submerged Cadillac, and the beginnings of the Ant Farm collective Cadillac Ranch in May of 1974, "a series of ten Cadillacs part submerged in the dirt of the Texas Panhandle."[7] *On the Beach* was released on July 16 that same year.

The importance of the automobile tailfin as cultural marker should not be overlooked. In his reading of the cover, Reich helps us begin to understand the presence of the car in the sand. Referring to the "latent tailfin" of the Cadillac, Reich calls the car an "icon of obsolescence" and argues that its presence indicates a radical break with the past. The tailfin, as Phil Patton and Karal Ann Marling explain, spoke brashly of American triumphalism— of living under a regime of such stunning abundance that cars could function not only as a practical mode of transportation but also as an object of overblown style.[8]

Marling writes that by the mid-1950s "nobody really knew what a car looked like anymore." Cars, she writes, could take virtually "any form that signified speed, modernity, and a ponderous luxury."[9] This added up, as Patton summarizes, to a "comic-book vision of travel."[10] These earthbound vehicles were meant, of course to evoke flight, and space flight more particularly. "Rocket" was a key word in car design by the late 1950s. The back end of the car was what communicated most loudly. Part of the implication built into this design choice was that the "fantastic and insolent chariot" (in the words of critic Lewis Mumford) was always going to be out front of whatever *you* were driving.[11] Here it is important to note that the production of these cars was also complexly tied up, as Bernard Gendron and others have shown, with the production of rock-and-roll music. "Cadillac" and "El Dorado" were names not only of a car brand and model but of doo-wop groups as well.[12] While Jackie Brenston's 1951 rhythm and blues song "Rocket 88" is often cited as a key text in this respect, the real anthem of this cultural investment was Chuck Berry's 1956 song "You Can't Catch Me." In this song, Berry—the poet laureate of the fast car—introduces a narrator who tells of a species of car he calls a "Flight Deville" (genus "air-mobile"), which manages to go airborne when the police appear on his tail. The United States may, as Reyner Banham put it, have been "debauching itself with tailfins" while the Soviet Union was busy building Sputnik, but the car/rocket nexus contributed to an American mythology of power and speed that few challenged.[13]

The meaning of the buried Cadillac on the cover of *On the Beach* is overdetermined to be sure. It is impossible to offer even a thumbnail sketch of the centrality of the Cadillac to American popular music; the subject, like the car, is huge. But I want to make sure to emphasize how cagey Young and his design team were in making the rocket tailfins a central element in the cover art for the record that includes his definitive work of Manson art. If the original tailfin acted, as Phil Patton argues, as a sort of punctuation on a number of political, social, and cultural trajectories of the 1950s, then Young's apocalyptic joke on the cover of *On the Beach* certainly repurposes the fins to serve a similar role for the 1960s.[14] Right after recording *On the Beach*, but before it was released, Young debuted a song at the Bottom Line, in New York's Greenwich Village, called "Long May You Run." The audience howled with laughter as Young sang this gorgeous folk song, a valentine to a lost love—his first car (which was actually a 1948 Buick Roadmaster hearse he called "Mort"). In this song Young wonders whether the car has ended up in the Beach Boys' possession. On the cover of *On the Beach* the cranky singer just buries the damn thing in the sand.[15] After Manson, there is no more "Fun, Fun, Fun."

On the cover, Young is staring at an ocean with no waves; the last one has broken and will soon reach the beach. The Beach Boys' two major signs of mobility, the car and the surfboard, have been rendered obsolete. The stagy surrealism of the cover invites speculation about the action directly preceding this scene. *On the Beach* was made during the time Young was living with Carrie Snodgrass, best known for her starring role in *Diary of a Mad Housewife* (1970), and includes a song called "Motion Pictures": there is plenty of reason to read the cover as if it were a still from a film. Young, for instance, seems to be dressed in character. That lemon-colored blazer is located fairly far outside of Young's usual sartorial repertoire, which could be described as "feral forest dweller." The "story" told by the cover, as I have been suggesting, is a post-crisis story. Something terrible has happened in Los Angeles and Young has walked away, seemingly unharmed. In this scenario,

Young plays—and seems to be dressed as a weird updated version of—*The Great Gatsby's* narrator, Nick Carraway. Young stares at the ocean, perhaps meditating on how "careless" the powerful people he knew in Hollywood and in the Los Angeles music scene were. As F. Scott Fitzgerald explained, "[T]hey smashed up things and creatures and then retreated back to their money or their vast carelessness . . . and let other people clean up the mess they had made." With "Revolution Blues" as a key track on *On the Beach*, it is clear that for Young the murders of August 1969 are the root of this Southern California apocalypse.

There is no cleaning up the mess that Los Angeles has become in Young's world, or in Roman Polanski's *Chinatown* (1974). *Chinatown* was Polanski's first Hollywood film after the murders, and led to much chatter about its connection to the events at Cielo Drive. A few years earlier Polanski's version of *Macbeth* (1971) had many critics searching for possible Manson resonances as well. As Charles Derry has put it, "the obvious relationship between *Macbeth* and the real-life tragedy of Sharon Tate . . . has been pointed out by critics as often as it has been denied by Polanski."[16] Bryan Reynolds, who has undertaken an especially careful reading of the film and its reception, says categorically that "Every review of *Macbeth* of which I am aware makes reference to the butchery of Polanski's wife, unborn child, and friends."[17] Critic Roger Ebert, for instance, found it "impossible to watch certain scenes without thinking of the Charles Manson case. It is impossible to watch a film directed by Roman Polanski and not react on more than one level to such images as a baby being 'untimely ripped from his mother's womb.'"[18] (The comparisons were rough ones, to be sure. Macduff was "untimely ripped" from his mother's womb, but this was an early version of a C-section. He lived to tell the tale and kill Macbeth.) Perhaps the ugliest twist came with Pauline Kael's review in the *New Yorker*, which dangerously flirted with blaming Polanski for the crimes of the Family: "Even though we knew that Roman Polanski had nothing whatever to do with causing the [crimes], the massacre seemed a vision realized from his nightmare movies." Historian Vincent Brook has echoed Kael's rhetoric, with a slightly different focus, in *Land of Smoke and Mirrors*: the "Satanic possession theme" of *Rosemary's Baby*, Brook writes, was "gruesomely reenacted in real life" when Sharon Tate was killed by Manson's associates.[19]

Chinatown has been widely accepted to represent an effort on Polanski's part to process his horror at the murder of Sharon Tate. Polanski's biographer, Christopher Sandford, argues that the "catharsis" of "the Manson murders was to be found here rather than in Macbeth." Sandford, for his part, reads the film's ending as an acknowledgment of the emotional poetics of being a bystander. As Polanski's screenwriter Robert Towne put it, "beautiful blondes always die in LA" and the movie, therefore, needed to have a "tunnel at the end of the light."[20] Most historians, appropriately, have focused on the larger politics of in the film. Mike Davis, for instance, is less concerned with the local details of the movie, valuing more its willingness to depict what he calls the "capitalized lineages of power" that came to define the politics of Southern California.[21] Steven Erie has been especially efficient in his description of the primary animus of *Chinatown*. Towne and Polanski, as Erie puts it, sculpted a story of a "larcenous land grab among Gothic family romance," essentially summarizing that *Chinatown*'s vision of the conspiratorial politics of water and power in California functions as an allegory of both Watergate and Vietnam.[22]

That said, the lure of drawing direct connections between the film's imagery and the more recent past in Los Angeles has proven to be powerful. Writing of two of the film's main characters, investigator Jake Gittes (Jack Nicholson) and Evelyn Mulwray (Faye Dunaway), Vincent Brook argues that viewers "can't help superimposing Polanski's likely horrified reaction to Sharon Tate's murder onto Jake's devastated expression as he stares at Evelyn's limp body in the driver's seat."[23] Foster Hirsch takes this interpretive tendency much further than Brook does; Hirsch takes it for granted that Gittes is a stand-in for Polanski, and that the detective's interactions with Evelyn Mulwray and her power-hungry and incestuous father Noah Cross represent the director's attempt to confront the loss of his mother (in Auschwitz) and his wife (in Los Angeles). "Jake's failure to rescue Noah's daughters," in Hirsch's reading, can be interpreted as "a metaphor of Polanski's inability to save his pregnant wife . . . and his mother." Hirsch achieves quite a bit of lift here in this bravura analytical leap, suggesting finally that Noah Cross, therefore, represents a "combination of Charles Manson and Adolf Hitler."[24] I support Hirsch's interpretive *impulse* (i.e., *Chinatown* can be read as an important entry in the catalog of "Manson art"), even as I do not want travel with him along his overblown psychoanalytic trajectory.

If Manson and the Tate killings were going to inflect the art of Terry Melcher (and so many others) it is hardly surprising to find available analogies connecting Roman Polanski's 1970s work with the terrible crimes that so afflicted him. As I have been suggesting all along, however, one did not have to suffer directly from the Family's murderous creepy crawl to feel compelled to make art that, in one way or another, engaged with the case. While much of the Los Angeles art of 1974 (and 1975 and 1976) was organized around an apocalyptic vision of some kind of end times, that was hardly a new trope post-Manson. As Mike Davis has explained in his book *Ecology of Fear*, "the destruction of Los Angeles has been a central theme or image in at least 138 novels or films since 1909" (and he didn't even count songs).[25] As I have been suggesting, though, what was new in the Manson-art world of the 1970s was the turn—as in Melcher and so many others—toward what film historian Peter Biskind has called, in reference to Warren Beatty's work in *Shampoo*, "auto-critique."[26]

Shampoo appeared on screen in 1975 as the Hollywood version of *Terry Melcher*'s emotional politics (with quite a bit of capital-P Politics in the mix as well). Warren Beatty, who starred in the movie and co-wrote it with Robert Towne, has made it clear that the vicious murders at Cielo Drive had shaped everybody working in Hollywood: "It was impossible to escape it in this town, even if you were not friends with the people involved"—which Beatty was.[27] Beatty explains that the "original version of *Shampoo*," a film about a Los Angeles hairdresser generally understood to be modeled on Jay Sebring (who cut Beatty's hair), was "strongly influenced by the killings." This script, Beatty claims, "stretched out over a period of months, got into drug running, and was headed towards an apocalyptic ending."[28] The film manages to feel apocalyptic as it stands, even without any direct reference to Manson, Tate, or the murders. Production designer Dick Sylbert, who also worked on *Chinatown*, helpfully describes *Shampoo* as a reversal of the earlier movie: "What you hide in *Chinatown*, you show in Beverly Hills." Sylbert goes on to explain that in order to capture this focus on "display, vanity, narcissism" he littered the design with mirrors—"two hundred or so."[29]

Shampoo is self-reflexive, to say the least. It is not only about an individual Los Angeles hairdresser who happens to be narcissistic; it is about the narcissism that Beatty thought plagued life in Hollywood. In thinking about the relationship of the movie to the events of August 1969, it is helpful to take note of film critic Karina Longworth's claim that Beatty was amazed that so many in the film community believed that it was the murder of an "actress and a hairdresser"—and not the election of Richard Nixon in 1968—that marked the end of the dreams of liberation that characterized the late 1960s.[30] *Shampoo* begins on the eve of the 1968 election, and that time-stamp is all over the movie. It features an election night party, and Richard Nixon on a television screen, celebrating his victory and promising that his administration will "bridge the generation gap." The movie opens with a sex scene scored by the Beach Boys' "Wouldn't It Be Nice" and hurtles toward the 1970s with Spiro Agnew talking about ending permissiveness and Nixon promising an "open" administration. Beatty and Towne have a forceful (if not light) touch. When Goldie Hawn's character Jill says, "Sometimes I get this terrible feeling that something's gonna happen" we could be on the pages of Joan Didion's "White Album." But Beatty generally does not want to mystify what is happening to his characters in Los Angeles in the late 1960s. He does not want to let them off the hook with an appeal to the sort of passive and apolitical (or anti-political, actually) doom-mongering Didion wears as armor.

Beatty's George defers taking responsibility for his actions: "Can we talk later?" is something of a mantra for him in *Shampoo*. And this is what Beatty, for his part, most wanted the audience of his film to notice. While his sexually popular hairdresser—"Let's face it. I fucked them all," he ultimately confesses—seems centrally placed in his particular subculture, he is destined to live on the outskirts of the political moment. Beatty explains George's marginality with a remarkable phrase; George is doomed, according to Beatty, because he does not participate in the "forensics of national survival."[31] The climactic line in *Shampoo* comes, as many observers have noted, when Lester Karp (Jack Warren) wonders aloud about George's motivation for having sex with so many women, including his own wife: "[D]o you get your kicks sneaking around behind people's backs taking advantage of them? Is that your idea of being anti-establishment?" Beatty's George looks baffled for a moment and then settles the matter with a simple explanation: "I'm not anti-establishment." This is a profound moment in the history of Manson art, representing as it does Beatty's rather sly (and cruel?) effort to project Jay Sebring into the 1970s in order to argue that the hairdresser's (and Sharon Tate's) dalliance with the Los Angeles counterculture should not be read as anything other than slumming. While George is, in some obvious ways, patterned after Jay Sebring, he also brings Terry Melcher to mind. As played by Warren Beatty, George is at once remarkably privileged and completely unable to enjoy his privilege. This is a movie about a powerful culture in decline, and George's main function is as the canary in the coal mine. If *he* is not having fun, then who possibly could be? With this one line of dialogue, *Shampoo* reminds its viewers of how little it took for the promises of liberation to be revealed as desperate, compulsory pleasure-seeking. "A thin line between love and hate" is how the Persuaders, a Philadelphia soul group, put it in 1971.

Wrecking Crews

"We're the wrecking crew." This is what David Herrle has Tex Watkins say in his crazy-quilt book of poems *Sharon Tate and the Daughters of Joy* (2014).[1] The "wrecking crew" mention is a good joke. That was the name, of course, of the loose assemblage of Los Angeles–based session musicians (including Terry Melcher's friend Mike Deasy) who laid down the tracks for so many recordings in the 1960s and 1970s. And it was the name of a Dean Martin movie that also featured Sharon Tate (1968). Herrle cannot leave things here—his book is a web of references and Manson is only one of the poet's many reference points, along with such avatars of creative destruction as Marie Antoinette and William Faulkner's Thomas Sutpen. But it is in the reference to the session musicians—an emblem of underappreciated artistic achievement—that Herrle locates his most poignant citation. After naming the Family after the session players, Watkins then points over to Jay Sebring's dead body and says that the carnage is "our poetry, our song, our sculpture." Herrle is building, it seems, on Ed Sanders's proposition that Charles Manson was a "performance killer." With one referential move after another, Herrle reminds us that the Manson murders were (among so many other things) acts of complex performance. This is the crux of the seduction and the frustration for creators of Manson art: they have so much competition from the man himself.

Manson was *literally* an artist of course—a writer and singer of songs. But his artistic legacy is not found in "Look at Your

Game Girl" or "Cease to Exist"/"Cease to Resist" but rather in his more curatorial efforts. Sanders began to articulate this idea in the early 1970s, and Zachary Lazar has more recently put punctuation on it. The *Sway* author has argued that the Tate-LaBianca murders have a "perverse aesthetic quality to them. They were orchestrated in a way that is calculatedly terrifying. . . . [Y]ou couldn't script a more terrifying scene."[2] Lazar goes on to note that Manson's instruction to his girls on that August night, as they left the former movie ranch to go kill the current movie star, to "do something witchy" should "essentially" be translated to mean "be creative."[3] The creativity of Manson and his Family has bedeviled artists working in their wake who are confronted with an inspiration at once so ripe for meditating upon but also so inconveniently articulate in its own right. Herrle's "wrecking crew" line is a good one, but it is no match after all, for Tex Watkins's own alleged words to Voytek Frykowski: "I am the Devil and I'm here to do the Devil's business." Watkins is equal parts Captain Ahab—baptizing his weapon not in the name of the father but in the name of the devil—and African American folk figure Peetie Wheatstraw, the Devil's son-in-law. Like Manson, Watkins is a "performance killer." As with Manson (who reputedly hollered "Don't draw on me," Western-movie style, at a drunk stuntman at Spahn Ranch) and the witchy Manson women who wrote in blood on the walls and wove their own hair into a vest for their leader, Tex Watson knew how to stage a scene. Ed Sanders, for his part, simply could not stop wondering what movies the Manson Family made at the ranch.

John Waters, whose early films and later sculpture are so indebted to Manson, finds evidence of the creative impulse well in advance of the murders: "Was Manson's . . . 'creepy crawling,' some kind of humorous terrorism that might have been fun? Breaking silently into the homes of middle-class 'pigs' with your friends while you are tripping on LSD and gathering around the sleeping residents in their beds, not to harm them but to watch them sleep. . . . It *does* sound like it could have been a mind-bending adventure. When the Mansonites went further and moved the furniture around before they left, just to fuck with the waking homeowners' perception of reality, was this beautiful or evil? Could the Manson Family's actions also be some kind of freakish 'art'?"[4]

No artist has engaged in a more sustained or complex relationship with Manson and the Family than the Baltimore filmmaker, sculptor, photographer, and agent provocateur. In this respect he is Raymond Pettibon's art-world doppelganger, though Waters has been much more upfront and articulate about his obsession: from the filming of *Multiple Maniacs* during the breaking-news days of 1969 through his twenty-first-century advocacy for the parole of his friend Leslie Van Houten, Waters has never left the Manson Family alone for very long. But rather than try to "beat" the performance killings directed by Manson, Waters has more regularly attempted to "join" them. In *Shock Value*, Waters explains that he began work on *Multiple Maniacs* before the "real killers" had been apprehended. As a result, he decided that "Divine would take credit for the murders in the film. I figured that if the murderers were never caught, there would always be the possibility that Divine really did do it."[5] As the filming progressed, and the members of the Family were arrested, Waters changed his plot, even as the mission remained the same: "We wanted to scare the world . . . but we used a movie camera instead of deadly weapons." According to his own account, Waters did not only "scare the world," but also sent a cast member around the bend. As the director explains, "one of our new actors flipped out in the middle of a scene and ran from the set, screaming: 'I know that's a police camera. You've tricked me into confessing to the Tate murders, and now I'll be arrested!"[6] Manson and members of his Family were, of course, arrested during the late fall of 1969 and Waters's actors—if not his plot—were safe. The ending to *Multiple Maniacs* was changed; as Waters puts it, nobody, "not even Divine, could upstage Charles Manson."[7]

The organizing principle of this book you are reading is meant to emphasize that the artistic expressions inspired by Manson, his Family, and their crimes, have often been compelled to engage with the Family's own dramatic bent. The creepy crawl was nothing if not theatrical. The rearranging of furniture and consciousness was devised as a sort of real-world guerrilla stage direction: "Square family members wake up from their nighttime stupor as Family members exit through doors and windows. They look around. On their faces we see that they are questioning everything they have believed in until this point." In his book on the Doors, Greil Marcus refers to the Manson Family as a "band," but a "troupe" is more like it. John Waters recognized how much his own company, the Dreamlanders, resembled the Manson Family, and he has spent decades unpacking the implications of this realization. "The Manson Family looked just like my friends at the time!" Waters has written. Recall how Charles "Tex" Watson reminded Waters of "the frat-boy-gone-bad pot dealer" who sold him his first joint in Catholic high school, and for whom he "had the hots."[8]

In two different memoirs, on film, and in his sculpture, Waters goes to great pains to draw connections between the theatricality of the real-world Manson Family and the guerrilla attack of his own early films. Years after evoking the Family in *Multiple Maniacs* (1970) and *Female Trouble* (1974) Waters apologized for his own use of "the Manson murders in a jokey, smart-ass way . . . without the slightest feeling for the victims' families or the lives of the brainwashed Manson killer kids who were also victims in this sad and terrible case."[9]

Whatever latter-day concerns Waters has expressed about his exploitation of the Manson moment, he remains perhaps our best interpreter of the Family's relentless theatricality. Except for their leader (who may or may not have responded to the name "Jesus Christ"), members of the Family lived in the world with what Waters rightly calls "stage" names; Charles Watson is a distinct person, Waters suggests, from the Family actor Tex Watson. Waters describes Watson as if the young Texan had been a wannabe star hanging out in Schwab's drugstore. Watson was, as Waters argues, "perhaps Manson's best piece of work; a high-school football star who turned hippy and came to L.A. like millions of other kids to find '60s grooviness. Instead he met Manson and was turned into a killer in just ten LSD, Belladona-drenched months."[10] Waters first really got to "know" the Family in the moment of the trial, and he was taken by their seemingly self-conscious efforts to create the media impact they desired. Waters has written that these "starlets were out to grab headlines and no press agent was necessary." According to Waters, one of the accused referred to the trial as "this play"; these young women—playing "girls"—seemed to understand that they were still being directed to "do something witchy." Some organized themselves into a sort of tourist attraction on Broadway and Temple, near the courthouse, spending their time "giggling and mugging for their fans as they sang Charlie's songs."[11] The women of the Family were, as Waters puts it, "the most style-conscious defendants I've ever seen" and their head-shaving strikes him as an early development of a punk aesthetic.[12] And all of this served, of course, as a supporting act for the main attraction; as Waters describes things, Manson always entered the scene last, as "a true star should."[13]

While Waters's use of the Manson crimes could certainly be criticized for being insensitive, it seems clear that his own evolving sense of responsibility (his concern for the Tate family, his serious engagement with Leslie Van Houten's rehabilitation, and so on) was rooted in an unusual willingness to engage with Manson and his Family as actual people and not as one-dimensional signs of terror. Waters's close friendship with Leslie Van Houten and his committed activism on her behalf, is one obvious fruit of his nonconforming approach to reintroducing Manson and his followers to his fans.

Waters's 2006 sculpture "Playdate" is every bit as audacious (and touching) as his public declarations of support for the convicted murderer Van Houten. The tableau is simple enough—baby Michael Jackson meets baby Manson—and consonant with Waters's carefully cultivated image as the Pope of Trash. With their tiny bodies clad in onesies, the toddlers are adorable. With carved forehead (Manson) and carved face (Jackson) they are unsettling. Waters insists on what he calls the "original innocence" of Manson and Michael Jackson: "Even Charles Manson had other goals as a toddler," Waters wrote in 1986.[14] This meeting of the toddlers (portrayed with their adult heads) enacts a simple plea on the part of the artist that his viewers practice emotional justice. Waters excuses Manson for none of the crimes he was convicted of, excuses Jackson for none of the crimes he was accused of, but he does demand that we imagine both (at least in part) as innocent children—innocent children who experienced terrifying levels of abuse and neglect. Waters's achievement is to reintroduce these icons as objects of repressed feelings—affection, concern, and so on. There is nothing creepy about the crawl enacted here. The sculpture acts as a renunciation of the dehumanizing rhetorics surrounding the vilified figures. Waters is also too much of a popular culture historian to overlook the fact that Jackson and *his* family arrived in Los Angeles—ready for the bigtime—in the summer of 1969, just as Manson's Family was spiraling out of control. The Jackson 5's first single was released on October 6, 1969, less than a week before Manson was arrested at Barker Ranch.

Perhaps the richest Manson art on the contemporary scene will be that which, like Waters's "Playdate," refuses to endow Manson with some kind of mystical or singular power. This does not require turning Manson back into a baby or taking an exculpatory stance toward the convicted culture leader. Audiences in 1972, for instance, did not seem to have much patience for a theatrical "rockumentary" titled *22 Years*. It seems likely that no one was ready yet to hear this work's argument about how Manson's bad behavior was rooted in his own (titular) years of incarceration.[15] But in more recent days a few visual artists have striven to reframe Manson as something other than a terrifying sexmad guru and his Family as something other than sexy robots. Cady Noland's work has been particularly important here. The installation artist's work *Mr. SIR* presents an enigmatic portrait of Manson. The title alone evokes a sense of ambiguity with respect to Manson's power. The defendant is on his way to court with his pad and two pencils (one of which he would use to attack Judge Older), but it is not at all clear whether the artist is addressing

Manson as "Mr. SIR" or evoking Manson's own rhetorical stance of Southern-born, jail-bred humility. The way Manson hides behind his mass of hair suggests deference; his allegedly hypnotic stare is neutered here. But the pose also suggests slyness. Manson is keeping his own counsel here, to be sure. Manson is also wearing the Family vest in Noland's portrait—the visual chronicle his followers spent so many hours constructing for him. While his left hand holds the two pencils (which look like drumsticks from a distance—perhaps another trophy taken from Dennis Wilson's house?) Manson's right hand is another story. With his thumb and pinky hidden, Manson's right hand looks like a claw—it is not certain how functional this hand would be (and of course by Manson's own testimony he never "growed up to . . . write too good"). The placement of "Mr. SIR" in the gallery also makes it difficult to know how to read the one other major visual element in the piece—the door. Is it simply a sign of the jail gates Manson will soon be locked behind? Or is it a reminder that he has already entered our homes and rearranged our furniture?

Noland has also created two major works about the Family that do not feature Manson at all. In *Manson Girls Sit-In* she presents a resolutely unthreatening image of Ouisch and Squeaky (and the top third or so of another Family member's head), protesting the persecution outside the Hall of Justice in Los Angeles. But for all the familiar and potential witchiness of Squeaky and Ouisch, the tab-in-slot architecture of the work, which is then placed on the checkerboard gallery floor, re-presents the young women as the picture on a board-game piece (or pawns in a chess match). The piece, off center and somewhat lost in the spacious gallery, cannot play by the rules. The title encourages us to position the Manson women in a broader landscape of political action of the 1960s.

Even more striking is another Manson-themed work Noland debuted in 1993–1994. *Not Yet Titled (Bald Manson Girls Sit-In Demonstration)* confronts viewers with the uncomfortable reality of how quickly the Manson Family became a tourist attraction. As with so many objects of the tourist gaze, the Manson girls are being enclosed, defined, tamed. With wire-service news copy presented above the image, the bald women are offered up as a freaky spectacle, but Noland urges us to look into their eyes. While the artist wants to remind us of how quickly members of the Family were turned into objects of fantasy projection and dark humor, their relentless staring challenges the voyeuristic pleasure viewers might otherwise take in the tableau.

Taken together, Noland's two "Manson Girls" pieces refuse ready-made interpretive frameworks (such as Bugliosi's Helter Skelter) in favor of a more nuanced approach to gender, power, and spectacle. Decades earlier Ed Sanders warned *Free Press* readers to relinquish their fantasies about the sexual radicalism and availability of the young women living at Spahn Ranch. Here these women are monks, they are witches, they are news. They are nobody's easy target or punch line.[16]

Photographer Joachim Koester puts a punctuation mark on various trajectories of Manson art by removing targets (i.e., people) altogether from his work. Koester's 2008 Barker Ranch series uses the Family's last hideout, a remote outpost near Death Valley, as it central concern. While not steeped in movie history as Spahn Ranch was, Koester encourages viewers to read Barker Ranch as also "rich in filmic allusions."[17] Koester's ranch is devoid of almost all life. The key "figure" in number 4 of the series is a dead tree, a mockery of the Tree of Life at the heart of so many folkloric and mythological traditions. The Danish artist has come to Barker neither to praise nor to bury. His mission is to capture this iconic landscape, teetering at the moment just before it transforms into ruins. In taking us "back to the ranch" in this manner Koester insists that we understand the Manson case as a cracked Western. His Barker Ranch photography, then, must be understood as a late entry into the tradition of revisionist Western popular arts that began its rise to prominence just as Manson was making himself known to the musicians and filmmakers of Los Angeles.

Koester's desolate landscape photography is not in any way meant to "represent" Manson and his Family so much as he wants to employ them and the case to repudiate the romanticizing of outlaw imagery in so much film and popular and music of the

Vietnam-era and beyond. Perhaps most notable here is the cover of the first Crosby, Stills, Nash and Young LP, *Déjà Vu*, from 1970. Historian Michael Langkjaer has written incisively of how "the cover motif with its costumed and heavily armed 'outlaws' is a response to an America rent by social tensions contiguous with the Civil Rights Movement, the Vietnam War, fears of revolutionary violence and of notorious murders committed by the Charles Manson 'family,' for example, while also suggesting an ironic sense of failure of the youth counterculture." The Eagles would present something similar a few years later on the cover of their third album, *Desperado* (1973). Aside from the silly gunslinger/guitarslinger analogy both bands are activating, the imagery here (especially in the CSN&Y cover, with its invocation of the Confederate "Lost Cause" in the person of Stephen Stills) is not only nostalgic, but rearguard.[18] Joe Walsh joined the Eagles in 1975 after leading the James Gang, who also (obviously) trucked with Confederate/Western imagery. Warren Zevon would join this loose movement with his own "Frank and Jesse James," which takes the fairly standard position that these ex-Confederates were Robin Hoods.

Koester's work, on the other hand, joins a more insurgent tradition—or set of overlapping traditions, to be more precise. Perhaps thinking of what Pauline Kael called the "acid western" in her review of Alejandro Jodorowsky's *El Topo* (1970), along with the more widely known "Spaghetti Westerns" of Sergio Leone and others, and the so-called "Outlaw" country music coming from Austin and elsewhere in the 1970s, Koester refuses the comforts of projecting images of good and bad guys. Instead he offers only a broken promised land, a place where abstract concepts like "justice" and "mercy" could not possibly find any purchase.[19] In the second photograph of the series, Koester shows an out-building at Barker Ranch, its exposed beams summoning up the bars of the jail cell that would become Manson's next (and most familiar) home. With this, the Anglo-American ideal of Western freedom is laid as bare as these beams—"light out for the territory ahead of the rest" like Huck Finn if you will, but Koester's picture reminds us that the forces that want to "sivilize" (and discipline) always know where you are.

This pragmatic doominess puts Joachim Koester in an artistic tradition that includes the filmwork of Sam Peckinpah and Dennis Hopper (whose fringe jacket and hat in *Easy Rider* marked him as both cowboy and Indian), the Firesign Theater (with its "electric western" version of Siddhartha in *Zacariah*), Alexander Jodorowsky, Monte Hellman, Arthur Penn, Jim McBride, Rudy Wurlitzer, and Jim Jarmusch's *Dead Man* (1995). It is there in the mournfulness of Townes Van Zandt's oft-covered ballad "Pancho and Lefty" and in the woefully underappreciated work of folk singer Mary McCaslin. Over the course of a few solo records and one collaboration with Jim Ringer, McCaslin sang as a Westerner at once deeply steeped in the available mythologies of liberation but with a bracing realism about hierarchies of gender and corporate power shaping the contemporary landscape.

There are no jokes in Koester's show. Koester's California is the landscape of Antonioni's *Zabriskie Point*—but without the fantasy scene that portrays the hippie orgy in Death Valley. Manson did not "end" the sixties, Koester's photographs suggest, but he did help close some frontiers. (Those frontiers are mournfully indexed in the first story in Claire Vaye Watkins 2013 collection *Battleborn*; in "Ghosts, Cowboys" Watkins—the daughter of Manson Family member Paul Watkins—runs through a history of the West that includes the doomed founding of Spahn Ranch in the 1940s.) Koester's Barker Ranch series is Manson art in the extreme aftermath. This is not the breathtaking horror of the river of blood and bodies hanging from rafters that open *El Topo*, but the desert after vengeance has been wreaked. The post-Manson landscape is a terrain grown "weary of her inhabitants" (as John Winthrop wrote of England, in 1631, justifying the Anglo settling of New England), a barren place, with no families, and no Family.

Endnotes

Notes to the Introduction

1 Margalit Fox, "Manson Dies at 83; Wild-Eyed Leader of a Murderous Crew," *New York Times*: November 20, 2017; Aja Romano, "The Life and Death of Notorious Cult Leader Charles Manson, Explained," *Vox*: November 20, 2017; Parker quotation found in Greg Kot, "Death as a Career Move," *Chicago Tribune*: October 12, 1995.
2 George Bishop, *Witness to Evil*, 146.
3 Sarah Churchwell, *Many Lives of Marilyn Monroe*, 7.
4 Joan Didion, *The White Album*, 47.
5 Barbara Grizzuti Harrison, "Only Disconnect" in *Off Center*, 113.
6 Deana Martin, *Memories Are Made of This*, 169.
7 Rob Sheffield, *Dreaming the Beatles*, 203.
8 Bernie Leadon, of the Eagles, says this in a BBC documentary *Hotel California*. Don McLean hints at the same mistake in his song "American Pie." The locus classicus is John Burks's account in *Rolling Stone*, "In the Aftermath of Altamont."
9 Michael Denning, *The Cultural Front*, 26.
10 BBC documentary *Charles Manson: The Man Who Killed the Sixties*.
11 "Hollywood: Where All Walks of Life Mingle," *Sandusky Register*, December 17, 1969: 46.
12 Vernon Scott "Hollywood Is Susceptible to Drifters Like Manson," *Raleigh Register* December 16, 1969: 13.
13 Quoted in Vincent Bugliosi with Curt Gentry, *Helter Skelter*, 647; and Tommy Udo, *Charles Manson*, 152.
14 Tony O'Neill, *Sick City*, 145.
15 Sawyer interview found here: www.youtube.com/watch?v=v4qZB2ytq10.

16 Quoted in Udo, *Charles Manson*, 153.

17 Curt Rowlett, "The Summer of Love."

18 Bill James, *Popular Crime*, 265.

19 Buck Henry in Peter Biskind, *Easy Riders* 79; Van Dyke Parks in Harvey Kubernik, *Canyon of Dreams*, 200; and Barney Hoskyns, *Hotel California*.

20 Peter Vronsky, *Female Serial Killers*, 395.

21 Phil Proctor, personal communication.

22 Jonathan Crary, *24/7* 112–114.

23 "Manson Admits Mansion Visits," *Fairbanks Daily News Mirror*: October 24, 1970: 3.

24 Anthony DeCurtis, "Peace, Love and Charles Manson."

25 Mike Rubin, "Summer of '69," 152.

Notes to Part I

Mother Father Sister Brother

1 Testimony found at www.cielodrive.com/susan-atkins-grand-jury-testimony.php.

2 www.cielodrive.com/archive/susan-was-a-good-kid-then-came-sadie-glutz/.

3 Robert Shellow and his co-authors in "Runaways of the 1960s" (1967) tried about as hard as anyone in their essay to reorient the study of these young people, but to little apparent avail. iii–iv, 1–51.

4 www.cielodrive.com/susan-atkins-grand-jury-testimony.php.

5 Kevin Kennedy, "Manson at 50"; also, testimony at www.cielo-drive.com/charles-manson-trial-testimony.php.

6 *Rolling Stone* article at www.rollingstone.com/culture/news/charles-manson-the-incredible-story-of-the-most-dangerous-man-alive-19700625.

7 Susan Atkins with Bob Slosser, *Child of Satan*, 75–80.

8 David Smith and Alan Rose, "The Group Marriage Commune."

9 Donald Nielsen, *Horrible Workers*, 79.

10 Ibid.

11 Christina Grogan, *Father-Daughter Incest*, 15.

12 Quoted in Steve Blush and George Petros, *.45 Dangerous Minds*, 39.

13 Vincent Bugliosi with Curt Gentry, *Helter Skelter*, 526.

14 Tommy Udo, *Music Mayhem Murder*, 153.

15 Vincent Bugliosi, *Helter Skelter*, 165.

16 Donald Nielsen, *Horrible Workers*, 84.

17 Betty Friedan, *Feminine Mystique*, 63.

18 Stephanie Coontz, *Way We Never Were*, 10.
19 Capote interview can be found here at www.capote.wordpress
    .com/2011/05/14/truman-capote-interviews-bobby-beausoleil-
    san-quentin-1973/. I am also relying on my own conversation
    with Beausoleil for this section.
20 Susan Atkins, *Child of Satan*, 77.
21 Ibid., 95.
22 Donald Nielsen, *Horrible Workers*, 70.
23 Vincent Bugliosi, *Helter Skelter*, 551.
24 Anita Stevens and Lucy Freeman, *I Hate My Parents*, 113, 117.
25 David Smith and Alan Rose, "The Group Marriage Commune."
26 Interview with Manson in Box 1, Folder 8 of John Gilmore papers
    at UCLA, page 25.
27 Karen Staller, *Runaways*, 93.
28 Ibid., 91.
29 Ed Sanders, *The Family* (2002), 15.
30 Natasha Zaretsky, *No Direction Home*, 2.
31 Ibid., 11.
32 Vincent Bugliosi, *Helter Skelter*, 510.
33 Natasha Zaretsky, *No Direction Home*, 12–13.
34 Tom Brinkman, *Bad Mags 2*, 446.
35 Ann Jones, *Women Who Kill*, 2–3.
36 Ibid., 11.
37 Video currently found here: www.youtube.com/watch?v=
    Agtau1zFUuM&t=181s.
38 "Report to the President" found at www.archive.org/stream/
    whitehouseconfer00inwhit/ whitehouseconfer00inwhit_djvu.txt.
    See also Barbara Chandler, "The White House Conference on
    Children."
39 www.mansondirect.com/transa.html.
40 Interview with Bobby Beausoleil in Box 1 of John Gilmore papers
    at UCLA, "Burning Is the End." 47.
41 Susan Atkins, *Child of Satan*, 72–73.
42 Micol Ostow, *Family*, 39.
43 Currently copies of the Manson *Life* issue ("The Love and Terror
    Cult") sell for around $20. Its text can be found here: www.eviliz1
    .rssing.com/chan-10867740/all_p5.html.
44 Jeff Guinn, *Manson*, 157.
45 Ed Sanders, *The Family* (2002), 26.
46 Jeff Guinn, *Manson*, 129.
47 Emma Cline, "See Me," *Paris Review*, found here: www.theparis-
    review.org/blog/2014/03/17/see-me/.

48 Bobby Beausoleil, personal communication.
49 Donald Nielsen, *Horrible Workers*, 79.
50 Brian Wilson, *I Am Brian Wilson*, 54–55.
51 Paul Watkins, *My Life*, 47.
52 From the documentary *Charles Manson: The Man Who Killed the Sixties*.
53 www.eviliz1.rssing.com/chan-10867740/all_p5.html.

The Family That Slays Together

1 On these films and Manson, see especially David Ray Carter, "It's Only a Movie?" and Jon Towlson, *Subversive Horror Cinema*, 134–135.
2 Nick Cull's great analysis of *The Exorcist* can be found here www .historytoday.com/nick-cull/exorcist.
3 For Nathan Rabin on *Billy Jack* see www.thedissolve.com/features/ forgotbusters/593-forgotbusters-billy-jackthe-trial-of-billy-jack/.
4 On Father Peyton, see Joseph Gribble, "Family Theater of the Air." on Spirit, see William Ruhlmann, "Spirit." Part's obituary is here: www.legacy.com/obituaries/latimes/obituary.aspx?n=marvin-lawrence-part&pid=139539359.
5 "Getting Cute with Charlie Manson," *Rolling Stone*.
6 Ibid.
7 The whole song is reprinted in John Aes-Nihil, et al. *The Manson File*, 67.
8 John Aes-Nihil, *The Manson File*, 67.
9 Theo Wilson, *Headline Justice*, 169.
10 Ibid., 182.
11 Ibid., 179.
12 Ibid., 178.
13 Ibid., 178–179.

Ranch, Hill, Farm

1 From the BBC documentary *Cease to Exist*.
2 "Hey dad" is from a Theo Wilson article in the *Daily News* found here www.nydailynews.com/news/crime/court-finds-manson-children-guilty-1971-article-1.2069176. Of course a number of variations of "dad" travel in counterculture circuits, in a number of tonal registers. Manson's trial speech can be found in John Aes-Nihil, et al., *The Manson File*.
3 Andres Killen, *1973 Nervous Breakdown*, 128.

4 On the Source Family, see Jodi Wille's documentary and the Isis Aquarian book, and Doug Harvey's "Father Yod Knew Best."

5 From the Jodi Wille's documentary.

6 David Felton, "The Lyman Family's Holy Siege," *Rolling Stone*.

7 Ibid.; see also Ryan Walsh, *Astral Weeks*.

8 Brian Burness, "Quiet Survivors," found here: www.trussel.com/lyman/quiet.htm.

9 Robert Levey, "Reinventing Life," found here: www.trussel.com/lyman/levey.htm.

10 Ellen Herst, "Mel and Charlie's Women," originally in *Boston After Dark*, found here: www.trussel.com/lyman/women.htm.

11 Ibid.

12 Brian Burness, "Quiet Survivors."

13 Lisa Law, *Flashing on the Sixties*, 91. See also Alice Echols, *Shaky Ground* 22.

14 I found this documentary at the UCLA Film and Television Archive.

15 Ellen Herst, "Mel and Charlie's Women."

16 Ibid.

17 Ibid.

18 Ibid.

19 Ibid.

20 Jeffrey Blum and Judith Smith, *Nothing Left to Lose*, 7.

21 Ibid.

22 Ibid.

23 Robert Houriet, *Getting Back Together*, 19.

24 Ibid., 21.

25 Ibid., 83.

26 Barry Miles, *Hippie*, 270.

27 Jerry LeBlanc and Ivor Davis, *5 to Die*, 49.

28 Jeffrey Sconce, "XXX: Love and Kisses," 213.

29 Ibid., 214.

30 Ibid., 209, 214.

31 Episodes 45 and 47 of Karina Longworth's *Charles Manson's Hollywood* are helpful here.

32 Gay Talese, "Charlie Manson's Home on the Range."

33 Paul Krassner, *Confessions*, 225.

34 This is from an order filed on behalf of Sandra Good claiming contempt against Bugliosi in September 1970, found in Box 2 of the John Gilmore papers at UCLA.

35 Tex Watson, *Will You Die for Me?* 51.

36 Quoted in Richard Cándida Smith, *Utopia and Dissent*, 368.

37 Timothy Miller, *Hippies and American Values*, 36.
38 www.thefarmcommunity.com/FAQ.html#17.
39 Jonathan Crary, *24/7*, 114.
40 Ibid., 115.
41 Judith Stacey, *Brave New Families*, 269.

Hush Little Dropout

 1 Robert Houriet, *Getting Back Together*, 19.
 2 Jeffrey Sconce, "XXX: Love and Kisses," 215.
 3 www.murdersofaugust69.freeforums.net/thread/654/terry-melcher-grand-jury-testimony.
 4 Jason Cherkis, "The Lost Girls."
 5 Charles M. Young's "RUN RUN RUN RUN RUNAWAYS," from *Crawdaddy*'s October 1976 issue. It is not easy to find online but is, currently, here: www.runawaysonline.proboards.com/thread/520/infamous-crawdaddy-article.
 6 Jeffrey Sconce, "XXX: Love and Kisses" 220.
 7 Abbie Hoffman, *Revolution for the Hell of It*, 74.
 8 Karen Staller, *Runaways*, 85.
 9 Ibid., 85, 89.
10 David McBride, "On the Fault Line," 96.
11 Karen Staller, *Runaways*, 69.
12 Bobby Beausoleil, personal communication.
13 Karen Staller, *Runaways*, 89, 109.
14 Ann Moses, "The Runaway Youth Act," 232.
15 Karen Staller, *Runaways*, 82.
16 Ibid., 111.
17 Richard Fairfield, *Communes USA*, 273.
18 Vincent Bugliosi, *Helter Skelter*, 315.
19 Ann Moses "The Runaway Youth Act," 236.
20 Per Karen Staller's framing in *Runaways*.
21 J. Anthony Lukas, "The Two Worlds of Linda Fitzpatrick"; Leticia Kent, "High on Life"; Richard Goldstein, "Love."
22 Leticia Kent, "High on Life"; Richard Goldstein, "Love."
23 Ada Calhoun, *St. Marks Is Dead*, 175–176.
24 Leticia Kent, "High on Life."
25 Arthur Gelb, *City Room*, 473.
26 Ada Calhoun, *St. Marks Is Dead*, 165–166.
27 Skip Hollandsworth, "The Lost Boys."
28 Ibid.
29 Ibid.

30 John Gurwell, *Mass Murder in Houston*, 112.
31 "Double Life of Corll Begins to Unravel."
32 Lillian Ambrosino, *Runaways*, 4.
33 Robert Shellow, et al., "Suburban Runaways of the 1960s" 16, 28.
34 Shellow et al., "Suburban Runaways of the 1960s" 32.
35 Robin Lloyd, *For Money or Love*, x.
36 Bibi Wein, *The Runaway Generation*, 201.
37 Robert Sam Anson, "The Last Porno Show," 289.
38 Ibid.
39 Judy Kutulas, *After Aquarius Dawned*, 150–151.
40 Greg Bennet, "Hidden Gem: Taking Off."
41 www.kirkusreviews.com/book-reviews/anonymous-3/go-ask-alice/.
42 Mark Oppenheimer, "Just Say 'Uh-Oh'"; *Go Ask Alice* 50, 83.
43 Brian Herrera, "*Go Ask Alice* Forty Years Later."
44 Ibid., 82.
45 Ibid., 46.
46 Ibid., 12, 55, 47.
47 Gretchen Lemke-Santangelo *Daughters of Aquarius*, 4.
48 Ben Fong-Torres, "FCC Discovers Dope."
49 Gretchen Lemke-Santangelo, *Daughters of Aquarius*, 12.
50 Lewis Yablonski, *The Hippie Trip*, 289.
51 Gretchen Lemke-Santangelo, *Daughters of Aquarius*, 5.
52 Carol Clover, *Men, Women, and Chain Saws*, 40.
53 J. Hoberman, "Off the Hippies."
54 Judy Klemesrud, "His Happiness Is a Thing Called 'Joe.'"
55 Donald Nielsen, *Horrible Workers*, 77.
56 Hillary Radner in the introduction to *Swinging Single*, 27.
57 Karlene Faith, *Long Prison Journey*, 110.
58 Scott's article found at www.cielodrive.com/archive/diane-abigail-sharon-linked-in-death/.
59 Quoted in Lisa Rhodes, *Electric Ladyland*, 197.
60 Amanda Petrusich, "We Support the Music."
61 Lisa Rhodes, *Electric Ladyland*, 168.
62 Jean Stafford quoted in Tom Brinkman, *Bad Mags 2*, 341; Max Lerner in Anita Stevens, *I Hate My Parents*, 89, 112.
63 Jerry LeBlanc and Ivor Davis, *5 to Die*, 49.
64 Susan Atkins, *Child of Satan*, 185.

The History of Consciousness

 1 Karlene Faith, *Unruly Women* 275–300; also Faith, *Long Prison Journey* 18–19, 78; and personal communication with Candace Falk.

2 Karlene Faith, *Unruly Women*.

3 Susan Atkins, *Child of Satan*, 185.

4 Karlene Faith, *Long Prison Journey*, 18.

5 Ibid., 19.

6 Karlene Faith, *Unruly Women* 275, 287.

7 Ibid., 298.

8 Ibid., 300.

9 Personal communication with Candace Falk.

10 Karlene Faith, *Long Prison Journey*, 291.

11 Ibid., 78.

12 Ibid., xviii.

13 Ibid., 18, 66.

14 Ibid., 9.

15 Gretchen Lemke-Santangelo, *Daughters of Aquarius*, 2.

16 Marisa Meltzer, "Cult Following."

17 Bobby Beausoleil, personal communication.

18 Gretchen Lemke-Santangelo, *Daughters of Aquarius*, 6.

19 Ibid., 89.

20 Emma Cline, *The Girls*, 41; Timothy Miller, *The 60s Communes*, 34–35.

21 Emma Cline, *The Girls*, 3.

22 Ibid., 4–5, 89.

23 Ibid., 248, 330.

24 Ibid., 33.

25 Ibid., 17.

26 Ibid., 17.

27 Ibid., 187.

28 Alison Umminger, *American Girls*, 5.

29 Ibid., 43.

30 Ibid., 42, 95.

31 Ibid., 233.

32 Ibid., 234.

33 Ibid., 260.

34 Jess Bravin, *Squeaky*, 43.

35 Alison Umminger, *American Girls*, 262.

36 Laura Elizabeth Woollett, *The Love of a Bad Man*, 118.

Notes to Part II

High Rollers

1 Alvin Karpis as told to Robert Livesey, *On the Rock*, 151.

2 Greg King, *Sharon Tate*, 121; Manson quoted in Steven Blush and George Petros, *.45 Dangerous Minds*, 202.

3 Hoskyns, *Waiting for the Sun*, 175.
4 Ed Sanders, *The Family*, (1971) 34.
5 David McBride, "On the Fault Line," 2.
6 Mark Jones and Gerry Carlin, "Unfound Footage and Unfounded Rumors," 175.
7 Harvey Kubernik, *Canyon of Dreams*, 202.
8 Jeff Guinn, *Manson*, 325.
9 Vincent Bugliosi with Curt Gentry, *Helter Skelter*, 488.
10 Joan Didion, *The White Album*, 41–42, 47.
11 Simon Reynolds and Joy Press, *The Sex Revolts*, 145.
12 Barney Hoskyns, *Waiting for the Sun*, 174.
13 Michael Walker, *Laurel Canyon*, 126.
14 Greil Marcus, *The Doors*, 146.
15 Ibid., 145–146.
16 Ivor Davis and Jerry LeBlanc, *5 to Die*, 223.
17 Ibid., 19.
18 J. D. Russell, *The Beautiful People*, 103, 100.
19 Ibid., 107, 131.
20 Lawrence Schiller, *The Killing of Sharon Tate*, 14.
21 Ivor Davis and Jerry LeBlanc, *5 to Die*, 222.
22 Vincent Bugliosi, *Helter Skelter*, 91.
23 Robert Stone, *Prime Green*, 200.
24 Greg King, *Sharon Tate*, 181.
25 Barney Hoskyns, *Waiting for the Sun*, 184.
26 This 1991 interview is widely available online.
27 Paul Krassner, *Confessions*, 197; Vincent Bugliosi, *Helter Skelter*, 48.
28 "Burning is the End," Box 1 of the John Gilmore Papers, UCLA Special Collections Library, 46.
29 Ed Sanders, *The Family* (2002), 163.
30 Marianne Faithfull with David Dalton, *Faithfull*, 212.
31 Jimmy McDonough, *Shakey*, 260, 287.
32 Nick Kent, *The Dark Stuff*, 310.
33 Ed Sanders, "Beausoleil, Manson, Death Row and the Gas Chamber, Revisited," *Los Angeles Free Press*: 3; see also Truman Capote, "Then It All Came Down."
34 A. L. Bardach's 1981 *Oui Magazine* interview, "Jailhouse Interview: Bobby Beausoleil."
35 Peter Biskind, *Easy Riders*, 79.
36 Howard Hampton, "Impressions of an Existential Stuntman," 36.
37 Nick Kent, *The Dark Stuff*, 287; Steven Gaines, *Heroes & Villains*, 215.

38 Greg King, *Sharon Tate*, 133; Ed Sanders, *The Family* (2002), 62.
39 Michael Walker, *Laurel Canyon*, xii; "celebrityism" is found in a documentary titled *Charles Manson: Journey Into Evil*.
40 Adam Webb, *Dumb Angel*, 79; Ed Sanders, *The Family* (2002), 96.
41 Harvey Kubernik, *Hollywood Shack*, 84.
42 Michael Walker, *Laurel Canyon*, 11; Harvey Kubernik, *Hollywood Shack*, 84.
43 Christopher Sharrett, "From the Archives: *Riot on Sunset Strip*."
44 Jeff Guinn, *Manson*, 159.
45 Harvey Kubernik, *Hollywood Shack*, 84.
46 Bob Fisher, *Easy Rider: 35 Years Later*.
47 J. D. Russell, *The Beautiful People*, 111.
48 Michael Walker, *Laurel Canyon*, xii.
49 Vincent Bugliosi, *Helter Skelter*, 48.

Hippies with Power

1 Barney Hoskyns, *Hotel California*, 18.
2 Barney Hoskyns, "The Meeting of the 'Twain."
3 Barney Hoskyns, *Hotel California*, 17.
4 Peter Biskind, *Easy Riders*, 59.
5 Thomas Frank, *Conquest of Cool*, 7.
6 Gregg Jakobson, personal communication.
7 Rachel Rubin, *Well Met*, 48–49.
8 Bobby Beausoleil, personal communication.
9 Steven Gaines, *Heroes and Villains*, 204.
10 Vincent Bugliosi, *Helter Skelter*, 335.
11 Greg King, *Sharon Tate*, 133.
12 Ed Sanders, *The Family* (2002), 38.
13 Greg King, *Sharon Tate*, 138; also John Phillips with Jim Jerome, *Papa John*, 229–230.
14 Michael Walker, *Laurel Canyon*, 11.
15 David Kamp, "Live at the Whisky."
16 Nick Kent, *The Dark Stuff*, 45.
17 Vincent Bugliosi, *Helter Skelter*, 336.
18 Barry Miles, *Hippie*, 274; Jakobson's estimate can be found in his testimony at Tex Watson's trial: www.cielodrive.com/gregg-jakobson-trial-testimony.php.
19 Simon Wells, *Charles Manson*, 151.
20 Adam Webb, *Dumb Angel*, 80.
21 Steven Gaines, *Heroes & Villains*, 215; Jeff Guinn, *Manson*, 212.
22 Melcher's comments here are from his testimony at Watson's trial found at www.cielodrive.com/terry-melcher-trial-testimony.php.

23 www.cielodrive.com/terry-melcher-trial-testimony.php.
24 Jeff Guinn, *Manson*, 221–222.
25 Ibid., 221; Ed Sanders, *The Family* (2002), 135; Dawn Eden Goldstein, "The Mike Deasy Story."
26 *The Byrds: Under Review.*
27 Dave Marsh, *The Heart of Rock and Soul*, 520.
28 From BBC documentary *Cease to Exist.*
29 Melcher testimony at www.cielodrive.com/terry-melcher-trial-testimony.php.
30 Ed Sanders, *The Family* (2002), 34.

Hungry Freaks

1 Ed Sanders, *The Family* (2002), 37, 63, 133; Paul Watkins with Guillermo Soledad, *My Life*, 38.
2 Ed Sanders, *The Family* (2002), 84
3 Frank Zappa, *The Real Frank Zappa Book*, 104.
4 David Toop, "Surfin' Death Valley," 406.
5 Rachel Rubin, *Well Met*, 48.
6 David Kamp, "Live at the Whisky."
7 Barry Miles, *Hippie*, 50.
8 Ibid., 66
9 Hoskyns, *Waiting for the Sun*, 111.
10 Barry Miles, *Hippie*, 66.
11 Pauline Butcher, *Freak Out!* 69.
12 David Kamp, "Live at the Whisky."
13 Michael Walker, *Laurel Canyon*, 127.
14 Greg King, *Sharon Tate*, 137.
15 Rachel Adams, *Sideshow U.S.A.*, 9.
16 Ibid., 9, 139, 145.
17 Chuck Eddy, *Accidental Evolution*, 2, Andrew Hannon, "Acting Out."
18 William Bishop, *Witness to Evil*, 275.
19 Tom Wolfe, *The Electric Kool-Aid Acid Test*, 11.
20 Frank Zappa, liner notes, *Freak Out!*
21 Ibid.
22 Kevin Courier, *Trout Mask Replica*, 25.
23 Don Was, "iTunes and the Death of Liner Notes."
24 Rachel Adams, *Sideshow U.S.A.*, 139, 141.
25 Weather Underground, "Declaration of a State of War."
26 Barry Miles, *Zappa*, 128.
27 Ibid., 128–129.
28 Michael Walker, *Laurel Canyon*, 127.

29 Harvey Kubernik and Kenneth Kubernik, *Perfect Haze*, 108.
30 Mike Barnes *Captain Beefheart*, 85.
31 Mike Barnes, *Captain Beefheart*, 87.
32 Gregg Jakobson testimony at www.cielodrive.com/gregg-jakob-son-trial-testimony.php.
33 Jeff Guinn, *Manson*, 7–9.
34 Paul Watkins, *My Life*, 18–19.
35 Carole Brightman, *Sweet Chaos*, 151.
36 Paul Watkins, *My Life*, 63, 123.
37 Frank Zappa, liner notes, *Freak Out!*
38 Rachel Rubin, *Well Met*, 48–49.
39 John Waters, *Role Models*, 46.
40 Paul Watkins, *My Life*, 37.
41 Ibid., 37–38.
42 Rachel Adams, *Sideshow U.S.A.*, 139.
43 Paul Watkins, *My Life*, 38.
44 Ibid., 37.
45 Ibid., 146.
46 For *Rolling Stone* article, see www.rollingstone.com/culture/news/charles-manson-the-incredible-story-of-the-most-danger-ous-man-alive-19700625.
47 Devon Powers, "Long-Haired, Freaky People," 12.

The Bad Fathers of the Feast

 1 Michael Walker, *Laurel Canyon*, xviii.
 2 Phil Proctor, personal communication.
 3 Peter Biskind, *Easy Riders*, 79.
 4 Curt Rowlett, "The Summer of Love."
 5 Michael Walker, *Laurel Canyon*, 124.
 6 Barney Hoskyns, *Hotel California*, 115.
 7 Peter Biskind, *Easy Riders*, 79.
 8 Barney Hoskyns, *Hotel California*, 95.
 9 Peter Biskind, *Easy Riders*, 78.
10 Ibid.
11 Robert Stone, *Prime Green*, 200.
12 Ibid., 202.
13 John Phillips, *Papa John*, 228.
14 Robert Stone, *Prime Green*, 202.
15 John Phillips, *Papa John*, 228.
16 Robert Stone, *Prime Green*, 200–201.
17 Ibid., 201.
18 Michael Walker, *Laurel Canyon*, 126.

19 David Felton, David Dalton, and Robin Green, *Mindfuckers*, 26.
20 Michael André Bernstein, *Bitter Carnival*, 171.
21 Tom Nolan, "Surf's Up!" 22.
22 Peter Biskind, *Easy Riders*, 79.
23 Harvey Kubernik, *Canyon of Dreams*, 200.
24 Barney Hoskyns, *Hotel California*, 96.
25 Harvey Kubernik *Canyon of Dreams*, 200.
26 John Kaye, "1972: Five Days in September."
27 Peter Biskind, *Easy Riders*, 57.
28 Allen Katzman, "Poor Paranoids," 5.
29 www.robertchristgau.com/get_artist.php?name=joni+mitchell;
    Sheila Weller, *Girls Like Us*, 281–285.
30 From the BBC documentary *Hotel California*.
31 Vincent Bugliosi, *Helter Skelter*, 394.
32 Manson testimony at www.cielodrive.com/charles-manson-trial-
    testimony.php.
33 Vincent Bugliosi, *Helter Skelter*, 335; Ed Sanders "Manson & the
    Missing Groin Clink," 3, 12.
34 David Leaf, *The Beach Boys*, 136.
35 Scott Timberg, "Drugs, Paranoia."
36 Vincent Bugliosi, *Helter Skelter*, 336.
37 www.rollingstone.com/culture/news/charles-manson-the-incred-
    ible-story-of-the-most-dangerous-man-alive-19700625.
38 Ed Sanders, *The Family* (2002), 61.
39 Jeff Guinn, *Manson*, 216.
40 Adam Webb, *Dumb Angel*, 54.
41 Gary Lachman, *Turn Off Your Mind*, 394.
42 Adam Webb, *Dumb Angel*, 85.
43 Ibid., 85.
44 www.murdersofaugust69.freeforums.net/thread/597/terry-
    melcher-trial-testimony.
45 Barney Hoskyns, *Hotel California*, 94.
46 www.murdersofaugust69.freeforums.net/thread/654/terry-
    melcher-grand-jury-testimony.
47 www.murdersofaugust69.freeforums.net/thread/597/terry-
    melcher-trial-testimony.
48 www.murdersofaugust69.freeforums.net/thread/654/terry-
    melcher-grand-jury-testimony.
49 Gay Talese, "Manson's Home on the Range."
50 Ed Sanders, *The Family* (2002), 33, 70.
51 Tommy Udo, *Music Mayhem Murder*, 97.
52 Peter Biskind, *Easy Riders*, 79–80.

53 www.murdersofaugust69.freeforums.net/thread/597/terry-melcher-trial-testimony.

54 Ibid.

55 www.cielodrive.com/terry-melcher-trial-testimony.php.

56 www.murdersofaugust69.freeforums.net/thread/597/terry-melcher-trial-testimony.

57 Ibid.

58 Ibid.

59 www.cielodrive.com/terry-melcher-trial-testimony.php.

60 www.murdersofaugust69.freeforums.net/thread/665/gregg-jakobson-trial-testimony.

61 Ibid.

Family Affairs

1 Greil Marcus, *The Doors*, 156.

2 Barney Hoskyns, *Hotel California*, 196.

3 John Phillips, *Papa John*, 210.

4 Steve Huey, "The Fifth Dimension"; Fred Bronson, *Billboard Book of Number One Hits*, 253.

5 William Ruhlmann, "The Fifth Dimension: The Age of Aquarius."

6 Maas's article originally appeared in the April 1970 issue of *Ladies' Home Journal* and can be found here: www.murdersofaugust69.freeforums.net/thread/675/ladies-journal-april-sharon-murders. Also, quoted in Vincent Bugliosi, *Helter Skelter*, 288.

7 www.cielodrive.com/terry-melcher-trial-testimony.php.

8 Ed Sanders, *The Family* (2002), 29.

9 Manson's speech has been reproduced frequently. It can be found in John Aes-Nihil, *The Manson File* and here www.murdersofaugust69.freeforums.net/thread/679/charles-manson-testimony-november-1970.

10 Thomas Pynchon, *Inherent Vice*, 209.

11 Joel Selvin, *Sly and the Family Stone*, 124.

12 Ed Sanders, *The Family* (2002), 331.

13 Ibid., 323.

14 Chuck Eddy, *Accidental Evolution*, 1–2.

15 Nile Rodgers, *Le Freak*, 109.

Notes to Part III

The Bug vs. the Fug

1 Rob Sheffield, *Dreaming the Beatles*, 222.

2 Michael André Bernstein, *Bitter Carnival*, 171; Nicholas Bromell, *Tomorrow Never Knows*, 124.

3 Devin McKinney, *Magic Circles*, 320.
4 George Bishop, *Witness to Evil*, 52.
5 Jean Murley, *Rise of True Crime*, 66–67.
6 Ibid., 63, 91, 95.
7 John Harrison, *Hip Pocket Sleaze*, 256.
8 Jean Murley, "Documenting Murder," 208.
9 Jean Murley, *Rise of True Crime*, 64.
10 Mark Seltzer, *True Crime*, 2.
11 Jean Murley, "Documenting Murder," 191.
12 Jean Murley, *Rise of True Crime*, 62–63.
13 Ibid., 63.
14 Michael Hannon, "Judge Revokes Manson's Right."
15 Found here: www.murdersofaugust69.freeforums.net/thread/666/kasabian-testimony-july-1970-session.
16 Ibid.
17 Ibid.
18 Vincent Bugliosi with Curt Gentry, *Helter Skelter*, 423.
19 www.murdersofaugust69.freeforums.net/thread/665/gregg-jakobson-trial-testimony and www.murdersofaugust69.freeforums.net/thread/669/kasabian-testimony-july-1970-session.
20 Cite in David Schmid, "Capote's Children," 219.
21 From 1981 parole hearing as reported in Vincent Bugliosi, *Helter Skelter*, 647.
22 Ed Sanders, *The Family* (2002), 150; Michael Hannon, "MANSON INTERVIEW!"
23 For Brussell's arguments, see www.maebrussell.com/Transcriptions/16.html.
24 *Rolling Stone* gave Stovitz a pseudonym taken from Doestoevsky's *Crime and Punishment*, but his identity did not stay secret for long. He was removed from the case soon after speaking to *Rolling Stone*.
25 These appeared on front page of Madison *Times* on December 4, 1969.
26 Lawrence Lipton, "An Open Letter to Piers Anderton."
27 Vincent Bugliosi, *Helter Skelter*, 261–262.
28 www.rollingstone.com/culture/news/charles-manson-the-incredible-story-of-the-most-dangerous-man-alive-19700625.
29 The *Los Angeles Times* story can be found here: www.cielodrive.com/archive/susan-atkins-story-of-2-nights-of-murder/.
30 Ibid.
31 Lawrence Schiller, et al., *The Killing of Sharon Tate*, 14.
32 Ibid., 14.

33 Ibid., 41.

34 Ibid., 72.

35 Ibid., 72–73,

36 Ibid., 114.

37 George Bishop, *Witness to Evil*, 232, 236.

38 Ibid., 44.

39 Ibid., 346.

40 Ibid., 122.

41 "Ivy League Hillbilly" is from the the *Sandusky Register*, December 4, 1970: 6.

42 George Bishop, *Witness to Evil*, 46–47, 139.

43 Ibid., 406.

44 Ibid., 351.

45 Vincent Bugliosi, *Helter Skelter*, 262.

46 Justin Gifford, "Harvard in Hell," 111–112.

47 Ivor Davis and Jerry LeBlanc, *5 to Die*, 16.

48 Ibid.

49 Ibid., 19–20.

50 Ibid., 223.

51 David Schmid, *Natural Born Killers*, 226.

52 Ivor Davis and Jerry LeBlanc, *5 to Die*, 143.

53 J. D. Russell, *The Beautiful People*, 94.

54 Ibid., 111.

55 Leslie Fiedler, *Love and Death*, 244.

56 Ivor Davis and Jerry LeBlanc, *5 to Die*, 212.

57 Ibid., 49.

58 Ibid., 54–55, 121.

59 Dunbar Van Ness, "Changing Focus on Manson"; John Lennon is quoted in Tommy Udo, *Music Mayhem*, 155; Karpis is in an article from *Winnipeg Free Press* from December 15, 1969: 4 ("Ex-Convict Terms Manson Product of Prison System").

60 Ivor Davis and Jerry LeBlanc, *5 to Die*, 146.

61 Ibid., 147.

62 Steven V. Roberts, "The Hippie Mystique."

63 Paul O'Neill, "The Wreck of a Monstrous Family" (part of *Life Magazine*'s December 1969 coverage): 24.

64 David Smith and Alan Rose, "The Group Marriage Commune."

65 "A Doctor and a Parole Office Remember Manson" (Sidebar to *Life Magazine*'s December 1969 coverage): 26.

66 Susan Faludi, *The Terror Dream*.

67 Vincent Bugliosi, *Helter Skelter*, 297; Mark Kermode, "We're Still Mad about Manson."

A Legion of Charlies

1   Rachel Rubin, *Well Met*, 41–45.
2   Lawrence Lipton, "An Open Letter to Piers Anderton."
3   Marvin Garson's letters can be found in the *Free Press* on January 9, 1970: 26, and January 16, 1970: 9.
4   Lawrence Lipton, "Radio Free America," in the *Free Press* on February 6, 1970: 3.
5   *Free Press* on January 23, 1970: 12.
6   Michael Hannon, "MANSON INTERVIEW!"; Jerry Rubin, *We Are Everywhere* 238.
7   Michael Hannon, "MANSON INTERVIEW!"
8   Michael Hannon, "Manson's Life: Jail Shadows."
9   "Cheap Head Prose" from *Kirkus Reviews*, November 11 1974.
10 www.rollingstone.com/culture/news/charles-manson-the-incredible-story-of-the-most-dangerous-man-alive-19700625.
11 *Free Press*, May 1–7, 1970: 1–2.
12 See here for Ed Sanders's *Investigative Poetry*: www.woodstock-journal.com/pdf/InvestigativePoetry.pdf.
13 *Free Press*, May 1–7, 1970: 2.
14 David Kamp, "Live at the Whisky."
15 *Free Press*, May 1–7, 1970: 2
16 Keith Clarke and Jeffrey Hemphill, "The Santa Barbara Oil Spill," www.www2.bren.ucsb.edu/~dhardy/1969_Santa_Barbara_Oil_Spill/Essays.html.
17 *Free Press*, March 13–19, 1970: 2.
18 Ibid., See also Michael Hannon "Judge Revokes Manson's Right to Defend Himself."
19 *Free Press*, November 6, 1970: 3.
20 Hector Tobar, "Finally, Transparency in the Ruben Salazar Case," *Los Angeles Times*, August 5, 2011.
21 Robert Christgau, "Lumpenhippies and Their Guru."
22 *Free Press*, August 14–20, 1970: 1, 4.
23 *Free Press*, January 8 1971: 4.
24 In *Charles Manson: The Man Who Killed the Sixties.*
25 Stew Albert found (from *Good Times,* April 2, 1971) found here: www.mansonblog.com/2013/08/charles-manson-and-lt-calley.html.
26 Allen Katzman, "Poor Paranoid's Almanac," *East Village Other*, August 27, 1969: 5.
27 From "Burning is the End," 72 found at UCLA in Box 1 of John Gilmore papers.
28 www.luckyfrogfarms.com/cook/NL/1970%27s/1971/1971_08.pdf.

29 www.comixjoint.com/legionofcharlies-1st.html.

30 Esther Sundell Lichti, "Richard Schechner and the Performance Group" 26–28.

31 Theodore Shank, *Beyond the Boundaries*, 98–99.

32 Esther Sundell Lichti, "Richard Schechner and the Performance Group," 151; Theodore Shank, *Beyond the Boundaries*, 100.

33 In Theo Wilson, *Headline Justice*, 192.

Hippie Ugly! Hippie Shit! Toothpaste Good!

1 *Free Press*, June 1 1970: 1–2.

2 *Free Press*, August 7, 1970: 1.

3 Joan Didion, *The White Album*, 44–45.

4 Ibid., 45.

5 www.rollingstone.com/culture/news/charles-manson-the-incredible-story-of-the-most-dangerous-man-alive-19700625.

6 Paul Watkins with Guillermo Soledad, *My Life*, 55.

7 Ibid.,

8 Ed Sanders, *The Family* (2002), 323.

9 Thomas Myers, "Rerunning the Creepy Crawl," 84.

10 Ed Sanders, *The Family* (1971), 11.

11 Robert Christgau, "Lumpenhippies and Their Guru."

12 Ed Sanders, *The Family* (2002), xi.

13 Thomas Myers, "Rerunning the Creepy Crawl," 85.

14 *Free Press*, August 28, 1970: 6; Ed Sanders, *The Family*, 105.

15 Ed Sanders, *The Family* (1971), 412.

16 Ed Sanders, *The Family* (2002), 420.

17 Ed Sanders, *The Family* (1971), 8.

18 Thomas Myers, "Rerunning the Creepy Crawl," 86.

19 Robert Christgau, "Lumpenhippies and Their Guru."

20 Peter Gilstrap, "On Top of the Underbelly," found here www.articles.latimes.com/2006/sep/17/magazine/tm-gilmore38.

21 Ed Sanders, *The Family* (2002), 88.

22 Clifford Geertz, *The Interpretation of Cultures*.

23 Ed Sanders, *The Family* (2002), 63, 201, 288.

24 www.rollingstone.com/culture/news/charles-manson-the-incredible-story-of-the-most-dangerous-man-alive-19700625.

25 Ibid.

26 Ibid.

27 *Free Press*, October 23, 1970: 12.

28 Ed Sanders *The Family* (2002), 30.

29 *Free Press*, November 6, 1970: 3.

30 Vincent Bugliosi, *Helter Skelter*, 526.
31 Tommy Udo, *Music Mayhem Murder*, 153.

A Newcomer, an Intruder

1 John Gilmore with Ron Kenner, *Garbage People*, i–ii.
2 Jean Murley *Rise of True Crime*, 93–94.
3 Ibid., 93.
4 Michael Rogers, "Manson Meets the Bug."
5 Ibid.
6 This all circulated in 1974. Some *Los Angeles Times* coverage can be found here: www.mansondirect.com/thebug.html, and here: www.dailymail.co.uk/news/article-3130075/Charles-Manson-prosecutor-secret-love-child-lover-23-years.html.
7 Vincent Bugliosi, *Helter Skelter*, 259.
8 Rob Sheffield, *Dreaming the Beatles*, 203.
9 Ibid., 203–204.
10 Bobby Beausoleil, personal communication.
11 David Schmid, "Capote's Children" 218–219.
12 Vincent Bugliosi, *Helter Skelter*, 165.
13 Christopher Lehmann-Haupt, "Prosecuting the Manson Case."
14 Jean Murley, *The Rise of True Crime*, 65–66.
15 Christopher Lehmann-Haupt, Prosecuting the Manson Case."
16 Ed Sanders, *The Family* (2002), 367.
17 Jerry Rubin, *We Are Everywhere*, 135.
18 From "Burning Is the End," 72, found in Box 1 of John Gilmore papers.

Not Just the Facts, Ma'am

1 David Schmid, *Natural Born Killers*, 193.
2 Vincent Bugliosi, *Helter Skelter*, 80.
3 From "Burning Is the End," 45–46, in Box 1 of John Gilmore papers.
4 Vincent Bugliosi, *Helter Skelter*, 79.
5 www.sirshambling.com/artists_2012/L/lotsa_poppa/index.php; In personal communication, Bobby Beausoleil has also made the case to me that the shooting of Bernard Crowe was a major engine of all the violence that the Manson Family engaged in for the rest of 1969.
6 Vincent Bugliosi, *Helter Skelter*, 54.
7 Ibid.
8 Ibid., 188–189.

9 Deana Martin, *Memories Are Made of This*, 163.
10 Steve Oney, "Manson: An Oral History," at www.lamag.com/long-form/manson-an-oral-history1/5/.
11 Jeffrey Sconce, "XXX: Love and Kisses," 214.
12 Grady Turner, "Raymond Pettibon" at www.bombmagazine.org/article/2257/raymond-pettibon.
13 Paul Watkins, *My Life*, 36.
14 Karlene Faith, *Long Prison Journey*, 9.
15 Elaine Woo, "Historian Curt Gentry."
16 Howard Becker, *Outsiders*, 9; Kai Erickson, *Wayward Puritans*; Jeffrey Melnick, *Black-Jewish Relations on Trial*, 48–50.
17 Vincent Bugliosi, *Helter Skelter*, 118, 159, 184–185, 331.
18 George Bishop, *Witness to Evil*, 57.
19 Nancy MacLean, "Leo Frank Case Reconsidered," 919.
20 Jim Knipfel, "Manson on Film."
21 Theo Wilson, *Headline Justice*, 182.
22 Steve Oney, "Manson: An Oral History" at www.lamag.com/longform/manson-an-oral-history1/5/.
23 Theo Wilson, *Headline Justice*, 182.
24 Jim Knipfel, *Manson on Film*.
25 Vincent Bugliosi, *Helter Skelter*, 101.
26 Ibid., 91.
27 Dana Parsons, "Barred from World He Loved."
28 Rory Carroll and Simon Hattenstone, "Defending the Indefensible."
29 In Vincent Bugliosi, *Helter Skelter*, 509–510.
30 Jerry Lembcke, *The Spitting Image*.
31 Michael Hannon, "Judge Revokes Manson's Right."

Notes to Part IV

Blood in a Swimming Pool

1 Editors of Phaidon, *PressPLAY*, 496.
2 Kliph Nesteroff, "The Mel Lyman Personality Cult Revisited."
3 Zachary Lazar, *Sway*, front matter.
4 www.artofthestate.co.uk/Banksy/banksy_anywhere.htm.
5 The Columbus, Ohio–based band DarkDixie also released a record in 1995 titled *The Manson-Nixon Line*.
6 See, for instance, here: www.digitalspy.com/tv/american-horror-story/news/a807911/is-charles-manson-a-character-in-american-horror-story-season-6/.

7 See Gerald Carlin and Mark Jones, "'Helter Skelter' and Sixties Revisionism" and their stunning website (www.helterskeltercovers.wordpress.com/) for a good overview.

8 See, for instance, Clara Livesey, *The Manson Women*, 32.

9 Gerald Carlin and Mark Jones, "'Helter Skelter' and Sixties Revisionism."

10 Ibid.

11 Vincent Bugliosi with Curt Gentry, *Helter Skelter*, 525.

12 June Thomas, "NBC's New Drama."

13 Ibid.

14 Adam Bryant, "Why David Duchovny."

15 Ibid.

16 Ibid.

17 Eric Avila, *Popular Culture in the Age of White Flight*, 234.

18 Ibid., 7.

19 Thomas Pynchon, *Inherent Vice*, 304.

20 Dana Spiotta, *Lightning Field*, 208.

21 Thomas Pynchon, *Inherent Vice*, 208.

They Are Still among Us

1 For more see my chapter on shout-outs in *9/11 Culture*.

2 Andrew Gross, *Eyes Wide Open*, 133.

3 Madison Smartt Bell, *Color of Night*, 62.

4 www.jungleredwriters.com/2011/07/eyes-wide-open.html.

5 Andrew Gross, *Eyes Wide Open*, 190.

6 John Harrison, "The Hip Pocket Sleaze Files."

7 Ibid.

8 Michael Perry, *Skelter*, 401–402.

9 Lary May, "Redeeming the Lost War," 23–24. What follows draws heavily from May, especially pages 35–40.

10 Bell's claims are here: www.huffingtonpost.com/madison-smartt-bell/american-terror_b_842036.html, and Lindgren's review is here: www.washingtonpost.com/entertainment/books/book-review-the-color-of-night-by-madison-smartt-bell/2011/04/11/AFWp715G_story.html.

11 John Kaye, *The Dead Circus*, epigraph.

12 Ibid., 124, 187, 218, 257.

13 Ibid., 91.

14 Ibid., 170.

15 Ibid., 170–171.

16 Ibid., 60, 171.

17 Ibid., 98.
18 Tony O'Neill, *Sick City*, 144–145, 147.
19 John Kaye, *The Dead Circus*, 270–271.
20 Ibid., 271.
21 Ibid., 290.
22 Amanda Petrusich, *Do Not Sell at Any Price*, 5.

He's a Magic Man

1 Karen Halttunen, *Murder Most Foul*, 5, 146.
2 Simon Wells, *Charles Manson*, 410.
3 Tom Brinkman, *Bad Mags 2*, 395.
4 Ibid., 443, 385.
5 Allan Kozinn, "Will the Manson Story Play as Myth."
6 Tommy Udo, *Music Mayhem Murder*, 178.
7 Jon Towlson, *Subversive Horror Cinema*, 131–132.
8 David Ray Carter, "It's Only a Movie?" 299.
9 John Cline and Robert Weiner, "Arch Hall," 199.
10 Jeffrey Sconce, "XXX: Love and Kisses," 207, 209, 213, 219.
11 Ibid., 223–31.

Waves of Mutilation

1 Sanders quoted in Manson quoted Steven Blush and George Petros, *.45 Dangerous Minds* 290-291; Bugliosi quoted in "Charles Manson: A Portrait in Terror" on KABC (in UCLA Film and Television Archive.)
2 See especially Mike Rubin's great account in "Summer of '69."
3 Ed Sanders in the *Los Angeles Free Press*, May 1–7, 1970: 1.
4 Mark Goodall, "Arise" 10–11, 17–18, 22.
5 Lewis Parker, personal communication.
6 Zachary Lazar, *Sway* 14.
7 Ibid., 9.
8 Ibid., 209.
9 Kory Grow, "Redd Kross"; Roger Ebert, "Beyond"; Mike Rubin, "Summer of '69"
10 Tommy Udo, *Music Mayhem Murder*, 43; Mike Rubin "Summer of '69."
11 Frank Black insights at www.genius.com/2247041.
12 Thomas Crow, *The Long March*, 366.
13 Mark Jones and Gerry Carlin, "Unfound Footage and Unfounded Rumors," 183.
14 Thomas Crow, *The Long March*, 366.

15 Ibid.

16 Ibid.; also Mark Goodall, "The 'Book of Manson.'"

17 Barney Hoskyns, *Waiting for the Sun*, 309.

18 Dewar MacLeod, *Kids of the Black Hole*, 127.

19 Tim Tonooka, Black Flag interview in *Ripper* 6 (1981). www.dementlieu.com/users/obik/arc/blackflag/int_ripper6.html.

20 "Is There Any Escape from Stupid?"

21 Cory Frye, "Negativland's 'Helter Stupid.'"

22 Robert Barry, "Key Tracks."

23 Kembrew McLeod, *Pranksters*, 208–209.

24 Kim Gordon, *Girl in a Band*, 57, 141.

25 Alec Foege, *Confusion Is Next*, 122–123.

26 Greil Marcus, *In the Fascist Bathroom*, 134.

27 Robert Barry, "Key Tracks."

28 Aram Sinnreich, *Mashed Up*.

29 Robert Barry, "Key Tracks."

30 Ibid.

31 Cory Frye, "Negativland's 'Helter Stupid.'"

32 Robert Barry, "Key Tracks."

33 "Is There Any Escape from Stupid?"

34 Ibid.

35 Kristine McKenna, "Eno." www.music.hyperreal.org/artists/brian_eno/interviews/musn82.htm.

36 On Christopher Wool, see Peter Schjeldahl, "Writing on the Wall: A Christopher Wool Retrospective," *New Yorker*, November 4, 2013; see also www.sothebys.com/en/auctions/ecatalogue/lot.5.html/2006/contemporary-art-evening-sale-n08201; and Ken Johnson, "Art in Review," *New York Times*, March 17, 2000.

Desperados under the Eaves

1 Michael Denning, *Mechanic Accents*.

2 JR Robinson, personal communication.

3 JR Robinson, "Beau Soleil."

4 Bud Scoppa review in *Rolling Stone*, June 6, 1974: 70.

5 George Lipsitz, *Midnight at the Barrelhouse*, 68.

6 Joel Selvin, *Sly and the Family Stone*, 125.

7 For background here see A. E. Hotchner, *Doris Day*; Joel Selvin, *Sly and the Family Stone*; and Karina Longworth's podcast, *Charles Manson's Hollywood*, episode 48.

8 Sean Nelson, *Court and Spark*, 42.

9 Greil Marcus, *Stranded*, 293.

Zeroville

1 Jimmy McDonough, *Shakey*, 441.
2 Daniel Durchholz and Gary Graff, *Long May You Run*, 81.
3 Jimmy McDonough, *Shakey*, 441.
4 Stephen Holden's review can be found here: www.thrasherswheat. org/tnfy/on_the_beach_rolling_stone_092674.htm.
5 Song counts found at www.sugarmtn.org/.
6 On Manson dedication, see www.thrasherswheat.org/fot/otb.htm.
7 See James Reich's work at www.jamesreichbooks.com/on-the-beach/.
8 Karal Ann Marling, *As Seen on TV*, 141–142; Phil Patton, "Tailfins."
9 Karal Ann Marling, *As Seen on TV*, 154.
10 Phil Patton, "Punctuation."
11 Karal Ann Marling, *As Seen on TV*, 131.
12 Bernard Gendron, "Theodor Adorno Meets the Cadillacs."
13 Karal Ann Marling, *As Seen on TV*, 133.
14 Phil Patton, "Punctuation."
15 Jimmy McDonough, *Shakey*, 104.
16 Charles Derry, *Dark Dreams*, 98.
17 Bryan Reynolds, *Performing Transversally*, 114.
18 Ibid.
19 Kael in Bryan Reynolds, *Performing Transversally*, 117; Vincent Brook, *Land of Smoke and Mirrors*, 142.
20 Christopher Sandford, *Polanski*, 200.
21 Mike Davis, *City of Quartz*, 114.
22 Steven Erie, *Beyond Chinatown*, 31.
23 Vincent Brook, *Land of Smoke and Mirrors*, 143.
24 Foster Hirsch, *Detours and Lost Highways*, 153.
25 Mike Davis, *Ecology of Fear*, 276.
26 Peter Biskind, *Star*, 217.
27 Ibid.
28 In episode 50 of Karina Longworth's podcast, *Charles Manson's Hollywood*.
29 Peter Biskind, *Star*, 196.
30 Episode 50 of Karina Longworth's *Charles Manson's Hollywood*.
31 In Peter Biskind, *Star*, 217.

Wrecking Crews

1 David Herrle, *Sharon Tate*, 183.
2 Christopher Sorrentino, "Zachary Lazar."

3 Ibid.

4 John Waters, *Role Models*, 50.

5 John Waters, *Shock Value*, 62.

6 Ibid.

7 Ibid.

8 Greil Marcus, *The Doors*, 42; John Waters, *Role Models*, 46.

9 John Waters, *Role Models*, 45.

10 Ibid., 54.

11 John Waters, *Shock Value*, 116–117.

12 Ibid., 119.

13 Ibid., 116.

14 John Waters, *Crackpot*, 47.

15 Dan Dietz, *Off Broadway Musicals*, 468.

16 On Cady Noland, see www.deh allen.nl/en/exhibitions/cady-noland-english/.

17 www.nicolaiwallner.com/texts.php?action=details&id=95.

18 Michael Langkjaer, "Déjà vu Desperados."

19 For Rosenbaum's elaboration of Kael's term see www.chicagoreader.com/chicago/acid-western/Content?oid=890861.

Works Consulted

Adams, Rachel. *Sideshow USA: Freaks and the American Cultural Imagination*. Chicago: University of Chicago Press, 2001.

Aes-Nihil, John, et al. *The Manson File*. 1988. Port Townsend, WA: Feral House, 2011.

Ambrosino, Lillian. *Runaways*. Boston: Beacon, 1971.

Anonymous [Beatrice Sparks]. *Go Ask Alice*. 1971. New York: Simon Pulse, 2006.

Anson, Robert Sam. "The Last Porno Show," in Leroy Schultz, *The Sexual Victimology of Youth*. Springfield, IL: Charles C. Thomas, 1980.

Atkins, Susan, with Bob Slosser. *Child of Satan, Child of God: Her Own Story*. San Juan Capistrano, CA: Menolorelin Dorenay, 1977.

Avila, Eric. *Popular Culture in Age of White Flight*. Berkeley: University of California Press, 2004.

Bardach, A. L. "Jailhouse Interview: Bobby Beausoleil and the Manson Murders," *Oui*. November, 1981.

Barker, Hugh and Yuval Taylor. *Faking It: The Quest for Authenticity in Popular Music*. New York: W. W. Norton, 2007.

Barry, Robert. "Key Tracks: Negativland's 'Helter Stupid.'" www.daily. redbullmusicacademy.com

Becker, Howard. *Outsiders: Studies in the Sociology of Deviance*. New York: Free Press, 1997.

Bell, Madison Smartt. *Color of Night*. New York: Vintage, 2011.

Bernstein, Michael André. *Bitter Carnival: Ressentiment and the Abject Hero*. Princeton, NJ: Princeton University Press, 1992.

Bishop, George. *Witness to Evil: The Inside Story of the Tate/La Bianca Murder Trial*. Los Angeles: Nash, 1971.

Biskind, Peter. *Easy Riders, Raging Bulls: How the Sex-Drugs-And-Rock 'N' Roll Generation Saved Hollywood*. New York: Simon & Schuster, 1998.

Biskind, Peter. *Star: How Warren Beatty Seduced America*. New York: Simon & Schuster, 2010.

Blum, Jeffrey, and Judith Smith. *Nothing Left to Lose: Studies of Street People*. Boston: Beacon, 1972.

Blush, Steven, and George Petros. *.45 Dangerous Minds: The Most Intense Interviews from Seconds Magazine*. New York: Creation, 2005.

Bravin, Jess. *Squeaky: The Life and Times of Lynette Alice Fromme*. New York: St. Martin's, 1997.

Brightman, Carole. *Sweet Chaos: The Grateful Dead's American Journey*. New York: Pocket, 1999.

Brinkman, Tom. *Bad Mags 2: The Strangest, Sleaziest, and Most Unusual Periodicals Ever Published!* London: Headpress, 2009.

Bromell, Nicholas. *Tomorrow Never Knows: Rock and Psychedelics in the 1960s*. Chicago: University of Chicago Press, 2000.

Brook, Vincent. *Land of Smoke and Mirrors: A Cultural History of Los Angeles*. New Brunswick, NJ: Rutgers University Press, 2013.

Bronson, Fred. *The Billboard Book of Number 1 Hits*. New York: Billboard, 1993.

Bryant, Adam. "Why David Duchovny Steals Charles Manson's Spotlight in NBC's *Aquarius*," *TV Guide*, May 28, 2015.

Bugliosi, Vincent, with Curt Gentry. 1974. *Helter Skelter: The True Story of the Manson Murders*. New York: W. W. Norton, 2001.

Burnes, Brian. "Quiet Survivors from the 1960s: The Lyman Family Sets Own Course on a Kansas Farm," *Kansas City Star*, March 27, 1986: 1B. www.trussel.com/lyman/quiet.htm.

Calhoun, Ada. *St. Marks Is Dead: The Many Lives of America's Hippest Street*. New York: W. W. Norton, 2015.

Capote, Truman. "Then It All Came Down," *Music for Chameleons*. New York: Random House, 1980. Found at www.capote.wordpress.com/.

Carlin, Gerald, and Mark Jones. "'Helter Skelter' and Sixties Revisionism," *Volume!: Les revues des musique populaires*, Volume 9.2: 2012. Found at www.volume.revues.org/.

Carroll, Rory, and Simon Hattenstone. "Defending the Indefensible: Lawyers on Representing Clients Accused of Nightmarish Crimes," *The Guardian*, June 27, 2014.

Carter, David Ray. "It's Only a Movie? Reality as Transgression in Exploitation Cinema," *From the Arthouse to the Grindhouse: Highbrow and Lowbrow Transgression in Cinema's First Century*, ed. John Cline and Robert Weiner. Toronto: Scarecrow, 2010, 297–315.

Chandler, Barbara. "The White House Conference on Children," *The Family Coordinator* 20.3 (July 1971): 195–207.

Cherkis, Jason. "The Lost Girls," *Huffington Post*. July 9, 2015.

Christgau, Robert. "Lumpenhippies and Their Guru," *New York Times*, October 31, 1971.

Churchwell, Sarah. *The Many Lives of Marilyn Monroe*. New York: Picador, 2004.

Clark, Keith, and Jeffrey Hemphill. "The Santa Barbara Oil Spill: A Restrospective," *Proceedings of the 64th Annual Meeting of the Association of Pacific Coast Geographers*.

Cline, Emma. *The Girls*. New York: Random House, 2016.

———. "See Me," *Paris Review*, March 27, 2014.

Cline, John, and Robert Weiner. "Arch Hall Jr., *The Sadist*, and the Ideal Teenager," In *From the Arthouse to the Grindhouse: Highbrow and Lowbrow Transgression in Cinema's First Century*, ed. John Cline and Robert Weiner. Toronto: Scarecrow, 2010, 188–201.

Clover, Carol. *Men, Women, and Chainsaws: Gender in the Modern Horror Film*. Princeton, NJ: Princeton University Press, 1992.

Coontz, Stephanie. *The Way We Never Were: American Families and the Nostalgia Trap*. 1992. New York: Basic, 2000.

Courier, Kevin. *Captain Beefheart's Trout Mask Replica*. New York: Bloomsbury, 2007.

Crary, Jonathan. *24/7: Late Capitalism and the Ends of Sleep*. New York: Verso, 2013.

Crow, Thomas. *The Long March of Pop: Art, Music, and Design, 1930–1995*. New Haven, Conn.: Yale University Press, 2014.

Davis, Ivor, and Jeffrey LeBlanc. *5 to Die*. Los Angeles: Holloway House, 1970.

Davis, Mike. *City of Quartz: Excavating the Future of Los Angeles*. New York: Verso, 1990.

———. *Ecology of Fear: Los Angeles and the Imagination of Disaster*. New York: Metropolitan, 1998.

Davis, Susan. "White Revolutionaries Settle in Roxbury," *Bay State Banner*, February 15, 1967.

DeCurtis Anthony. "Peace Love and Charlie Manson," *New York Times*, August 1, 2009.

Denning Michael. *Mechanic Accents: Dime Novels and Working-Class Culture in America*. New York: Verso, 1987.

Derry, Charles. *Dark Dreams 2.0: A Psychological History of the Modern Horror Film from the 1950s to the 21st Century*. Jefferson, NC: McFarland, 2009.

Didion, Joan. *The White Album.* New York: Simon & Schuster, 1979.

Dietz, Dan. *Off Broadway Musicals, 1910–2007.* Jefferson, NC: McFarland, 2010.

"A Doctor and a Parole Officer Remember Manson," *Life* Magazine, December 19, 1969: 26.

"Double Life of Corll Begins to Unravel," *Lakeland Ledger*, August 19, 1973.

Durchholz, Daniel, and Gary Graff. *Neil Young: Long May You Run— The Illustrated History.* Minneapolis: Voyageur, 2010.

Ebert, Roger, "Beyond the Valley of the Dolls." www.rogerebert .com/ reviews/beyond-the-valley-of-the-dolls-1980.

Echols, Alice. *Shaky Ground: The 60s and Its Aftershocks.* New York: Columbia University Press, 2002.

Eddy, Chuck. *The Accidental Evolution of Rock 'n' Roll: A Misguided Tour through Popular Music.* Cambridge, MA: Da Capo, 1997.

Editors of Phaidon. *PressPLAY: Contemporary Artists in Conversation.* London: Phaidon, 2005.

Erickson, Kai. 1966. *Wayward Puritans: A Study in the Sociology of Deviance.* Boston: Allyn & Bacon, 2004.

Erie, Steven. *Beyond Chinatown: The Metropolitan Water District, Growth, and the Environment in Southern California.* Palo Alto, CA: Stanford University Press, 2006.

Fairfield, Richard. *Communes USA: A Personal Tour.* Baltimore: Penguin, 1972.

Faith, Karlene. *Unruly Women: The Politics of Confinement and Resistance.* Vancouver: Press Gang, 1993.

———. *The Long Prison Journey of Leslie Van Houten: Life Beyond the Cult.* Boston: Northeastern University Press, 2001.

Faithfull, Marianne, with David Dalton. *Faithfull: An Autobiography.* New York: Little, Brown, 1994.

Faludi, Susan. *The Terror Dream: Fear and Fantasy in Post-9/11 America.* New York: Metropolitan, 2007.

Felton, David. "The Lyman Family's Holy Siege of America," *Rolling Stone*, December 23, 1971.

Felton, David, and David Dalton. "Charles Manson: The Incredible Story of the Most Dangerous Man Alive," *Rolling Stone*, June 25, 1970.

Felton, David, Robin Green, and David Dalton. *Mindfuckers: A Source Book on the Rise of Acid Fascism in America Including Material on Charles Manson, Mel Lyman, Victor Baranco, and Their Followers.* San Francisco: Straight Arrow, 1972.

Fiedler, Leslie. *Love and Death in the American Novel*. 1960. Champaign, IL: Dalkey Archive, 1998.

Fisher, Bob. "Easy Rider: 35 Years Later," *MovieMaker*. June 22, 2004.

Foege, Alex. *Confusion is Next: The Sonic Youth Story*. New York: St. Martin's, 1994.

Fong-Torres, Ben. "FCC Discovers Dope, Does Darndest Thing," *Rolling Stone*, April 1, 1971.

Frank, Thomas. *The Conquest of Cool: Business Culture, Counterculture, and the Rise of Hip Consumerism*. Chicago: University of Chicago Press, 1998.

Friedan, Betty. *The Feminine Mystique*. 1963. New York: Norton, 2001.

Frye Cory. "Negativland's 'Helter Stupid' 20 Years Later." www.archive. li/000Z7.

Gaines, Steven. *Heroes and Villians: The True Story of the Beach Boys*. New York: New American Library, 1986.

Geertz, Clifford. "Thick Description: Toward an Interpretive Theory of Culture," *The Interpretation of Cultures: Selected Essays*. New York: Basic Books, 1973. 3–30.

Gelb, Arthur. *City Room*. New York: Putnam, 2003.

"Getting Cute with Charlie Manson," *Rolling Stone*, May 14, 1970, 10.

Gendron, Bernard. "Theodor Adorno Meets the Cadillacs," *Studies in Entertainment: Critical Approaches to Mass Culture*, ed. Tania Modleski. Bloomington: Indiana University Press, 1986. 18–36.

Gifford, Justin. "'Harvard in Hell': Holloway House Publishing Company, *Players Magazine*, and the Invention of Black Mass-Market Erotica," *MELUS* 35.4 (2010): 111–137.

Gilmore, John, with Ron Kenner. *The Garbage People: The Trip to Helter-Skelter and Beyond with Charlie Manson and Family*. 1971. Los Angeles: Amok, 1995.

Gilstrap, Peter. "On Top of the Underbelly," *Los Angeles Times*, September 17, 2006.

Goldstein, Richard. "Love: A Groovy Idea While He Lasted," *Village Voice*, October 19, 1967.

Goldstein, Dawn Eden. "The Mike Deasy Story," *The Dawn Patrol*.

Goodall, Mark. "Arise: The Music of Charles Manson," *Headpress*, July 2010.

———. "'The Book of Manson': Raymond Pettibon and the Killing of America," *Journal of Graphic Novels and Comics* 3.2 (2012): 159–170.

Grogan, Christine. *Father-Daughter Incest in Twentieth-Century American Literature: The Complex Trauma of the Wound and the Voiceless*. Madison, NJ: Fairleigh Dickinson University Press, 2016.

Gross, Andrew. *Eyes Wide Open*. New York, William Morrow, 2011.

Grow, Kory. "Redd Kross on the Pop Culture Obsessions That Shaped Them," August 17, 2012. www.mtv.com/.

Guinn, Jeff. *Manson: The Life and Times of Charles Manson*. New York: Simon & Schuster, 2013.

Gurwell, John. *Mass Murder in Houston*. Houston: Cordovan Press, 1974.

Halttunen, Karen. *Murder Most Foul: The Killer and the American Gothic Imagination*. Cambridge, MA: Harvard University Press, 1998.

Hampton, Howard. "Impressions of an Existential Stuntman: Looking Back at Dennis Hopper," *Film* Comment 49.3 (2013): 36–41.

Hannon, Andrew. "Acting Out: Performative Politics in the Age of the New Left and the Counterculture." (PhD diss., Yale University, 2016).

Hannon, Michael. "Judge Revokes Manson's Right to Defend Himself," *Los Angeles Free Press*, March 13–19, 1970:

————. "Manson Interview!" *Los Angeles Free Press*, January 30–February 4: 1.

————. "Manson's Life: Jail Shadows," *Los Angeles Free Press*, February 13, 1970: 4.

Harvey, Doug. "Father Yod Knows Best," *LA Weekly*, August 29, 2007.

Harrison, Barbara Grizzuti. "Only Disconnect" in *Off Center: Essays*. New York: Dial, 1980.

Haupt, Christopher Lehmann. "Prosecuting the Manson Case," *New York Times*, November 8, 1974.

Harrison, John. *Hip Pocket Sleaze: The Lurid World of Vintage Adult Paperbacks*. London: Headpress, 2013.

Herrle, David. *Sharon Tate and the Daughters of Joy*. St. Louis: Time Being, 2013.

Herst, Ellen. "Mel & Charlie's Women: The Souring of Street Life," *Boston After Dark*, February 15–21, 1972: 1, 12, 13.

Herrera, Brian. "Go Ask Alice—40 Years Later," *Performations*, September 23, 2011.

Hirsch, Foster. *Detours and Lost Highways: A Map of Neo-Noir*. New York: Limelight, 1999.

Hoberman, J. "Off the Hippies: 'Joe' and the Chaotic Summer of '70," *New York Times*, July 30, 2000.

Hoffman, Abbie. *Revolution for the Hell of It*. 1968. New York: Thunder's Mouth, 2005.

Hollandsworth, Skip. "The Lost Boys," *Texas Monthly*, April 2011.

Hoskyns, Barney. *Hotel California: The True-Life Adventures of Crosby, Stills, Nash, Young, Mitchell, Taylor, Browne, Ronstadt, Geffen, the Eagles, and Their Many Friends*. Hoboken, NJ: Wiley, 2005.

————. *Waiting for the Sun: Strange Days, Weird Scenes and the Sound of Los Angeles*. New York: St. Martin's, 1996.

————. "The Meeting of the 'Twain: Monterey Pop and the Great California Divide," booklet, *The Criterion Collection* (*The Complete Monterey Pop Festival*).

Hotchner, A. E. *Doris Day: Her Own Story*. New York: William Morrow, 1975.

Houriet, Robert. *Getting Back Together*. 1971. New York: Avon, 1972.

Isis Aquarian with Electricity Aquarian. *The Source: The Untold Story of Father Yod, Ya Ho Wa 13 and the Source Family*. Los Angeles: Process, 2007.

"Is There Any Escape From Stupid," Interview with Don Joyce and Mark Hosler of Negativland from *Mondo 2000*.

James, Bill. *Popular Crime: Reflections on the Celebration of Violence*. New York: Scribner, 2011.

Jones, Ann. *Women Who Kill*. 1980. New York: Feminist Press, 2009.

Jones, Mark, and Gerry Carlin. "Unfound Footage and Unfounded Rumors: The Manson Family Murders and the Persistence of Snuff." In *Snuff: Real Death and Screen Media*. Neil Jackson, Shaun Kimber, Johnny Walker, and Thomas Joseph Watson, ed. New York: Bloomsbury, 2016. 173–187.

Kamp, David. "Live at the Whisky," *Vanity Fair* (November 10, 2000).

Karpis, Alvin, as told to Robert Livesey. *On the Rock: Twenty-Five Years in Alcatraz*. New York: Beaufort, 1980.

Katzman, Allen. "Poor Paranoids," *East Village Other*, August 27, 1969, 5.

Kaye, John. *The Dead Circus*. New York: Grove, 2002.

————. "1972: Five Days in September," *Los Angeles Review of Books*, June 27, 2013.

Kennedy, Kevin. "Manson at 50," *California Magazine*, May 1985.

Kent, Leticia. "High on Life and Deader Than Dead," *Village Voice*, October 12, 1967.

Kent, Nick. *The Dark Stuff: Selected Writings on Rock Music 1972–1993*. Cambridge, MA: Da Capo, 2002.

Kermode, Mark. "We're Still Mad about Manson," *The Guardian*, July 10, 2004.

Killen, Andres. *1973 Nervous Breakdown: Watergate, Warhol, and the Birth of Post-Sixties America*. New York: Bloomsbury, 2006.

King, Greg. *Sharon Tate and the Manson Murders*. New York: Barricade, 2000.

Klemesrud, Judy. "His Happiness Is a Thing Called 'Joe,'" *New York Times*, August 2, 1970.

Knipfel, Jim. "Manson on Film," *The Chiseler*. www.chiseler.org

Kozinn, Alan. "Will the Manson Story Play as Myth, Operatically at That," *New York Times*, July 17, 1990.

Krassner, Paul. *Confessions of a Raving, Unconfined Nut: Misadventures in the Counterculture*. New York: Simon & Schuster, 1993.

Kubernik, Harvey. *Canyon of Dreams: The Magic and Music of Laurel Canyon*. New York: Sterling, 2009.

———. *Hollywood Shack Job: Rock Music in Film and on Your Screen*. Albuquerque: University of New Mexico Press, 2006.

Kutulas, Judy. *After Aquarius Dawned: How the Revolutions of the Sixties Became the Popular Culture of the Seventies*. Chapel Hill: University of North Carolina Press, 2017.

Lachman, Gary. *Turn Off Your Mind: The Mystic Sixties and the Dark Side of the Age of Aquarius*. New York: Disinformation, 2003.

Langkjaer, Michael. "Déjà vu Desperados: Embattled Survivor Imagery of Crosby, Stills, Nash and Young in the Setting of Youth Rebellion America, c. 1967–1973," *Catwalk: The Journal of Fashion, Beauty and Style*, 4.2 (2015): 71–98.

Law, Lisa. *Flashing on the Sixties*. Santa Rosa, CA: Square Books, 2000.

Lazar, Zachary. *Sway*. 2008. New York: Little, Brown, 2009.

Leaf, David. *The Beach Boys and the California Myth*. New York: Grosset and Dunlap, 1978.

Livesey, Clara, M.D. *The Manson Women: A Family Portrait*. New York: Richard Marek, 1980.

Lembcke, Jerry. *The Spitting Image: Myth, Memory, and the Legacy of Vietnam*. New York: New York University Press, 1998.

Lemke-Santangelo, Gretchen. *Daughters of Aquarius: Women of the Sixties Counterculture*. Lawrence: University Press of Kansas, 2009.

Levey, Robert. "Re-inventing Life on a Hilltop in Roxbury," *Boston Globe*, February 1, 1970. www.trussel.com/lyman/levey.htm.

Lichti, Esther Sundell. "Richard Schechner and the Performance Group: A Study of Acting Technique and Methodology." (PhD diss., Texas Tech University, 1996).

Lipsitz, George. *Midnight at the Barrelhouse: The Johnny Otis Story*. 2010. Minneapolis: University of Minnesota Press, 2013.

Lipton, Lawrence. "An Open Letter to Piers Anderton," *Los Angeles Free Press*, December 19, 1969: 3.

Lloyd, Robin. *For Money or Love: Boy Prostitution in America*. New York: Ballantine, 1977.

Longworth, Karina. "Charles Manson's Hollywood," *You Must Remember This*. www.youmustrememberthispodcast.com.

"The Love and Terror Cult," *Life*, December 19, 1969.

Maas, Peter. "The Sharon Tate Murders," *Ladies Home Journal*, April 1970.

MacLean, Nancy. "The Leo Frank Case Reconsidered: Gender and Sexual Politics in the Making of Reactionary Populism," *Journal of American History* 78.3 (December 1991): 917–948.

MacLeod, Dewar. *Kids of the Black Hole: Punk Rock in Postsuburban California*. Norman: University of Oklahoma Press, 2010.

Marcus, Greil. *The Doors: A Lifetime of Listening to Five Mean Years*. New York: Public Affairs, 2011.

———. *Mystery Train: Images of America in Rock 'N' Roll*. 1975. New York: Plume, 2015.

Marcus, Greil, ed. *Stranded: Rock and Roll for a Desert Island*. 1979. Boston: Da Capo, 2007.

Marling, Karal Ann. *As Seen on TV: The Visual Culture of Everyday Life in the 1950s*. Cambridge, MA: Harvard University Press, 1996.

Marsh, Dave. *The Heart of Rock and Soul: The 1001 Greatest Singles Ever Made*. 1989. Cambridge, MA: Da Capo, 1999.

Martin, Deana. *Memories are Made of This: Dean Martin through His Daughter's Eyes*. New York: Three Rivers, 2005.

May, Lary. "Redeeming the Lost War: Backlash Films and the Rise of the Punitive State," *Punishment in Popular Culture*, ed. Charles Ogletree Jr., and Austin Sarat. New York: New York University Press, 2015. 23–54.

McBride, David. "On the Fault Line of Mass Culture and Counterculture: A Social History of the Hippie Counterculture in 1960s Los Angeles," (PhD diss., UCLA, 1998).

———. "Death City Radicals: The Counterculture in Los Angeles," *The New Left Revisited*, ed. John McMillan and Paul Buhle. Philadelphia: Temple University Press, 2003. 110–136.

McDonough, Jimmy. *Shakey: Neil Young's Biography*. New York: Anchor, 2003.

McKinney, Devin. *Magic Circles: The Beatles in Dream and History*. Cambridge, MA: Harvard University Press, 2003.

McLeod, Kembrew. *Pranksters: Making Mischief in the Modern World*. New York: New York University Press, 2014.

Melnick, Jeffrey. *9/11 Culture: American Under Construction*. Malden, MA: Wiley, 2009.

Miller, Timothy. *The Hippies and American Values*. Knoxville: University of Tennessee Press, 1991.

———. *The 60s Communes: Hippies and Beyond*. Syracuse, NY: Syracuse University Press, 1999.

Miles, Barry. *Hippie*. 2003. London: Sterling, 2005.

_____. *Zappa: A Biography*. 2004. New York: Grove/Atlantic, 2005.

Moses, Ann. "The Runaway Youth Act: Paradoxes of Reform," *Social Service Review* 52.2 (June 1978): 227–243.

Murley, Jean. "Documenting Murder before *In Cold Blood*: The 1950s Origins of True Crime," *Violence in American Popular Culture. Volume 2: Representations of Violence in Popular Culture Genre*, ed. David Schmid. Santa Barbara, CA: Praeger, 2016. 191–209.

Murley, Jean. *The Rise of True Crime: 20th-Century Murder and American Popular Culture*. Westport, CT: Praeger, 2008.

Myers, Thomas. "Rerunning the Creepy-Crawl: Ed Sanders and Charles Manson," *Review of Contemporary Fiction 19.1* (Spring 1999): 81–90.

Nelson, Sean. *Court and Spark*. New York: Continuum, 2007.

Nesteroff, Kliph. "The Mel Lyman Personality Cult Revisited," *WFMU Beware of the Blog*, March 27, 2011.

Nielsen, Donald. *Horrible Workers: Max Stirner, Arthur Rimbaud, Robert Johnson, and the Charles Manson Circle*. Lanham, MD: Lexington, 2005.

Nolan, Tom. "Surf's Up! Melcher's Nightmare Is Over," *Rolling Stone*, May 9, 1974.

O'Neill, Paul. "Flattery, Fear and Sex," *Life*, December 19, 1969: 20.

O'Neill, Tony. *Sick City*. New York: Harper Perennial, 2010.

Oney, Steve. "Manson: An Oral History," *Los Angeles* Magazine, July 1, 2009.

Oppenheimer, Mark. "Just Say Uh Oh," *New York Times*, November 15, 1998.

Ostow, Micol. *Family*. New York: Egmont, 2011.

Parsons, Dana. "Barred from World He Loved, Just Getting By Is a Trial," *Los Angeles Times*, October 25, 1998.

Patton, Phil. "Tailfins at Their High Point," *New York Times*, August 1, 2009.

_____. "The Punctuation at the End of the '50s," *New York Times*, July 30, 2009.

Perry, Michael. *Skelter*. New York: Pocket, 1994.

Petrusich, Amanda. *Do Not Sell at Any Price: The Wild, Obsessive Hunt for the World's Rarest 78rpm Records*. 2014. New York: Scribner, 2015.

_____. "'We Support the Music': Reconsidering the Groupie," *New Yorker*, December 29, 2015.

Phillips, John, with Jim Jerome. *Papa John: An Autobiography*. Garden City, NY: Doubleday, 1986.

Powers, Devon. "Long-Haired Freaky People Need to Apply: Rock Music, Cultural Intermediaries, and the Rise of the 'Company Freak," *Journal of Consumer Culture* 12.3 (2012): 3–18.

Pynchon, Thomas. *Inherent Vice*. New York: Penguin, 2009.

Radner, Hillary, and Moya Luckett, eds. *Swinging Single: Representing Sexuality in the 1960s*. Minneapolis: University of Minnesota Press, 1999.

Reich, James. "On the Beach: Dali, Ballard, Neil Young and Cadillac Ranch." www.jamesreichbooks.com/2014/05/21/on-the-beach/.

"Report to the President: White House Conference on Children." Washington, DC, 1970. www.archive.org/stream/whitehouseconfer-00inwhit/whitehouseconfer00inwhit_djvu.txt.

Reynolds, Bryan. *Performing Transversally: Reimagining Shakespeare and the Critical Future*. New York: Palgrave Macmillan, 2003.

Reynolds, Simon, and Joy Press. *Sex Revolts: Gender, Rebellion and Rock 'n' Roll*. Cambridge, MA: Harvard University Press, 1995.

Rhodes, Lisa. *Electric Ladyland: Women and Rock Culture*. Philadelphia: University of Pennsylvania Press, 2005.

Roberts, Steven. "The Hippie Mystique," *New York Times*, December 15, 1969: 1.

Robinson, JR. "Beau Soleil," September 2014. www.futuristika.org/jr-robinson-beau-soleil/.

Rodgers, Nile. *Le Freak: An Upside Down Story of Family, Disco, and Destiny*. New York: Spiegel & Grau, 2011.

Rogers, Michael. "Manson Meets the Bug," *New York Times*, November 17, 1974.

Rosenbaum, Jonathan. "Acid Western [Review of *Dead Man*]," *Chicago Reader*, June 27, 1996.

Rowlett, Curt. "The Summer of Love Breeds a Season of Hate: The Effects of the Manson Murders on Public Perceptions of the Hippie Lifestyle." www.steamshovelpress.com/fromeditor48.html.

Rubin, Jerry. *We Are Everywhere*. New York: Harper and Row, 1970.

Rubin, Mike. "Summer of '69: Exploring the Cultural Battle between Charles Manson and Woodstock," *Spin Greatest Hits: 25 Years of Heretics, Heroes, and the New Rock 'n' Roll*. Hoboken, NJ: Wiley, 2010: 28–44.

Rubin, Rachel. *Well Met: Renaissance Faires and the American Counterculture*. New York: New York University Press, 2014.

Russell J. D. *The Beautiful People: The Pacesetters of the New Morality*. New York: Apollo, 1970.

Sanders, Ed. *The Family: The Story of Charles Manson's Dune Buggy Attack Battalion*. New York: Dutton, 1971.

———. *The Family*. New York: Thunder's Mouth, 2002.

———. "Investigative Poetry." www.woodstockjournal.com/pdf/ InvestigativePoetry.pdf.

Sandford, Christopher. *Polanski: A Biography*. New York: St. Martin's, 2009.

Schiller, Lawrence. *The Killing of Sharon Tate with the Exclusive Story of the Crime by Susan Atkins (Confessed Participant in the Murder of Sharon Tate)*. New York: New American Library, 1970.

Schmid, David. *Natural Born Killers: Serial Killers in American Culture*. Chicago: University of Chicago Press, 2005.

———. "Capote's Children: Patterns Of Violence in Contemporary American True Crime Narratives," *Violence in American Popular Culture. Volume 2: Representations of Violence in Popular Culture Genres*, ed. David Schmid. Santa Barbara, CA: Praeger, 2016. 211–226.

Sconce, Jeffrey. "XXX: Love and Kisses from Charlie," *Swinging Single: Representing Sexuality in the 1960s*, ed. Hilary Radner and Moya Luckett. Minneapolis: University of Minnesota Press, 1999. 207–223.

Selvin, Joel. *Altamont: The Rolling Stones, the Hells Angels, and the Inside Story of Rock's Darkest Day*. New York: HarperCollins, 2016.

Selvin, Joel. *Sly and the Family Stone: An Oral History*. New York: Avon Books, 1998.

Seltzer, Mark. *True Crime: Observations on Violence and Modernity*. New York: Routledge, 2007.

Shank, Theodore. *Beyond the Boundaries: American Alternative Theater*. Ann Arbor: University of Michigan Press, 2002.

Sheffield, Rob. *Dreaming the Beatles: The Love Story of One Band and the Whole World*. New York: HarperCollins, 2017.

Shellow, Robert, et al. "Suburban Runaways of the 1960s," *Monographs of the Society for Research in Child Development*, 32.2 (1967): iii–iv and 1–51.

Sinnreich, Aram. *Mashed Up: Music, Technology, and the Rise of Configurable Culture*. Boston: University of Massachusetts Press.

Smith, David, and Alan Rose. "The Group Marriage Commune: A Case Study," *Journal of Psychedelic Drugs*, 3.1 (1970).

Smith, Richard Cándida. *Utopia and Dissent: Art, Poetry, and Politics in California*. Berkeley: University of California Press, 1995.

Sorrentino, Christopher. "Zachary Lazar," *BOMB* 13 (Spring 2008).

Spiotta, Dana. *Lightning Field*. New York: Scribner, 2001.

Stacey, Judith. *Brave New Families: Stories of Domestic Upheaval in Late-Twentieth-Century America*. 1990. Berkeley: University of California Press, 1998.

Stevens, Anita, and Lucy Freeman. *I Hate My Parents: The Real and Unreal Reasons Why Youth Is Angry*. New York: Tower, 1970.

Staller, Karen. *Runaways: How the Sixties Counterculture Shaped Today's Practices and Policies*. New York: Columbia University Press, 2006.

Stone, Robert. *Prime Green: Remembering the Sixties*. New York: Harper Collins, 2007.

"The Surrealism of Neil Young's On the Beach Album." www.neilyoung-news.thrasherswheat.org/2011/11/surrealism-of-neil-youngs-on-beach.html.

Talese, Gay. "Charlie Manson's Home on the Range," *Esquire*, March 1970.

Thomas, June. "NBCs New Drama Is a Strange, Cheap Exploitation of the Charles Manson Murders," *Slate*, May 28, 2015.

Timberg, Scott. "Drugs, Paranoia and a Creepy Charles Manson Connection," *Salon*. June 5, 2015.

Toop, David. "Surfin' Death Valley USA: The Beach Boys and Heavy Friends," *Collusion*, February–April 1982. In *The Sound and the Fury: A Rock's Backpages Readers; 40 Years of Classic Rock Journalism*, ed. Barney Hoskyns. New York: Bloomsbury, 2003. 399–406.

Towlson, Jon. *Subversive Horror Cinema: Countercultural Messages of Films from* Frankenstein *to the Present*. Jefferson, NC: McFarland, 2014.

Turner, Grady. "Raymond Pettibon," *Bomb*, 69 (Fall 1999).

Udo, Tommy. *Charles Manson: Music Mayhem Murder*. London: Sanctuary, 2003.

Umminger, Allison. *American Girls*. New York: Flatiron, 2016.

Van Ness, Dunbar. "Changing Focus on Manson," *Los Angeles Free Press*, January 23, 1970: 9, 12.

Vronsky, Peter. *Female Serial Killers: How and Why Women Become Monsters*. New York: Berkley Books, 2007.

Walker, Michael. *Laurel Canyon: The Inside Story of Rock-and-Roll's Legendary Neighborhood*. New York: Faber and Faber, 2006.

Was, Don. "iTunes and the Death of Liner Notes," *Huffington Post*, December 17, 2010.

Waters, John. *Role Models*. New York: Farrar, Straus and Giroux, 2010.

———. 1981. *Shock Value: A Tasteful Book about Bad Taste*. New York: Thunder's Mouth, 2005.

———. 1987. *Crackpot*. New York: Scribner, 2003.

Watkins, Paul, with Guillermo Soledad. *My Life with Charles Manson.* New York: Bantam, 1979.

Watson, Tex, as told to Chaplain Ray. *Will You Die for Me?: The Man Who Killed for Charles Manson Tells His Own Story.* Old Tappan, NJ: Fleming H. Revell, 1978.

Weather Underground. "Declaration of a State of War." www.lib.berkeley.edu/MRC/pacificaviet/scheertranscript.html.

Webb, Adam. *Dumb Angel: The Life and Music of Dennis Wilson.* Creation Books, 2001.

Wein, Bibi. *The Runaway Generation.* New York: McKay, 1977.

Weller, Sheila. *Girls Like Us: Carole King, Joni Mitchell, Carly Simon and the Journey of a Generation.* New York: Atria, 2008.

Wells, Simon. *Charles Manson: Coming Down Fast.* London: Hodder, 2010.

Wilson, Brian, with Ben Greenman. *I Am Brian Wilson.* Boston: Da Capo, 2016.

Wilson, Theo. *Headline Justice: Inside the Courtrom—The Country's Most Controversial Trials.* 1996. New York: Thunder's Mouth, 1998.

Wolfe, Tom. *The Electric Kool-Aid Acid Test.* 1968. New York, Picador, 2008.

Woo, Elaine. "Curt Gentry Dies at 83," *Los Angeles Times,* July 23, 2014.

Woollett, Laura Elizabeth. *The Love of a Bad Man.* London: Scribe, 2016.

Yablonski, Lewis. *The Hippie Trip.* New York: Pegasus, 1968.

Zappa, Frank. Liner Notes. The Mothers of Invention, *Freak Out!* Verve Records, 1966.

Zaretsky, Natasha. *No Direction Home: The American Family and the Fear of National Decline, 1968–1980.* Chapel Hill: University of North Carolina Press, 2007.

Video Documentaries

The Byrds: Under Review (2007)

Cease to Exist (2007)

Charles Manson: Journey into Evil (1995)

Charles Manson: The Man Who Killed the Sixties (1994)

Gimme Shelter (1970)

Groupies (1970)

Hotel California (2007)

Manson (dir. Robert Hendrickson and Laurence Merrick, 1973)

Manson (History Channel, 2009)

Mondo Hollywood (1967)
Mondo Mod (1967)
Neil Young: Don't Be Denied (2009)
Six Degrees of Helter Skelter (2009)
The Source Family (2012)
Truth and Lies: The Family Manson (2017)

A Note on Sources

This is primarily a work of cultural history and analysis, and as such my main objects of study are often widely available published works, popular culture artifacts, and so on. There is no major "Manson archive" to speak of, though I learned much from John Gilmore's papers at UCLA's Special Collections in the Charles E. Young Library and from an amazing trove of television clips—mostly local news coverage—also at UCLA. Gilmore's papers include early interviews with Charles Manson and Bobby Beausoleil, a manuscript Beausoleil appears to have intended as an afterword for Gilmore's book ("Burning is the End"), and many other rich resources.

With respect to archival materials, I also learned quite a bit from some truly, madly, wildly (dis)organized boxes of trial documents and related correspondence at the Los Angeles Superior Court Archives and Records Center. Among other finds here are copies of subpoenas served to potential witnesses and a collection of notes potential jurors wrote to the judge in the hopes they would be excused from serving. (Favorites? The older person who explained that his doctor worried that even his prescribed nitroglycerin would not protect his heart from the potential shocks of this work, and the note from a scholar who explained that the day he was supposed to appear for jury selection he had a previous commitment—a "luncheon" with an editor from a press that had interest in publishing his manuscript. I followed the lead and discovered that he seems to have landed the deal!)

One of the real challenges facing students of Manson and the Family is that there is not even a generally available transcript of the 1970 and 1971 major trials. The Archives and Records Center *does* have daily minutes of the trial. Manson's own speech at his trial has been reproduced widely and numerous websites have posted important selections from the Grand Jury and trial proceedings. The few researchers and webmasters who have gained access to the main trial transcript (which is, allegedly, 24,000 pages long) seem to have done so through connections to either Vincent Bugliosi himself or other members of his original team.

I learned, ultimately, that it might be possible to engage in legal proceedings to try to find out more about the extant records, but this was not a road I wanted to go down. I contacted a number of webmasters whose sites have published excerpts and mostly not heard back. One of the few who responded explained that Bugliosi had personally shared his copy but that the process of scanning the thousands of pages would take some time! This webmaster stopped answering my emails when I asked if I could help expedite the process in any way in the hopes of obtaining a copy for myself. Since Bugliosi's death in 2015 there has been no announcement from his estate about the donation of his papers, so the transcript question remains unresolved. Since I am the kind of historian who is most interested in "stories about" events—rather than some elusive "actual" truth of the event—the mysterious case of the missing transcript has struck me as fascinating in its own right.

Decades ago, Ed Sanders wrote about areas of silence in and around the case and it struck me as a fitting that Sanders himself is one of these areas. Sanders himself won't talk much about the case anymore; I know for sure that I am not the only contemporary researcher who has been rebuffed by the cranky old Fug. His series of articles for the *Free Press*— all of its coverage in fact—are a crucial resource. For a while the Freep used to offer up all of its Manson-related material in a compact digital portfolio for a small price. That seems to have disappeared, as things do online, but at least one Manson-omnibus site still has it posted (see website listings below for more information on this). The *East Village Other* also had fascinating regular coverage, but is harder to access. I found a complete run at New York University's Fales Library.

If you study the Manson Family and trials you have to accept that your work will be upsetting to some people who either want to guard the materials they own or want to lock down (or define the parameters) of historical discussion. This is just how it is in Mansonland. In my years of research I have met an impressive number of incredible people who were willing to share their stories and their work, but also a few who not only refused, but felt the need to critique the project right out of the gate. (My favorite here came from the musician and Beach Boy associate Van Dyke Parks who responded to my query about a possible interview by sending me the following email two days running: "No time for this. I view it as a trivial pursuit, and redundant at best.") In this light I want to invite students, scholars, and other interested parties to get in touch if you think I might have any materials or insights that could help you with your own work. I'm at jeffrey.melnick@umb.edu.

Manson on the Web

It will come as no surprise to most readers that the Manson Family has a huge presence on the Internet. In my years of work on the Family I came to appreciate deeply the denizens of the net who donated so much of their energy to constructing sites open to all comers—no paywalls! Most of the sites listed here have, in addition to posted documents, photographs, videos, and so on, very robust communities of commenters. Reading comments on these sites offers some very good hints as to how Manson and the Family continue to live in contemporary culture. Without the generosity of these webmasters it would take unlimited time for travel and deep pockets for eBay to get at some of the most important Manson research materials. Here are some of the most important sites.

www.murdersofaugust69.freeforums.net
A turn-of-the-century style discussion board with a very robust collection of documents, photographs, and trial records, as well as a particularly lively commenting community.

www.lsb3.com
This "Tate-LaBianca Homicide Research Blog" has an impressive trove of research materials.

www.cielodrive.com
This is probably the best of the Manson omnibus sites. In addition to major portions of trial (and Grand Jury) testimony, cielodrive.com is notable for being the most professionally laid-out and most easily navigable online Manson collection.

www.mansonblog.com
The blog is not particularly easy to navigate but it is another example of a site that will offer up many riches to the patient surfer.

www.law2.umkc.edu/faculty/projects/ftrials/ftrials2printable.htm
was created by Professor Douglas Linder and others at University of Missouri-Kansas City Law School. With a good overview of the trial and samples of some of the most important testimony—not to mention records of parole hearings—this is absolutely indispensable.

www.trussel.com/f_mel.htm
This is a Lyman Family site, which has plenty of Manson-related material as well. Constructed and maintained by Steve Trussel, this is a truly unmatched archive.

www.truthontatelabianca.com
For many years this was a crucial omnibus site and I still have reams of notes taken from materials found there. But this is the Internet, folks, and the site disappeared.

Personal Communication

This book is not organized around interviews but I have been very fortunate to have the research enriched by in-person, telephone, and email conversations with a range of people with interests in the case—from direct participants in this historical moment, to artists inspired by the events in and around the Family, to other scholars working in the area. With gratitude, I list the people whose insight I have benefited from:

Gregg Jakobson
Bobby Beausoleil
Phil Proctor
Candace Falk
Lewis Parker
JR Robinson
David Felton
Karlene Faith
Lonnie Martin
Erik Forrest Jackson

On Quoting Songs

Permission to quote popular songs is prohibitively expensive—that is when the owners of the copyright are actually willing to allow it: Neil Young was a surprise "no"! The good news is the lyrics to all the songs I mention are widely available online; just remember to trust your ears before you trust the crowd-sourced transcriptions.

Acknowledgments

Part of the burden of this book has been to demonstrate why and how the Manson Family have come to be such a pervasive presence in our culture. The ubiquity of the Family in fact and fiction meant that I had literally dozens of comrades along the way. I have been honored by all of the people who have shared their personal encounters with Manson, who have helped me make my way over and through Mansonland, and who have shared leads, links, and lore. Especially important to my research and writing process has been the generosity of those who, in one way or another, have been actors in, and creators of, the cultural dramas I explore here. In this light I offer my deep gratitude to Gregg Jakobson, Bobby Beausoleil, David Felton, Karlene Faith, Phil Proctor, Candace Falk, Lewis Parker, Erik Forrest Jackson, Lonnie Martin, and JR Robinson. The process of getting the book from manuscript to print has been shockingly free of drama and actually pleasant! For this I want to thank my wise agent, Don Fehr, and the wonderful work done by all the folks I have worked with at Arcade/ Skyhorse—most notably the sharp and committed editors Lilly Golden and Maxim Brown.

Creepy Crawling is also built on the foundation of the remarkably supportive American Studies department at University of Massachusetts, Boston. My department chairs, Lynnell Thomas and Aaron Lecklider, have helped make it possible for me to balance teaching responsibilities and research. Shauna Manning, the department administrator, has been a crucial part of all of my work at UMB. My undergraduate and graduate students make me feel hopeful and inspired just about every day. I also feel grateful to find myself working a part of a robust public sector union. I am grateful to have received financial support from the University in the form of a Joseph P. Healey Grant and a College of Liberal Arts Dean's Fund award. I appreciate the support I have received from key staff in the Dean's office, especially Kim Ho, Eddie Sze, and Lauren Brackett.

I thank David Shafer, of California State, Long Beach, for his enthusiastic support and careful reading of the manuscript, as well as Brett Mizelle, a colleague of David's, for inviting me to talk about the work in progress to an energetic audience at CSULB. The manuscript also benefited greatly from a close reading by scholar David Schmid, who offered his incredible analytic acumen and amazing attention to detail just because I wrote him an email and asked him to. Old friends Gary Wilder, Audrey Vernick, Scott Fabozzi, Dan Itzkovitz, and Susannah Ringel have offered the kinds of support that matter most. I am glad to have this chance to thank some newer friends as well, especially a group I have come to know first through a shared interest in popular music and mostly as incredibly smart virtual presences. I want to take this moment to remember the wise and warm Ali Belz, no longer with us. Sincere thanks are also due to Vincent Maganzini, Tom Johnston, and Larry Blum, all of whom shared information, insights, and enthusiasm. I have also drawn energy from the support of my mother Iris Swimmer and stepfather Len Swimmer, and my siblings Melnick (Dan, Dave, and Debby) and Rubin (Larry and Lucy). To my academic role model, dear colleague, and friend, Judy Smith, I owe a debt of gratitude for her close reading, incisive comments, and high standards. Above all, I have drawn as much as I can from the example Judy provides as a brilliant scholar and as the most ethically evolved person I have ever known.

Which brings me to my Cambridge/Somerville family. None of the rest of this matters much without these four people: Cindy Weisbart, Jessie Rubin, Jacob Rubin, and Rachel Rubin. There has been no greater honor or reward in my life than sharing a home with Jessie and Jake as they grew into the kind and brilliant adults they are today. They both know how insanely much I love them and how much I have drawn from their camaraderie and their critical intelligence. I thank Jessie Rubin especially for sharing her musical expertise to help me parse some intractable texts, and to Jacob Rubin for his deep knowledge and skills in teaching me to understand visual texts of all kinds. (And for saying to me: "It's time to stop researching and start writing. Otherwise you just have a very strange hobby.") Cindy is the teacher I aim to be and if my reach exceeds my grasp I'm still so lucky to have her establishing the goals; she is the kind of friend you read about in books. Rachel Rubin has been my partner at home and in all sorts of work for a blessedly long time and continues to set the bar for the kind of engaged scholarship I value most. Grateful beyond words for this family, I will end by noting that I am not a religious person but I am a superstitious person so I will just say: *kinehora.*

Index